AFRO-CUBAN JAZZ

AFRO-CUBAN JAZZ

SCOTT YANOW

San Francisco

Published by Miller Freeman Inc
600 Harrison Street, San Francisco, CA 94107
An imprint of Music Player Network
  www.MusicPlayer.com
  Publishers of *Guitar Player, Bass Player, Keyboard,*
      Gig, MC2, and *EQ* magazines

Distributed to the book trade in the U.S. and Canada by
Publishers Group West
1700 Fourth Street, Berkeley, CA 94710

Distributed to the music trade in the U.S. and Canada by
Hal Leonard Publishing
P.O. Box 13819, Milwaukee, WI 53213

Cover Design by Richard Leeds
Text Design by Wilsted & Taylor Publishing Services
Composition by Nancy Tabor
Front Cover Photo of Mongo Santamaria by Lee Tanner
Back Cover Photo of Tito Puente by Bradley Niederman

Library of Congress Cataloging-in-Publication Data
Yanow, Scott
    Afro-Cuban jazz / Scott Yanow.
        p. cm. — (Third Ear)
    Includes bibliographical references, discographies, and index
    ISBN 0-87930-619-X
    1. Latin jazz—History and criticism. 2. Jazz musicians—Bio-bibliography.
    I. Title. II. Series

    ML3506.Y37 2000
    781.65'089'687291—dc21   00-049025

Printed in the United States of America

00 01 02 03 04 05   5 4 3 2 1

Contents

INTRODUCTION

Most styles of jazz have a symbolic opening event that signals its birth. Swing caught on after Benny Goodman's orchestra was a surprise sensation at Los Angeles' Palomar Ballroom in 1935. Bebop began to form as a truly independent music at after-hours jam sessions during 1940-42 at Minton's Playhouse and Monroe's Uptown House in New York. And jazz's start can be considered to have taken place in 1895, when the legendary (and unrecorded) New Orleans cornetist Buddy Bolden formed his first band.

Although, as with the other styles, the exact moment of conception of Afro-Cuban Jazz is not really known and there were earlier events of importance, its symbolic beginning took place in 1947, when Mario Bauzá introduced Dizzy Gillespie to Chano Pozo. Gillespie had expressed to Bauzá his desire to add a Latin percussionist to his big band, an unprecedented step for a jazz orchestra (although Stan Kenton was starting to move along similar lines). After some initial adjustments between the American rhythm section and the conguero, the chemistry that occurred between Pozo (who did not speak English), the trumpeter, and his big band was pure magic. Afro-Cuban Jazz quickly caught on, and its evolution has not stopped yet.

A clarification of a few terms is necessary from the start. In this book Afro-Cuban Jazz means the mixture of jazz improvisations with Cuban and African rhythms. This style of jazz is generally bebop-oriented, but it can be more modern or even tied to an earlier form, such as swing. Quite often the idiom is called Latin Jazz, but I have decided to forego that term for three reasons: (1) Latin Jazz is already the name of a fine book by John Storm Roberts. (2) Both Ray Barretto and the late Mario Bauzá hated the term. (3) Since bossa novas from Brazil, tangos from Argentina, and various local folk musics that have some improvising can all be called Latin Jazz but are outside the confines of this particular book, a slightly more restrictive term was needed.

Though one of the most consistently popular forms of jazz, Afro-Cuban Jazz has suffered from critical neglect through the years. While many jazz history books state that 1920s jazz evolved into swing, which became bebop and was "succeeded" by cool jazz, hard bop, the avant-garde, fusion, and whatever terms can be thought of to describe the past 20 years of jazz, Latin music does not fit easily into that simplistic narrative. Afro-Cuban Jazz began to mature during the bebop era and since then has coexisted alongside the other jazz styles, influenced by and in turn influencing most later developments of jazz. It never really decreased in popularity and, unlike bop and later styles, it never cut its tie with the dancing audience.

Due to its constant popularity and the fact that it works perfectly as party music, Afro-Cuban Jazz has often not been taken seriously by the more somber members of the jazz community, some of whom write it off as mere dance music. Surprisingly little has been written about Afro-Cuban Jazz, particularly in jazz history books. Mark Gridley's *Jazz Styles* (now in its seventh edition) says virtually nothing about Latin rhythms. Other than John Storm Roberts' fine books *The Latin Tinge* and *Latin Jazz,* along with a recent biography on Tito Puente by Steve Loza, extensive reading material in English about Afro-Cuban music is quite scarce. Do not expect to find more than a cursory reference to this idiom in most of the jazz reference guides (although in *The All Music Guide to Jazz,* we did our best not to overlook this infectious music and its main innovators). The major jazz magazines now and then will have an article on the bigger names, but only *Latin Beat* magazine has historical pieces (particularly those by Max Salazar) that dig into the music's past and present. So clearly there is a gap waiting to be filled.

As with the books *Swing* and *Bebop,* the most difficult aspect to putting together this overview is deciding what to include and how far to stretch the definition of the style. One of the main problems was deciding what to do with Salsa. The word (meaning "spicy sauce") was used in some song titles as early as the 1930s, made a comeback in the 1960s, and then was applied by some to most Latin music that occurred in the 1970s, particularly in New York, whether it was jazz or not. For the purpose of this book, Salsa can be thought of as the pop equivalent of Afro-Cuban Jazz. Often the rhythms are similar, but the emphasis is on vocalizing in Spanish rather than jazz improvising. The tricky part is that most performers of Latin music since 1940 (such as Tito Puente) have performed both Afro-Cuban Jazz and Salsa, often alternating the two or mixing them together. So, when in doubt about whether someone should have an entry in this book, the question came down to whether the individual's or group's music has much jazz to it. In the case of Los Van Van, a major Latin dance band, the answer had to be no, since they are purely a vocal ensemble (with their strong backup musicians restricted to background riffing). Celia Cruz was clearly a borderline case because, although her singing was never jazz, she did perform frequently with Tito Puente in later years and her contributions to Latin music in general are difficult to deny, but one can certainly argue against her inclusion. There was also a question as to whether to include Carlos Santana in a book on Afro-Cuban Jazz. Santana has long been principally a Latin rock (rather than jazz) guitarist, but since his music has often overlapped with jazz and his recording of Tito Puente's "Oye Como Va" made that song into a standard, he deserves to have an entry.

Afro-Cuban Jazz is designed as an introductory guide for listeners who wonder who the main innovators of the wide-ranging style have been and which recordings are most representative. Because there has been relatively little written about the idiom, my early fear was of leaving someone major out altogether, although I am now confident that, possible minor omissions aside, every significant figure appears somewhere in this book. As with the other books in the series, not every recording by each artist is here. In fact, in some cases the artist's recordings are difficult to obtain, particularly those made for such legendary labels as Fania, Tico, and Seeco. Hopefully the recordings that are most highly recommended in this book will whet readers' appetites to explore fully their favorite artist's other work.

To hear a cooking trumpet, saxophone, or piano jamming on top of overheated polyrhythms played by a percussion section of congas, bongos, and timbales is one of the thrills of music. I hope that in this book I have done the music justice.

I used a ten-point rating system for the CD reviews. Here are what the ratings mean:

10 A gem that belongs in every serious jazz collection
9 Highly recommended
8 A very good release
7 An excellent acquisition
6 Good music but not quite essential
5 Decent but not one of this artist's more important works
4 So-so
3 A disappointing effort with just a few worthwhile moments
2 A weak release
1 Stinks!

I would like to thank a few people whose help has been invaluable. Richard Ginell (a top classical and jazz critic) and Al Cresswell (a fine bebop pianist) were kind enough to lend me several important CDs and LPs from their huge record libraries to use in this book. Susie Hansen not only let me go through her CD collection but lent me her nearly complete collection of *Latin Beat* magazines. All fans of Afro-Cuban Jazz should immediately subscribe to this valuable bilingual publication (Latin Beat, 15900 Crenshaw Blvd., Suite 1-223, Gardena, CA 90249), which covers all styles of Latin music. Also of strong assistance was the talented writer Patricia Albela.

Thanks are also due to Dorothy Cox and Matt Kelsey of Miller Freeman for trusting in me and believing in this important project, to Brian Ashley who got me started in the jazz writing business back in 1976 when he formed *Record Review,* to the many much-maligned but invaluable jazz publicists (including Terri Hinte of Fantasy Records, Ann Braithwaite, Lynda Bramble, and Lori Hehr), who make life much easier for jazz journalists, and to the first Afro-Cuban Jazz artist I ever heard, Cal Tjader. In addition, a special thanks to my wife Kathy and my daughter Melody for their love and support.

A BRIEF HISTORY OF AFRO-CUBAN JAZZ

Although Afro-Cuban Jazz symbolically began when Dizzy Gillespie and Chano Pozo met in 1947, the same can be said about Mario Bauzá's composing of "Tanga" for Machito's orchestra in 1943, Machito's putting together of his first successful big band in 1940, Don Azpiazu's arrival in the United States in 1930, pianist Jelly Roll Morton's utilization of a tango rhythm in his 1923 recording of "New Orleans Blues," or W.C. Handy's use of a habanera syncopation for the "B" section of "St. Louis Blues" during the 1910s. Latin music has been around for a long time. It just took time for the jazz world to discover it (and vice versa).

Latin rhythms appeared now and then in jazz before seeming to explode out of nowhere in the 1940s. Way before recordings were being made, Nigerian slaves brought their polyrhythmic chants and drums to the Caribbean islands. In Cuba the rhythms were combined with the language and song of Spain and the *clavé* was developed. The clavé is the basis for all Cuban music, an offbeat rhythmic pattern over two bars, made originally by the clashing together of two little wooden sticks (also known as the clavés). To count out the clavé rhythm, one can assign the two bars eight beats apiece and clap on 1-4-7 in the first bar and 3-5 in the second. Or, with four beats in a bar, the pattern would be 1-2½-4 followed by 2-3. Sometimes (usually during solos), this 3/2 pattern is reversed to 2/3. Although it sounds complex, the rhythm is quite catchy and can be heard (at least beneath the surface) in all Cuban music.

The influence of Cuban music was first heard in the United States in the music of Louisiana's classical composer and piano virtuoso Louis Moreau Gottschalk, who visited Cuba in 1854 and wrote several works that used Cuban rhythms. An early rhythm, the *habanera,* was a descendant of the *contradanza* (a Spanish line dance), adding syncopation and soon influencing (and overlapping with) the Argentinean tango. In the mid-1860s, Sebastian Yradier's "La Paloma" (which uses the habanera) became the first major Latin hit in the United States through its sheet music sales. Manuel Ponce's "Estrellita" had similar success starting in 1909, and the habanera (or tango) rhythm pops up in several ragtime pieces of the early 20th century (including Scott Joplin's "Solace") and most famously in W.C. Handy's "St. Louis Blues."

The *son,* which would be the basis for the rumba, was one of the first rhythms invented by Cubans. It originated in Havana around the time of World War I and has two simultaneous levels. Percussionists improvise over an African rhythm while a Spanish rhythm is utilized for the playing of a nine-string Cuban guitar (known as the *tres*) and a bass, with Spanish lyrics usually being sung (sometimes by a *coro,* a Spanish term for chorus) over the instruments. The overall effect is quite polyrhythmic, infectious, and exciting. Sexteto Habanero's *Las Raices de Son* (Tumbao 009) is an intriguing CD featuring the son being played in its early days (1925-31) by a group consisting of tres, guitar, bass, bongo, clavé, and maracas; five of the musicians also sing throughout the performances.

In the early 1920s, the septeto was a common group in Cuba, consisting of trumpet, at least one singer, tres, bass, maracas, clavés, and bongo (a small double-drum with conical or cylindrical hardwood shells and heads that are tuned a fourth apart). Also increasingly popular were *charangas,* Cuban dance orchestras featuring a flute in the lead joined by violins, piano, bass, and timbales (two small metal drums on a stand with two tuned cowbells and an occasional cymbal).

Meanwhile in the United States, the tango was the first South American dance to really catch on. Jelly Roll Morton stated that the "Spanish tinge" was an essential musical ingredient that separated jazz from ragtime, and he used the tango rhythm in several of his piano pieces, including "The Crave" and "New Orleans Blues." The tango rhythm was also used as a novelty in quite a few American jazz records of the 1920s when an "exotic" device was called for. By the end of the decade Latin dance bands (usually in watered-down form) were becoming more common in larger American cities.

On April 26, 1930, Don Azpiazu's Havana Casino Orchestra debuted on Broadway at New York's Palace Theatre and introduced authentic Cuban dance music to the United States for the first time. Azpiazu was the first to record "The Peanut Vendor" and "Green Eyes" ("Aquellos Ojos Verdes"), also making strong-selling recordings of "Mama Inez" and "Marta," using a rhythm section that included *maracas* (rattles filled with seeds), clavés, *guiro* (a scraper, made from a serrated gourd, with a distinctive sound), bongos, and timbales. Although Azpiazu's name would soon become obscure, the songs that he helped make famous are still well known today. "The Peanut Vendor" in particular was a sensation at the time, being recorded by countless groups, including Duke Ellington and Louis Armstrong, and helping to start the popularization of the rumba, a slow, sensual variety of the son that caught on very big during the decade.

The success of "The Peanut Vendor" resulted in many other Latin-flavored songs being written, including "La Cucaracha," "Alla en el Rancho Grande" (better known as simply "Rancho Grande"), "Cuando Vuelva a Tu Lado" ("What a Difference a Day Makes"), and Cole Porter's "Begin the Beguine." During the Swing era such Latin-flavored numbers were recorded as "The Rumba Jumps" (by Glenn Miller), "Chili-Con Conga" (Cab Calloway), "Rhumboogie" (Freddie Slack), "The Peanut Vendor" (the John Kirby Sextet), "La Paloma" and "Estrellita" (Harry James), "Caravan" and "Conga Brava" (both composed by Juan Tizol for Duke Ellington), and "Green Eyes" (Jimmy Dorsey), among many others. But although Latin bands began to proliferate in the United States (Xavier Cugat became a national celebrity with his blending of sweet music with Latin rhythms), and many Hollywood musicals gave an idealized view of Central and South America, in general Latin music and jazz stayed separate. American musicians were not prepared yet to play Latin rhythms, and while Cuban and Latin American bands often played swing hits, they usually did not feature much soloing.

Meanwhile four important events occurred in the late 1930s/early '40s that would permanently affect the music:

(1) In Cuba, Arsenio Rodriguez introduced the *conjunto,* an expansion on the septeto. Rodriguez's group consisted of several trumpets, piano, tres, bass, conga, bongo, and voices, being much more extroverted than most of the more polite Latin dance bands.

(2) The conga began to be accepted as a major instrument in Latin music. Previously it had been associated primarily with carnivals and religious cults. But when Arsenio Rodriguez added a conga to his conjunto, it was a major step forward. And when the charismatic Desi Arnaz adopted the conga and introduced it to American audiences, the conga gained a permanent spot in Afro-Cuban bands. The conga, which originated in the Congo, has a tapered or barrel-shaped shell and a single head. In addition to the conga itself,

some congueros use the higher-pitched *quinto* or the larger (and lower-voiced) *tumbadora*. Since the conga has a fatter tone and a lower pitch than the bongo, its addition added a great deal to the rhythm section of Latin bands.

(3) Although it would not reach the height of its popularity until the mid-1950s, the mambo rhythm began to be developed in the late 1930s by Arsenio Rodriquez's conjunto and Antonio Arcaño's charanga. In the latter group, bassist Cachao and his brother pianist Orestes López originated the catchy and repetitious rhythm, years before pianist Pérez Prado (who at one point claimed to have invented the mambo himself) arranged for the rhythm to be played in a big band context.

(4) After a false start in 1939, Machito organized his orchestra (the Afro-Cubans) in 1940. The following year his brother-in-law, Mario Bauzá, joined the band as musical director, arranger, and trumpeter, encouraging Machito to hire technically skilled jazz musicians in the horn sections. Although originally emphasizing ensembles and vocals, by 1943, when Bauzá wrote what is considered the first Afro-Cuban Jazz song ("Tanga"), Machito's orchestra was becoming jazz oriented. The Afro-Cuban rhythms were better suited to bebop than to swing, so when bop began becoming prominent in 1945, Machito's ensemble was leading the way in the Latin music world, inspiring both Stan Kenton and Dizzy Gillespie to expand the sounds, vocabularies, and rhythms of their orchestras.

The year 1947 was key for Afro-Cuban Jazz. Dizzy Gillespie added Chano Pozo to his big band and recorded "Manteca." His "A Night in Tunisia" (written in 1943 before he was well acquainted with Cuban rhythms) was already becoming a standard. Stan Kenton recorded such numbers as "Machito" and "The Peanut Vendor" and in January 1948 played opposite Machito's orchestra at a Town Hall concert. The new and unusual music was dubbed "Cubop." Other orchestras that would soon be playing the style included those of Pupi Campo (inspired by Stan Kenton), José Curbelo, Noro Morales, René Touzet (whose sidemen in 1949 included Art Pepper and Johnny Mandel), and most significantly Tito Puente and Tito Rodriguez. From this point on, Afro-Cuban and Latin jazz would be a major style of music, even if the jazz media's attention was sometimes difficult to gain.

For the next few years some of the most significant mixtures of jazz and Latin music were made with Machito's orchestra. In August 1948 Machito appeared in New York clubs with guest soloists Howard McGhee on trumpet and tenor saxophonist Brew Moore. During 1948-50, Machito recorded on a few occasions with Charlie Parker, Flip Phillips, and Buddy Rich, including Chico O'Farrill's "Afro-Cuban Jazz Suite." And other jazz greats regularly popped up as guests.

Chico O'Farrill was everywhere in those days, arranging a couple Afro-Cuban Jazz charts for Benny Goodman, writing "Cuban Episode" for Kenton, and recording some of his finest work as a bandleader. Charlie Parker's *South of the Border* album was more routine, but it did introduce his "My Little Suede Shoes" and he utilized percussionists José Mangual and Luis Miranda. Bud Powell's "Un Poco Loco" showed how the top bebop players were beginning to utilize Latin rhythms. Stan Kenton recorded "23 Degrees North, 82 Degrees West" (the location of Havana!), British tenor saxophonist Kenny Graham formed a band called the Afro-Cubists, and Shorty Rogers recorded the tongue-in-cheek "Viva Zapata" in 1953.

With the hit records of Pérez Prado adding to its momentum, there was a strong mambo craze during the first half of the 1950s. Close behind was the cha-cha-cha (often simply called the cha-cha), developed in 1949 by violinist-composer Enrique Jorrin, who cut the tempo of the mambo in half and utilized a double slap of the conga on beats four and eight. His 1953 hit "La Enganadora" made the dance popular for the remainder of the decade, while Orquesta Aragon helped make the cha-cha-cha famous in Cuba.

West Coast cool jazz did not have that much of an effect on Afro-Cuban Jazz; it was more significant as an inspiration for 1960s Brazilian bossa nova. However, Cal Tjader emerged from the West Coast to become one of the most important of the music's leaders, and tenor saxophonist José "Chombo" Silva's main inspirations were Lester Young and Stan Getz. In the 1950s for the first time conga players started appearing often on otherwise-straightahead jazz combo dates, with Ray Barretto, Candido, Patato Valdés, and Sabu Martinez gaining a great deal of freelance work, as would Mongo Santamaria and Willie Bobo in the future. And the series of *descargas* (Cuban jam sessions) led by bassist Cachao starting in the mid-1950s were the Cuban equivalent of America's Jazz at the Philharmonic, all-star jams in which soloists played over a *montuno* (a repetitive vamp).

In the late 1950s several trends were going on simultaneously in Afro-Cuban Jazz. The mambo fad had passed its peak, but the big bands of Tito Puente and Tito Rodriguez were still quite popular, often sharing the bill (and fighting over their billing) at New York's Palladium. Cal Tjader had one of his strongest groups, and Herbie Mann led an impressive Afro-Cuban outfit. At the same time, pianist Charlie Palmieri's Charanga Duboney (which originally had flutist Johnny Pacheco and four violins) brought back the traditional charanga sound, which unexpectedly became popular for a few years. Other charanga groups were formed, including units by Pacheco, Ray Barretto, and Mongo Santamaria.

The isolation of Cuba starting in 1960 (after dictator Fidel Castro's relations with the United States ended) meant that few new musicians would emigrate from the island country during the next 15-20 years. Puerto Rico, which had always been significant in the development of the music, now became one of its main centers, along with New York City. While avant-garde jazz had little influence on Afro-Cuban music (even if Willie Bobo recorded on Herbie Hancock's mostly free album *Succotash*), soul jazz and soul music would soon have a major impact. Starting with Ray Barretto's "El Watusi" in 1962 and continuing with Joe Cuba's "Bang Bang" in 1966, Pete Rodriguez's "Pete's Boogaloo," and Johnny Colon's "Boogaloo Blues," contemporary Afro-Cuban Jazz began to be affected by R&B and pop music (in addition to soul jazz), and many of the recordings made the best-seller charts for brief periods. The new mixture was called *boogaloo* (or *bugalú*), catchy music (often cover tunes with lyrics in English) that could be described as cha-cha-cha with a backbeat.

In the past, Cuban and Latin bands tended to have a strict instrumentation, but that really began to change in the 1960s. Eddie Palmieri had a flute and two-trombone frontline (La Perfecta) that was dubbed "trombanga" by Charlie Palmieri. Eddie's adventurous piano playing (which in time would be influenced by McCoy Tyner, Chick Corea, and to a lesser extent in spots by Cecil Taylor) and often-unusual bands were influential and led the way toward increased experimentation. The 1970s were a strange time for Afro-Cuban music. The word *Salsa* was everywhere and was applied by some to all things Latin. The word had been used as early as 1933, when Ignacio Pineiro's Sexteto Nacional introduced "Echale Salsita" and was revived in 1962 by Joe Cuba (who recorded "Salsa y Bembe") and in 1964 by Cal Tjader, whose "Soul Sauce" ("Salsa del Alma") was a hit. It really describes Latin pop/dance music dominated by Spanish vocals, an idiom that had already existed for decades. Because the demographics of the United States were changing, with a major increase in Spanish-speaking people from Latin and South America, Salsa became quite popular in the '70s and has remained so to this day. Some of the leaders of Afro-Cuban Jazz (including Ray Barretto and Tito Puente) emphasized Salsa during the 1970s, while the jazz segment of the Latin music world became a bit buried in electronic fusion, rock, funk, and other mixtures of styles. But, just when it seemed that the music would be completely swamped by commercialism and the dominance of other idioms, things began to change again.

In 1977 Dizzy Gillespie, Ray Mantilla, Stan Getz, David Amram, and a few other American jazz musicians took a rare visit to Cuba, where they discovered a particularly fertile music scene, best exemplified by the group Irakere. In 1979 American and Cuban musicians played together openly at a recorded series of concerts in Havana. Although relations between the two countries would soon sour, the secret was out about Cuba's homegrown musicians. Soon Paquito D'Rivera had defected (immediately becoming a top jazz star), and others gradually followed, including Arturo Sandoval in 1990. Irakere began to appear at European festivals, and the release of a few of its recordings stateside inspired others in the United States to mix post-bop jazz solos with Cuban rhythms and folkloric singing. Jerry González's Fort Apache Band in the United States was among those that showed that Afro-Cuban rhythms could mix in well with soloing much more advanced than bebop.

The Concord Picante label was started in 1979 by Concord head Carl Jefferson to record the music of Cal Tjader and other top Afro-Cuban players. In time Tito Puente, Mongo Santamaria, and Ray Barretto would be among those veterans who returned to Cubop and recorded for Picante. The death of Cal Tjader in 1982 ended an era but started a new one as his conguero Poncho Sanchez had great success with his own band. The rise of world fusion (as the world became a smaller place) resulted in styles from various countries being mixed together. New names on the scene included pianists Michel Camilo and Danilo Perez.

Afro-Cuban Jazz came close to flourishing in the 1990s. Arturo Sandoval defected from Cuba and was soon recognized as one of the world's top trumpeters. Cuba loosened its doors a bit, and such musicians as pianists Gonzalo Rubalcaba and Chucho Valdés were eventually not only free to play in the United States but able to return to Cuba to record. Ry Cooder discovered that a group of forgotten veterans in Cuba (loosely called the Buena Vista Social Club) were still capable of playing classic music. Canadian Jane Bunnett worked hard to arrange American tours for talented Cuban musicians with her Spirits of Havana band. Such survivors as Tito Puente, Mario Bauzá, Mongo Santamaria, and Ray Barretto were continually honored. And the legacy of Afro-Cuban Jazz continued to grow as it was accepted not only as a viable form of music but as a strong influence on other modern styles of jazz.

The future looks bright for this danceable, inventive, and fun music in the 21st century!

AFRO-CUBAN JAZZ: 1930-2000

MEMO ACEVEDO

b. Santa Fe de Bogota, Colombia

A fine drummer and timbale player, Memo Acevedo has performed during the past 15 years with singer Mark Murphy, saxophonist Tom Scott, Irakere, and various rock and pop performers. Acevedo, who teaches percussion at the Drummers Collective Program in New York, has recorded with bassist Harvie Swartz and singer Sherri Roberts, in many commercial situations, and on *Building Bridges,* his lone CD so far as a leader.

7 *Building Bridges / Feb. 28, 1993 + Mar. 7, 1993 / The Jazz Alliance 10022*

Much of the music on Memo Acevedo's debut set as a leader finds his ten-piece group from Canada (which includes two trumpets, one trombone, a flute, and two saxophonists) sounding like a small big band. Among the sidemen are trumpeters Dave Dunlop and Kevin Turcotte, flutist Bill McBirnie, and Alex Dean on tenor, with Acevedo and Marcus Chonsky on conga supplying the percussion work. The music (which includes seven pieces written by Acevedo and/or trombonist Terry Promane) is primarily straightahead jazz with a Latin flavor; the one exception is "Heartbeat," which is a feature for the leader's percussion. There are guest spots for Gonzalo Rubalcaba (outstanding on an intriguing rendition of "Cherokee"), Dave Valentin, and Tito Puente on timbales (heard on Tadd Dameron's "Lady Bird"). A swinging set with enough fiery moments to make it recommendable.

ALEX ACUÑA

b. Dec. 12, 1944, Pativilca, Peru

An exciting drummer (also very skilled on timbales and congas) who is often heard in commercial settings when not playing Afro-Cuban Jazz, Alejandro Necisup Acuña started first on trumpet and piano (taught to him by his father) in his native Peru but was self-taught on drums. At 16, he became a studio musician in Lima, Peru. Acuña was in Las Vegas with Pérez Prado's band during part of 1964-65 and spent 1966-75 primarily as a studio musician and freelancer in Puerto Rico and Los Angeles. In 1975 he became a member of Weather Report, working as a percussionist during October 1975-April 1976 (recording *Black Market* with the group) and then switching to drums through October 1977, appearing on *Heavy Weather* (including the original version of "Birdland"). Since spending a five-year stint with singer Al Jarreau, Acuña has freelanced mostly in the Los Angeles area. He has worked in countless settings, including with Clare Fischer, singer Tania Maria, keyboardist Chick Corea, the Yellowjackets, guitarist Lee Ritenour, keyboardist Lyle Mays, pianist Bobby Enriquez, and many of Los Angeles' top Latin players. Acuña, who led the Latin fusion band Koinonia in the 1980s (they recorded four albums), has in recent times been heading Alex Acuña and the Unknowns, a band of Latin studio players he met while making the Eddie Murphy movie *Coming to America.* They have recorded two albums (*Alex Acuña and the Unknowns* and *Thinking of You*) for JVC.

7 *Top Percussion / 1999 / DCC Compact Classics 185*

Subtitled "Rhythms for a New Millenium," Alex Acuña's set is primarily rhythm, along with occasional vocal chants. Up to seven percussionists (including Giovanni Hidalgo and Luis Conte) are heard on each selection with the only other instruments being (on one or two songs apiece) guitarist Felix Cassaverde, bassists Mariane Liy, Abraham Laboriel and Pee Wee Hill, and pianist Albert Salas; "So Be It" is a duet by Acuña and pianist Otmaro Ruiz. Otherwise, this is mostly one long percussion feast with complex polyrhythms galore. Listeners who enjoy percussion solos and close interaction between Acuña and his masterful sidemen will want this spirited if purposely limited outing.

AFROCUBA

Founded in 1978, Afrocuba effectively mixes modern post-bop jazz styles (most notably fusion) with Cuban folk melodies and heated percussion. Based in Cuba and filled mostly with musicians who had studied at the Havana Conservatoire of Music, the band is led by trumpeter Roberto Garcia López and is usually a two-horn septet (with saxophonist David Suarez Merlin), although for some projects it has been expanded. Shortly after being formed, Afrocuba won the UNEAC prize for popular music and appeared at the World Festival of Youth and Students in Cuba. They made their first trip outside of Cuba when they visited Ronnie Scott's club in London in 1982 and have since returned several times.

7 *Acontecer / July 1992-Oct. 1992 / Discmedi Blau 75*

Afrocuba's 1992 session (which is a bit brief at 37 minutes) finds the group combining late '70s fusion horn lines (played by trumpeter Roberto Garcia López, who also contributes some electric keyboards for atmosphere, and David Suarez Merlin on tenor and soprano) with the fiery percussion of Leonardo Garcia López and Mario Luis Pino and occasional group singing. There are no great virtuosos among the soloists (their statements are generally quite short) and the horn lines are as much

R&B as jazz, but this band has an appealing spirit and a strong ensemble sound. Amaury Gutierrez's scat singing on "Amor Blindado" is a highlight.

6 *Eclecticism / June 1987-Mar. 1994 / Jazz House 039*

Eclecticism features Afrocuba on eight selections from 1994 along with three cuts that are reissued from 1987. The later date finds Afrocuba sounding much more conventional than they did on 1992's *Acontecer*. Most of the fusion elements were dropped, with a greater emphasis on vocals, repetition, and fairly typical rhythms. Their music is infectious but not all that distinctive. However, the three numbers from 1987 (placed at the end of this CD) are all fairly strong instrumentals. The group is heard with a completely different lineup than it would have five years later (other than leader-trumpeter López) and was expanded to a nonet that includes Oriente López on keyboards and flute, Edino Montero on second trumpet, and Fernando Acosta on tenor and soprano. Those selections, which find the musicians stretching out and playing fairly unpredictable Afro-Cuban Jazz, had originally been released in full on the LP *Eclipse de Sol* (JRH 004), so listeners should search for the LP instead.

FRANCISCO AGUABELLA

b. 1925, Matanzas, Cuba

One of the most significant Cuban percussionists of the 1950s, Francisco Aguabella has remained quite busy up to the present time. He began to play the sacred Batá drum at age ten. Two years later Aguabella dropped out of school to work with his father on the docks, playing music at night. By the mid-'40s he was a full-time musician, moving to Havana. In 1950 Aguabella worked at the Cabaret Sansuci with the musical revue Sun Sun Ba Ba Ey. Katherine Dunham in 1953 hired him to play percussion for her dancers, and he spent the next four years primarily in Italy, working on the film *Mambo* (1953-54) and performing for her shows.

In 1957 Aguabella moved to the United States, where his friend Mongo Santamaria introduced him to Tito Puente. He appears on Puente's notable RCA recording *Top Percussion* and contributed two songs to Puente's *Dancemania* album.

Aguabella spent time living in Oakland (playing conga with the Duran Brothers) and Los Angeles, where he worked with René López, René Touzet, and Pérez Prado. He played with Mongo Santamaria (including recording *Yambu and Mongo,* to which he contributed some arrangements), led his own set (*The Latin Way*) for Fantasy in 1961 and recorded *The New Continent* with Dizzy Gillespie's orchestra in 1962; Aguabella would gig with Gillespie on several occasions through the years.

Aguabella worked regularly with Peggy Lee during 1963-70 and Frank Sinatra (1970), playing with the Latin rock group Malo (1971-74). Otherwise he has worked with virtually everyone at one time or another. His list of credits include trumpeter Don Ellis, tenor saxophonist Joe Henderson, the Jazz Crusaders, Emil Richards, trumpeter Al Hirt, Rosemary Clooney, Tito Rodriguez, Tito Puente (recording El Rey), Eddie Palmieri (1989's *Sueño*), Carlos Santana, Cal Tjader, Machito, Cachao, and vibraphonist Bobby Hutcherson, among many others. Based in California since 1987 and leading three albums for Cubop in the late 1990s (*Hitting Hard, Agua de Cuba,* and *H₂O*), the veteran percussionist is portrayed in the Les Blank film *Sworn to the Drum: A Tribute to Francisco Aguabella.*

9 *Agua de Cuba / 1999 / Cubop 0018*

The percussion work is so dense, complex, and exciting on the opening, "Dajomy Blue," that listeners could be excused for thinking that the rest of this CD (just Francisco Aguabella's fourth as a leader) would be anticlimactic. However, the solos of trumpeter Ramon Flores, trombonist Isaac Smith, and Charles Owens on tenor and flute (even if his spots on tenor are sometimes over the top) keep the momentum flowing. A strangely unidentified pianist is also a major asset. Aguabella, whose conga playing is joined in the rhythm section by Humberto Hernández on timbales and Joséy de Leon on bongos (drummer-timbale player Tiki Pasillas is sometimes in Hernández's place) plus an unlisted bassist, is heard throughout in peak form. The repertoire, which includes "Watermelon Man," "Manteca," "Milestones," and Aguabella's "Salsa Latina" among the highlights, is particularly strong. Highly recommended.

JUSTO ALMARIO
b. Feb. 18, 1949, Sincelejo, Colombia

A fine saxophonist whose own recordings tend to be commercial but who can be a very valuable sideman, Justo Almario has long been a fixture in the Los Angeles area. The son of a percussionist, Almario was playing on Colombian television by the time he was 14. He first visited the United States with a Colombian folklore group when he was 15. Almario studied at Berklee during 1969-70, was Mongo Santamaria's musical director (1971-75), and worked regularly with vibraphonist Roy Ayers (1976-79). After traveling with Henry Mancini's orchestra (where he was well featured as a soloist), he settled in L.A. to become a studio musician.

Skilled on tenor, alto, soprano, and flute, Almario was a member of trumpeter Freddie Hubbard's band during 1980-81. He has since worked with quite a few notables, including Cal Tjader, bassist Charles Mingus, Poncho Sanchez, Machito, Tania Maria, and Tito Puente, in addition to being a member of Koinonia for ten years. Almario, who considers John Coltrane, Cannonball Adderley, and Charlie Parker to be important influences, can play anything from Latin crossover to hard bop. He has recorded with Roy Ayers, Mongo Santamaria, Cachao, Humberto Ramirez, singer Kevyn Lettau, Poncho Sanchez, Tania Maria, Dianne Reeves, Luis Bonella, and Bobby Shew plus many others. Since the early 1980s he has often teamed up with Alex Acuña in the group Tolu. As a leader, Justo Almario has recorded for Uno Melodia (1981), Meadowlark (1985-87), MCA (1989), Blue Moon (1992), and Integrity (1994), although he is best heard as a sideman.

4 *Heritage / 1992 / Mesa / Bluemoon 79343*
6 *Justo & Abraham / 1994 / Integrity 00822*

Justo Almario is a fine saxophonist who can play fiery solos. *Heritage,* however, is a mostly commercial crossover effort. Although the backup group has Abraham Laboriel Sr. on bass, drummer Abraham Laboriel Jr., percussionist Alex Acuña, and pianist Otmaro Ruiz among others, the Latin aspect of the music is quite minor. Almario, who is heard on tenor, flute, soprano, and alto, comes across best here on soprano, particularly on "Rhapsody in Rio" and the thoughtful "Something of You." Most of the other selections are funky and danceable but rather simplistic and forgettable, with an overemphasis on the rather routine melodies (most of them by the leader), little adventure to Almario's playing, and the main goal clearly being to get radio airplay.

Justo & Abraham, which is co-led by bassist Abe Laboriel Sr., is a set that the principals consider a gift to God, with titles that proclaim their faith. All of the songs are of recent vintage (no traditional hymns are included) and, with the exception of one song that uses a coro ("Yahweh"), the music is instrumental. That fact probably adds to the accessibility of the performances! Almario is heard on tenor, soprano, and flute with a little bit of his alto and clarinet also being heard. The backing rhythm section includes pianist Greg Mathisson, both

Laboriels, guitarist Michael Thompson, Harlan Rogers on keyboards, and percussionist Luis Conte, with occasional additions and alterations. The music, which has a Latin feel and some good solos from Almario, is pleasing. But once again it is a pity that the saxophonist never completely cuts loose.

ARMANDO "CHOCOLATE" ARMENTEROS
b. April 4, 1928, Ranchuelo, Santa Clara, Las Villas Province, Cuba

Considered one of the top veteran trumpeters from Cuba, Chocolate Armenteros has been featured with many bands through the years. He grew up in a musical family and played with a local orchestra from the time he was 11. After relocating to Havana, Armenteros worked with Septeto Habanero, and he made his recording debut in 1949 with René Alvarez y su Conjunto Los Astros; he also recorded with Arsenio Rodriguez that year. While with Julio Gutierrez's group, he gained the lifelong nickname of "Chocolate" when a woman thought that he was the 1932 world featherweight boxing champion Kid Chocolate; Armenteros would have had to have been champ when he was four to be that person!

In the 1950s Armenteros worked in Cuba's studios and with many groups, including those led by his cousin Beny Moré, singers Joséito Fernandez, Cheo Marquetti, and Rolando La Serie, Bebo Valdés, and Chico O'Farrill. Armenteros was part of the band used on Nat King Cole's album *Cole Español,* which was cut in Cuba. He first appeared in the United States in the late 1950s and worked with José Fajardo, Cesar Concepcion, Machito, Mongo Santamaria, Orlando Marin, Johnny Pacheco, the Tico All-Stars, Charlie Palmieri, Joe Quijano, Ismael Rivera, and Eddie Palmieri, among many others. Chocolate has kept quite busy through the decades, finally having his recording debut as a leader in 1974 when he was 46, working as a session musician (appearing on countless records), and performing with Grupo Folklorico y Experimental Nuevayorquino, La Sonora Matancera (1976-81), Machito, Cachao, and his own groups. One of his few recordings outside of the Cuban music world was a hard bop date with pianist Cedar Walton's Sextet (*Eastern Rebellion 4*). Chocolate Armenteros recently appeared on *Paquito D'Rivera Presents 40 Years of Cuban Jam Sessions.*

DESI ARNAZ

b. Mar. 2, 1917, Santiago de Cuba, Cuba,
d. Nov. 2, 1986, Los Angeles, CA

Immortal for his role as Lucille Ball's husband, Ricky Ricardo, in the classic television series *I Love Lucy* (1951-59), Desi Arnaz earlier on gained fame for his work as a bandleader, singer, and conga player. Born Desiderio Alberto y de Acha III, young Desi was part of a rich family, since his father (who owned three ranches and an island in Santiago Bay) was one of the founders of Bacardi Rum. There were plans for him to attend law school, but the Batista revolution of August 1933 wiped out the family fortune. By 1935 Arnaz's family was forced to flee to the United States, where he enrolled in high school in Miami so he could learn English. Struggling in poverty at first, Arnaz had a job cleaning bird cages! However, he proved to be a charismatic singer and was soon singing rumbas in a local hotel. He was discovered by Xavier Cugat, who immediately hired him for his world-famous orchestra. Arnaz spent six months during 1936 performing with Cugat, and his exciting conga solos helped to introduce that instrument to the American public. He led his own group for a couple of years (even appearing for a time as the leader of a house band at a New York nightclub called La Conga!) but was just struggling along when he was offered a part in the Rodgers and Hart Broadway musical *Too Many Girls*. The show was a hit, and Arnaz also appeared in the film version, whose star

was Lucille Ball. By 1940 the two were married.

Desi Arnaz, who also appeared in such films as *Bataan, Father Takes a Wife, Four Jacks and a Jill, The Navy Comes Through, Cuban Pete,* and *Holiday in Havana,* never became a movie star; there were few worthwhile roles for Latin performers. However, his band in the 1940s was one of the most popular of all Latin groups, even though its jazz content was generally not that high. After serving in the Army (1943-45), Desi Arnaz made his best recordings for RCA during 1946-49, including having hits in two numbers that became trademarks for him: "Babalu" and "Cuban Pete." Due to his great popularity in later years, when music was secondary, the Desi Arnaz Orchestra, which had strong musicianship and put on colorful shows, tends to be overlooked and written-off today.

Lucille Ball had a popular radio show (*My Favorite Husband*) during 1949-50 that would be the basis for *I Love Lucy.* In the spring of 1950 Lucy and Desi put together a humorous vaudeville act that they took on the road, and soon they founded Desilu Productions; Arnaz ended up being a very skilled businessman. CBS TV was interested in having Lucy star in a *My Favorite Husband* television series, but they were initially against having Desi play opposite her, due to his accent. However the couple borrowed $8,000 to produce a pilot film, the executives at CBS saw the potential of the show, and during 1951-57 *I Love Lucy* became a legendary television series; 180 half-hour episodes were made. During 1958-59 the series became monthly hour-long specials. But it all ended in 1960 when Lucy and Desi were divorced. Desi Arnaz remained famous throughout the remainder of his life, occasionally performing with a Latin band in later years.

8 *Cuban Originals / 1946-1949 / BMG 74321-69936*

Desi Arnaz's most significant recordings were the

43 that he cut for RCA Victor during 1946-49, and this 16-song CD has the cream of that period. Four selections (including memorable renditions of "Tico Tico," "The Peanut Vendor," and "Brazil") are instrumentals, while the very likable singer is heard on most of the other tunes; Jane Harvey also takes two vocals. Although the music sometimes is a bit sweet (thanks to the strings) and there are a couple novelties (including "Carnival in Rio"), the performances are stronger than expected and the rhythm section (with Arnaz on conga) is frequently exciting. Among the other highlights are "Cuban Pete," "Guadalajara," and "Babalu." A fine sampling from Desi Arnaz's underrated musical career.

DON AZPIAZU

b. 1893, Cuba, d. 1943, Cuba

His name might be forgotten today, but Don Azpiazu was largely responsible for the introduction of Cuban music to the United States, and he took the first early steps toward forming Afro-Cuban Jazz. After playing successfully in Cuba, Don Azpiazu's Havana Casino Orchestra (with the important Cuban singer Antonio Machin) came to the United States in 1930. Cuban music had been heard previously in the United States in watered-down form, but when Azpiazu's ensemble appeared on Broadway, using maracas, clavés, bongos, and timbales in its instrumentation and playing some jazz, it was a historic occasion. Azpiazu's recording of "The Peanut Vendor" was a hit as was his version of "Green Eyes." He was among the first to record "Mama Inez," a song often satirized by American bands (who used silly novelty effects). He also made his music a little more accessible by using Chick Bullock and Bob Burke to sing songs in English while Machin took care of the Spanish vocals. Azpiazu's success started a brief Latin music fad (suddenly many New York studio orchestras had "Havana" in their name) and led to the formation of many rumba bands.

After touring Europe in 1932, Azpiazu's orchestra returned home and was quickly forgotten in the United States. In the late 1930s he returned to New York, where he led a band at the Seville Biltmore Hotel. But the management discouraged him from playing jazz, wanting him to stick to Cuban dance music, and he never emerged again from obscurity. However, in his original dream of combining Cuban music and jazz, Don Azpiazu was 15 years ahead of his time.

GATO BARBIERI

b. Nov. 28, 1934, Rosario, Argentina

Leandro "Gato" Barbieri has always been best known for his huge and often-ferocious sound on the tenor. Barbieri started out in his native Argentina studying and playing alto and clarinet at age 12 after hearing Charlie Parker's recording of "Now's the Time." He moved to Buenos Aires with his family in 1947 and soon became a prominent local musician, playing with Lalo Schifrin (1953), among others, and permanently switching to tenor in 1955. Barbieri's career since then can easily be divided into three periods. In 1962 he started his early period as a fiery avant-gardist, spending time living in Rome and Paris, working and recording with cornetist Don Cherry (for Blue Note), soprano saxophonist Steve Lacy, pianist Dollar Brand, vibraphonist Gary Burton (*Genuine Tong Funeral*), Charlie Haden's Liberation Orchestra, and the Jazz Composers Orchestra in addition to making his first recordings as a leader.

Having abandoned his Argentinean roots as he explored free improvising and intense sound explorations, Barbieri moved into the second part of his career, which ended up being his most artistically satisfying. Barbieri switched his attention back to Argentinean and South American music, combining folk melodies with the improvising of jazz and recording several classic albums for Flying Dutchman and Impulse during 1969-75.

After writing and playing the romantic themes used throughout the soundtrack of 1972's *Last*

Tango in Paris (and appearing briefly in the film), Barbieri gained a surprising amount of fame. From the mid-1970s on his music became much more commercial, emphasizing melodies and his warm sound, with only rather basic improvising; his poppish A&M albums sold quite well. Barbieri's own erratic health and the death of his wife led to the tenor's being mostly retired from active performing from the mid-1980s to the mid-'90s. He returned in 1997 with his Sony recording *Que Pasa,* but this effort was clearly aimed at the commercial pop/jazz market. Whether there will be a significant fourth period in Gato Barbieri's career is not known yet.

5 *In Search of Mystery / Mar. 15, 1967 / ESP 1049*

5 *Last Tango in Paris / Nov. 20-25, 1972 / Rykodisc 10724*

10 *Latino America / Apr. 18, 1973-Oct. 17, 1973 / Impulse 2-236*

10 *Chapter 3: Viva Emiliano Zapata / June 25, 1974 / GRP/Impulse 111*

4 *Que Pasa / 1997 / Sony*

4 *Che Corazon / 1999 / Columbia 69690*

In Search of Mystery is from Barbieri's early years. He romps through four of his originals, with musical commentary provided by cellist Calo Scott, bassist Sirone, and drummer Bobby Kapp. This is passionate music that is admirable for its chance taking, but sometimes it is almost unlistenable due to its intensity!

The soundtrack from *Last Tango in Paris* was reissued in deluxe form by Rykodisc, including 11 themes from the movie (three of which are the "Last Tango in Paris" theme at different tempos) plus a lengthy "The Last Tango in Paris Suite," which has 29 cues used for the film. But despite its success in making Gato famous, the music wears pretty thin after a while and often does not stand up apart from the film.

The classics of Gato Barbieri's career were his *Chapters 1, Chapter 2, Chapter 3,* and *Chapter 4* for Impulse during 1973-75. *Chapter 4* has not yet been reissued on CD, but *Chapter 3* came out individually while *Chapter 1* and *Chapter 2* have been combined on the two-CD set *Latino America.* In addition to the original program, five previously unreleased selections have been included on *Latino America* along with four now-complete songs that were formerly released in edited form. Recording in both Buenos Aires and Los Angeles, Gato and a variety of mostly lesser known (but talented) South American musicians perform highly rhythmic music and lengthy vamps with spirit and passion. Barbieri, who often punctuates his fiery solos with eccentric vocal outbursts, is heard at the peak of his powers. *Chapter 3* is perhaps even better. For this project, Barbieri is joined by an 18-piece orchestra that includes Victor Paz and Randy Brecker on trumpets, Howard Johnson on tuba, keyboardist Eddie Martinez, drummer Grady Tate, and four percussionists, including Ray Armando and Ray Mantilla. The arrangements, by Chico O'Farrill, fit perfectly Barbieri's solo flights on six of his originals, "Milonga Triste," and "Cuando Vuelva a Tu Lado" ("What a Difference a Day Makes").

Ironically Barbieri's commercial A&M dates (such as *Caliente, Ruby Ruby,* and *Tropico*), which were among his bigger sellers, have not been reissued on CD. When he returned after a long period off the scene, Barbieri came back with *Que Pasa* and *Che Corazon,* two albums that are often quite close to being easy-listening pop music. Sticking mostly to melody statements with only an occasional growl, Barbieri sounds as if he were playing by a rulebook, being careful not to disturb any radio program directors! Get his Impulse sets instead.

LPs to Search For:
Gato Barbieri's early avant-garde period can be heard on *Gato Barbieri & Don Cherry* (Inner City 1039) and a 1967 raging trio set, *Obsession* (Affinity 12). *Confluence* (Freedom 1003), duets from 1968

with pianist Abdullah Ibrahim (then known as Dollar Brand), is moderately more mellow. *El Pamperio* (Flying Dutchman 10151), recorded at the 1971 Montreux Jazz Festival, was near the beginning of the "new" Barbieri as he rediscovered his roots; on it he plays four lengthy numbers, including "Brasil," with a five-piece rhythm section that includes pianist Lonnie Liston Smith and both Na-Na and Sonny Morgan on percussion. *The Third World Revisited* (BMG 6995) teams Barbieri on four numbers (including "Yesterdays" and "A John Coltrane Blues") with keyboardist Jorge Dalto, bassist Ron Carter, guitarist Paul Metzke, drummer Bernard Purdie, Babafemi on congas, and Ray Mantilla on timbales in 1974. The following year, Barbieri recorded the now-elusive *Chapter 4— Alive in New York* (ABC 9303), a live septet date (with Howard Johnson tripling on flügelhorn, tuba, and bass clarinet!) that is up to the level of his first three "Chapters." From a much later period (1983), *Apasionado* (Doctor Jazz 40183) is less adventurous than the "Chapters" but still has its moments as Barbieri caresses such tunes as "Latin Lovers," "Habanera," and "Last Tango in Paris."

RAY BARRETTO

b. Apr. 29, 1929, Brooklyn, NY

An important bandleader during the past 40 years, Ray Barretto first gained fame during the second half of the 1950s, when he helped the conga to become accepted as a jazz instrument by playing as a sideman on quite a few jazz records. Although the music was generally hard bop rather than Afro-Cuban Jazz, Barretto's conga added a Latin flavor and made jazz listeners more aware and accepting of his instrument than they had been previously.

While serving in the Army in Germany during 1946-49, Barretto first heard a recording of Chano Pozo with Dizzy Gillespie's orchestra and was inspired to take up the conga. After he settled in New York, Barretto worked with Charlie Parker (during a two-week engagement), Eddie Bonnemere's Latin Jazz Combo (1953-54), Pete Terrace (1954), José Curbelo (1955-57), and most notably with Tito Puente (1957-61 as the replacement for Mongo Santamaria) and Herbie Mann (1961-62). He was a sideman on records by pianist Red Garland (*Manteca*), tenor saxophonist Gene Ammons, Dizzy Gillespie, altoists Lou Donaldson, Cannonball Adderley, Sonny Stitt, and Oliver Nelson, guitarist Wes Montgomery, and tenorman Stanley Turrentine. Barretto's first album as a leader was in 1961, *Pachanga with Barretto* (originally for Riverside). After the success of that project, Barretto formed his band, Charanga Moderna, a flute-and-strings group.

Barretto would continue working as a sideman now and then, including making recordings with guitarist Kenny Burrell, trumpeter Freddie Hubbard, Cal Tjader, guitarist George Benson, and even the Rolling Stones and the Bee Gees, but his most significant work was as a leader. The year 1962's *Latino* is considered one of his best Latin jazz albums, and his Tico record from the same year, *Charanga Moderna,* included a pop hit in "El Watusi." Barretto recorded other albums for Tico and United Artists throughout the 1960s, some of which were rhythm and blues-oriented and trying to duplicate the commercial success of "Watusi," without success. *Acid* (Fania 346), from 1967, really established him as a bandleader and began his association with the Fania label, for which he recorded over 20 albums, among them 1973's *The Other Road* (which included the hit "Guarare"). In 1975 Barretto became the musical director for the Fania All-Stars. Barretto's music for Fania ranged from jazz oriented to pure Salsa, while his two mid-1970s sessions for the Atlantic label were mostly Latin fusion.

In the 1980s Barretto performed and recorded Salsa, Afro-Cuban Jazz, and R&B. But since signing with the Concord Picante label in the 1990s

Whether as a leader or sideman in Salsa, bebop, or Afro-Cuban Jazz, the versatile Ray Barretto has been a major musical force for 45 years.

(and more recently recording for Blue Note), Ray Barretto has mostly performed Afro-Cuban Jazz, particularly in his projects with his New World Spirit Band. Throughout his career Ray Barretto has recorded over 1,000 studio dates and 50 albums as a leader.

10 *Carnaval / June 1, 1961-Sept. 20, 1962 / Fantasy 24173*

Ray Barretto's first two albums as a leader (and two of his finest) are reissued on this CD. *Pachanga With Barretto* is comprised of ten compositions by Héctor Rivera, high-quality music meant to accompany dancers who performed the Pachanga, a new Latin dance of the era. Although the playing and writing is a bit formal and traditional, the music is quite lively. Barretto is joined by flutist José Canoura, violinist Mike Stancerone, trumpeter "El Negro" Vivar, Frank Mercado on tenor (Vivar and Mercado have very minor roles), pianist Alfredito Valdez, Jr., bassist Ricky Jackson, Ray Mantilla on timbales, and Willie Rodriguez and Rudy Caldazo on additional percussion. The playing of Canoura and Stancerone (along with the coro) are most impressive. However the *Latino* album also included on this disc is even better, more of a descarga with looser playing and hotter solos. The group is the same except that José "Chombo" Silva is on tenor, Wito Korthwright is added on guido and the group singing is absent. The band jams such tunes as "Manha De Carnaval," "Exodus" and "Summertime," stretching out on "Descarga La Moderna," "El Negro Y Ray," and "Cocinando Suave." A gem, this CD is essential for all Afro-Cuban Jazz collections.

7 *La Cuna / Aug. 1979 / Legacy/Epic 66126*
7 *Handprints / Mar. 1991 / Concord Picante 4473*
8 *Ancestral Messages / Dec. 1992-Jan. 1993 / Concord Picante 4549*
8 *Taboo / Feb. 26-27, 1994 / Concord Picante 4601*
9 *My Summertime / July 1-3, 1995 / Owl 35830*

Originally recorded for producer Creed Taylor's CTI label, *La Cuna* has some of the later CTI trappings, with a slick sound in spots, but overall this is a fairly high-quality Afro-Cuban date. In addition to Barretto, the lineup includes such notables as Tito Puente on timbales, Joe Farrell (on tenor, soprano, and flute), and Charlie Palmieri and Carlos Franzetti alternating on piano. This is Cubop that does not overlook later developments in both jazz and Latin music.

Ray Barretto's three Concord Picante releases feature his New World Spirit Band, although his group did not yet have its name at the time of *Handprints*. Actually, other than Barretto, the only musicians on all three dates are pianist-keyboardist Hector Martignon and bassist Jairo Moreno. The septet (which also includes Steve Slagle on reeds, trumpeter Tim Ouimette, trombonist Barry Olsen, and drummer Ed Uribe) performs ten spirited group originals on *Handprints*. *Ancestral Messages* has Barretto at the head of a band with Ray Vega, tenor saxophonist and flutist Jay Rodriguez, drummer Satoshi Takeishi, and Alfredo Gonzales on guiro, in addition to Martignon and Moreno. The material (which includes "Freedom Jazz Dance," "Killer Joe," and plenty of catchy originals) is particularly strong, consistently stimulating the soloists. *Taboo,* which has Adam Kolker in Jay Rodriguez's place and drops the guiro, is on the same level, highlighted by "Work Song," "Lazy Afternoon," and McCoy Tyner's "Effendi."

My Summertime features the 1995 version of New World Spirit (with trumpeter Michael Mossman and drummer Vince Cherico) and shows that Ray Barretto's band really can turn practically any piece of music into Afro-Cuban Jazz. Among the songs successfully "Latinized" on this CD are

Duke Jordan's "No Problem," Dave Brubeck's "In Your Own Sweet Way," "Autumn Leaves," Thelonious Monk's "Off Minor," and even "When You Wish Upon a Star." Barretto takes a half-spoken vocal on "Summertime."

8 *Contact! / Apr. 3-9, 1997 / Blue Note 56974*
9 *Portrait in Jazz and Clavé / Mar. 6-14, 1999 / Blue Note 68452*

Although the liner notes to *Contact!* claim that it is not a "Latin jazz" date (Barretto hates that term), but a jazz date with Latin overtones, it sure sounds like the former to me. The jazz content is strong, with fine playing from the Lee Morgan/Freddie Hubbard-inspired trumpet and occasional trombone of Michael Mossman, plus many hard bop solos from Adam Kolker on tenor and soprano and pianist John Di Martino. However, the rhythm section (which consists of bassist Jairo Moreno or Hans Glawishnig, drummer Vince Cherico, percussionist Ray Vega, and Barretto on conga) mostly plays Afro-Cuban rhythms. The material includes "Caravan," "Serenata," "Poinciana," Horace Silver's "Sister Sadie" plus a few originals and a prayer on "La Bendicion." Whatever it is called (check out the Afro-Cuban groove to Michel Legrand's "The Summer Knows"), this is music that succeeds on its own terms.

The same can be said for *Portrait in Jazz and Clavé,* which has New World Spirit (Barretto, Kolker, trumpeter John Bailey, Di Martino, Cherico, and percussionist Bobby Sanabria) in 1999 joined by four featured guests: Kenny Burrell, tenor saxophonist Joe Lovano, Steve Turre on trombone and shells, and bassist Eddie Gomez. The repertoire is intriguing, including Latinized versions of four Duke Ellington songs (highlighted by "The Mooche" and "Cotton Tail"), a song apiece by Thelonious Monk, Wayne Shorter, and John Coltrane, and a couple of obscurities; Kolker, Di Martino, and former band member Michael

Mossman provided the arrangements. High-quality Afro-Cuban Jazz, with the guests sounding inspired by the unusual (for them) setting.

MARIO BAUZÁ

b. Apr. 28, 1911, Havana, Cuba, d. July 11, 1993, New York, NY

One of the giants of Afro-Cuban Jazz, Mario Bauzá could be considered its unofficial founder; he was certainly (at an absolute minimum) one of the most significant important early instigators of the style. Adopted as a youth by his godparents, he began music lessons when he was five and attended Havana's Municipal Academy starting at age seven. A very skilled musician, Bauzá debuted on clarinet with the Havana Philharmonic when he was nine

Mario Bauzá, the behind-the-scenes founder of Afro-Cuban Jazz.

and was made a regular member of the orchestra three years later on bass clarinet. He originally met Machito around 1923-24 and visited New York as early as 1926 with the orchestra of pianist Antonio Maria Romeu. It gave the teenager a chance to see American jazz for the first time and to make his recording debut with Romeu's Charanga Orchestra. After graduating from Havana's Municipal Conservatory in 1927, Bauzá (who by then was also playing alto-sax and bassoon) played with Los Jovenes Rendencion, an ensemble that also included Machito.

In 1930 Bauzá decided to move to the United States, and he was coincidentally on the same ship as Don Azpiazu's Havana Casino Orchestra, which included the legendary singer Antonio Machin. When Machin left Azpiazu and offered Bauzá a job to play with his quartet if he would switch to trumpet, the 19-year-old reportedly learned to play the instrument in just a couple of weeks! He recorded often with Machin during the first half of the 1930s and worked with many orchestras, including those led by Cuban trumpeter Vicente Sigler, Noble Sissle (playing saxophone with the singer's big band during 1931-32), and Hi Clark (his Missourians) at the Savoy Ballroom. Switching permanently to trumpet, Bauzá was with Chick Webb's orchestra during 1933-38 and introduced Webb to Ella Fitzgerald, helping to convince the drummer to hire the unseasoned singer. Bauzá, who became Webb's musical director in 1934, returned briefly to Cuba in 1936 to marry Machito's sister, Estella, a marriage that lasted until her death in 1983. After leaving Webb, Bauzá played with Don Redman (1938-39) and in 1939 joined Cab Calloway's big band. One night he faked being ill so his friend Dizzy Gillespie could sub for him and Calloway could hear Dizzy. The ploy worked and Gillespie was soon added to the band. The Bauzá-Gillespie friendship a few years later resulted in musical history.

In January 1941 Mario Bauzá joined Machito's Afro-Cubans (which had been formed the year before) as musical director. Soon he helped reorganize the band and made it more jazz-oriented, adding technically skilled readers and jazz improvisers. In 1943 when Machito was temporarily in the military, Bauzá kept the Afro-Cubans working. During that period he composed and arranged "Tanga" (Spanish for marijuana) which is considered the first Afro-Cuban Jazz song. A few years later his "Mambo Inn" became a standard. In 1947 when Dizzy Gillespie (who was quite impressed by Machito's music) mentioned to Bauzá that he would like to add a percussionist to his own orchestra, Bauzá introduced Gillespie to Chano Pozo; that would be the official start of "Cubop" or Afro-Cuban Jazz.

Mario Bauzá was an important part of Machito's orchestra up until 1975, rarely ever soloing but being responsible for some of the arrangements and the ensemble's general musical direction. Bauzá also recorded on Chano Pozo's rare dates as a leader in 1947 and with Tito Rodriguez. However, in 1975 he had an argument with Machito about the bandleader's agreeing to take an important tour of Europe with a small group. The promoter could not afford the full orchestra, and Bauzá felt that the Machito sound could not be duplicated in a combo. Due to this disagreement, Bauzá left Machito after 34 years. Years later he would admit that he was wrong and would reconcile with Machito.

Bauzá freelanced as a writer (retiring from active playing), led albums in 1977 and 1986, made guest appearances, commissioned Chico O'Farrill to develop "Tanga" into the four-movement "Tanga Suite," and during his last years led his own orchestra. Mario Bauzá's Afro-Cuban Jazz Concert Orchestra recorded three albums for Messidor and performed on the *Mambo Kings* soundtrack, giving the Afro-Cuban Jazz founder a last hurrah before his death from cancer at the age of 82.

10 *Tanga / Dec. 1991 / Messidor 15819*
9 *944 Columbus / May 27-28, 1993 / Messidor 15828*

Mario Bauzá's final period began with *Tanga,* the first of three recordings by his 1990s big band. His famous "Tanga" was expanded into five movements (counting a brief opening lullaby) for the occasion by arranger Chico O'Farrill. This version, with solos by ten of Bauzá's players (including trumpeters Victor Paz and Larry Lunetta, trombonists Conrad Herwig and Gerry Chamberlain, and tenor saxophonist Dioris Rivera) is quite exciting. Also on the CD are six briefer pieces, three of which have vocals, including some wild Latin scat singing by Rudy Calzado. Paquito D'Rivera guests on alto during his "Chucho." Highly recommended.

944 Columbus was recorded two months before Bauzá's death, and he knew it would be his final project, saying, "This is the last thing I'm going to do for the new generation." Bauzá's 19-piece Afro-Cuban Jazz Orchestra (with its four percussionists plus drummer Bobby Sanabria) feature such soloists on this disc as trumpeter Michael Mossman, flügelhornist Manny Duran, flutist Enrique Fernandez, a few fine saxophonists, and pianist Marcus Persiani. The two lead vocalists are Graciela (Bauzá's sister-in-law) and Rudy Calzado, who would take over the orchestra after the leader's death. Most of the selections on this final album are group originals, although there are major exceptions in "Heat Wave" and "A Night in Tunisia." It is fitting that the final song, "Chano," was dedicated to Chano Pozo, Mario Bauzá's contemporary who helped popularize Afro-Cuban Jazz nearly a half-century before.

STEVE BERRIOS

b. Feb. 24, 1945, New York, NY
An influential and versatile drummer, Steve Berrios has appeared in many settings since the mid-1960s.

His father, Steve Berrios Sr., played drums with Marcelino Guerra, Noro Morales, Miguelito Valdés, and Pupi Campo in addition to being part of the house bands of several New York City mambo clubs. After seeing Dizzy Gillespie play, the younger Berrios began playing trumpet when he was 11. At 16 he appeared at the Apollo Theatre with George Wheeler's Jazz Disciples, and he spent time playing with Pucho and the Latin Soul Brothers, Hugo Dickens and Joe Panama. However, Berrios was also very interested in the drums (he enjoyed playing his father's percussion instruments at home), and at 19 he gave up trumpet altogether, playing drums in a hotel band for four years. After he worked opposite Mongo Santamaria, he was invited to join the congueros band, where he played drums and timbales off and on for 20 years.

Berrios had the opportunity to work with many top musicians in addition to Santamaria, including singers Miriam Makeba and Leon Thomas, pianists Kenny Kirkland, Randy Weston, and Hilton Ruiz, trumpeter Wallace Roney, altoist Bobby Watson, tenor saxophonist Michael Brecker, Art Blakey's Jazz Messengers, Paquito D'Rivera, Tito Puente, Ray Mantilla's Space Station, Max Roach's M'Boom (starting in 1991), and others. He was an original member of Jerry González's Fort Apache Band (starting in 1981), working with that group for over 15 years. Considered one of the top drummers in Afro-Cuban Jazz today, Steve Berrios has led two albums of his own for Milestone.

9 *First World / Nov. 1994 / Milestone 9234*
7 *And Then Some! / Dec. 1995-Jan. 1996 / Milestone 9235*

First World, Steve Berrios' debut as a leader has plenty of variety, to say the least. There are some relatively straightforward jazz performances (Joe Ford's "Mafranbingo" and Walter Davis Jr.'s "Uranus"), guest appearances by warm singer

Freddy Cole and Grover Washington Jr. on soprano (for Antonio Carlos Jobim's "Once I Loved" and "Once in a While"), four percussion displays (three are very brief) by the leader, an unusual transformation of Ornette Coleman's "Lonely Woman," and some Cuban-oriented vocal pieces. Berrios even takes a lyrical trumpet solo on the ballad "Wild Is the Wind" with pianist Larry Willis and bassist George Mraz in a trio. Altoist Joe Ford and trumpeter Eddie Henderson are assets on a few selections. The style, mood, and atmosphere change from song to song, but Berrios' obvious comfort level in all of these idioms makes the disc quite successful.

And Then Some! is a much more intimate date, with most of the selections involving only three or four musicians. A few cuts have Wayne Wallace overdubbing on several trombones, singer Elisabeth Monder (the drummer's wife) becoming a coro, and Berrios overdubbing extra percussion. There are several pieces with Julio Collazo on lead vocal, a duet rendition of Thelonious Monk's "Bemsha Swing" with Joe Ford on soprano and Berrios on timpani, and a trio on "Blues for Sarka" with Ford and bassist George Mraz. Although there are certainly some strong moments on this disc, overall *First World* is on a higher level.

IGNACIO BERROA

b. July 8, 1953, Havana, Cuba

Ignacio Berroa has probably had his greatest fame due to his association with Dizzy Gillespie, but his drums have uplifted many dates through the years. Berroa started on violin before switching to drums. He studied at the Cuban National School of Arts (1964-67) and the National Conservatory of Music (1968-70) before playing in a Cuban Army band. He was with Felipe Dulzaides (1972-75) and the ICAIC (1975-79), also working regularly in the studios. In 1980 Berroa moved to New York, where he has since worked with Paquito D'Rivera, Dizzy

Gillespie (1981-83 and with Dizzy's United Nation Orchestra during 1987-91), pianist McCoy Tyner, Machito (1983-87), Clark Terry, Dave Valentin, Hilton Ruiz, Daniel Ponce, David Amram, altoist Lou Donaldson, James Moody, electric bassist Jaco Pastorius, and many others. Ignacio Berroa remains in great demand.

RUBÉN BLADES

b. July 16, 1948, Panama City, Panama

As famous for being a political activist as for his musical skills, Rubén Blades has been involved in Cuban music for many years, as both a singer and a bandleader. Both of his parents were musicians, and Blades sang with Conjunto Latino while in school in 1966 before working with Los Salvajes del Ritmo (1967-69). He graduated from the University of Panama, worked as a lawyer, moved to Miami in 1974, relocated to New York, and worked in the mailroom of the Fania label until he joined Ray Barretto's band in 1975. Blades had strong success as a songwriter, writing hits for (among others) singer Ismael Miranda, Tito Puente, Ricardo Ray, and Bobby Rodriguez. He recorded often with Willie Colón (including "El Cazangero"), the Fania All Stars, and Barretto. Blades' "Pedro Navaja" (a Latin transformation of "Mack the Knife") and "Plastico" are among his best-known songs, and his album *Siembra* became a best-selling Salsa album. Blades, who creates Cuban-oriented folk music full of social commentary (sometimes mixing in pop elements), became involved in films, acting in 1985's *Crossover Dreams, Critical Condition, The Milagro Beanfield War,* and *Dead Man Out.* He took time from music and acting to run for president of Panama in 1994 (finishing third). As a singer, Rubén Blades falls into the area of Salsa, but his bands have often performed high-quality Afro-Cuban Jazz, as they showed during a successful set at the 2000 Playboy Jazz Festival in Hollywood.

WILLIE BOBO

b. Feb. 28, 1934, New York, NY, d. Sept. 15, 1983, Los Angeles, CA

One of the most popular performers in Afro-Cuban Jazz, Willie Bobo was a colorful showman who was also a superior Latin percussionist. Born William Correa to a Puerto Rican family, Willie's father played the cautro (a ten-stringed guitar) on weekends. Bobo started on the bongos as a teenager, soon adding congas, timbales, and drums. He worked as Machito's band boy in 1947 so he could gain entrance to see the band, sometimes sitting in on bongos or drums during the last set. He played with Pérez Prado, had a few informal lessons from Mongo Santamaria in 1948 and 1950, and recorded with Mary Lou Williams in 1952; she was the first one to call him Willie Bobo. Bobo became well known while playing bongos with Tito Puente (1954-57), as part of his famous percussion unit with Mongo Santamaria that was dubbed "Ti-Mon-Bo." Bobo, who guested with George Shearing's band on the 1955 album *The Shearing Spell,* switched to timbales whenever Puente took vibes solos.

After appearing on Cal Tjader's album *Mas Ritmo Caliente* in 1957, Bobo left Puente, co-leading a short-lived group with Mongo Santamaria called Conjunto Manhattan before they both became members of Cal Tjader's band (1958-61). Bobo recorded with Tjader often and was also on Santamaria's dates of the era, including the one that resulted in the original version of "Afro Blue." After stints with Santamaria (1961-62) and Herbie Mann (1962-63), Bobo had his own Latin band, recording for Tico and Roulette.

Although that particular band group broke up in 1964, his important contributions as part of Cal Tjader's *Soul Sauce* recording resulted in Bobo's forming a more successful group in 1965. He recorded for Verve for the rest of the decade, including the hit album *Spanish Grease*. His 1970s

recordings (for Blue Note and CBS) were often influenced by R&B and pop, and Bobo occasionally sang in later years (including his favorite song, Antonio Carlos Jobim's "Dindi"). In 1980 he was diagnosed with cancer but kept it quiet until near the end, performing regularly until his death in 1983 at the age of 49. Willie Bobo recorded as a sideman with many jazz and Latin bands, including those led by Herbie Mann, Miles Davis, arranger Gil Evans, Stan Getz, Cannonball Adderley, Sonny Stitt, vibraphonist Terry Gibbs, pianists Herbie Hancock (*Inventions and Dimensions*), Les McCann, and Mary Lou Williams, drummer Chico Hamilton, saxophonists Ike Quebec, Oliver Nelson, and James Moody, guitarist Wes Montgomery, and trumpeters Howard McGhee and Thad Jones, in addition to Tito Puente, Cal Tjader, and Mongo Santamaria.

8 *Spanish Grease/Uno Dos Tres / June 6, 1965-Apr. 26, 1966 / Verve 314 521 664*

6 *Talkin' Verve / Feb. 4 1965-Dec. 23, 1968 / Verve 314 537 575*

Willie Bobo's two best-known albums as a leader, *Spanish Grease* and *Uno Dos Tres,* have been combined as one CD. Listeners looking for classic Afro-Cuban Jazz will be a bit disappointed because the music is much more pop-oriented, in the boogaloo vein, rather than displaying Bobo's roots in Tito Puente and Cal Tjader. However, there are plenty of catchy cuts along the way, including "Spanish Grease," "Fried Neck Bones and Some Home Fries," "The Breeze and I," and, surprisingly, Benny Golson's "I Remember Clifford." On the other hand, covers of such pop tunes as "It's Not Unusual" and "Our Day Will Come" are a little more difficult to sit through! Bobo's key sidemen include trumpeter Melvin Lastie, Bobby Brown on alto and tenor, and Patato Valdés on conga.

Talkin' Verve is a sampler with some of the highlights of Willie Bobo's Verve recordings, drawing its

15 selections from such albums as *A New Dimension, Bobo Motion, Juicy,* and *Spanish Blues Band* in addition to *Spanish Grease* and *Uno Dos Tres.* Some of the songs sound quite dated, but the CD does include such memorable numbers as "Evil Ways" (which Santana would soon largely copy), "Spanish Grease," Eddie Harris' "Sham Time," and "Fried Neck Bones and Some Home Fries." This is a solid introduction to Willie Bobo's music of the era, even though the original complete programs are preferred.

BONGO LOGIC

The main logic of Bongo Logic, founded by timbale player-musical director Brett Gollin in 1987, has been to combine traditional Cuban dance music (the charanga) with post-bop jazz, funk, and classical influences. Gollin (born May 27, 1952, in Los Angeles) visited Cuba in late 1985 and became inspired to form a flute, piano, and strings charanga group, but one that sounded contemporary. Bongo Logic debuted in 1987, they recorded for the Rocky Peak label the following year, and their early personnel consisted of Gollin, flutist Art Webb, pianist Joe Rotondi, violinist Harry Scorzo, keyboardist John Douglas, bassist Guillermo Guzman, Johnny Crespo on guiro, and Michito Sanchez on congas. By the time they made *Despierta* ("Wake Up") for Rhythm Safari in 1991, Gollin, Webb, Rotondi (now playing keyboards), Scorzo, Crespo, and Guzman were still present, along with percussionist Alfredo Ortiz, singers Tata Ramos and Ricardo Pasillas, trumpeter John Fumo, and trombonist Claude Caillet. The spirited group has since also recorded for the Montuno label.

LUIS BONILLA

b. 1956, Los Angeles, CA
The son of Costa Rican émigrés, Luis Bonilla started on trombone in high school and considered his main early influences to be J.J. Johnson, Curtis

Fuller, and Frank Rosolino. He played locally with Afro-Cuban, Brazilian and straightahead jazz bands (including Gerald Wilson's orchestra in 1985), graduated with a music degree from Cal State L.A., and recorded with Wilson, the Garcia Brothers, and Kenny Goldberg. Luis Bonilla, who worked with Poncho Sanchez and with his own groups, made his recording debut as a leader in 1991 for Candid.

8 *Pasos Gigantes / Feb. 26, 1991 / Candid 79507*

Luis Bonilla (doubling on bass trombone) leads an impressive octet on this consistently stimulating set. Joined by trumpeter Tony Lujan, Justo Almario (tenor, soprano, and flute), Ken Goldberg (alto, baritone, flute), Otmaro Ruiz, electric bassist Abraham Laboriel, Alex Acuña on drums and timbales, and Michito Sanchez on conga, Bonilla performs a wide variety of high-quality Afro-Cuban Jazz tunes. In addition to four group originals and "The Dolphin," the repertoire includes Wayne Shorter's obscure "Deluge," "Caravan," "If You Could See Me Now," and a Latinized version of John Coltrane's "Giant Steps" arranged by Almario that was renamed "Pasos Gigantes." Every musician gets opportunities to solo, with Bonilla, Lujan, Ruiz, and the percussionists often taking honors. Easily recommended.

JIMMY BOSCH

b. 1960, Jersey City, NJ
An important trombonist known to some as "El Trombon Criollo," Jimmy Bosch has uplifted the music of many groups. He grew up in Hoboken, New Jersey, one of 11 children raised in a poor family. Bosch began playing trombone when he was 11 and within two years was working locally in Latin bands. In 1978 he enrolled in the classical music department at Rutgers University but, more importantly, became a member of Manny Oquendo y Libre, with whom he made his recording debut and performed on and off for 20 years. Bosch has also

been a member of singer Marc Anthony's horn section and worked with Cachao, Ray Barretto, Eddie Palmieri, Rubén Blades, India, Machito, Tito Puente, the Fania All-Stars, Celia Cruz, and others. Considered a very valuable sideman, Bosch formed his own band (the Masters) in 1996. He has since recorded *Soneando Trombon* and *Salsa Dusa* for the Rykodisc label.

7 *Salsa Dusa / 1999 / Rykodisc 1007*

This is a fine effort that blends jazz solos by Bosch, trumpeter Felix Vega, and Jeff Lederer on tenor with Spanish vocals from Frankie Vazque, Herman Olivera, and Frankie Morales and spirited percussion. Bosch's lyrics are listed in both Spanish and English in the liner notes and are quite intelligent and purposeful. The strong ensembles (which are full of improvised riffs), the infectious singing, and the worthy material (which, along with the originals, includes Wayne Shorter's "Speak No Evil") make this set of interest to a wide audience.

SONNY BRAVO

b. Oct. 7, 1936, New York, NY

A fine pianist who is best known as a sideman, Sonny Bravo, born Elio Osacar, is always a strong asset, even if he is underrated. His father played bass professionally with Latin groups. A top baseball prospect in his youth and winner of a baseball scholarship to the University of Miami, Bravo injured his arm in 1956 and had to retire from sports. Fortunately, playing piano was also a strong interest of his, so he was soon working for El Casino de Miami, Conjunto Caney, Mandy Campo, and José Fajardo. Bravo worked for a few months with Tito Puente (recording on Tito's Roulette LP *My Fair Lady*), played with Vicentico Valdés, recorded with Bobby Paunetto, and worked for a couple of years with singer Raul Marrero. He recorded *The New York Latin Scene* for Columbia in 1968. Bravo worked with the Louie Ramirez-Pete Bonet

Orchestra for two years, played with Tipica 73, freelanced, and in the early 1980s became a long-time member of Tito Puente's orchestra, where he succeeded Jorge Dalto. Sonny Bravo, who spent nearly 20 years with Puente, has also freelanced on an occasional basis, including recording *The Latin Connection* with vibraphonist Terry Gibbs.

JANE BUNNETT

b. Oct. 22, 1956, Toronto, Canada

Jane Bunnett was originally thought of as an avant-garde soprano saxophonist and flutist. Her strong interest in Cuban music has resulted in her touring and recording with some of Cuba's best during the past decade, becoming a champion of Cuban musicians.

Bunnett originally studied classical piano and clarinet, but a bout with tendonitis forced her to quit. After seeing Charles Mingus' band at Keystone Korner in San Francisco in 1975, she was inspired to play adventurous jazz, taking up the soprano (studying with Steve Lacy, an early influence) and flute. From the time of her debut recording in 1988, Bunnett has consistently utilized major jazz musicians, including her husband (trumpeter Larry Cramer), pianist Don Pullen, tenor saxophonist Dewey Redman, and singers Sheila Jordan and Jeanne Lee, recording a duet album with pianist Paul Bley and playing in 1990 with the Kenny Wheeler Big Band.

After performing at the Havana Jazz Festival in 1990 (she had first visited Cuba in 1982), Bunnett became very interested in the island nation's music. Her 1991 *Spirits of Havana* recording was a major turning point, and since then she has frequently toured with bands under that title, meeting Cuban music on its own terms and adding her distinctive horns to the rhythms and vocals. She has also recorded with the Havana Flute Summit and on dates led by pianists Marilyn Lerner, Hilario Duran, and D.D. Jackson. Bunnett and Larry

Cramer have raised quite a bit of money through the years to buy instruments for Cuban students. So immersed has Jane Bunnett become with the Cubans' music that she was nicknamed "Havana Jane," but she is a versatile musician able to excel in many settings.

8 *New York Duets / 1989 / Music & Arts 629*
8 *Live at Sweet Basil / 1990 / Denon 9009*
10 *Spirits of Havana / Sept. 27, 1991-Oct. 4, 1991 / Denon 9011*

At the beginning of her career, Jane Bunnett was originally an avant-garde flutist and soprano saxophonist. Bunnett's second recording, *New York Duets* (her first has probably not yet been reissued on CD), teams her with one of her favorite pianists, the late Don Pullen. The repertoire consists mostly of their originals (including Pullen's "Double Arc Jake") plus two Thelonious Monk songs and a lone Cuban theme, "For Merceditas." Although Pullen often plays atonally, his solos are so rhythmic as to be more accessible than listeners might expect. This combination works well. *Live at Sweet Basil* is in the same vein (both "For Merceditas" and "Double Arc Jake" are repeated) but this time the music is performed by an excellent quintet consisting of Bunnett, Pullen, trumpeter Larry Kramer, bassist Kieran Overs, and drummer Billy Hart.

Spirits of Havana and the recordings that follow are the reasons that Jane Bunnett is in this book. Bunnett performs Cuban music (jazz, traditional dance music, and accompanying folkloric vocals) without losing her own musical personality. On *Spirits of Havana*, she ventured to Havana, where, with Cramer and bassist Overs, she used such top Cuban players as pianists Gonzalo Rubalcaba, Hilario Duran, and Emilio Rodriguez, quite a few percussionists, the Grupo Yoruba Andabo singers, lead vocalist Merceditas Valdés, and guitarist Ahmed Barroso. A few originals and

Monk's "Epistrophy" alternate with Cuban standards. The spirit of this recording did a great deal to revive interest in Cuban music, and the results are both heartwarming and quite special.

7 *The Water Is Wide / Aug. 18-19, 1993 / Evidence 22091*
9 *Jane Bunnett and the Cuban Piano Masters / Sept. 15-16, 1993 / World Pacific 32695*
7 *Rendez-Vous Brazil/Cuba / Mar 20-21, 1995 / Justin Time 74*
8 *Chamalongo / 1997 / Blue Note 23684*
8 *Ritmo + Soul / Sept. 19-21, 1999 / Blue Note 24456*

The Water Is Wide was a change of pace for Jane Bunnett in 1993, a non-Latin date that matched her horns with Larry Cramer, Don Pullen, Kieran Overs, and Billy Hart with guest vocals by Sheila Jordan and Jeanne Lee. Bunnett pays tribute to Rahsaan Roland Kirk on "Serenade to a Cuckoo," plays a couple of Thelonious Monk tunes à la Steve Lacy ("Pannonica" and "Brake's Sake"), explores diverse moods and styles on some originals, and wraps things up with Duke Ellington's "Rockin' in Rhythm." Jordan (on an emotional "You Must Believe in Spring") and Lee have individual features and come together on the title cut.

On her World Pacific release, Bunnett collaborates with pianists José Maria Viter and Frank Emilio Flynn plus bassist Carlitos del Puerto in a variety of settings, including three songs that feature both pianists. Everyone plays well, but it is the rich and memorable (if little-known) melodies (five by Viter, one from Flynn, and four other songs) that steal the show and make this a very winning program. *Rendez-Vous* is an unusual album in that it mixes together Cuban and Brazilian music, performed by musicians from both countries. Hilario Duran and bassist Carlos del Puerto represent

Cuban music, while guitarist-vocalist Fil Jachado and singer-percussionist, Celso Machado infuse the proceedings with a strong Brazilian flavor, including six originals; Bunnett brought in two other pieces. The melodic results are infectious and recommended to listeners open to a wide variety of styles. *Chamalongo* was the follow-up to *Spirits of Havana*. Some of the same musicians (Bunnett, Cramer, and Duran) are present, along with tenor saxophonist Yosvany Terry, percussionist Tata Guines, and the Cuban Folkloric All-Stars (which consists of five singers and five percussionists). Merceditas Valdés takes three vocals, her last on record before her death, making this spirited outing particularly historic.

The solos throughout *Ritmo + Soul* by Jane Bunnett (particularly on soprano), Larry Cramer, and Hilario Duran (who often takes honors) are consistently rewarding and explorative. Dean Bowmen's occasional vocals are also strong and, along with the percussionists (Dafnis Prieto, Lucumi, Pancho Quinto, and El Gato Gatell plus Njacko Backo on the kalimba), give the set much of its Cuban flavor. With the exception of three songs in the public domain, all of the compositions are by Bunnett and/or Cramer. A fine fusion of advanced jazz with Cuban music, just like most of Jane Bunnett's important and heartfelt recordings.

LPs to Search For:

In Dew Time (Dark Light 9001), Jane Bunnett's debut, features the up-and-coming player in 1988 with some very impressive company, including Don Pullen, tenor saxophonist Dewey Redman, Vincent Chancey on French horn, and Larry Cramer. The six numbers (which include Pullen's "Big Alice," a Carla Bley piece, and "As Long As There's Music") are played with groups as large as a septet and, although not hinting at her soon-to-blossom interest in Cuban music, this was a very impressive first step in Jane Bunnett's career.

CACHAO

b. Sept. 14, 1918, Havana, Cuba

Because he plays bass (rather than percussion, piano, or trumpet) and since he is soft-spoken, Israel "Cachao" López has spent much of his life in obscurity. However, in reality he has been one of the most important contributors to Cuban music. Cachao has not only been one of Afro-Cuban Jazz's finest bassists, but he was one of the founders of the mambo and recorded some of the first *descargas* (Cuban jam sessions). Although he has also played trumpet, piano, guitar, trombone, and bongos at various times, Cachao probably felt that he did not have much of a choice about choosing to play bass; 35 of his relatives were bass players! His brother Orestes (b. August 29, 1908) and sister Coralia (b. May 6, 1911) were also musicians. As early as 1926 (when he was seven), Cachao was playing guitar and bongos for the youth band El Conjunto Miguel de Seste. He played bass with the Ignacio Villa Orchestra for silent movies at a local theater and was a member of the Havana Philharmonic during 1932-1963. In the 1930s he worked in Havana with Pedro Sanjuan's Havana Philharmonic Orchestra and with violinist Marcelino Gonzales' ensemble, where his bass solos gained him the nickname "Cachao," short for *Cachandeo*, which in Spanish means "lively with joy."

During 1934-37 Cachao played with Ernesto Munoz, Antonio Maria Cruz, and Fernando Collazo. In 1938 he and his brother Orestes López (on piano) were members of Arcaño's La Primera Maravilla del Siglo. The two brothers combined to form the mambo rhythm for the first time in 1938, with Cachao's "Gloria Maceo" and Orestes' "Mambo" being among the earliest mambos. It took about a year to catch on, helped by the addition of a conga to the orchestra, and was initially opposed by purists of Cuban music. But the mambo eventually placed Arcaño's orchestra among the most popular in Cuba, predating by a decade the worldwide mambo craze fueled by Pérez Prado. Cachao played bass and arranged for the very busy group until he left in 1949 due to exhaustion.

After a long rest, Cachao became a busy freelancer in Cuba, playing with (among others) Marian Merceron's orchestra, José Fajardo, and Bebo Valdés. The first *descarga* (Spanish for "discharge," meaning "jam session") in Cuba was recorded by Bebo Valdés (with Cachao on bass) in 1952, and in 1957 Cachao's two volumes of Cuban jam sessions caught on and started a trend. Cachao worked steadily in Cuba until 1963, when he moved to the United States. He played with the who's who of Cuban music in New York into the early 1980s, including with Machito, Johnny Pacheco, Tito Rodriguez (1964-66), Candido, Fernando Mullens, Joe Quijano, Chico O'Farrill, Eddie Palmieri, Julio Guttierrez, Lou Pérez, Pupi Campo, and the Tico All-Stars. In addition Cachao was involved in quite a bit of session work, including with Patato and Totico, Hubert Laws, Mongo Santamaria, Lou Pérez, and Charlie Palmieri.

In the 1980s Cachao settled in Miami, where he remained active but for a time slipped into obscurity. He worked with Angel René, Joe Cain, Marco Rizo, the Miami All-Stars, the Fania All-Stars and the Miami Symphony Orchestra, but was often thought of as just another veteran bassist. However, actor Andy Garcia became aware of his historical importance and produced a 1993 documentary called *Cachao: Como Su Ritmo No Hay Dos* ("Like His Rhythm There Is No Other"). The film's release resulted in Cachao's rediscovery and to his finally gaining his deserved recognition. Since then he has been used on several special recording sessions (including Gloria Estefan's tribute to the founders of Cuban music, *Mi Terra*), working and recording with Paquito D'Rivera and Tito Puente in addition to leading his own groups. Now in his early 80s, Cachao remains one of the last significant pioneers of Afro-Cuban Jazz to be quite active still.

9 *Master Sessions Volume 1 / 1994 / Crescent Moon/Epic 64320*

After years of being overlooked and having fairly anonymous jobs, in the early '90s Cachao was finally recognized as an important founder of Afro-Cuban Jazz, in addition to being one of Latin music's top bassists. This "comeback" disc, which is full of delightful melodies, has inspired playing by quite a few all-stars along with a strong celebratory air. Among the musicians who help keep the momentum flowing are Paquito D'Rivera (mostly on clarinet), Justo Almario on tenor, Jimmy Bosch, Néstor Torres (in top form throughout), and a variety of percussionists and vocalists. The set runs out of gas a little during the final three numbers, but it starts out so strong that the CD is essential for all lovers of Afro-Cuban Jazz.

MICHEL CAMILO
b. Apr. 4, 1954, Santo Domingo, Dominican Republic

A powerful and virtuosic pianist who loves to challenge himself, Michel Camilo is one of the most exciting performers in jazz today, combining bebop with his Dominican Republic musical heritage. His partly Cuban family was very musical (all nine of his uncles were musicians), and he started on the accordion when he was four. Camilo, who studied piano at the National Conservatory starting when he was nine, first heard jazz (Art Tatum's recording of "Tea for Two") when he was 14 and was soon playing both jazz and classical music. At 16 he was the youngest member of the Dominican National Symphony Orchestra of Santo Domingo, as a percussionist.

In 1979 Camilo moved to the United States, where he met Mario Bauzá, who lent him Ernesto Lecuona's music for a year, an important influence on his playing. Camilo studied at Juilliard and Mannes College of Music and joined an all-star studio group called French Toast (with whom he

Bassist, Cachao was an important, if sometimes overlooked, pioneer of Afro-Cuban Jazz

recorded in 1984). Camilo's song "Why Not?" caught on as a standard and became a hit for the Manhattan Transfer, while his "Caribe" was performed by Dizzy Gillespie. He worked with Tito Puente, gained recognition while with Paquito D'Rivera's band (1982-86), and since then has mostly led his own trios. Michel Camilo has recorded regularly as a leader since 1985, has written for films and television, and has never lost his fire or his desire to stretch himself in both straightahead and Afro-Cuban Jazz settings.

7 *Why Not / Feb. 25-27, 1985 / Evidence 22002*

7 *Suntan / June 29-30, 1986 / Evidence 22030*

9 *On Fire / Jan. 20-25, 1989 / Epic 45295*
7 *On the Other Hand / Apr. 1990 / Epic 46236*

Michel Camilo's debut as a leader, *Why Not*, was cut in 1985, when he was 30, following a slightly earlier album with French Toast. The pianist's often-hyper style was very much formed by this time, and the set (originally cut for the Japanese King label but reissued domestically in 1992 by Evidence) is an excellent showcase for his talents. Camilo is joined by electric bassist Anthony Jackson, drummer Dave Weckl, trumpeter Lew Soloff, Chris Hunter on alto and tenor, and percussionists Sammy Figueroa and Guarionex Aquino. The group performs six of Camilo's originals, including his hit "Why Not?," which the Manhattan Transfer had made famous two years earlier.

Camilo's second album as a leader, *Suntan*, gave him the opportunity to really stretch out with his working trio of the period, a unit with Weckl (just prior to his joining Chick Corea) and Jackson; two of the five songs have Joel Rosenblatt filling in on drums. Originally made for the Japanese Suntan label and put out previously in the United States for a only brief time by Projazz, this 1992 reissue features the trio playing two songs by Camilo, a pair from bassist Jaco Pastorius (including "Used to Be a Cha-Cha"), and Airto Moreira's "Tombo in 7/4." Three of the five numbers are over ten minutes long, giving the Camilo Trio many opportunities to really develop their ideas and explore different rhythms.

After an album for Portrait (which has not been available in quite a few years), Camilo signed with Epic. *On Fire* lives up to its name, showing just how powerful a two-handed pianist Camilo has always been. He is heard in trios with Michael Bowie or Marc Johnson on bass and Marvin "Smitty" Smith or Dave Weckl on drums; two songs add a percussionist, and "Hands & Feet" is a duet with the flamenco dancer Raul. All of the selections other than "Softly As in a Morning Sunrise" are Camilo originals. The music on *On the Other Hand* is mostly laid back, other than the calypso title cut. Camilo is featured in a variety of settings with bassist Bowie, drummer Cliff Almond, trumpeter Michael Mossman, tenorman Ralph Bowen, and altoist Chris Hunter; two R&Bish vocalists are also on "Forbidden Fruit." Hunter's soprano is featured on the ballad "City of the Angels," there are two versions of the tender "Silent Talk," and most of the rest of the music features Camilo in a quiet or at least supportive role, making this a different type of Michel Camilo album, much more introspective than usual.

7 *Rendezvous / Jan. 18-20, 1993 / Columbia 53754*

9 *One More Once / May 20-26, 1994 / Columbia 66204*

8 *Spain / Aug. 1999 / Verve 314 561 545*

For his debut on the Columbia label, *Rendezvous*, Michel Camilo had a reunion with his 1986 trio of Anthony Jackson and Dave Weckl. The music is not strictly Afro-Cuban Jazz, although Camilo's expertise at polyrhythms always shows off the influence of his musical roots in the Dominican Republic. For the project, Camilo performs an obscurity, "Caravan," and seven of his more stimulating (if lesser-known) originals. The close communication among the musicians makes it sound as if the trio was a regularly working group rather than just a one-time reunion set. *One More Once* is an inspired idea, featuring the pianist at the head of a big band. Since he has a powerful orchestral attack, this is a very successful outing, whether Camilo pays tribute to Count Basie ("One More Once"), revives "Why Not," performs "Caribe" (probably his second best-known original), or takes "The Resolution" as an unaccompanied solo. The well-rounded effort also features such fine players as Paquito D'Rivera, Chris Hunter, Ralph Bowen, and Michael Mossman plus the conga of Giovanni Hidalgo.

Spain is a set of duets between Camilo and the virtuosic flamenco guitarist Tomatito. Whether setting an introspective mood or featuring heated interplay, the musicians sound quite relaxed and comfortable with one another. The duo explores Chick Corea's "Spain," "Besame Mucho," three originals, and two songs by Luis Salinas, building in momentum and power as the set progresses. Well worth several listens.

LPs to Search For:
Michel Camilo (Portrait 44482) is a now-obscure effort from 1988 that has Camilo romping in trios

with Marc Johnson or Lincoln Goines on bass and Dave Weckl or Joel Rosenblatt on drums. There are also some guest spots for Mongo Santamaria's congas. The repertoire includes "Nostalgia," "Blue Bossa," and "Caribe."

CANDIDO

b. Apr. 22, 1921, San Antonio De Los Baños, Cuba

One of several key conga players who appeared on many jazz dates in the 1950s and '60s (leading to the acceptance of Latin percussion as an optional part of jazz combos), Candido Camero gave a Latin feel to many bop dates yet was just as at home in purely Cuban settings. He started out playing bongos at age four, learned bass and tres as a youth, and switched to the drums when he started working professionally at age 14. Self-taught on all of his instruments, Candido mostly played tres, bass, and drums in his early days, before switching to conga in 1940. He recorded in Cuba, including with Machito, backed the dance team of Carmen and Rolando during 1940-46, and made his first visit to the United States with them, in 1946. Candido was a member of the house band at the Tropicana Club in Havana for five years (1947-52). Dizzy Gillespie heard him and convinced him to move to the United States. Candido took his advice, playing with Gillespie for a time in the States in 1952; he would record the album *Afro* with the trumpeter in 1954 and play with him on and off through the years.

Candido gained some recognition when he worked regularly with the Billy Taylor Trio (1953-54), was on George Shearing's first Latin jazz recording in 1953, and toured and recorded with Stan Kenton in 1954. Candido led his own band later in the 1950s (tenor saxophonist Al Cohn and altoist Phil Woods spent short periods as his sidemen) but became much better known for his many recordings with jazz greats. He appeared on records with Erroll Garner (1954), Gene Ammons (1956), guitarist Kenny Burrell (1956), Art Blakey (*Drum Suite* in 1957), tenor saxophonist Sonny Rollins (1962), singer Dinah Washington, pianist Wynton Kelly (1964), tenor saxophonist Illinois Jacquet (1965), Wes Montgomery (1965), drummer Elvin Jones (1969 and 1973), and vibraphonist Lionel Hampton (1977), among many others. In addition, he made appearances with Charlie Parker (captured live during a radio broadcast), bassist Charles Mingus, baritonist Gerry Mulligan, Woody Herman, Ella Fitzgerald, Duke Ellington, Count Basie, pianist Randy Weston, David Amram, singer Joe Williams, Machito, Tito Puente, Joe Loco, the Lecuona Cuban Boys, Miguelito Valdés, Lou Pérez, Mongo Santamaria, and Chico O'Farrill (with whom he recorded in 1995). In the 1960s, Candido's quintet (with Cachao on bass) worked at El Liborio, and he later led a group at the Chateau Madrid for 14 years. He has also worked extensively in the studios and led his own albums for Tico, ABC-Paramount, Roulette, Solid State, Blue Note, Polydor, and Salsoul, most of which are currently difficult to find.

4 *Thousand Finger Man / Sept. 4 + 9, 1969 / Blue Note 22664*

Candido plays quite well throughout the six selections on this CD reissue, but otherwise the music is a complete waste. The songs are immediately forgettable, there are few other solos from the nonet of mostly no-names (other than an out-of-tune soprano solo from Joe Grimm), and Frank Anderson's organ sounds quite dated. This set (originally from Solid State) would have been better if it had been all-percussion, for the other players add little if anything to the lightweight music.

EDDIE CANO

b. June 6, 1927, Los Angeles, CA, d. Jan. 30, 1988, Los Angeles, CA

A fine pianist influenced by both Erroll Garner and Noro Morales, Eddie Cano was for a time quite popular, playing Afro-Cuban Jazz in small groups. He actually started off with bass lessons from his grandfather (a bassist for the Mexico City Symphony) before switching to piano, also playing trombone in high school. Cano discovered jazz, served in the Army (1945-46), and after his discharge worked with the Miguelito Valdés Orchestra (1947-48). In addition to playing regularly with Bobby Ramos (1949-53), Cano had opportunities to sit in with Tito Puente, Machito, José Curbelo, and Noro Morales. He recorded with Les Baxter (1952) and wrote some of the more exotic arrangements used by Baxter on his famous mood music dates. Cano was part of Cal Tjader's group in 1954 (later recording with Tjader in 1956 and 1960) and led his own bands. In addition to recording with Jack Costanzo, vibraphonist Tony Martinez, and flutist Buddy Collette, Cano headed quite a few albums of his own for RCA, GNP, Reprise, Atco, and Dunhill, having a hit in 1961 with "A Taste of Honey." He faded in popularity in the late 1960s but continued working into the 1980s, including with Poncho Sanchez. Eddie Cano, who was the first president of the Hispanic Musicians Association (HMA), died after heart surgery at age 60.

CARIBBEAN JAZZ PROJECT

One of the most intriguing Latin-oriented jazz groups to be formed in the 1990s, the Caribbean Jazz Project, in its original version, had three co-leaders: Dave Samuels on vibes and marimba, steel drummer Andy Narell, and Paquito D'Rivera on alto and clarinet. In the summer of 1993, Samuels was asked to assemble a band for a concert at the Central Park Zoo in New York. He called Narell, D'Rivera, and a rhythm section, the musical magic was obvious, and by 1994 the group was officially formed, making its recording debut the following

year. Performing originals inspired by the music of Latin America, Cuba, the Caribbean, and Brazil, the band filled its own musical niche. In the late 1990s, due to the busy schedules of Narell and D'Rivera, Samuels became the Caribbean Jazz Project's sole leader, using Dave Valentin and guitarist Steve Khan as the other key voices.

9 *The Caribbean Jazz Project / Apr. 1995 / Heads Up 3033*

8 *Island Stories / Sept. 1996 / Heads Up 3039*

7 *New Horizons / Aug. 15-17, 1999 / Concord Picante 4878*

The Caribbean Jazz Project, the debut recording by the Caribbean Jazz Project, is the best of their trio of recordings. The combination of alto, steel drums, and vibes/marimba is quite unique. With the assistance of pianist Dario Eskenazi, bassist Oscar Stagnaro, drummer Mark Walker, and Luis Conte on congas, bongos, and timbales, each set by this group tended to be a tour of Latin and South America. They perform nine originals and two obscurities on their self-titled CD with spirit and plenty of variety. The follow-up set, *Island Stories* (using the same personnel except that Pernell Saturnino was in Conte's place) is a little wider ranging in its choice of material which includes Ernesto Lecuona's "Andalucia" (a D'Rivera clarinet specialty) and Astor Piazzola's "Libertango"; Samuels' "Tjader Motion" is a highlight.

The third CD by this intriguing group has a very different personnel than the first. Paquito D'Rivera's spot is taken by flutist Dave Valentin, and, in a major loss, the steel drum of Andy Narell is gone, succeeded by guitarist Steve Khan. The sextet (which also includes Dave Samuels, bassist John Benitez, and both Richie Flores and Robert Vilera on percussion) is still impressive, and the material (group originals other than "A Night in Tunisia" and Alec Wilder's "Moon and Sand") is melodic and catchy. The unusual vibes-steel drum-alto blend is missed but, taken on its own terms, the music (which shows off the influence of both Afro-Cuban Jazz and Caribbean styles) is quite enjoyable.

WILLIAM CEPEDA

b. Puerto Rico

Part of an important musical family in Puerto Rico, William Cepeda has long sought to combine his Puerto Rican musical heritage with advanced jazz. The trombonist has played with many top jazz and Cuban artists, including trumpeters Donald Byrd and Lester Bowie, saxophonists Jimmy Heath, David Murray, and Paquito D'Rivera, trombonist Slide Hampton, Celia Cruz, Oscar DeLeon, Eddie Palmieri, and Tito Puente, among many others. In 1989 he was in Dizzy Gillespie's United Nation Orchestra. Since returning to his native Puerto Rico in 1990, William Cepeda has remained quite active, creating what he calls Africanrican Jazz.

9 *My Roots and Beyond / 1998 / Blue Jackel 5028*

For his first CD as a leader, William Cepeda gathered players from Puerto Rico, Cuba, and the United States to perform a particularly strong jazz set. Cepeda (who also plays conch shell and percussion in addition to participating in the occasional group vocals) heads an octet (including tenor saxophonist Donny McCaslin, trumpeter Omar Kabir, and pianist Uli Gussendderfer) that is augmented on various selections by vocalists, percussionists, and such notables as Slide Hampton, Paquito D'Rivera, Luis Bonilla, and Tony Lujan. The solos are adventurous and post-bop (rather than Cubop), the rhythms are stirring, and there is plenty of variety in Cepeda's originals and grooves. Highly recommended.

WILLIE COLÓN

b. Apr. 28, 1950, Bronx, NY

A major name since the late 1960s, Willie Colón is a producer, bandleader, composer, vocalist, and trombonist. Born William Anthony Colón Roman, he started on trumpet when he was 12, switching to trombone two years later. While in school Colón directed a big band called the Latin Jazz All-Stars. His first professional group had two trombones (instead of trumpets or a flute) in the frontline, à la Eddie Palmieri. Colón signed with the Fania label when he was just 17 and soon had hits in "Jazzy" and "I Wish I Had a Watermelon"; his debut album, *El Malo*, sold 30,000 copies. His recordings since then (which often feature socially relevant lyrics) have mixed Latin jazz with other idioms, including songs from Africa, Brazil, the Caribbean, and Panama, and the influences of Puerto Rican country music, pop, and rock. Among his more highly rated albums are 1974's *The Good, the Bad, the Ugly,* 1978's *Siembra* with Rubén Blades (the biggest seller in Fania's catalog), and 1982's *Canciones del Solar de los Aburriodos,* although many of his recordings are outside of the realm of Afro-Cuban Jazz, including some that are collaborations with David Byrne.

Colón was perhaps at the height of his fame and influence in the 1970s, when he was considered one of the most significant contributors to Salsa and was working regularly on projects for the Fania label. In 1974 Colón began a long-time musical partnership with Rubén Blades and (by the late '70s) Celia Cruz, whose recordings he produced (including 1981's *Celia and Willie*) He worked steadily in the 1980s and '90s, particularly as a producer, had a late '80s band called *Legal Aliens,* and recorded for Sony in the early '90s. Willie Colón also ran for Congress in 1994, gaining 40 percent of the vote in the Democratic primary.

CONEXION LATINA

Founded in Germany in the late 1980s by trombonist Rudi Fuesers, Conexion Latina teams musicians from Germany, Puerto Rico, Venezuela, Denmark, and the United States to play both Afro-Cuban Jazz and Salsa. Thus far the band has recorded four albums for the Enja label.

8 *Mambo 2000 / July 9-10, 1992 / Enja 7055*
6 *La Conexion / Oct. 17, 1995 / Enja 9065*

Mambo 2000 is a particularly strong Afro-Cuban Jazz record. This live set features Conexion Latina as a mighty 15-piece orchestra with seven horns and four percussionists plus four vocalists. Four of the nine selections involve singing (with Anthony Martinez and Javier Plaza taking turns as lead vocalist), while the instrumentals have solos from trumpeter Benny Bailey (in top form) and tenor saxophonist Bobby Stern. The ensembles are stirring, and the multinational group is often quite exciting. The music on *La Conexion,* from three years later, is more run-of-the-mill. Bailey and Stern were gone, all nine songs emphasize singing (with Martinez and Plaza still the main voices), and, although the ensembles have their heated moments, it is frustrating how little solo space there is for the individual players. But be sure to pick up *Mambo 2000*!

LUIS CONTE

b. Nov. 16, 1954, Santiago, Cuba

A valuable percussionist who has played in a wide variety of settings (including jazz, R&B, and pop), Luis Conte has remained quite busy in the studios for many years. He started playing guitar as a child in Cuba but soon switched to percussion. In 1967 he was sent to Los Angeles by his parents so he could avoid serving in the Cuban Army. Los Angeles was the perfect place for this versatile musician to be based, for he studied at L.A. City College, played locally in clubs starting in 1973, and became a very busy studio musician. Conte worked in the '70s with the Latin fusion band Caldera, toured with Madonna, Andy Narell and

guitarist Al DiMeola, and has appeared on countless recordings, including his own in the late '80s for Denon. As a sideman Luis Conte has recorded with (among many others) drummer Louie Bellson (1977's *Ecue/Ritmos Cubanos* for Pablo), Clare Fischer, Justo Almario, Poncho Sanchez, Alex Acuña, Dave Valentin, drummer Roland Vásquez, altoists Brandon Fields and Eric Marienthal, guitarist Jeff Linsky, singers Tania Maria and Dianne Reeves, and pianist David Benoit.

7 *La Cocina Caliente / Oct. 12-13, 1987 / Denon 2237*
4 *Black Forest / June 6-11, 1989 / Denon 74100*

La Cocina Caliente, Luis Conte's debut as a leader, reflects his wide range of interests in jazz-influenced Latin styles. The music ranges from light funk/fusion and danceable grooves to Cubop (including "Killer Joe") and a closing jam by six percussionists on "Spankin'." Conte makes a strong contribution to each selection without being dominant, and such intriguing players as trumpeter Walt Fowler, tenor saxophonist Larry Klimas, keyboardist David Garfield, and Alex Acuña also make strong contributions. The electric keyboards at times sound a bit dated, but in general this music still sounds quite spirited more than a dozen years later.

Black Forest is of lesser interest, particularly from the Latin standpoint. The music is funky, often commercial, and not too memorable. The best selections are a Latinization of Chopin's "Susarasa," "Mere Wotimbo," and the closing percussion feature, "El Solar," although tenorman Larry Klimas does an excellent (if unintentional) imitation of Ernie Watts on "Krimson and Khaos." Otherwise the music (which often has David Witham's keyboards setting the grooves) is quite routine, sounding as if it was geared for radio airplay, obviously without much success. Luis Conte plays well but is often a minor character on his own CD.

JACK COSTANZO

b. Sept. 24, 1922, Chicago, IL

Due to his highly visible position as the bongo player with the Nat King Cole Trio (actually quartet), Jack Costanzo was for a time one of the best-known Latin players on the music scene. He started off as a dancer in a team with his wife, spending his spare time teaching himself bongos and studying congas. After serving in the Navy in 1945, Costanzo taught dancing at the Beverly Hills Hotel. On bongos and (to a lesser extent) congas he played with the Bobby Ramos Orchestra, Lecuona's Cuban Boys, Chuy Reyes, Desi Arnaz, and René Touzet. An important period with Stan Kenton (1947-48) gained Costanzo some fame, and he appeared on Kenton's first recording of "The Peanut Vendor" plus "Bongo Riff," "Monotony," "Abstraction," and other numbers.

Joining Nat King Cole in 1949, Costanzo was well featured for the first year, sitting out on the ballads but being heard quite prominently on the often-boppish swingers and taking "Calypso Blues" as a duet with Cole's voice. After Nat's recording of "Mona Lisa" became very big in 1951, the singer began to de-emphasize both his piano playing and his combo, and Costanzo ended up working as part of Cole's orchestra, staying with him until 1953. After leaving Cole, Costanzo worked mostly with pop groups and singers in addition to appearing with Kenton a few additional times until 1957, recording with Charlie Barnet (1954) and Pete Rugolo (1955 and 1958) and playing with Peggy Lee, Harry James, and Pérez Prado. Jack Costanzo led five record albums of his own during 1954-61 (best known is *Mr. Bongo*), settling in San Diego, where he has led his own group ever since.

MARK "SNOWBOY" COTGROVE

b. England

Based on their recent release, Snowboy and the Latin Section is one of the better Afro-Cuban bands currently active in England. Mark "Snowboy" Cotgrove is based in North London, where, at his Hi-Hat Club each Sunday, his impressive group performs for enthusiastic dancers and he DJs. Cotgrove, a fine conga player who considers Tito Puente, Ray Barretto, and the music of Eddie and Charlie Palmieri to be his main influences, has been active as a musician and DJ for over 20 years.

8 *Snowboy and the Latin Section Play Afro Cuban Jazz / 1999 / Cubop 026*

Snowboy's band consists of three fine horn players (trumpeter Sid Gauld, trombonist Paul Taylor, and tenor saxophonist Gary Plumley), Neil Angilley on electric piano and organ, bassist Nico Gomez, David Giovannini on drums and timbales, Dave Pattman on bongos, and Snowboy on congas. Their second release (following their earlier *Mambo Rage*) consists of eight group originals, with the music sometimes featuring Salsa singing from Snowboy, Giovannini, and Pattman but also including many opportunities for the musicians to stretch out. Well worth picking up.

CELIA CRUZ

b. Oct. 21, 1924, La Habana, Cuba

Although Celia Cruz has never sung jazz, she is included in this book due to her occasional associations with jazz-oriented performers (including Tito Puente), her lengthy career, and her position as one of Cuba's most famous singers. The future "Queen of Latin Music" was part of a family that had 14 children. She studied literature at a teachers' training college but, after winning a radio talent show, was soon studying music full time at Havana Conservatory of Music. Cruz (who was inspired by vocalist Paulina Alvarez) started out singing Afro-Cuban religious music but won so many amateur radio talent contests that she was hired as a featured vocalist on Radio Cadena, switching to secular music.

In 1949 Cruz toured Mexico and Venezuela with the revue Las Mulatas de Fuego. The following year she joined La Sonora Matancera, one of Cuba's top bands. Cruz starred with that ensemble for 15 years. She made her recording debut in 1951, had such hits as "Cao Cao Mani Picao" and "Mata Siguaraya," and became world famous. In 1960 she was touring Mexico with the band when she and her musicians decided not to return to Cuba, which was undergoing the U.S. blockade. Instead they moved to the United States, where she soon became a regular at New York's Palladium, married trumpeter Pedro Knight (who became her manager), and often shared the bill with Tito Puente, recording quite a few albums with him. By the late 1960s Celia Cruz was one of the top stars in the Salsa movement, recording for Fania, often working with the Fania All-Stars and Willie Colón, and in 1974 recording a gold record (*Celia y Johnny*) with Johnny Pacheco.

Celia Cruz has remained quite busy up to the present time, traveling the world, recording for RMM, appearing in the movie *The Mambo Kings,* and getting a star on Hollywood's Walk of Fame.

JOE CUBA

b. Apr. 22, 1931, New York, NY

Born Gilberto Calderon, this conga player is best known for leading the Joe Cuba Sextet. He originally became inspired to play Latin music after hearing Tito Puente's "Abaniquito." Calderon began playing conga professionally with La Alfarona X in 1950, Noro Morales, and Joe Panama (whose group patterned itself after Joe Loco's quintet). After Panama's band broke up in 1953, the musicians (without Panama) regrouped as the Cha

Cha Boys. When the band two years later was hired at Bronx's Starlight Ballroom, the ballroom owner spontaneously renamed the group the Joe Cuba Sextet. When Calderon called to ask who this Joe Cuba person was, he was told, "You!"

The band in the mid-1950s consisted of Calderon, vibraphonist Tommy Berrios (later Oscar Garcia), pianist-arranger-composer Nick Jimenez, bassist Jules "Slim" Codero, drummer-percussionist Jimmy Sabater, and singer Willie Torres (succeeded by José "Cheo" Feliciano in 1957, although Torres returned in 1965). Their 1956 recording *Mambo of the Times,* coupled with the band's decision to sing mostly in English, helped it become very popular and a major attraction. "To Be with You," "El Pito," "Oh Yeah," and "Bang Bang" were all hits in the 1960s, with the last one selling over a million copies. The group initially recorded for Mardi Gras, but their most famous albums were made for Seeco and Tico. After reaching the peak of their popularity in the late '60s, the Joe Cuba Sextet underwent a lot of turnover during the following decade but managed to work steadily until the late '70s, when it broke up and its members scattered. Joe Cuba became a licensed paralegal. The Joe Cuba Sextet had a reunion in 1984, and Cuba formed New Generation in 1992 (recording in 1995), although he remained a part-time player. In recent times, "Bang Bang" was revived and recorded by David Sanborn, but the band's recordings are currently somewhat scarce.

CUBANISMO

Led by trumpeter Jesus Alemany, Cubanismo is an all-star band featuring some of Cuba's best musicians. Alemany, born in Guanabacoa, Cuba, gained important experience playing traditional Cuban music for Sierra Maestra from the age of 15. The fiery trumpeter (who has a wide range) eventually relocated to London. Another key player in the band is pianist Alfredo Rodriguez, who left Cuba at a young age in 1960, living in New York and Miami before moving to Paris in 1983. Rodriguez has long been an important pianist in the Afro-Cuban scene, recording with Celia Cruz, Tito Puente, Johnny Pacheco, Mario Bauzá, and Dizzy Gillespie among others. Also included in Cubanismo are some of the musicians from Irakere and Tata Guines, one of Cuba's top percussionists. Cubanismo, which is based in Cuba (even though Alemany and Rodriguez live elsewhere), has toured the United States on a few occasions in recent times.

10 *Jesus Alemany's Cubanismo / May 1995 / Hannibal 1390*

The ten pieces on Cubanismo's debut showcase such Cuban dances as the rumba, cha-cha-cha, son, danzo, and pa'ca plus the Cuban descargas. Although the liner notes claim that the mostly instrumental music is much different than what is called Latin jazz, in reality it practically defines modern Afro-Cuban Jazz. Trumpeter-leader Jesus Alemany's solos are full of power, emotion, and occasional high notes. Pianist Alfredo Rodriguez really drives the rhythm section with his polyrhythms, the percussionists (led by Tata Guines) are explosive, and there are also hot solos from several of the sidemen, including trombonist Carlos Alvarez and Efraim Rios on tres. Stirring music from a very exciting 14-piece ensemble.

9 *Malembe / 1996 / Hannibal 1411*

After the strong success of Cubanismo's debut release, Jesus Alemany and Alfredo Rodriguez returned to Cuba for this almost-equally successful follow-up date. It is difficult not to be impressed with Cubanismo's trumpet section, the colorful arrangements, the memorable originals (even if "Cubanismo Llego" has a section taken from "Darn That Dream" that is not acknowledged), the spirited ensembles, and the solo work of Alemany (an underrated giant of the trumpet), Rodriguez, and

saxophonist Yosvany Terry Cabrera. The occasional singing (usually by a coro) is integrated well into the music rather than being dominant. There is not a slow moment on this disc!

XAVIER CUGAT

b. Jan. 1, 1900, Gerona, Spain, d. Oct. 27, 1990, Spain

In the 1930s and '40s, there was no more famous name in Latin music than that of Xavier Cugat, with his only competition being the Brazilian bombshell Carmen Miranda. Cugat's commercial success was so widespread (his was the one Latin band known to nearly all Americans) that his brand of Cuban dance and pop music tends to be underrated today. In reality, Cugat's orchestra (which never featured jazz) was always very musical, exotic without seeming dangerous, and did a fine job of representing Cuban music to the rest of the world in the pre-Cubop days.

Born in Spain, Cugat moved to Cuba with his family when he was four. He started playing violin in Havana cafes when he was just eight, often performing with a trio for silent movies. Cugat was skilled enough a violinist to play with the Havana Symphony. But after he had made it as a bandleader, he rarely ever soloed, just playing in ensembles. In 1921 he moved to the United States, having a second career for a time as a cartoonist for the *Los Angeles Times;* Cugat was a skilled caricaturist. He became friends with silent film star Rudolph Valentino, who encouraged him to form a tango orchestra. Cugat took his advice, forming the Gigolos, and was soon being billed as "The King of the Tango." His early band had three or four violins, trumpet, piano, accordion, marimba, guitar, and drums; it was gradually expanded through the years. By the 1930s he had added bongo and both Latin and American singers (including Dinah Shore in 1939). During 1934-35, Cugat's was one of three orchestras (along with Del Murray's and the then-unknown Benny Goodman's) to be featured on NBC's *Let's Dance* radio series.

Among Xavier Cugat's more popular records were "The Lady in Red" (1935), "Perfidia" (1941), "Brazil" (1943), and "South America Take It Away" (1946), although he was always a steady seller. The rise of the rumba in the 1930s enhanced Cugat's popularity, and he added mambos to his repertoire after they caught on big in the '40s. His band's style was said to have inspired Cole Porter to write "Begin the Beguine" (which Cugat recorded in 1935, three years before Artie Shaw). It was common for top Cuban musicians newly arrived in the United States (and those who were up-and-coming) to spend time in Cugat's orchestra. These included Desi Arnaz (who while with Cugat helped to popularize the conga), Machito, Tito Rodriguez, and Charlie Palmieri. Miguelito Valdés was Cugat's star singer during 1940-42, and his recording of "Babalu" made the tune famous before Desi Arnaz adopted it as his trademark song.

Although he does not seem to have recorded until 1933, Xavier Cugat appeared on film as early as 1927 (in some musical shorts) and made appearances in many full-length movies through the years, including *In Gay Madrid* (1930), *Ten Cents a Dance* (1931), *Go West Young Man* (1937), *You Were Never Lovelier* (1942), *Bathing Beauty* (1944), *Holiday in Mexico* and *A Date with Judy* (1948), all the way up to *The Phynx* (1969). He usually had a small supporting role in these films, playing a good-humored bandleader and always having at least one or two specialty numbers.

In addition to their film appearances and many first-class dance records, Xavier Cugat and his orchestra put on exciting visual shows and were a popular attraction for over four decades, having no difficulty rising above the current musical trends. Cugat, who had five glamorous wives during his life, retired in 1970 and moved to Spain in 1980. Despite health problems, he occasionally put

together an orchestra, including one as late as 1986 to celebrate his 87th birthday; he made it to 90. Due to his appearances in quite a few big-budget motion pictures in the 1940s, Xavier Cugat is still famous today.

JOSÉ CURBELO
b. 1919, Cuba

José Curbelo was the leader of one of the more popular Cuban orchestras of the mid- to late 1940s. A child prodigy on piano, he graduated from the Molinas Conservatory at 15. After gaining experience working in Cuba with the orchestras of Los Hermanos Lebartard, Gilberto Valdés, and Havana Riverside, Curbelo departed for New York in May 1939. The pianist freelanced for a time, including with Xavier Cugat, Juancito Sanabria, and Oscar De La Hoya. In 1942 he organized a nine-piece group consisting of two trumpets, three saxes, his piano, bass, timbales, drums, and Polito Galindez as lead singer, and was a mainstay in New York until 1959. Curbelo recorded for Coda (including in 1946 with singer Tito Rodriguez, Tito Puente on timbales, Chino Pozo on bongo, and Carlos Vidal on conga), RCA, Tico, and Fiesta. Sabu Martinez was his conguero in the mid-1950s, and Al Cohn played tenor with the band for a time. Tiring of performing, in 1959 Curbelo broke up his group and founded the Alpha Artists, a booking agency that handled most of the top Latin groups throughout the 1960s. José Curbelo left music for real estate in 1971, reformed his booking agency in 1976, and retired altogether to Miami in the early 1980s.

JORGE DALTO
b. 1948, Roque Pérez, Argentina, d. Oct. 27, 1987

A versatile pianist and keyboardist, Jorge Dalto could play Afro-Cuban Jazz, Brazilian music, tangos, straightahead jazz, and commercial music with equal skill. He was born 100 miles north of Buenos

Aires, where his father, Eliseo Dalto, led a tango orchestra and encouraged his son to learn piano. The youth played locally in rock groups, served for a year in the Argentinean Army, and then in 1971 moved to Chicago to gain experience as a musician. He made his recording debut with the fusion group Second Coming. Shortly after moving to New York in 1973, Dalto recorded with Gato Barbieri (appearing on the *Yesterdays* album), spending four months touring with the tenor's band.

After two years of freelancing, in 1975 Dalto joined George Benson's band, recording three albums with him including the guitarist's hit record of "This Masquerade." He also worked with Mario Bauzá during this period and in 1977 put together his Inter-American Quintet, recording *Chevere* for United Artists. During the next decade Dalto worked for a long period with Tito Puente and also played with Machito, Paquito D'Rivera, Grant Green, Dizzy Gillespie (appearing with Gillespie and Machito on *Afro-Cuban Jazz Moods*), Carmen McRae, Grover Washington Jr., and Spyro Gyra. He recorded additional albums as a leader for Gaia (1978), Cheetah (1983), and finally Concord Picante (1985). The 1980s version of the Inter-American Band included Patato Valdés on congas, Nicky Marrero on timbales, and Jorge's wife, Adela Dalto, on vocals. But shortly after the release of the Concord Picante CD, Jorge Dalto was stricken with cancer. He died in 1987 at the age of 39.

8 *Urban Oasis / Jan. 1985 / Concord Picante 275*

Jorge Dalto's last recording was one of his strongest. Using a septet (with flutist Artie Webb, bassist Sal Cuevas, drummer Buddy Williams, Patato Valdés, and Nicky Marrero as the nucleus), Dalto often changes the instrumentation (guitarist José Neto, bassists Andy González and Sergio Brandao, and José Mangual Sr. on bongos make appearances) and plays two songs without any per-

cussionists. Heard on both acoustic and electric pianos, Dalto performs such numbers as his "Samba All Day Long," "Killer Joe," Freddie Hubbard's "Skydive," and "Ease My Pain" (which features his wife, Adela, on vocals) during a well-rounded but, sadly, final effort.

PAQUITO D'RIVERA
b. June 4, 1948, Havana, Cuba

One of the great alto saxophonists in jazz, a very talented clarinetist, and an underrated soprano saxophonist (who also makes rare appearances on flute and tenor), Paquito D'Rivera has had a very successful and important career since escaping from Castro's Cuba. In addition to his championing of Cuban music and his mastery of Bebop, D'Rivera has often focused on music from other Latin and South American countries, reviving many worthy obscurities.

His father, Tito Rivera (a classical saxophonist), originally bought him a tenor sax, gave him his first lessons (at age five), and introduced him to jazz. Paquito developed very quickly, and he was performing in public by the time he was six, playing the Webern Clarinet Concerto No. 2 at Havana's National Theatre when he was just ten. D'Rivera started listening to jazz regularly after discovering Willis Conover's program on *Voice of America*. Starting in 1960 he studied at the conservatory in Havana. When he served in the Cuban military during 1965-67, he was fortunate enough to be able to play in an army band. After his discharge, D'Rivera was one of the founding members of the Orquesta Cubana de Musica Moderna, switching with the better players in 1973 to Irakere. He played and recorded regularly with Irakere in addition to making two solo albums of his own, and he met and jammed with Dizzy Gillespie when the trumpeter visited Cuba in 1977. But the restrictions of the Communist regime were a constant irritant and led D'Rivera to make plans. Traveling aboard with

Irakere, in 1980 he defected when the band was visiting Spain.

It did not take long for D'Rivera to become established in the United States. He played with Dizzy Gillespie, was signed to a contract with Columbia, and was soon leading his own Afro-Cuban Jazz ensemble. D'Rivera's group helped introduce Hilton Ruiz, Claudio Roditi, Danilo Perez, and particularly Michel Camilo. Even after his Columbia period ended in 1987 (the year that the altoist became an American citizen), he maintained a high profile, gigging constantly and recording for other labels.

D'Rivera worked as a sideman for short periods with McCoy Tyner, Lionel Hampton, Tito Puente, Freddie Hubbard, and others, in addition to playing with Dizzy Gillespie on an occasional basis, most notably with Dizzy's United Nation Orchestra during 1988-91, while also leading his own groups. After Gillespie's death in 1992, D'Rivera became the musical director of the United Nation Orchestra (which works on a part-time basis). He also co-led (with Dave Samuels and Andy Narell) the Caribbean Jazz Project in the mid-1990s and produced recordings by several musicians, including J.P. Torres and Bebo Valdés. But it is as an altoist (where his range is quite outstanding) and clarinetist that Paquito D'Rivera continues to make his strongest mark on jazz and Latin music.

7 *Taste of Paquito / 1981-Oct. 1987 / Columbia/Legacy 57717*

8 *Return to Ipanema / Mar. 1-2, 1989 / Town Crier 516*

8 *Tico! Tico! / June 28, 1989-Aug. 16, 1989 / Chesky 34*

10 *Reunion / Aug. 1990 / Messidor 15805*

9 *Who's Smoking?! / May 21-22, 1991 / Candid 79523*

8 *Havana Café / Aug. 28-29, 1991 / Chesky 60*

Paquito D'Rivera's recordings as a leader range from bebop and advanced straightahead jazz to lots of Afro-Cuban Jazz, some Brazilian music, and melodies from other South and Latin American countries. His output has been both numerous and consistently rewarding, with equal doses of fire and lyricism. He began his American recording career with a series of seven albums for Columbia, none of which have yet been reissued in full. *Taste of Paquito* is a worthwhile single-CD sampler that has music from five of the seven LPs, including such selections as "On Green Dolphin Street," "Manteca," Michel Camilo's "Why Not," and four of D'Rivera's originals. Among the key sidemen are such major players as Claudio Roditi, Michel Camilo, Hilton Ruiz, Jorge Dalto, bassist Eddie Gomez, Ignacio Berroa, and Daniel Ponce. But when are these valuable albums going to be reissued in full?

Return to Ipanema has a strong dose of Brazilian music, with Claudio Roditi co-starring, but the music also hints strongly at D'Rivera's roots in Cuban music. The octet includes Ralph Moore on tenor, trombonist Jay Ashby, and Danilo Perez. The melodic repertoire has two songs apiece from Lobo (including the memorable "Pra Dizer Adeus"), Antonio Carlos Jobim, and Roditi, plus D'Rivera's "To Brenda," and a fresh reworking of "Summertime." *Tico! Tico!* finds D'Rivera (on clarinet, alto, and his rarely played tenor) performing with two different five-piece rhythm sections that include Danilo Perez and percussionist Raphael Cruz. The program has Paquito exploring "Three Venezuelan Waltzes," recent classical-flavored pieces, some rewarding if little-known tunes, and the famous title cut with equal success.

Although D'Rivera had had an accident shortly before recording *Reunion* and would soon be hospitalized for a few days (successfully), the session was a happy occasion. It was the first time that D'Rivera and his former Irakere partner, Arturo

Sandoval, had recorded together since the altoist's defection in 1980; Sandoval followed him a decade later. Performing with a superb band also including Danilo Perez, acoustic guitarist Fareed Haque, bassist David Finck, drummer Mark Walker, and Giovanni Hidalgo, the group (with the leader switching between alto and clarinet) sticks mostly to originals, other than a couple of Chucho Valdés songs, "Tanga," and "Body and Soul" (the last a feature for Sandoval). D'Rivera and Sandoval clearly inspired each other, as can be heard throughout this classic outing. Another reunion is long overdue!

Who's Smoking?! also has plenty of heated moments. For the bop-oriented session, D'Rivera is joined by Roditi, flügelhornist Mark Morganelli, Perez or Pedrito López on piano, bassist Harvie Swartz, drummer Al Foster, and (on four of the nine numbers) tenor saxophonist James Moody. John Coltrane's "Giant Steps" and Thelonious Monk's "I Mean You" are revitalized, "Out of Nowhere" is taken as a clarinet-bass duet, and the other selections include the blazing title cut (cowritten by D'Rivera and Roditi) and Perez's "You Got It, Diz!" *Havana Café* includes mostly high-quality originals by band members, featuring D'Rivera (on clarinet, alto, and soprano), Fareed Haque or Ed Cherry on guitar, Perez, bassist David Finck, drummer Jorge Rossy, and percussionist Sammy Figueroa. The results are often fiery, always stirring, and never less than stimulating, with the highlights including "Havana Café," "Who's Smoking?," "Jean Pauline," and "Bossa do Brooklyn."

9 *40 Years of Cuban Jam Session / Feb. 1993 / Messidor 15826*

8 *A Night in Englewood / July 1993 / Messidor 15829*

8 *Portraits of Cuba / Feb. 6-7, 1996 / Chesky 145*

7 *Live at MCG / Feb. 14, 1997 / Blue Jackel 1003*

8 *100 Years of Latin Love Songs / Sept. 8-9, 1998 / Heads Up 3045*

7 *Tropicana Nights / 1999 / Chesky 186*

7 *Live at the Blue Note / Aug. 20, 1999 / Half Note 15095-4911*

40 Years of Cuban Jam Session is not a reissue featuring 40 years of music but instead a gathering of 23 top Cuban expatriates organized by Paquito D'Rivera (who is actually only on six of the 11 selections). The personnel and instrumentation change from song to song, and among the many great Cuban players heard from are Cachao, Chocolate Armenteros, J.P. Torres, José "Chambo" Silva on tenor (one of his last recordings), drummer Horacio "El Negro" Hernández, and guitarist René Toledo, along with many lesser-known but talented players. The results are respectful, heartfelt, and often exciting.

After Dizzy Gillespie's death in 1992, Paquito D'Rivera took over his United Nation Orchestra (which had been formed in 1988). The following year they recorded *A Night in Englewood*. The orchestra's Latin connection was even stronger than it had been earlier, and D'Rivera chose to feature group originals rather than the usual Gillespie repertoire. The 16-piece ensemble includes as key soloists trombonist Conrad Herwig, Mario Rivera on tenor, and D'Rivera, with guest spots for trombonist Slide Hampton, Claudio Roditi, and Dave Samuels on marimba and vibes; D'Rivera's "I Remember Diz" is a highlight of the spirited program.

Portraits of Cuba has D'Rivera (on soprano, clarinet, and alto) backed by Carlos Franzetti's arrangements for three reeds, six brass (including French horn), and a rhythm section. The repertoire is diverse and includes "The Peanut Vendor," pieces by Josh White ("La Bella Cubana"), René Touzet, and Ernesto Lecuona, three by D'Rivera, and even the "Theme from 'I Love Lucy'." the colorful charts and D'Rivera's fine playing (his soprano playing at that point had reached the same level as his alto and clarinet solos) make this a highly enjoyable listen.

Paquito D'Rivera's second recording as the leader of the United Nation Orchestra documents a live concert. Although the ensemble is definitely strong, Dizzy is missed, and the big band does not display that distinctive a personality. The more notable players include D'Rivera, trombonists Conrad Herwig and William Cepeda, Fareed Haque, and trumpeter Diego Urcola. Many of the songs on this disc come from band members, but the most notable ones actually originated elsewhere, including Emiliano Salvador's "Puerto Padre," "A Night in Tunisia," and especially Ernesto Lecuona's "Andalucia Medley" (taken from Lecuona's "Andalucia Suite"), which is played as a clarinet-bass duet.

100 Years of Latin Love Songs has one number apiece from each of the ten decades of the 20th century, with the songs originating from Argentina, Chile, Colombia, Mexico, Cuba, the Dominican Republic, Brazil, Puerto Rico, and Venezuela. Although "La Morocha" is from 1905 and "Ay Ay Ay" was composed in 1915, all of the music sounds quite contemporary. Bob Belden arranged the selections for a 13-piece string section, a rhythm section with pianist Dario Eskenazi, plus Roberto Perera on Paraguayan harp and the acoustic guitars of Fareed Haque, Aquiles Baez, and David Oquendo. Some of the performances are quite intimate (particularly the five on which D'Rivera plays soprano), while "Sin Tu Carino" really cooks. A well-rounded effort featuring mostly underrecognized but rewarding material.

On *Tropicana Nights,* Paquito D'Rivera pays tribute to both what was once called "the most beautiful nightclub in the world" and the type of music played in Havana in the 1950s. D'Rivera heads a 21-piece orchestra that includes among the names trumpeter Urcola, trombonists William

Cepeda and Jimmy Bosch, and such percussionists as Milton Cardona and Ralph Irizarry. The music is traditional yet swinging and highlighted by "Mambo à la Kenton," D'Rivera's "Chucho," "Siboney," "Mambo Inn," and "The Peanut Vendor." For his *Live at the Blue Note* CD, D'Rivera leads a sextet/septet of mostly lesser-known talented Latin and South American players that comprise his regular band of the period. The group includes Urcola (a fine up-and-coming player), pianist Dario Eskenazi, bassist Oscar Stagnaro, drummer Mark Walker, percussionist Pernell Saturnino, and guest flutist Oriente López, with five of the seven selections being originals by these musicians. D'Rivera (on alto except for taking "Buenos Aires" on clarinet) is in a happy state of mind (as can be heard from his announcements to the audience), and the musicians play with plenty of spirit, even if none of these songs seem destined to become standards.

LPs to Search For:

During 1981-1987, Paquito D'Rivera (newly arrived from Cuba) recorded seven excellent albums for Columbia, none of which have yet been fully reissued. The music is generally high-quality bebop with a strong dash of Cuban influences. *Blowin'* (Columbia 37374) has D'Rivera assisted by a few overlapping rhythm sections that sometimes include Jorge Dalto (featured on a duet with D'Rivera on "El Dia Que Me Quieras"), Hilton Ruiz, bassist Eddie Gomez, and Ignacio Berroa. *Mariel* (Columbia 38177) features similar personnel plus a couple of appearances (including on John Coltrane's "Moment's Notice") by trumpeter Randy Brecker. *Live at Keystone Korner* (Columbia 38899) teams D'Rivera for the first time on record with Claudio Roditi; the sextet also includes keyboardist Carlos Franzetti, bassist Steve Bailey, Berroa, and Daniel Ponce. The live date from 1983 has plenty of sparks, particularly from D'Rivera, who sticks throughout to alto. *Why Not* (Columbia

39584) focuses on D'Rivera's sextet with Roditi and Michel Camilo, which is augmented by extra percussionists and (on four numbers) harmonica virtuoso Toots Thielemans; the repertoire includes "Manteca," "Samba for Carmen" (dedicated to Carmen McRae and featuring the leader's clarinet), and Camilo's "Why Not." *Explosion* (Columbia 40156) has D'Rivera's writing for a string section on three numbers, but it is the fiery Afro-Cuban numbers that are most memorable, including "Just Kidding" (based on "Salt Peanuts"), Mario Bauzá's "Mambo Inn," and "The Lady and the Tramp." D'Rivera's group with Roditi and Camilo is joined by a few guests, including Howard Levy's harmonica on "Christmas Without You." There is a lot of variety on *Manhattan Burn* (Columbia 40583), including some easy-listening selections with mundane synthesizers, two fiery matchups with tenor saxophonist George Coleman ("Paquito" and "À la Tristano"), some spots for Roditi, and "Two Venezuelan Waltzes" (featuring D'Rivera's clarinet and acoustic guitarist Fareed Haque). The last of Paquito D'Rivera's seven Columbia releases, *Celebration* (Columbia 44077), celebrated the fact that he had just become an American citizen. With Roditi, pianists Roger Kellaway and Makoto Ozone, and Giovanni Hidalgo plus a string section on four of the seven selections, the music (all group originals) avoids predictability and is full of the Cuban fire that epitomizes Paquito D'Rivera's playing.

HILARIO DURAN

b. 1953, Cuba

One of the great Cuban pianists around today, Hilario Duran (who sometimes shows the influence of McCoy Tyner and Chick Corea) has been nicknamed "Con Tumbao" for his creative use of the *Tumbao,* repetitive bass figures. Duran graduated from Amadeo Rodan Conservatory in Havana in 1981 and spent most of the decade working with Arturo Sandoval (before the trumpeter's defection) as pianist, the main arranger, and musical director. Duran's appearance on Jane Bunnett's famed *Spirits of Havana* recording in 1990 gained him recognition. In the 1990s he led Perspectiva (Sandoval's former band), recorded three albums as a leader for Justin Time (starting with 1995's *Francisco's Song*), and moved to Toronto, Canada. Hilario Duran currently teaches in the jazz studies program of Humber College and tours with Bunnett's Spirits of Havana band.

8 *Killer Tumbao / Jan. 10-11, 1997 / Justin Time 101*

9 *Habana Nocturna / Oct. 31, 1998-Nov. 1, 1998 / Justin Time 125*

Hilario Duran sounds in top form on both of these colorful projects. *Killer Tumbao,* which has fine solos from Jane Bunnett (on flute and soprano), trumpeter El Indio, tenor saxophonist Carlos Averhoff, and altoist Gerrtman Velazco in addition to Duran, also includes some folkloric singing. Highlights include such pieces as "Homage to Chano Pozo" (with fine percussion work from José Luis Quintana and Tata Guines) and a lengthy descarga, "Timba Mabo."

Habana Nocturna is particularly intriguing, because Duran performs such numbers as Billy Strayhorn's "U.M.M.G.," the beautiful "Autumn Nocturne," "Harlem Nocturne," and "Like Someone in Love" in addition to three of his originals. The instrumental set has strong improvising from Bunnett and trumpeter Larry Cramer, the inventive use of a string quartet, plus colorful rhythms from Horacio "El Negro" Hernández and Rodolfo Valdés Terry. Hilario Duran deserves much greater recognition for his talented playing.

FRANK EMILIO

b. 1921, Cuba

The appearance of Frank Emilio, one of the top

pianists living in Cuba during the past few decades, as the leader of a Blue Note album in 1998 (when he was 77) was a happy surprise, resulting in some recognition that he had deserved decades before. Born Frank Emilio Flynn, he taught himself piano at the age of ten, placing first in an amateur contest in Havana just a year later. He became blind at the age of 13 but continued his piano study, learning to read music (including classical works) in Braille. In the late 1930s he worked during the day as a music teacher while at night appearing on radio with his own group. Emilio worked in the 1940s with Antonio Maria Romeu, Ignacio Pineiro's Septeto Nacional, José Antonio "King" Mendez and on the radio in Havana.

When American jazz artists visited Cuba in the 1950s, they often played with Emilio, including Sarah Vaughan, drummer Philly Joe Jones, and tenor saxophonist Zoot Sims. A fixture on Cuban radio and television in the 1960s and '70s, Emilio and percussionist Guillermo Barreto founded Quinteto Cubana de Musica Moderna, one of the top Cuban jazz bands and one that was succeeded in 1973 by Irakere. Emilio has remained quite active up until the present time, recording and performing with Jane Bunnett's Spirits of Havana (including being one of the stars on the CD *Jane Bunnett and the Cuban Piano Masters*), recording with his Los Amigos for Milan and Blue Note, and occasionally touring Europe and Canada. Frank Emilio gave two well-received concerts at Lincoln Center (with guest Wynton Marsalis) in 1998.

9 *Ancestral Reflections / Nov. 20-24, 1998 / Blue Note 98918*

Frank Emilio's Blue Note debut finds the 77-year-old pianist sounding quite creative on a variety of traditional-sounding material, including Cachao's mambo "Juventud de Pueblo Nuevo," Ernesto Lecuona's "La Conga Se Va," and a few melodic originals. Emilio leads a charanga with Joaquin Gavilan and (on two songs) Orlando Valle on flute and Lazaro Enriquez (who takes a couple fine solos) and Pablo Suarez on violins, along with bass, timbales, congas, guiro, and two background singers. Barbaro Torres Delgado is a special guest on "El Arroyo Que Murmura," playing some beautiful lute. The music overall is quite modern and creative, with many excellent jazz solos (highlighted by Emilio's strong work) heard throughout the nine pieces.

PETE ESCOVEDO
b. July 13, 1935, Pittsburg, CA

Percussionist Pete Escovedo has been a major force in the Latin music of the San Francisco Bay area (whether it be Afro-Cuban Jazz, Salsa, rock, or pop music) since at least the late 1960s. He grew up in Oakland and was surrounded by music throughout his childhood; his father sang with Latin big bands. Pete played the saxophone in high school, soon switched to vibes, and, when pianist Ed Kelly needed a percussionist, quickly learned timbales. Escovedo played on and off with pianist Carlos Federico's band for 12 years, was with Chico Ochoa's big band for a year, and recorded with Mongo Santamaria. Pete and his younger brother, the late Coke Escovedo, both developed into skilled percussionists and were greatly in demand for local gigs. With their younger sibling, Phil Escovedo, playing bass, the Escovedo Bros. Latin Jazz Sextet was formed, and they worked regularly in the mid-'60s. The group disbanded in 1967 when Carlos Santana hired Pete and Coke for his Latin rock group. After touring with Santana for the next three years (Pete has rejoined him a few times since), Coke and Pete founded the 14-piece Latin rock-oriented big band Azteca, recording two albums for Columbia. The ensemble at various times included such notables as saxophonist Mel Martin, trumpeter Tom Harrell, drummer Lenny White, and Pete's 15-year-old daughter, Sheila E., on percussion. However, when the band grew to 24 members in 1974, it became too expensive to keep together and broke up.

Pete and his daughter, Sheila E., started working together regularly. They were discovered by drummer Billy Cobham, who used them on one of his Atlantic records and produced two albums by the Escovedos for Fantasy (*Solo Two* and *Happy Together*). Although Sheila E. would eventually switch to pop and rock music (working with Prince), she frequently rejoins her dad in his Afro-Cuban Jazz bands and has recently led her own Latin jazz group, The E Train. Pete Escovedo since the late 1970s has worked in many different settings, including in the studios, touring, recording with George Duke, Herbie Hancock, Woody Herman, Cal Tjader, and Tito Puente and working with more pop-oriented acts. In 1983 he formed Esgo Records, and he has often used his other children (Juan, Pete Michael, and Zina) in his groups. Although Coke Escovedo passed away in 1986, Pete has remained quite active, recording for Concord (its Crossover subsidiary in 1985 and 1987 and for Concord Picante and Vista in 1995, 1997 and 2000), becoming involved in community affairs in the San Francisco Bay Area and doing what he can to spread the joy of Afro-Cuban music.

8 *Solo Two/Happy Together / Sept. 1976-1978 / Fantasy 24747*
Billy Cobham sponsored the two Fantasy albums by Pete and Sheila Escovedo, which, with the exception of one selection (left out due to lack of space), are reissued on this single CD. A strong rhythm section (with Pete on timbales, Sheila on congas, keyboardist Mark Soskin, guitarist Ray Obiedo, either Abraham Laboriel or Randy Jackson on bass, and Cobham himself playing drums on the second date) is joined by several guests from the Bay Area on some cuts, including trumpeter Tom Harrell, trombonist Julian Priester,

and the reeds of Mel Martin. The Escovedos perform boundary-crossing music that includes fusion, Latin jazz with pop sensibilities, and some slightly commercial instrumental music. Those with an open mind towards mixing Latin music with pop and rock will find this historic set of great interest.

7 *E Music / Feb. 2000 / Concord Picante 4892*
On this wide-ranging set, Pete Escovedo interprets Afro-Cuban Jazz, Salsa, bits of pop, and some straightahead sections, all with equal enthusiasm. His regular band (pianist Joe Rotundi, Justo Almario on reeds, trumpeter Ramon Flores, trombonists Francisco Torress and Arturo Velasco, and son Peter Escovedo on drums) is joined on some cuts by quite a few guests including trumpeter Ray Vega, guitarist Ray Obiedo, pianist George Duke, and Sheila E. on vocals, drums, and percussion. The music is not for jazz purists due to the diversity and pop elements, but the overall results are fiery, infectious, and fun.

ESTRADA BROTHERS

The Estrada Brothers have been a popular attraction in the Los Angeles area since the mid-1950s but did not have an opportunity to record for a major jazz label until 1997. The sons of a violinist (Louis Estrada), the Estrada Brothers grew up in Oxnard, California, and have always been inspired by the music of Cal Tjader, Tito Puente, and Stan Kenton. The band was founded by Ruben (who played trumpet and drums before switching to his Tjader-influenced vibes), Henry (on saxophones and flute), and Angel (who left music in the 1970s). Raul Rico Jr. became the group's percussionist in 1976, and a decade later the group solidified with the addition of Ruben's son Cougar on drums, pianist Joe Rotondi Jr., and bassist Malcom Ian Peters. In 1995 the band finally made its first recording, *About Time,* on their own Rumba Jazz label. The success of that CD resulted in

Milestone's signing the Estrada Brothers and recording *Get Out of My Way* in 1997. Although the band still remains primarily a regional favorite, it continues working regularly, keeping the legacy of Cal Tjader and the 1950s Afro-Cuban Jazz pioneers alive.

8 *Get Out of My Way / Mar. 16-17, 1996 / Milestone 9260*

The Estrada Brothers perform most of their best material on this spirited CD, which can easily be enjoyed by fans of the Cal Tjader sound. Ruben Estrada (on vibes, percussion, and occasional trumpet) and Henry Estrada (on various reeds) are joined by pianist Joe Rotondi Jr., bassist Malcom Ian Peters, drummer Ruben Estrada Jr., and Raul Rico, the sparkplug of the group, on congas. The band sings on the humorous "Get Out of My Way," but otherwise this is a purely instrumental set. Standards such as "Tin Tin Deo," a Latinized "Blue Moon," "Blue Bossa," and "Besame Mucho" alternate with a few melodic originals. The music overall is consistently infectious, rhythmic, and hot.

GARCIA BROTHERS

Led by pianist Robert Garcia, bassist Raul Garcia, Rudy Garcia on timbales, and Peter Garcia on vocals, the Garcia Brothers were initially inspired and encouraged by Poncho Sanchez. The Garcias received their earliest musical training from their father, have long played locally in Los Angeles, and first met Sanchez in 1979. Their debut recording in 1994 featured the group as an octet with three horns, piano, bass, and three percussionists, including Rolando Mendosa, who occasionally takes vocals.

7 *Jazz con Sabor Latino / 1994 / Discos Dos Coronas 9406*

This CD is an enjoyable set of Afro-Cuban Jazz pieces by an excellent if not particularly distinctive group. Pianist Robert, bassist Raul, and timbale player Rudy Garcia are the co-leaders (singer Peter is absent). However, the most significant players are the horn soloists (trumpeter Tony Lujan, trombonist Luis Bonilla, and tenor saxophonist Rob Lockhart) plus singer Rolando Mendosa (who also plays conga). The excellent jazz solos, the occasional cheerful group vocals, and the cooking but relaxed rhythms make this a fine acquisition.

DIZZY GILLESPIE

b. Oct. 21, 1917, Cheraw, SC, d. Jan. 6, 1993, Englewood, NJ

Dizzy Gillespie was one of the greatest jazz trumpeters of all time, was considered (along with altoist Charlie Parker) the founder of bebop, and was an important bandleader, an occasional but significant composer, a master at showmanship, and one of jazz's most famous jazz musicians for many decades. In addition, he was a natural comedian, a remarkable scat–singer, and an important teacher and inspiration to younger generations of jazzmen. As if that were not enough, Gillespie is considered one of the most important pioneers of Afro-Cuban Jazz. Although he was involved primarily in straightahead jazz throughout his career, during several different periods he did a great deal to make Latin rhythms an integral part of modern jazz.

He was born John Birks Gillespie to a poor family as the last of nine children. Nicknamed Dizzy early in his career due to his wit and sly brilliance, Gillespie started on trombone, switching to trumpet at age 12. He won a scholarship to an agriculture school (the Laurinburg Institute in North Carolina) where he studied music until he dropped out in 1935 in hopes of becoming a professional musician. His early inspiration was the dramatic and chance-taking swing trumpeter Roy Eldridge. After playing in Philadelphia with Frankie Fairfax's

Dizzy Gillespie's enthusiasm for Latin rhythms helped make Afro-Cuban Jazz possible

orchestra, Dizzy took Eldridge's old spot with Hill's big band in 1937, making his recording debut on "King Porter Stomp." Initially he sounded quite similar to Eldridge, but within a couple of years he was clearly developing his own unusual style. Gillespie often stretched himself during solos and was criticized for taking wild chances.

After touring Europe with Hill's orchestra, Dizzy freelanced for a year and then spent 1939-41

with Cab Calloway's big band. Mario Bauzá, whom he had met earlier, helped him get him into the orchestra and introduced him to Latin rhythms. Much to Calloway's chagrin, Dizzy often experimented during his short solos. And although Dizzy was gradually developing his own radical style, Cab often accused him of playing "Chinese music." Calloway's problems with Gillespie's solos are quite understandable for Dizzy tended to improvise over more complex chords than the rhythm section was actually playing! Despite that, Dizzy is heard taking short solos on many Calloway recordings of the period, including "Pickin' the Cabbage"; writer John Storm Roberts has pointed out that Gillespie's arrangement of this piece has spots that are reminiscent of "A Night in Tunisia." Dizzy's period with Cab's band was cut short when he was mistakenly accused of throwing a spitball at the singer during a performance (trumpeter Jonah Jones was actually the culprit). A fight broke out and Gillespie was soon unemployed.

Dizzy, who had met Charlie Parker (whom he called "my heartbeat") in 1940, played with quite a few orchestras during 1941-42, including those led by Ella Fitzgerald (the Chick Webb ghost band), Coleman Hawkins, Benny Carter, Charlie Barnet, Fess Williams, Les Hite, Claude Hopkins, Lucky Millinder, Calvin Jackson, and Duke Ellington (where he subbed for four weeks). He sat in with Machito's orchestra on a few occasions during 1942-43 and also worked with the Alberto Socarrás Latin ensemble for a week in 1943. In addition, Dizzy took part in the after-hours jam sessions at Monroe's Uptown House and Minton's Playhouse. By 1943 Gillespie largely had his style together, but the Musicians Union recording strike kept his association with the Earl Hines Orchestra (which also featured Charlie Parker on tenor) completely off of records, along with their version of his first Afro-Cuban song, "A Night in Tunisia." It also resulted in the 1944 Billy Eckstine big band's only making a few sides with Gillespie, most notably "Blowin' the Blues Away" and "Opus X."

Dizzy Gillespie, who led the first bop-oriented combo on 52nd Street in late 1943 and participated in the first full-fledged bebop recording date (two sessions in 1944 led by tenor saxophonist Coleman Hawkins, including the initial version of Gillespie's "Woody 'n You"), had opportunities to record "A Night in Tunisia" during late 1944/early 1945 with both the Boyd Raeburn Orchestra and singer Sarah Vaughan, the latter as a vocal piece called "Interlude."

Nineteen-hundred-forty-five was the breakthrough year for the 27-year-old trumpeter. He recorded a series of very influential bebop records with Charlie Parker (including "Hot House," "Salt Peanuts," "Dizzy Atmosphere," "Shaw Nuff," and "Groovin' High") that upset the swing-oriented jazz establishment, and soon "Bird & Diz" were the talk of the jazz world.

Gillespie organized his first big band that year, but it struggled and flopped during a Southern tour because swing fans felt that they could not dance to the music; no recordings exist of the legendary orchestra. Dizzy took a small band with Charlie Parker to the West Coast later in the year, with mixed results. The local musicians were very impressed, but the audiences at Billy Berg's in Hollywood were generally small and much more interested in Slim Gaillard's comedy jive band. After a few recordings and appearances with Jazz at the Philharmonic, Gillespie and his sidemen (other than Parker, who cashed in his plane ticket) returned to New York.

However, bebop was here to stay. In 1946 Dizzy Gillespie had much better luck with his second big band, an influential orchestra that lasted for over three years. The following year, Gillespie mentioned to Mario Bauzá that he would like to add a percussionist to his band. Bauzá soon introduced Dizzy to Cuban conga player and vocalist Chano Pozo, who had been in the United States for nearly a year without much success. A historic if short-lived musical partnership began. At first Pozo's role with the bebop orchestra (which included arranger Gil Fuller and such major sidemen as tenor saxophonist Big Nick Nicholas, baritonist Cecil Payne, pianist John Lewis, vibraphonist Milt Jackson, bassist Al McKibbon, and drummer Kenny Clarke) was relatively minor. Pozo's rhythms did not always mesh well with the standard rhythm section (and vice versa), although after some adjustments they were able to learn from each other; McKibbon in particular became adept at Latin rhythms. However on September 29, 1947, the Dizzy Gillespie big band played at Carnegie Hall, and with Pozo on conga and Chiquito on bongos, musical history was made. Most memorable was the debut of George Russell's "Afro-Cuban Drum Suite," which was renamed "Cubana Be" and "Cubana Bop" when it was recorded commercially three months later. Pozo's conga rhythms and haunting chants/vocals became a featured part of the big band's perform-ances for the next year, which included a European tour. Among the Gillespie recordings that featured Pozo were the classic "Manteca" (which he cowrote with Dizzy) and "Algo Bueno" (a Latin reworking of "Woody 'n You"). In concert the "Afro-Cuban Suite" (a different piece than the "Afro-Cuban Drum Suite") was a showcase for Pozo. Chano Pozo also cowrote "Tin Tin Deo" but did not live long enough to record it. He was killed in a bar brawl on December 2, 1948.

After Pozo's death, Gillespie at first used Sabu Martinez on bongo, with drummer Joe Harris sometimes switching to conga. Vince Guerra was on conga for part of 1949, but eventually the extra percussion was dropped. "Manteca" would always be in Gillespie's repertoire along with "A Night in Tunisia," but he de-emphasized Afro-Cuban rhythms for the next decade, with a few exceptions. The Dizzy Gillespie big band broke up in early-1950, and the trumpeter switched to leading a bop quintet that also played some more accessible R&Bish numbers when he was not touring with JATP or being involved in all-star sessions recorded for the Verve label. However, for some recordings in Paris in 1952, Gillespie utilized either Humberto Morales or Umberto Canto on conga. In 1954 for a recording project called *Afro,* he was joined by a big band that included Candido and Ramon

Santamaria on congas, José Mangual on bongo, and Ubaldo Nieto on timbales, performing the four-part "Manteca Suite" (arranged by Chico O'Farrill), "Caravan," "A Night in Tunisia," and the debut of Dizzy's "Con Alma." But surprisingly, when he led a major orchestra during 1956-58 that toured the world under the sponsorship of the U.S. State Department, the music was strictly bebop.

After the Dizzy Gillespie big band broke up in 1958, Dizzy gradually became more interested in Latin-oriented projects again. His 1959 sextet album, *Have Trumpet, Will Excite,* utilized Patato Valdés' conga on a few numbers and Argentinean pianist Lalo Schifrin, whom Gillespie had met ear-lier in South America and persuaded to move to the United States, became a regular member of his quintet. Schifrin's five-part "Gillespiana" originally utilized Candido on conga, Jack Del Rio on bongo, and the timbales of Willie Rodriguez for a suite that included both South American and African rhythms. Gillespie's recorded Carnegie Hall con-cert of 1961 had Ray Barretto, Julio Collazzo, and John Mangual on percussion, and Latin rhythms were heard often during Schifrin's period in his band, even during regular performances by Diz's regular quintet.

Lalo Schifrin went out on his own in 1963, and Gillespie mostly explored bop for the next decade, when not stuck recording commercial funk-orient-ed dates. Among the exceptions was a 1970 Perception LP called *Portrait of Jenny* that had bassist Andrew González, both Jerry González and Patato Valdés on congas, and Nicholas Marrero on timbales. A long-awaited recording with Machito's orchestra in 1975, *Afro-Cuban Jazz Moods,* unfortu-nately fell short of being the expected classic, and a 1980 concert recording co-led by Mongo Santamaria (with drummer Steve Berrios) was just ok. However, Gillespie's 1977 visit to Cuba had a major impact, indirectly resulting in Paquito D'Rivera's and Arturo Sandoval's eventual move to the United States. Gillespie's final big band project, the United Nation Orchestra, was formed in 1988 and was very Latin-oriented, including such major players as D'Rivera, Sandoval, Claudio Roditi, Steve Turre, Mario Rivera, Danilo Perez, Ignacio Berroa, and Giovanni Hidalgo in the all-star cast. Although expensive to maintain, the United Nation Orchestra made a live recording for Enja and performed at a series of special concerts.

After a final burst of activity (and several recordings with all-star groups) in January 1992, Dizzy Gillespie was struck down by bad health. He was inactive during his last year, passing away at the age of 75, a much-beloved figure whose contributions to bebop, Afro-Cuban Jazz, and music in general are difficult to overstate. Since his death, his United Nation Orchestra has been led on a part-time basis by Paquito D'Rivera.

10 *The Complete RCA Victor Recordings / May 17, 1937-July 6, 1949 / Bluebird 66528*

9 *Diz 'n Bird at Carnegie Hall / Sept. 29, 1947 / Roost 57061*

8 *Dizzy Gillespie/Max Roach in Paris / Feb. 28, 1948 + May 15, 1949 / Vogue 68213*

9 *Dizzy Gillespie and His Big Band / July 19, 1948 / GNP/Crescendo 23*

Dizzy Gillespie's recording career is covered in great depth in the book *Bebop* in this series. The releases discussed in this section are significant from an Afro-Cuban standpoint. The two-CD set *The Complete RCA Victor Recordings* has all of Gillespie's recordings for that label. In addition to including his three initial recorded solos (cut with Teddy Hill's orchestra in 1937, including "King Porter Stomp"), "Hot Mallets" with a 1939 Lionel Hampton all-star group, an exciting 1946 septet date (which includes "A Night in Tunisia"), and a session by the 1949 Metronome All-Stars, the bulk of this twofer features the classic Dizzy Gillespie big band of 1946-49, which had also recorded earlier

for Musicraft before Chano Pozo had joined. Pozo actually recorded only eight numbers with the big band, and those are all here, including "Manteca," "Cubana Be/Cubana Bop," and "Algo Buena." In addition, the first session after Pozo's death has his composition "Guarachi Guaro" played by the band, with Sabu Martinez and Joe Harris on bongos and conga. Otherwise there are many examples of exciting big band bop to be heard on this essential reissue.

The Dizzy Gillespie big band was also recorded live on several occasions during Pozo's period. *Diz 'n Bird at Carnegie Hall* has a remarkable 25-minute five-song set by a quintet with Gillespie and Parker that is highlighted by "Confirmation" and "Ko Ko." There are also ten selections from the 1947 Dizzy Gillespie Orchestra, including "One Bass Hit" (featuring Al McKibbon), "Cubana Be/Cubana Bop," and "Things to Come." The Vogue CD has the 1948 big band in Paris playing some of the same songs plus "Two Bass Hit" and Pozo's showcase on the "Afro-Cuban Drum Suite"; there are also four numbers by the 1949 Max Roach Quintet with Kenny Dorham and tenor saxophonist James Moody. The GNP/Crescendo set is the last issued recording of Chano Pozo with the Dizzy Gillespie big band, and it is a well-recorded and exciting program that is highlighted by "Emanon," "Good Bait," and "Manteca."

9 *Gillespiana and Carnegie Hall Concert / Nov. 14, 1960-Mar. 4, 1961 / Verve 314 519 809*

8 *An Electrifying Evening with the Dizzy Gillespie Quintet / Feb. 9, 1961 / Verve 314 557 544*

6 *Jambo Caribe / Nov. 4-6, 1964 / Verve 314 557 492*

5 *Dizzy Gillespie and His Quintet / Nov. 24, 1965 / RTE 1008*

The single-CD *Gillespiana and Carnegie Hall*

Concert combines two former LPs from 1960-61. Lalo Schifrin was encouraged by the trumpeter to write new music, and he came up with the five-movement "Gillespiana," a work that uses a 21-piece group (including four French horns and three percussionists) and grows in interest with each listen. The studio version of this piece (which Schifrin has revived in recent years) is joined by other music cut at a Carnegie Hall concert, where the work was actually debuted with a similar band. Gillespie, who is in top form throughout, performs "Manteca," a rather silly version of "Ool Ya Koo" (with singer Joe Carroll), "Tunisian Fantasy," "Kush," and "This Is the Way."

An Electrifying Evening is most notable for Gillespie's rather incredible trumpet break on "A Night in Tunisia," following a very Cuban melody statement, with altoist Leo Wright switching to flute. Otherwise this is a high-quality bebop quintet set that also includes "Kush," "Salt Peanuts," and a definitive version of "The Mooche." *Jambo Caribe* features the post-Schifrin quintet joined by Kansas Fields on percussion for a set of music associated with or influenced by the Caribbean. There is not much stretching out here by Gillespie and James Moody (heard on tenor and flute), but the results are fun and "And Then She Stopped" became part of Gillespie's repertoire. The RTE concert disc does not live up to expectations. The quintet outing, which includes Latin- and Brazilian-oriented material, never catches fire and sounds rather routine, other than "Chega De Saudade" and Dizzy's good-natured vocal on the calypso "Oh Joe."

6 *Afro-Cuban Jazz Moods / June 4-5, 1975 / Original Jazz Classics 447*

9 *To a Finland Station / Sept. 9, 1982 / Original Jazz Classics 733*

8 *Live at the Royal Festival Hall / June 10, 1989 / Enja 79658*

Afro-Cuban Jazz Moods, a late-period meeting between the great trumpeter, Machito's Afro-Cuban orchestra, and composer-arranger Chico O'Farrill, is not the classic it should be. The use of Dana McCurdy's synthesizer is distracting, and the rock rhythms in "Three Afro-Cuban Jazz Moods" are unfortunate and somewhat frivolous. Where are the exciting Afro-Cuban rhythms that were Machito's trademark? However, Dizzy (who was still at 80-90% of his peak) uplifts the brief (32-minute) program with consistently inventive solos, and the ensembles by the augmented 23-piece Machito Orchestra are full of fire.

To a Finland Station is much better. Dizzy Gillespie may have been nearly 65 but he sounds quite inspired, sharing the spotlight with the great Arturo Sandoval, who was still nearly a decade away from defecting to the United States. With fine support from a Finnish rhythm section, the trumpeters push each other on five originals, including Gillespie's "Wheatleigh Hall" and "And Then She Stopped." A very memorable effort by two of the all-time greats.

Dizzy Gillespie's trumpet chops were pretty weak by 1989, but his spirit uplifts *Live at the Royal Festival Hall,* the only recording released thus far by the United Nation Orchestra with its original leader. James Moody, Paquito D'Rivera, Slide Hampton, Arturo Sandoval, Claudio Roditi, Steve Turre, singer Flora Purim, and percussionist Airto are all well featured. Gillespie is largely an inspiring figurehead, just taking a few short solos, but his sidemen play at the top of their game. Among the selections on this highly enjoyable set are "Tin Tin Deo," "Tanga," and an 18½ minute version of "A Night in Tunisia."

LPs to Search For:
Bebop Enters Sweden 1947-1949 (Dragon 34) features the Gillespie Orchestra during a February 2, 1948, concert in Stockholm, including a version of "Manteca." Also on this LP are three songs from

Chubby Jackson's Fifth Dimensional Jazz Group (a bop sextet with vibraphonist Terry Gibbs and trumpeter Conte Candoli) in 1947 and three numbers in which James Moody in 1949 is featured with a group of Swedish all-stars. *Good Bait* (Spotlite 122) has a couple of rare broadcasts from the Dizzy Gillespie big band during its final year (December 1948-July 1949), including solo spots for trombonist J.J. Johnson, altoist Ernie Henry, tenorman Yusef Lateef, and singer Johnny Hartman. Sabu Martinez or Vince Guerra is on conga, and they add a Cuban flavor to "Algo Buena" and Ernest Lecuona's "Tabu."

ANDY GONZÁLEZ

b. Jan. 1, 1951, New York, NY

The younger brother of trumpeter-percussionist Jerry González, bassist Andy González has been on many high-quality Latin sessions through the years. The co-leader of Libre with Manny Oquendo, he has also been a member of his brother's Fort Apache Band since its beginning. Although he has not led his own record dates and is seemingly content to be a stimulating sideman, Andy González has recorded with many major jazz and Latin players, including Charlie Palmieri, Eddie Palmieri, Charlie Sepúlveda, Alfredo Rodriguez, the Latin Jazz Orchestra, Chico O'Farrill, Arturo O'Farrill, Conrad Herwig, Danilo Perez, David Amram, David Sanchez, keyboardist Don Grolnick, Hilton Ruiz, J.P. Torres, pianist Kenny Kirkland, Papo Vazquez, Patato Valdés, Ray Barretto, Rumba Club, Steve Turre, Tito Puente, trumpeter Tom Harrell, Willie Colón, and many others. It is a good bet that if Andy González is on a session, the music is going to be significant!

JERRY GONZÁLEZ

b. June 5, 1949, Bronx, NY

Jerry González's Fort Apache Band at its best is a superb mixture of post-bop (as opposed to bebop) jazz improvising and stirring Afro-Cuban rhythms, fueled by González's ability to play both trumpet (influenced by Miles Davis and Dizzy Gillespie) and conga with equal ability. González's father sang in Latin bands, his uncle was a guitarist, and his younger brother, Andy González, is a superior bassist who has often played in his groups.

González started on trumpet when he was 12, but early on, inspired by Mongo Santamaria, he began doubling on conga. He studied at New York City's Music and Art High School (1964-67), cofounded the Latin Jazz Quintet in 1964 with brother Andy, and earned a scholarship to the New York College of Music, where he befriended veteran trumpeter Kenny Dorham. González worked with Pupi Legarreta and Monguito Santamaria (Mongo's son), toured with the Beach Boys (on trumpet), and gigged with Dizzy Gillespie when he was 20, recording the *Portrait of Jenny* album (on conga) with the great trumpeter in 1970.

In the 1970s Gonzales worked with Eddie Palmieri for four years, was a founding member of Manny Oquendo's Conjunto Libre, and played with trumpeter Clifford Thornton's Grupo Experimental, Machito, Ray Barretto, Tito Puente, Paquito D'Rivera, drummer Tony Williams, tenor saxophonist Archie Shepp, drummer Joe Chambers, trumpeter Woody Shaw, and pianist Kirk Lightsey, among others.

In 1980 Jerry González began leading his own group which by 1982 had become the Fort Apache Band, a pacesetting ensemble that updates the Cubop tradition by mixing Latin rhythms with modern jazz solos that stretch beyond bebop. In addition, González has freelanced up to the present time with many top all-stars, including Tito Puente, Chico O'Farrill, pianist McCoy Tyner, trumpeter Franco Ambrosetti, arranger Bob Belden, clarinetist Don Byron, and pianist James Williams, being a major asset in both jazz and Latin settings.

©Susan Rosmarin

Jerry González moved Afro–Cuban Jazz beyond bebop.

7 *Ya Yo Me Cure / July 1980-Aug. 1980 / Pangea 6242*

10 *Rumba Para Monk / Oct. 27-28, 1988 / Sunnyside 1036*

9 *Obatala / Nov. 6 1988 / Enja 79609*

8 *Earthdance / Oct. 2-3, 1990 / Sunnyside 1050*

7 *Crossroads / Apr. 1994-May 1994 / Milestone 9225*

7 *Pensativo / Apr. 1995-Aug. 1995 / Milestone 9242*

8 *Fire Dance / Feb. 2-4, 1996 / Milestone 9258*

Jerry González's debut as a leader, *Ya Yo Me Cure*, finds him leading a group similar to Fort Apache in musical intent if not instrumentation. In addition to three originals by singer Frankie Rodriguez, there is such unusual material as Wayne Shorter's "Nefertiti," Thelonious Monk's "Evidence," and the "I Love Lucy Theme." González is joined by Rodriguez, Hilton Ruiz, Andy González, Steve Turre, Papo Vásquez, Mario Rivera, and five percussionists for an ambitious and enjoyable early set.

Rumba Para Monk was the first full-length Latin tribute to the music of Thelonious Monk. At the time, the Fort Apache Band was a quintet consisting of tenor saxophonist Carter Jefferson, pianist Larry Willis, Andy González, and Steve Berrios. The percussion spots work well as a contrast to the straight-ahead solos on such numbers as "Monk's Mood," "Nutty," "Little Rootie Tootie," and "Jackie-ing"; Jerry González did not let the band coast by picking out any "easy" Monk tunes! Larry Willis' very un-Monklike piano is also a major asset. A classic of its kind.

Obatala, recorded live in Zurich in 1988, finds González using a larger group than normal, with tenor saxophonist John Stubblefield (who would later become a regular member of Fort Apache), Papo Vásquez, Larry Willis, guitarist Edgardo Miranda, Andy González, Steve Berrios, and three percussionists. The extra players in the rhythm section are a major asset that should have been retained in future recordings, for the balance is quite even here between post-bop jazz and Afro-Cuban music. Among the high points of this stimulating set are remakes of "Evidence," "Nefertiti," and "Jackie-ing" plus a 14-minute exploration of Ron Carter's "Eighty-One."

The Fort Apache Band's personnel eventually stabilized as Jerry González on trumpet, flügelhorn, and congas, Joe Ford on alto and soprano, Carter Jefferson (replaced after his death in 1993 by John Stubblefield), Willis, Andy González, and Steve Berrios. *Earthdance* has its adventurous moments, with such songs as Wayne Shorter's "Fe Fi Fo Fum," Thelonious Monk's "Let's Call This," and Ron Carter's "Eighty-One" being explored. In general, when the leader plays trumpet, the band performs advanced hard bop. But when he switches to congas, the Afro-Cuban influence becomes stronger. Both *Crossroads* and *Pensativo* often find the band sounding like a mildly Latin version of Art Blakey's Jazz Messengers, essentially a straight-ahead jazz group with an occasional Latin interlude. *Crossroads,* which has a few very brief percussion pieces, includes Willis' "Malandro," Ford's "Thelingus" (dedicated to Monk, Mingus, and Ellington), a transformation of "Ezekiel Saw the Wheel," Cal Tjader's "Viva Cepeda," and Jackie McLean's tribute to the band, "Fort Apache." *Pensativo* is highlighted by another Wayne Shorter piece ("Dance Cadaverous"), Billy Strayhorn's "A Flower Is a Lovesome Thing," González's trumpet on Monk's "Ruby, My Dear," and a variety of superior group originals.

Fire Dance, an inspired live recording, gets the edge. The musicians stretch themselves on six lengthy pieces (four are over ten minutes, with Monk's "Let's Call This" being over 18). The Afro-Cuban element (often absent) is quite secondary to the straightahead post-bop solos (an additional percussionist in the band might have kept it from sounding so conventional), but the playing is generally strong, with each of the horn players getting plenty of space and González often emulating Miles Davis.

RUBEN GONZÁLEZ

b. Apr. 1919, Santa Clara, Cuba

A veteran pianist who would most certainly have been famous worldwide were it not for the isolation of Cuba, Ruben González was discovered by the outside world in the late 1990s thanks to Ry Cooder's Buena Vista Social Club project. González graduated from the Cienfuegos Conservatoire by the time he was 15. However, instead of becoming a concert pianist, González chose to play popular music. After performing locally, in 1941 he moved to Havana, where he worked with La Orquesta Paulina, Conjunto

Camayo, Los Hermanos, Raul Planas, and the young Mongo Santamaria. González first recorded with Arsenio Rodriguez in 1943 and spent time in Panama performing with Las Estrellas Negras ("The Black Stars"). Back in Cuba, he played with many top dance bands, including Enrique Jorrin's orchestra in the 1960s, a band that he took over after Jorrin's death.

At the time that Ry Cooder visited Cuba, González had been retired for a few years, was in danger of being forgotten, and did not even own a piano. However, he was found to be in both enthusiastic and prime form, and he became a major sparkplug in the "comeback" of the veteran players, recording and performing with both the Buena Vista Social Club and Juan De Marcos González' Afro-Cuban All-Stars. He also recorded his own delightful album for Nonesuch (his recording debut as a leader), cut when he was a very youthful 77! Ruben González has since toured the world, including appearing in the United States, and recorded two additional albums: *Indestructible* (Egrem) and *Estrellas de Arieto* (Eden Ways).

10 *Introducing . . . Ruben González / April 1996 / World Circuit/Nonesuch 79477*
This CD is impossible not to love. Although Ruben González was 77 at the time and did not even own his own piano, he plays quite brilliantly, performing a variety of traditional melodies plus two originals, often quoting other songs and really stretching himself. His chord voicings are distinctive and very inviting, his control of the piano is quite impressive, and the music sings its heart out. This recording, made spontaneously over a two-day period, has González as the lead voice much of the time, although trumpeter Manuel Mirabal takes some fine solos. The group also includes bassist Orlando "Cachaito" López, Carlos Puisseaux on guiro, the percussion of Amadito Valdés, Roberto Garcia, Carlos González, and Alberto Valdés and occasion-

ally three background singers; flutist Richard Egues pops up on one song. A gem.

MARCELINO "RAPINDEY" GUERRA
b. Apr. 26, 1914, Cienfuegos, Cuba, d. June 30, 1996, Alicante, Spain
Marcelino Guerra had a multifaceted career, as vocalist, composer, self-taught guitarist, and bandleader. The youngest of nine children, he picked up the lifelong nickname of "Rapindey" as a child due to his ability to run fast. After listening to local groups and learning many lyrics, he sang for the first time in public with a band when he was 14. In 1931 Guerra was Septeto Cinefuegos' lead vocalist for a few months, and he spent a year singing with Sexteto Cauto. He teamed up with dancer Julio Blanco (they cowrote songs for a few years), and he freelanced both as a singer and as a composer. Guerra worked and recorded with Arsenio Rodriguez, Ignacio Pineiro's Septeto Nacional, Mariano Merceron, Chano Pozo, Machito, and the La Playa Sextet.

After moving to New York in the early '40s, Guerra sang with Machito for a period. He led popular orchestras of his own during 1945-54 (Doc Cheatham was in the trumpet section for a time), recording for the Verne and Coda labels. After giving up on the band business, Guerra spent several years in the U.S. Merchant Marines. He made some guest appearances with Machito in the 1960s and also sang with La Playa Sextet but mostly worked outside of music. Ironically, Marcelino Guerra's song "Pare Cochero" was first recorded in 1990 and became a standard, many years after he had left the music world.

SUSIE HANSEN
b. Chicago, IL
One of the few violinists to lead a band playing Afro-Cuban Jazz (in addition to Salsa and dance

music), Susie Hansen is the daughter of James Hansen, who played violin in the Chicago Symphony for 37 years. Inspired by her father, Susie played violin as a child, put it down when she was 13, and then resumed her studies with much more enthusiasm when she was 18. She earned degrees in mathematics, electrical engineering, and computer science but eventually chose music. Susie originally played classical chamber music and rock before discovering jazz. After working in Boston with Strings Attached and in West Virginia with the Trapezoid Folk Band, she organized a jazz quintet in Chicago. At one concert she played opposite Victor Parra's Mambo Express All-Stars and was hired for that band, soon falling in love with Latin music. Susie moved to the Los Angeles area in 1988 and in September 1989 formed the Susie Hansen Charanga Jazz Ensemble. Since then, Susie Hansen has worked regularly in Southern California with her versatile group, recording *Solo Flight* in 1993.

8 *Solo Flight / 1993 / Jazz Caliente 222*

Susie Hansen's recording debut as a leader finds her leading a group filled with fine Los Angeles-based musicians. The band includes trombonist David Stout, Pedro Eustache on tenor and flute, a spirited rhythm section (with at least two percussionists), and the vocals of Cheo Negron and Mike Jimenez. Most of the songs are originals by Hansen and/or Stout, and the music alternates between Afro-Cuban Jazz and Salsa, with the leader taking many excellent solos and leading the appealing ensembles. Susie Hansen is long overdue to record again!

LARRY HARLOW

b. Mar. 20, 1939, Brooklyn, NY

A popularizer of Salsa in the 1970s who sought to stretch the music into other areas, Larry Harlow has been important as a musician, as a bandleader, and in the studios. Harlow (whose original name was Lawrence Kahn) began piano lessons at age five, loved jazz from an early age, and discovered Latin music soon afterwards. He studied the records of Noro Morales and Joe Loco so he could get the right rhythmic feel to play Latin jazz and dance music. Harlow first started leading his own group in 1957, worked with Randy Carlos' orchestra, and recorded an early LP as a leader for Fiesta, *Having a Ball.* After he graduated from Brooklyn College in 1962, Harlow worked with Johnny Pacheco. In 1964 he formed a popular band, recording *Heavy Smokin'* for Fania and in 1967 he hired Ishmael Miranda as his singer. Harlow was an original member of the Fania All-Stars (1968-76). His 1969 Fania album, *Me and My Monkey,* yielded a hit in "El Malecon." He recorded regularly for the Fania label until 1983 (sometimes on electric piano), including *A Tribute to Arsenio* (for Arsenio Rodriguez) and 1974's *Salsa.* In addition to producing many albums for other artists, in 1973 he debuted *Hommy—A Latin Opera,* which was his version of *The Who's Tommy.* Since the early 1980s, Larry Harlow has been less active as a Latin musician, staying behind the scenes running a recording studio, recording jingles, working for K-Tel, and often teaching Afro-Cuban music.

GIOVANNI HIDALGO

b. 1963, San Juan, Puerto Rico

Ever since he was a teenager, Giovanni Hidalgo has been considered one of the top conga players. Hidalgo's father, José "Manengue" Hidalgo, was also a conguero who worked with Ricardo Ray's group for many years. Giovanni began playing music when he was five and was a professional by the age of 12, playing with the Salsa bands of Mario Ortiz and Luigi Texidor. He was only 13 when he started working jobs with Charlie Palmieri. In 1980 Hidalgo became one of the founding members of

Batacumbele. He spent a long and beneficial period working with Eddie Palmieri (1982-88), and he also freelanced, including with Dave Valentin, trumpeter Freddie Hubbard, drummer Art Blakey, and others. Hidalgo was a member of Dizzy Gillespie's United Nation Orchestra for several years and has often worked as a session player, sometimes appearing on pop dates. As an occasional bandleader, Giovanni Hidalgo has headed dates for Messidor, Sony, and RMM.

7 *Villa Hidalgo / 1991 / Messidor 15817*
9 *Worldwide / 1993 / RMM/Tropijazz 81056*
8 *Time Shifter / 1995 / RMM/Tropijazz 81585*

Giovanni Hidalgo's debut as a leader, *Villa Hidalgo,* features the arrangements of trumpeter Tommy Villarini, who also contributed four of the nine selections. Hidalgo's conga, bongo, and timbales are showcased in a variety of settings, with his solos usually being brief and supportive of other players. "Villa Hidalgo" has a guest solo by Dizzy Gillespie (a decent effort that was one of his last on record), altoist Paquito D'Rivera uplifts "Bahia San Juan," David Sanchez has several spots, "Yuliria" is a piano-conga duet with Eric Figueroa, and "Ianmanuel" features five percussionists plus Figueroa's keyboards. Some of the music is funky and some is more traditional, with the styles and instrumentation changing from cut to cut.

Worldwide is a real gem. Hilton Ruiz, Marty Sheller, and Eric Figueroa contributed the colorful arrangements for a septet/octet that includes Dave Valentin, trumpeter Lew Soloff, tenor saxophonist Craig Handy, Hilton Ruiz or Figueroa on piano, bassist Eddie Rivera, and Ignacio Berroa plus guest Mario Rivera on various reeds. Hidalgo plays a large number of percussion instruments, and the band revitalizes such numbers as "It Don't Mean a Thing," Sonny Clark's "Blue Minor," "Canadian Sunset," "Summertime," and "Seven Steps to Heaven." The consistently rewarding solos and the surprising arrangements make this set highly recommended.

Time Shifter is nearly at the same level. Utilizing groups that range in size from 9 to 14 pieces, Hidalgo presides over dense ensembles that perform a variety of complex frameworks with apparent ease. "From This Moment On" (which has a surprisingly effective vocal by Jill Amesbury that at first seems out-of-place) and "Yesterdays" are the only standards. Among the many soloists are Mario Rivera on tenor, Lew Soloff, flutist David Rodriguez, pianist Figueroa, and trumpeter Jerry González (on "Call of the Jungle Bird"). A rather creative set full of unusual twists and turns.

H.M.A. SALSA/JAZZ ORCHESTRA

In 1985, the Hispanic Musicians Association (a nonprofit organization) was organized to help educate the public about Latin music and to stand up for the rights of its musicians. Eddie Cano was its first president (1986-87), to be succeeded by Elmo Questell (1988) and Bobby Rodriguez (starting in 1989). In 1991 its 22-piece Salsa/Jazz Orchestra made its recording debut for Sea Breeze, and a second CD, *California Salsa II*, was recorded in 1994 for the Dos Coronas label.

7 *California Salsa / 1991 / Sea Breeze 110*

The H.M.A. Salsa/Jazz Orchestra in 1991 featured some of the better L.A.-based Latin musicians, including trumpeters Bobby Rodriguez and Tony Lujan, tenor saxophonist Larry Covelli, keyboardists David Torres and Billy Mitchell, and a large percussion section. For their debut recording, the group plays Paul López arrangements on three of his originals and contributions from other band members plus Clare Fischer's "Pensativa," "Blue Skies," and "A-Train Mambo"; two numbers feature vocalists. A worthy effort from an ensemble that is much larger than most Afro-Cuban Jazz groups.

IRAKERE

In 1967 Chucho Valdés, Arturo Sandoval, and Paquito D'Rivera were among the musicians who formed the Orquesta Cubana de Musica Moderna (the Cuban Modern Music Orchestra). Six years later, that trio of greats plus several other top players broke away to form Irakere (Spanish for "forest"), which ever since has been considered Cuba's #1 music group. An experimental band that at its best features advanced jazz improvising, exciting rhythms, group singing, and plenty of original music, Irakere infuses even its most modern performances with strong doses of traditional Cuban melodies and stretches that are influenced by European classical music. The medium-size band (usually 10-11 pieces) first recorded in 1975 and created a stir in 1977 when Dizzy Gillespie and Stan Getz visited Cuba and discovered the group. Since there was a temporary thaw in United States-Cuban relations during the period, in 1978-79 Irakere appeared in the States and made a few recordings for Columbia. Among Irakere's other key members of the era were guitarist Carlos Emilio Morales, trumpeter Jorge Varona, and saxophonist Carlos Averhoff. D'Rivera defected in 1980, and Sandoval left the band a few years later (moving to the United States in 1990), but Irakere has managed to retain its high quality through the years. The biggest loss was in 1998, when leader Chucho Valdés departed to devote time to his own solo career. His son, Jesus Valdés, replaced him on piano, while drummer Enrique Pla and guitarist Morales (original members) took over as co-leaders. Irakere, which has visited the United States on an infrequent basis since 1996 and often plays in Europe, has recorded quite a few albums, including for Columbia, Milestone, Jazz House, World Pacific, Bembe, Harmonia Mundi, and Blue Note.

9 *The Best of Irakere / June 28, 1978-Apr. 1979 / Columbia/Legacy 57719*

8 *The Legendary Irakere in London / Oct. 1, 1987 / Jazz House 017*

8 *Live at Ronnie Scott's / Sept. 1991 / World Pacific 80598*

9 *Afrocubanismo! / Aug. 27, 1994-Sept. 4, 1994 / Bembe 2012*

4 *Indestructible / 1998 / Harmonia Mundi 3006 036*

8 *Yemaya / 1998 / Blue Note 98239*

The Best of Irakere has the most rewarding cuts from Irakere's first two Columbia recordings. The album *Irakere* is represented by four of its five original selections, including the 17½ minute "Misa Negra ("Black Mass")," while *Irakere II* (which was a bit more commercial and scattered) has six of its numbers reissued. The early Irakere magic was very much intact at the time, and there is quite a bit of excitement to be heard throughout this recommended release, with most of the tunes (other than "Adagio on a Mozart Theme") being group originals.

Irakere has played Ronnie Scott's club in London regularly since 1985 (when their initial appearance was considered sensational), and they have recorded several CDs at that venue in the years since. *The Legendary Irakere in London,* which starts out with a throwaway Salsa vocal piece, has two notable showcases for German Velazco, one apiece on alto and soprano. "Stella by Starlight ("Estella Va a Estallar")" is swung hard in its own fashion, and the closing, nearly 17-minute rendition of Dave Brubeck's "The Duke" has explosive yet lyrical piano playing by Chucho Valdés, an unusual arrangement (that during one stretch becomes "Satin Doll"), and some shouting choruses that find Irakere emulating the Count Basie Orchestra. *Live at Ronnie Scott's* is one of the most jazz-oriented of all the Irakere releases. With the exception of the departed D'Rivera, the two trumpets, and a percussionist, the group's lineup is the same as a dozen

Part of the rhythm section of Irakere, Cuba's premiere band.

years earlier. The many rehearsals and performances definitely show, with Irakere sounding very much at home during the 1991 performance that comprises this CD. Five of the six selections are individual features, including spots for flutist Orlando Valle, altoist Cesar López, and Valdés (who contributed all six originals and is showcased on "Mr. Bruce").

Recorded live at the Banff Center in Alberta, Canada, *Afrocubanismo!* is taken from several concerts during a festival. The 1994 version of Irakere (a septet with Valdés, Carlos Averhoff on tenor, trumpeter Juan Angel Munguia Cubas, altoist Cesar Alejandro López Martinez, bassist Carlos Del Puerto, drummer Enrique Pla, and Miguel Diaz on congas) stretches out on five of Valdés' originals, including the delightful "Cha Cha Chá," (with guest flutist Richard Egues), the adventurous "Neurosis," and "Estella a las Estrellas," which is really "Stella by Starlight." All three horn players

are outstanding, as is Valdés. Changuito sits in on timbales during two numbers, and several Canadians plus drummer Memo Acevedo help out on "Building Bridges." In addition, this CD includes a voice-and-percussion piece by Grupo Ilu Ana ("Rumba Tonada") and a closing selection ("Xiomaza") in which Irakere is joined by the members of Los Munequitos de Matanzas, a percussion, voice, and dance ensemble. The music is of high quality throughout, making this an easily recommended disc.

Indestructible is rather disappointing from a jazz standpoint. Irakere is essentially used as a conventional backup dance band behind the vocals of Mayra Caridad Valdés, singer-percussionist Oscar Valdés, and a three-voice chorus. The ten selections are all concise (between three and five minutes). And although the vocals are happy, the band has no opportunity to sound individual other than briefly on "Te Doy." In its own odd way, this CD is reminiscent of some of the Count Basie Orchestra recordings of the 1960s, where his big band served merely as a prop behind pop singers.

However, on *Yemaya,* Irakere is allowed to be Irakere. Mayra Caridad Valdés opens up the date with a heartfelt vocal on "Yemaya," but this is a rewarding cameo rather than the prelude to her being a dominant force. The other six songs are instrumentals that include Chucho Valdés' feature on "Mister Bruce," a workout on the chord changes of "Love for Sale" (retitled "La Explosion"), and an opportunity for guitarist Carlos Emilio Morales to freak out a bit on "Son Montuno." The other main soloists on this rewarding effort include Alfredo Thompson on tenor, altoist Cesar López, and trumpeter Mario Fernandez.

LPs to Search For:
El Coco (Milestone 9111) features the 1980 version of Irakere, a tentet that includes Sandoval and Jorge Varona on trumpets, saxophonists Carlos Averhoff and German Velazco, and a six-piece rhythm section with Valdés. The leader contributes two of the songs, and the spirited band also performs a pair of obscurities and a Cuban jazz reinterpretation of a Beethoven theme.

RALPH IRIZARRY
b. Brooklyn, NY

A versatile and exciting timbale player, Ralph Irizarry in recent times has emerged as a potentially important ·bandleader after years as a sideman. Growing up in Brooklyn, Irizarry was initially attracted to the conga drum when a friend introduced him to Latin music. Discovering that his father had a set of timbales in the closet, the teenager began to practice diligently, teaching himself the intricate Latin rhythms. He played with Jorge Maldonado's band in Brooklyn for nine months, moved with his family to Puerto Rico, and gigged locally. When he was 19, Irizarry returned to New

York City, where he worked with La Tipica New York, Charanga America, and other groups. Irizarry's big break was when he was hired for Ray Barretto's band, a stint that lasted four years (1979-83) and gave him a great deal of valuable experience, in addition to allowing him to make his recording debut. Irizarry became an important member of Rubén Blades' Seis del Solar in April 1983, staying not only for eight years with Blades but for a few additional years after the group went out on its own. Ralph Irizarry, who had an acting role in the film *Mambo Kings,* has led Timbalaye since 1996, recording for Shanachie.

9 *Best-Kept Secret / Dec. 1999 / Shanachie 66026*

On evidence of this recording, Ralph Irizarry's Timbalaye is certainly one of the world's best-kept secrets in Afro-Cuban Jazz. The musicians (trumpeter Alex Norris, trombonist Ozzie Melendez, tenor saxophonist Bob Franceschini, pianist Luis Perdomo, electric bassist Waldo Chavez, Roberto Quintero on congas and bongos, and Irizarry on timbales) are mostly all obscure, other than the leader, but prove to be expert ensemble players and colorful soloists. The nine originals on their CD are very jazz-oriented and modern, with the Latin rhythm section really pushing the lead voices. *Best-Kept Secret,* which does not have any slow moments, is easily recommended both to post-bop listeners and to fans of stirring Afro-Cuban rhythms.

STAN KENTON
b. Dec. 15, 1911, Wichita, KS, d. Aug. 25, 1979, Los Angeles, CA

The excitement of Afro-Cuban rhythms always appealed to Stan Kenton, and in the mid-1940s he and Dizzy Gillespie were virtually the only big bandleaders from jazz who went out of their way to embrace the new style. As with Gillespie, Kenton played Latin-oriented jazz only on a part-time basis throughout his career, but he was responsible for several very historic recordings along the way.

Always a controversial figure, Stan Kenton led a succession of highly original orchestras that often emphasized emotion, power, and advanced harmonies over swing. A pianist who was influenced by Earl Hines but never reached the level of being a virtuoso, Kenton played in the 1930s in the dance bands of Vido Musso and Gus Arnheim. However, he had too much charisma to be a sideman for long. After much planning, in 1940 he formed his first orchestra. One of his main goals was to play "serious" jazz for concert audiences rather than to be accompanying dancers. His first key soloist was trumpeter Chico Alvarez, and there were a few Latin numbers in his early repertoire, including "Lamento Gitano," "La Cumparsita," "Taboo," "El Choclo," and "Adios," but his versions were generally more swing than Latin. Kenton gained a strong following in the summer of 1941 when he played regularly at the Rendezvous Ballroom in Balboa Beach, California. Kenton enjoyed high-note trumpeters (being influenced by Jimmie Lunceford) and thick-toned tenors, and his arrangements were often somewhat bombastic but never dull. After its initial success, the Stan Kenton Orchestra struggled for a time, cutting a few titles for Decca that did not sell all that well. A period as Bob Hope's backup radio band offered some steady work but was unsatisfying.

The turning point came when Kenton signed with Capitol in late 1943, an association that would last 25 years. His orchestra's first recording date for the label resulted in a hit in the catchy "Eager Beaver" plus the original recorded version of his theme, "Artistry in Rhythm." Due to its unique style and the leader's personal magnetism, the Stan Kenton Orchestra would be one of jazz's few big band successes during the 1944-48 period, a time when the swing era ended and most jazz orchestras broke up. With singer June Christy having popular hits (including "Tampico" and "Across the Alley from the Alamo"), Kenton was able to afford more ambitious projects that he called "progressive jazz," often featuring the adventurous arrangements of Pete Rugolo.

In 1946 Stan Kenton first heard the orchestras of Nora Morales and Machito, and he was quite impressed. On January 2, 1947, he recorded a novelty tune, "His Feet Too Big For De Bed," that used José Mangual on bongos and Pedro Allende on maracas; this was before Dizzy Gillespie first met Chano Pozo. Surprisingly, when Kenton recorded Pete Rugolo's "Machito" on February 13, there were no extra percussionists, although the second, March 31, version has Ivan López on bongo and Eugenio Reyes on maracas. Later in the year Jack Costanzo on bongos became a regular member of Kenton's ensemble, as did Brazilian guitarist Laurindo Almeida. René Touzet guested on maracas for "Fugue for Rhythm Section" on September 25 and "Lament (for Guitar)" on October 22. But it was the December 6, 1947, session that really put Kenton in the Cubop Hall of Fame. Adding Machito himself on maracas, Carlos Vidal on conga, and the timbales of José Mangual (along with Costanzo's bongos), Kenton recorded "Cuban Carnival" and a classic version of "The Peanut Vendor"; the latter song would remain in his repertoire permanently. Finishing up the year's recordings during December 21-22, Kenton utilized Machito's maracas and Carlos Vidal's congas on the "Prologue Suite" and "Bongo Riff."

Due to these recordings, Tito Puente would consider Kenton to be a strong influence on his own orchestra in future years, as would Pupi Campo and René Touzet.

In early 1948, Kenton's orchestra shared the bill with Machito's Afro-Cubans at a well-publicized Town Hall concert, an engagement that gave Machito a great deal of exposure. The Kenton Afro-

Cuban recordings might have continued except that 1948 brought a Musicians Union recording strike, and by the end of '48 the bandleader decided to take the following year off. In 1950, when Kenton came back, he put together his most radical band, the 39-piece Innovations in Modern Music Orchestra. Carlos Vidal was on conga initially (the conga position was dropped the following year). But, other than "Cuban Episode" and 1951's "Viva Prado," the Afro-Cuban style was de-emphasized in favor of modern classical works and some rather unclassifiable music. Kenton had a more bop-oriented band during much of the 1950s, introducing only occasional new Latin pieces (such as 1954's "Hava-a-Havana" and "Bacante," both of which used Candido's conga). Versions of "Malagueña" and "Dark Eyes" in 1955 had Jack Costanzo, René Touzet, and José Guerrero added on Latin percussion, while Chico Guerrero's timbales and bongo helped out on 1956 versions of "The Peanut Vendor" and "Unison Riff."

The 1956 *Cuban Fire* album, which featured Johnny Richards' arrangements and compositions, was really Kenton's last full-fledged exploration of Cuban music. No less than six percussionists joined the Kenton Orchestra for this stirring project, which is rightfully considered a classic. Although he would continue to be quite active and involved in many projects during his final 20 years (including an orchestra with four mellophoniums, his memorable *West Side Story* recording, an unusual album of classical composer Richard Wagner's music, and the college stage band movement), Stan Kenton had made his final major statement in Afro-Cuban Jazz with *Cuban Fire.*

10 *The Complete Capitol Studio Recordings of Stan Kenton 1943-1947 / Nov. 19, 1943-Dec. 22, 1947 / Mosaic 7-163*

10 *Retrospective / Nov. 19, 1943-July 18, 1968 / Capitol 97350*

10 *Cuban Fire / May 22-24, 1956 / Capitol 96260*

10 *West Side Story / Mar. 15, 1961-Apr. 11, 1961 / Capitol 29914*

The seven-CD limited-edition Mosaic box set of *The Complete Capitol Studio Recordings of Stan Kenton 1943-1947* is magnificent but will be difficult to find. It includes all of the studio sides from Kenton's 1943-47 band plus radio transcriptions that he made for the Capitol label. Of greatest interest from the Latin standpoint are "Tampico," "Ecuador," "His Feet Too Big For De Bed," both early versions of "Machito," "Fugue for Rhythm Section," "Unison Riff," "Lament (for Guitar)," "Cuban Carnival," "The Peanut Vendor," and "Bongo Riff."

Retrospective is a four-CD set containing highlights from Kenton's entire period on the Capitol label. "Tampico" and one version of "Machito" are repeated from the Mosaic box, plus there is also "Viva Prado," the 1956 version of "The Peanut Vendor," two of the selections from *Cuban Fire,* a 1959 rendition of "Mexican Jumping Bean" (which has three added Latin percussionists) and two songs from Kenton's *West Side Story* album.

Cuban Fire is a six-part suite, composed and arranged by Johnny Richards, in which the Kenton orchestra was expanded to 27 pieces, including six percussionists (Willie Rodriguez, Sol Gubin, George Laguna, Tommy López, Mario Alvarez, and Roger Mozian), tuba, and two French horns. The raging ensembles and heated solos (by tenors Lucky Thompson and Bill Perkins, trombonist Carl Fontana, altoist Lennie Niehaus, and trumpeters Sam Noto and Vinnie Tanno) make this a classic set. Stan Kenton's interpretation of ten themes from *West Side Story* may not technically be Afro-Cuban Jazz, but since George Acevedo (conga), Mike Pacheco (bongos), and either Larry Bunker or Lou Singer (tympani) augment the orchestra's personnel and the music deals with a Puerto Rican gang, it qualifies for inclusion in this book! Kenton's shouting brass fits the music perfectly, and there are fine short solos from altoist Gabe Baltazar, tenor saxophonist Sam Donahue, and trumpeter Conte Candoli. It is a pity that the producers of the movie did not think of using Kenton's band on the soundtrack; they realized their oversight when it was already too late!

A CD sampler featuring Stan Kenton's key Latin-oriented recordings is long overdue.

LATIN JAZZ ORCHESTRA

Co-led by trumpeter Armando Rodriguez and Victor Rendon (doubling on drums and timbales), the Latin Jazz Orchestra has recorded two impressive albums. Rodriguez and Rendon first met while attending North Texas State University in the early 1970s. They played in the school's lab bands and worked in local Tex-Mex bands, moving in 1980 to New York, where they have played on countless sessions ever since. In 1991 they teamed up to form the Latin Jazz Orchestra, a fine ensemble that blends Latin melodies, jazz, and dance music. In addition to its co-leaders, the mid-'90s version of the ten- to twelve-piece band included pianist Arturo O'Farrill.

8 *Juarez / Feb. 22, 1992-Apr. 25, 1992 / Tortilla Flat 001*
8 *Havana Blues / Aug. 16, 1994-Nov. 23, 1996 / Palmetto 2034*

The Rodriguez-Rendon Latin Jazz Orchestra often sounds very much like a Latin big band of the 1950s on its two CDs, other than for the sophistication of the bass lines and the improved recording quality. The orchestra may not have any "big" names in the 13-piece lineup heard on their recording debut, *Juarez* (pianist Arturo O'Farrill was just beginning to get known), but its repertoire (which

includes "Bernie's Tune," "Here's That Rainy Day," Gato Barbieri's "Lluvia Azul," Horace Silver's "Nutville," and a few newer pieces) is fresh, the arrangements (by Victor Rendon, Armando Rodriguez, and Louis Bauzo) are colorful, the soloists are uniformly strong, and the band definitely has a joyous group spirit. Its follow-up, *Havana Blues,* has arrangements by Chico O'Farrill and the two co-leaders that find the band often sounding a bit similar to Machito and Tito Puente, although also being more boppish in general. In addition to some originals, the big band performs O'Farrill's "Havana Blues," Jimmy Rowles' "The Cobra," Chick Corea's "Guajira," Kenny Dorham's "Afrodisia," and Horace Silver's "Where You At?". There are several guest soloists on the set, including altoist Jerry Dodgion, trombonist Papo Vásquez, vibraphonist Victor Mendoza, and (on "Where You At?") and singer Adela Dalto. But even on the numbers where the band is heard sans guests, the music swings hard and is full of concise, exciting solos.

THE LATIN JAZZ QUINTET

The Latin Jazz Quintet has an odd history. The short-lived group, which was strongly influenced by Cal Tjader's band and the George Shearing Quintet (with conga in place of guitar), was born in the late 1950s and led by conga player Juan Amalbert. The early lineup consisted of Amalbert, vibraphonist Charlie Simmons, pianist Gene Casey, bassist Bill Ellington, and Manny Ramos on drums and timbales, expertly mixing light bop with Afro-Cuban rhythms. Their recording debut was the first of two unusual meetings with the great Eric Dolphy (heard on alto sax, flute, and bass clarinet). In both cases, the lightly swinging quintet did not react in the slightest to the fiery and eccentric flights of Dolphy, or vice versa. It was almost as if they were in separate rooms!

The band's second and third dates (from 1960-61) showcased the quintet, although the personnel was quite a bit different, with Amalbert and Ellington joined by vibraphonist Willie Coleman, Artie Jenkins or José Ricci on piano, and Phil Newsom on drums and timbales; Bobby Capers was sometimes added on alto. A fourth recording, a rather scarce effort made for Tru-Sound in 1962, had Amalbert, Ellington, and Capers assisted by vibraphonist William Bivens, pianist Willie Gardner, Manny Ramos on timbales, and Victor Allende on bongos. By the time the group had a "reunion" recording with Eric Dolphy (most likely in 1963) for United Artists, it had undergone a 100% turnover and now consisted of Felipe Diaz (the new leader) on vibes, pianist Arthur Jenkins, bassist Bobby Rodriguez, Tommy López on conga, and Louis Ramirez on timbales. Juan Amalbert, who played during the era with tenor-saxophonist Willis Jackson and organist Shirley Scott in addition to Duke Ellington's 1963 My People show, had left the band by then. Within a short time after its second Dolphy date, the Latin Jazz Quintet itself had passed into history.

7 *Caribe / Aug. 19, 1960 / Original Jazz Classics 819*

8 *Hot Sauce / Prestige 24128*

Caribe matches multi-instrumentalist Eric Dolphy with the early version of the Latin Jazz Quintet, an unlikely team to say the least. While the Quintet's playing is relaxed and tasteful on five of their basic originals plus "Spring Is Here," Dolphy is explosive, very speechlike, often atonal, and full of fire. No matter, the Latin Jazz Quintet performs as if he were not even present. And when Dolphy is finished with his solo, the Quintet continues in its soothing, Cal Tjader-influenced way. Definitely an oddity!

Hot Sauce has all of the music recorded by the Quintet during their second and third dates and is quite definitive of the band. The music alternates between standards (including "Red Top," "Summertime," "Blue Moon," and "Milestones") and basic originals. Bobby Capers' alto adds some fire (although nothing on Dolphy's level!) to eight of the 15 numbers.

LPs to Search For:
The Latin Jazz Quintet's fourth recording (cut for Tru-Tone) remains out of print. Its fifth and final set, cut for United Artists but reissued by Palladium, is simply called *The Latin Jazz Quintet* (Palladium 145). However, since Eric Dolphy again dominates, the album title is a bit inaccurate. On such numbers as "Speak Low," "A Night in Tunisia," "Cha Cha King," and "Lover," Dolphy is fiery and intense, while the Latin Jazz Quintet (which had a completely different personnel than during its first encounter with the unique reed soloist) essentially ignores him.

LATIN X-POSURE

Comprised of musicians and singers from Puerto Rico, Mexico, Peru, Cuba, and the United States, the Cincinnati-based Latin X-Posure (which was formed in 1997) consists of four horns, musical director Patrick Kelly on piano, bassist Michael Sharfe, timbales, congas, bongos, and four singers (Marible Andrade, Laura Toscaris, Lillian Valdés, and Maria Alvarez). Their soloists (particularly trumpeters Gary Winters and Brian Schwab) are strong and the group excels at both Salsa (three of their vocalists alternate singing lead in the coro) and Afro-Cuban Jazz plus some merengue and boleros. Their debut recording in 1999 launched J Curve's subsidiary Sabroso.

7 *Donde Estas? / June 1999 / J Curve Sabroso 6001*

For their first recording, Latin X-Posure interprets a wide-ranging program of Latin music that features plenty of vocals but also three strong instrumentals. The ten pieces range from a Latinized version of a Chopin classical melody ("Esta Noche Donde Estas"), the romantic "I Thought I Heard You Call My Name" (a bolero that has Laura Toscaris singing in English), the heated instrumental "Smokin' In Havana," and a few spots for guest saxophonists Rick VanMatre to a rather unusual version of the Beatles' "Ob La Dee, Ob La Da," which is turned into a jubilant dance number. A pretty strong beginning for this colorful ensemble.

ERNESTO LECUONA

b. Aug. 7, 1896, Guanabacoa, Cuba, d. Nov. 29, 1963, Tenerife, Canary Islands

One of the most important of all Cuban composers, Ernesto Lecuona wrote over 600 songs during his career, several of which became notable standards. He started out as a child prodigy, first performing in public on piano when he was five. Lecuona was already writing songs when he was 11 (an age when he began playing piano in silent movie houses) and teaching piano when he was 15. He graduated from Cuba's National Conservatory in 1917 and was soon touring as a concert pianist, appearing in New York that same year. However, Lecuona was more interested in popular music than in becoming a classical pianist, so he organized the Havana Orchestra, composing for operettas and musical comedies. He led the Palau Brothers Cuban Orchestra, which appeared in the 1931 movie musical *The Cuban Love Song,* playing "The Peanut Vendor." Lecuona formed Orquesta Cubana in 1932 but gave up playing piano so as to stick to composing and arranging. Although he returned to Cuba in 1934, he oversaw the band, which was renamed the Lecuona Cuban Boys, for decades; in fact a later edition of the group was still touring in the mid-1970s. Although he wrote musical shows and the scores for four Hollywood films, Lecuona was most significant as a songwriter. Among his

tunes are "Malagueña," "Andalucia" (better-known as "The Breeze and I"), "Siboney," "Always in My Heart," "Para Vigo Me Voy," "Canto Karabali" ("Jungle Drums"), and "La Comparsa." Lecuona left Cuba in 1960 after Fidel Castro took over, vowing not to perform until Cuba was free; he never played again. Ernesto Lecuona lived for a short time in Tampa, Florida, settled in Spain, and passed away on the Canary Islands during a vacation.

MARK LEVINE

b. Oct. 4, 1938, Concord, NH

Mark Levine has alternated between straightahead hard bop and Afro-Cuban Jazz throughout his career. He graduated from Boston University with a music degree in 1960, studying privately with Jaki Byard, Hall Overton, and Herb Pomeroy. Levine moved to New York shortly after, relocating to Los Angeles in 1967. Among his more important associations were sideman gigs with tenors Houston Person (1966) and Joe Henderson (1973), guitarist Gabor Szabo, Mongo Santamaria (1969-70), and Willie Bobo (1971-74). Levine moved to San Francisco in 1975, played with trumpeter Woody Shaw (1975-76), the Blue Mitchell-Harold Land Quintet (1975-79), Joe Henderson, Stan Getz, vibraphonist Bobby Hutcherson, Moacir Santo, and trumpeter Luis Gasca and had a long association with Cal Tjader (1979-83). Since then Levine has primarily led his own groups. For a few years he de-emphasized the piano and sought to make a living as a valve trombonist, but eventually he realized that he could get more work on his original instrument. Mark Levine has led sets for Catalyst (1976), Concord (1983 and 1985), and Left Coast Clavé (2000), the latter being his first full-fledged Afro-Cuban Jazz recording as a leader. He remains a very valuable and versatile pianist, based in the San Francisco Bay Area.

8 *Hey, It's Me / May 16, 2000-June 14, 2000 / Left Coast Clavé 001*

On this highly enjoyable effort, Mark Levine Latinizes a wide variety of material including songs by pianists Mulgrew Miller and Ronnie Mathews, drummer Victor Lewis, Sonny Rollins ("Airegin"), and trumpeter Charles Tolliver plus a few standards (including "Without A Song" and "You and the Night and the Music"). Levine is joined in his quartet by bassist Peter Barshay, drummer Paul Van Wageningen, and percussionist Michael Spiro. The musicians have a real feel for both the songs and the rhythms, making this an easily recommended set.

LPs to Search For:
Mark Levine's *Up 'Til Now* (Catalyst 7614), a 1977 sextet set with trumpeter Tom Harrell and the reeds of Ray Pizzi, 1983's *Concepts* (Concord Jazz 234), which features him on valve trombone with a San Francisco quintet, and *Smiley & Me* (Cameo 601), an unusual duet date of standards with drummer Smiley Winters, all lack any overt Latin elements. But as a sideman with Mongo Santamaria, Willie Bobo, Cal Tjader, and others, Levine has consistently shown how strong an Afro-Cuban pianist he can be.

JOE LOCO
b. Mar. 26, 1921, New York, NY, d. Mar. 7, 1988, San Juan, Puerto Rico

Although barely remembered today, during the 1950s and the first half of the '60s, the Joe Loco Trio was one of the more popular groups in Afro-Cuban Jazz. Joe Loco (who was born Joe Estevez) started dance and violin lessons when he was eight. At the age of 13 he stopped going to school so he could dance in vaudeville. It took three years, but in 1937 a truant officer caught him and he was forced to attend Harlem High School. This turned into a lucky break because while at school, Estevez learned both trombone and piano. After playing trombone with the New York Amateur Symphony,

he settled on piano. He began freelancing as a pianist in 1939, working with Ciro Rimac, Montecino's Happy Boys, Enric Madriguera, Xavier Cugat, and Machito (1943-45). He gained the lifelong name of Joe Loco after composing "Cada Loco Con Su Tema" for Machito in 1943.

Drafted into the U.S. Air Force in November 1945, Loco spent his year in the military quite usefully, teaching himself how to arrange music and writing charts for Vincent López, Noro Morales, and Xavier Cugat, among others. Discharged in early 1947, he studied music at Juilliard and worked with Ramon Argueso, Fernando Alvarez's Copacabana Samba Band (Tito Puente was in the group at the time), Jack López's big band, and Pupi Campo. While playing with Julio Andinio during 1949-50, Loco wrote arrangements for Tito Rodriguez, Machito, Marcelino Guerra, Noro Morales, and Tito Puente. During a second stint as pianist-arranger with Pupo Campo (1950-51), he subbed for Tito Rodriguez on a 1951 record date when Tito came down with laryngitis. The Joe Loco Trio's version of "Tenderly" was such a big hit that he soon left Campo and went out on his own.

Leading a quintet featuring vibraphonist Pete Terrace, Loco enjoyed turning swing tunes (such as "Blue Moon," "Love for Sale," and "How High the Moon") into mambos, and the general public loved his musical transformations. Loco's Latinized versions of American standards were so popular that the Joe Loco Quintet became a regular at jazz clubs where Latin music had not been played before. For a 15-year period, Loco and his group worked regularly, recording for Tico, Columbia, Ansonia (*The Music of Rafael Hernández*), Fantasy (as the Pete Terrace Quintet), Imperial, GNP, Liberty, and Orfeon. With the change in musical tastes by the late 1960s, Joe Loco settled in 1968 in Puerto Rico, where he spent his last couple of decades playing regularly at San Juan hotels.

8 *Loco Motion / 1960 / Fantasy 24733*

Two very different Joe Loco albums are reissued in full on this CD. The earlier set, *Going Loco,* is a strong example of how the pianist usually sounded. He heads a quintet also including vibraphonist Pete Terrace, bassist Juan Andino Garcia, Bobby Flash (mostly on bongos), and Freddie Aguilera on conga. In addition to four originals, the easy-listening music includes Latin versions of such standards as "September Song," "Autumn Leaves," and "I've Got You Under My Skin," often sounding a bit reminiscent of the George Shearing Quintet (although without a guitar). The other half of the CD finds Loco doing his best (on an album originally simply titled *Joe Loco*) to keep up with the pachanga craze of the early 1960s. He utilizes a charanga band comprised of flutist José Lozano, three violins (including José "Chombo" Silva), bassist Victor Venegas, Mongo Santamaria on conga, Willie Bobo on timbales, the guiro player Nicolas Martinez, and the vocals of Bayardo Velarde and Rudy Calzado. While Loco wrote five of the dozen selections (which include three by Santamaria), the spirited vocals often dominate so the leader is often merely a minor player on his own date. But since few Joe Loco recordings are easily available, this generous set is well worth picking up.

LOS HOMBRES CALIENTES

A very promising band, Los Hombres Calientes in 1998 consisted of trumpeter Irvin Mayfield, pianist Victor Atkins III, bassist David Pulphus, and drummer Jason Marsalis (younger brother of Wynton, Branford, and Delfeayo), with Bill Summers and Yvette Bostic-Summers on percussion and vocals. Although born and based in New Orleans, Los Hombres Calientes is very much an Afro-Cuban (rather than a New Orleans jazz or R&B) group although influenced by its surroundings. The idea behind the band was conceived by Mayfield (then just 20) and Summers (well known for his work with Herbie Hancock's Headhunters), and they soon recruited Marsalis, Pulphus (who had recorded previously with Terence Blanchard), Atkins, and Bostic-Summers. Performing mostly original material grounded in traditional Cuban music but looking forward, Los Hombres Calientes has thus far recorded two excellent discs for Basin Street and has a great deal of potential.

7 *Los Hombres Calientes / Mar. 1998 / Basin Street 0201*

8 *Vol. 2 / 1999 / Basin Street 202*

The band was only a couple months old when they recorded their debut disc, but Los Hombres Calientes already was fairly distinctive, as shown on its self-titled debut. The tight rhythm section, Mayfield's enthusiastic horn (which sometimes hints at Wynton Marsalis), and the spirited singers make this a strong debut. Guest vocalists are utilized on four of the selections, but overall the music is instrumental, including appealing Latin versions of "Stardust" and "After You're Gone." *Vol. 2* finds Los Hombres Calientes stretching beyond Afro-Cuban Jazz into New Orleans parade rhythms, funk, R&B, and even reggae. Bill Summers (who plays all types of percussion instruments) is the most significant performer in the group although trumpeter Irvin Mayfield gets in his spots and the rest of the group (the personnel had not changed yet) is impressive too. Other than a few numbers (including a medley of "Chameleon" and "We Want The Funk"), Los Hombres Calientes sticks to their wide-ranging originals including Mayfield's three-part "Cuban Suite." The rhythmic music is largely unclassifiable and is full of spirit and surprises. Jason Marsalis went out on his own shortly after this set was recorded, a pity for the band was really developing its own sound.

TONY LUJAN

b. 1957, Albuquerque, NM

An excellent trumpeter and flügelhornist inspired by Lee Morgan and Freddie Hubbard, Tony Lujan has worked in both Latin and boppish settings through the years. He studied at New Mexico State University and the University of Las Vegas, recorded two strictly straightahead dates for the Capri label (1990's *Magic Circle* and 1992's *Zulu*) and has become a fixture in the Los Angeles area. Among the many top artists with whom he has worked and/or recorded have been flügelhornist Clark Terry, arranger Bill Holman, Ray Charles, bassist Henry Franklin, arranger Gerald Wilson, Luis Bonilla, William Cepeda, the Garcia Brothers, the H.M.A. Salsa/Jazz Orchestra, Eddie Palmieri, and Tito Puente.

MACHITO

b. Feb. 16, 1912, Tampa, FL, d. Apr. 15, 1984, London, England

One of the most important contributors to Afro-Cuban Jazz and a major bandleader for over 40 years, Machito was a singer and occasional maracas player who was wise enough to let Mario Bauzá set the musical direction for his pioneering Afro-Cuban big band. He was born Frank Grillo in Florida but raised in Cuba. His mother nicknamed him "Macho," a title that stuck for two decades before a friend in New York urged him to add "ito" to it, à la Tito. He first met Bauzá in 1926 and sang with the Miguel Zavalle Sextet in the mid-1920s, advancing to the teenage band Los Jovenes Rendencion in 1928. Machito spent much of the 1930s performing in Cuba, including with El Sexteto Nacional at Havana's Montmartre Club. After Bauzá (who had moved to the United States in 1930) came home to marry Machito's sister Estella, his stories about New York inspired Machito to save money so he could emigrate too.

Machito left for the United States in October 1937 and a week later was already singing for Las Estrellas Habanera. In 1938 he made his recording debut (as part of a chorus with El Conjunto Moderno), and he soon recorded with Xavier Cugat (eight numbers), Noro Morales, and a few other New York-based Cuban bands. In 1939 Machito and Bauzá tried to start an orchestra, but it soon failed, so Machito worked for a time with Orquesta La Siboney, while Bauzá joined Cab Calloway. In 1940 Machito tried again, playing for a few months at the Club Cuba in Manhattan before, on December 3, 1940, Machito's Afro-Cubans had a very successful debut at the Park Palace Ballroom. Originally a vocal and ensemble-oriented unit, the band's music began to change when Bauzá joined in 1941 as trumpeter and its key arranger. Over time, Bauzá hired jazz-oriented soloists (including a 17-year-old drummer named Tito Puente) and constantly upgraded the band's musicianship. The band (which soon consisted of three saxophones, two trumpets, piano, bass, bongos, and timbales) was signed to Decca, and its records sold well, including an extensive series in 1942 in which it backed singer Miguelito Valdés. Although Machito was drafted in April 1943, it was decided to keep the increasingly popular orchestra together in the interim under Bauzá's temporary leadership.

A few changes were made by Bauzá, who added Carlos Vidal's conga to the instrumentation, sent to Cuba for Machito's sister Graciela to sing with the band, and that year wrote "Tanga," which is considered the first Afro-Cuban Jazz song. An accident at an army camp resulted in Machito's shattering his right knee; he was honorably discharged on October 27, 1943, and immediately went back to New York, where he resumed leading the band.

Machito's orchestra really caught on during the mid- to late 1940s, when it became Latin music's #1 band. Pianist René Hernández's arrangements were important to the group's sound, as was Bauzá's constant push to add more jazz to the band's music. Stan Kenton was very impressed, and on February 13, 1947, he recorded "Machito."

Dizzy Gillespie, Machito, and Louis Armstrong.

Kenton used Machito on maracas (along with Carlos Vidal on congas, José Mangual on timbales, and the bongos of Jack Costanzo) for his December 6, 1947, recording of "The Peanut Vendor." On January 24, 1948, the orchestras of Kenton and Machito shared the bill at a Town Hall concert in New York, and this resulted in Cubop's really catching on for a time. The term was adopted after a 1948 Machito recording of "Tanga" was made under the name of "Cubop City." That year Machito's orchestra often performed at the Royal Roost, using trumpeter Howard McGhee and tenor saxophonist Brew Moore as major soloists.

Producer Norman Granz became interested in recording Machito for his Clef label, and in December 1948 Charlie Parker and tenor saxophonist Flip Phillips recorded with Machito for the first time. So highly rated was Machito by this time as a symbol of Latin-oriented jazz that he appeared at a Jazz at the Philharmonic concert at Carnegie Hall on February 11, 1949, opposite Duke Ellington, Charlie Parker, Lester Young, Bud Powell, and Coleman Hawkins. During 1948-58 Machito recorded with such major guest soloists as Parker, Phillips, Buddy Rich, Dizzy Gillespie, trumpeter Harry "Sweets" Edison, altoist Cannonball

Adderley, Herbie Mann, trombonist Curtis Fuller, and tenor saxophonist Johnny Griffin.

Machito also recorded and performed frequently without any jazz guests, with a repertoire that ranged from traditional Cuban dance music and vocal pieces to bebop-oriented jazz, appearing regularly at the Palladium starting in 1954. In 1957 Machito and Bauzá were in Havana for the 50 Years of Cuban Music celebration and were treated as national heroes. With the change in popular tastes, Machito's orchestra had a lower profile as the 1960s progressed, but it remained a legendary name. The 1970s found the Afro-Cuban Jazz institution still quite busy, including a 1975 recording with Dizzy Gillespie. In 1976, after 35 years with the band, Mario Bauzá left Machito when he was angered that the bandleader had accepted an offer to take an octet to Europe. Bauzá felt that the Machito sound could not be duplicated with a smaller group, but in this case he was mistaken, for it was the start of Machito's nearly annual visits to Europe; years later Bauzá admitted that his departure was rash. Despite the loss of Bauzá, Machito's band worked regularly during its last years, with Machito hiring his son Mario as the group's musical director and his daughter Paula as the female vocalist. Machito was in London to play at Ronnie Scott's club in 1984 when he suffered a fatal stroke at the age of 72. A documentary film by Carlo Ortiz, *Machito: A Latin Jazz Legacy*, was released in 1987.

10 *Mucho Macho / 1948-1949 / Pablo 2625-712*

8 *Tremendo Cumban / 1949-1952 / Tumbao 004*

10 *Kenya / Dec. 17-24, 1957 / Roulette 22668*

8 *At the Crescendo / 1961 / GNP Crescendo 58*

8 *1983 Grammy Award Winner / Feb. 6-7, 1982 / MCA/Impulse 33106*

Machito's 1948-49 recordings with Charlie Parker have generally been reissued under Bird's name, while his 1950 recording of "Afro-Cuban Jazz Suite" (featuring Parker, Phillips, and Rich) has most recently been reissued under its composer's name on Chico O'Farrill's *Cuban Blues*. While many of Machito's most famous recordings have matched his orchestra with top guests from the jazz world, *Mucho Macho* is particularly significant because it shows how Machito's 1948-49 band sounded by itself, without any outsiders. At the time the orchestra consisted of three trumpeters (including Bauzá), two altoists, tenor saxophonist José Madera, baritone, pianist René Hernández, bass, bongos (José Mangual), conga (Luis Miranda), and timbales plus Graciela on occasional vocals. The 24 selections include both originals (including the popular "Asia Minor") and Latinized versions of such standards as "Jungle Drums," "At Sundown," "Tea for Two," and "St. Louis Blues." Classic music.

Tremendo Cumban has 20 additional titles from the era, with René Hernández's piano and arrangements, Mario Bauzá's direction, and the vocals of Machito, Graciela, and the Rugual Brothers all making an impact. Among the more memorable selections are Chico O'Farrill's "Holiday Mambo," "Bongo Fiesta," "Mambo Inn," "Carambola" (composed by Dizzy Gillespie), "Mambo à la Savoy," Chano Pozo's "Blen, Blen, Blen," and "Oboe Mambo," which features guest oboeist Mitch Miller!

Kenya is one of Machito's best recordings of the 1950s. The well-recorded performances consist of a dozen songs arranged by either A.K. Salim or the team of Bauzá and René Hernández, all originals written for the project except Chano Pozo's "Tin Tin Deo." Altoist Cannonball Adderley and trumpeter Joe Newman are the featured guests, and the orchestra also includes trumpeter Doc Cheatham, trombonist Eddie Bert, and a percussion section with up to seven players (including Candido, José Mangual, and Patato Valdés). The band sounds particularly inspired and powerful throughout this memorable effort.

It is a pity that the packaging of *At the Crescendo* is so abysmal (no personnel or date listing), for the music gives listeners a good idea what Machito's orchestra sounded like in the early 1960s. The selections alternate between jazz (including "Varsity Drag Mambo," "Cuban Fantasy," "Bernie and the Wolf," and "Pent-Up House"), superior dance music, and Salsa vocal features for Machito and Graciela. Aaron Sachs is the occasional cool-toned tenor soloist. Hopefully someday this highly enjoyable outing will be reissued properly!

Recorded in Holland two years before his death, Machito's Impulse CD finds his orchestra still in pretty strong form. Machito's vocals are joyful, his daughter Paula Grillo has a feature, and the 14-piece orchestra includes Chocolate Armenteros, who takes a few trumpet solos. Even this late, the infectious, open-minded spirit was still quite present in Machito's timeless music.

LPs to Search For:

Afro-Cubop (Spotlite 138) has seven selections that feature Machito's orchestra in 1949 broadcasting live from the Royal Roost club in NYC with guests Howard McGhee, Brew Moore, and (on the brief "Boppin' the Vibes") vibraphonist Milt Jackson, including "Cubop City," "How High the Moon," and "Tanga." In addition, an orchestra that is probably Machito's backs singer Harry Belafonte on "Lean on Me" and, most intriguingly, there are three live numbers by an unknown Afro-Cuban band (possibly Machito's or Tito Puente's) from 1950; two of the songs, "Mambo" and "Lament for the Conga," feature Charlie Parker!

JOSÉ MANGUAL

b. Mar. 18, 1924, Juana Diaz, Puerto Rico, d. Sept. 24, 1998, New York, NY

A versatile percussionist who often specialized on bongos, José Mangual is also the father of two notable percussionists: Luis Mangual and José Mangual Jr. The senior Mangual moved to New York in 1933 with his family and first discovered Cuban music on the radio, particularly enjoying *Casino de la Playa.* He gained experience playing locally, mostly on bongos but also occasionally bass. In 1942 Mangual replaced Tito Puente on timbales with Machito's orchestra. When Puente returned a month later, Mangual switched to bongos, becoming a fixture with Machito for the next 17 years. He can be seen performing with the Machito band in the 1946 movie *The Thrill of Music,* and he also participated in Chano Pozo's recordings of February 4, 1947. After leaving Machito in 1959, Mangual toured with Herbie Mann, and he later worked with Miles Davis (recording *Sketches of Spain*), Count Basie, Dizzy Gillespie, Stan Kenton, Chico O'Farrill, Erroll Garner, Tito Puente, Gato Barbieri, and Mario Bauzá's Big Band, among others. Later in life José Mangual mastered the tres guitar, but he will always be best known for his colorful bongo playing.

HERBIE MANN

b. Apr. 16, 1930, Brooklyn, NY

Throughout his long career, Herbie Mann, one of the most popular jazz flutists of all time, has been nothing if not musically curious, exploring cool-toned bebop, Afro-Cuban Jazz, Brazilian music, R&B, soul, reggae, fusion, and even disco. Mann's Afro-Cuban period lasted roughly from 1959 until fading out in 1967. He started off on clarinet when he was nine (after seeing a Benny Goodman performance in 1939), soon switching to flute (an instrument rarely used in jazz at that time) and tenor. After serving in the Army (1948-52), Mann debuted with accordionist Mat Mathews' Quintet (1953-54) and then led his own bands as one of jazz's first significant flutists. His work during 1954-58 was primarily bebop and included collaborations with guitarist Joe Puma, altoist Phil

Woods, tenor saxophonist Charlie Rouse, and fellow flutists Buddy Collette, Sam Most, and Bobby Jaspar. Mann also recorded on bass clarinet and tenor and in 1957 made a rare unaccompanied flute album for Savoy.

In 1959 Mann formed his Afro-Jazz Sextet, a group initially consisting of his flute, John Rae on vibes and timbales, bassist Knobby Totah, drummer Santo Miranda, and both Patato Valdés and José Mangual on percussion. Although there would be quite a bit of turnover during the next couple of years, the band caught on and made Mann famous. With Doc Cheatham added on trumpet, Mann toured Africa in 1960. During the first half of the 1960s such musicians as percussionists Ray Mantilla, Olantunji, Chief Bey and Ray Barretto, vibraphonists Hagood Hardy and Dave Pike, bassists Ahmed Abdul-Malik and Ben Tucker (who wrote the hit "Comin' Home Baby"), drummers Rudy Collins and Willie Bobo, and (in 1965) pianist Chick Corea spent time in Mann's band; Charlie Palmieri was on one recording date.

Quite typically, Mann eventually became bored with the music and started exploring Brazilian jazz instead, particularly after a trip to Brazil in 1961. However, his group (which included Patato Valdés for years) still had a strong Afro-Cuban flavor up until 1967, at which point he began spending more time exploring R&B and soul music. Herbie Mann, who had 25 albums reach the top 200 on the pop charts during 1962-79, has remained active to the present time and is still one of the world's most famous and influential flutists.

8 *Jazz Masters 56 / 1957-July 5, 1960 / Verve 314 529 901*

7 *Flautista / June 25, 1959 / Verve 314 557 448*

4 *The Herbie Mann Anthology / Aug. 3, 1960-Apr. 18, 1992 / Rhino 71634*

8 *65th Birthday Celebration / Apr. 25-30, 1995 / Lightyear 54185*

When one considers how popular Herbie Mann was, particularly during his Atlantic years, it is surprising how little of this material is currently available on CD. Many of his bebop dates from the 1950s are around, but few of his Afro-Cuban sessions (which were among his most important work) are currently in print. *Jazz Masters 56* draws its material from Mann's three Verve albums of 1957-60, one of which (*The Magic Flute of Herbie Mann*) actually predates his Afro-Cuban period, although one of the seven songs included from that album ("Evolution of Mann") has two percussionists added to the ensemble. There are also three selections from 1960's *Flute, Brass, Vibes and Percussion* (an underrated classic) and all five selections that originally comprised 1959's *Flautista*, one of Mann's strongest Afro-Cuban sessions. This date, which also includes Johnny Rae, Knobby Totah, Santo Miranda, José Mangual, and Patato Valdés, is also available separately with two previously unissued "bonus" tracks from the same session. The *Jazz Masters* set (which, in addition to "Cuban Patato Chip" and "Caravan," includes "The Peanut Vendor," "St. Louis Blues," and "Star Dust") is the better buy, but hopefully the *Flute, Brass, Vibes and Percussion* album will someday also become available on CD.

The two-CD *The Herbie Mann Anthology* looks attractive and seems like it should be definitive, but it falls far short. While the first disc has some gems from the 1960s (including "Comin' Home Baby," "Blues Walk," and "Memphis Underground"), the second CD is mostly stuck in the 1970s, and much of that material is quite dated and commercial. Considering Mann's intriguing and episodic career, this sampler should have been much stronger.

Herbie Mann's *65th Birthday Celebration,* recorded at New York's Blue Note, is a better summation of the flutist's musical interests. Over 50 top musicians join Mann for various selections, including trumpeters Randy Brecker and Claudio Roditi, Paquito D'Rivera, Dave Valentin, and percussionists Milton Cardono and Tito Puente, among many others. The music ranges from boppish and funky to Afro-Cuban and Brazilian, with the selections including workouts on "Jungle Fantasy," Charlie Parker's "Au Privave," and "Memphis Underground." Obviously a great time was had by all.

LPs to Search For:
Since Herbie Mann's Atlantic albums sold quite well during the 1960s and '70s, they turn up often in used record stores for inexpensive prices. Quite a few are well worth picking up, especially those from his Afro-Cuban era. Particularly recommended are *The Family of Mann* (Atlantic 1371), *Herbie Mann at the Village Gate* (Atlantic 1380), which includes his hit version of "Comin' Home Baby" and a nearly 20-minute rendition of "It Ain't Necessarily So," *Herbie Mann Returns to the Village Gate* (Atlantic 1407), *Standing Ovation at Newport* (Atlantic 1445) with Chick Corea on piano, *My Kinda Groove* (Atlantic 1433), and *New Mann at Newport* (Atlantic 1471).

RAY MANTILLA

b. June 22, 1934, New York, NY

A colorful percussionist who plays primarily conga and occasional timbales, Ray Mantilla has appeared in countless settings through the years. Mostly self-taught, Mantilla worked in many Latin bands in the 1950s, including with La Playa Sextet, Xavier Cugat, Lou Pérez, René Touzet, and Miguelito Valdés, in addition to accompanying singer Eartha Kitt. Mantilla was with Herbie Mann's Afro-Cuban group in 1960, played with drummer Max Roach a bit that year, and was with tenor saxophonist Al Cohn in 1961. After a period leading a Latin band in Puerto Rico (1963-69), Mantilla appeared with Max Roach's M'Boom in 1970 (and occasionally in later years) and spent two years as a member of Art Blakey's Jazz Messengers, the only conga player to be a regular part of that jazz institution.

Since the early 1970s, Mantilla has worked and/or recorded with Gato Barbieri, Ray Barretto, saxophonists Joe Farrell, Richie Cole, Bobby Watson, James Spaulding, Sonny Stitt, Stan Getz, and Lou Donaldson, pianists Don Pullen, Walter Bishop, Muhal Richard Abrams, Billy Taylor, Cedar Walton, and Mose Allison, bassist Charles Mingus (1977-78), singers Morganna King and Urszula Dudziak, trumpeter Freddie Hubbard, drummer Buddy Rich, guitarists Kenny Burrell and Joe Beck, organist Shirley Scott, arranger Bob Belden, and the Mingus Big Band, among others; quite a list! In addition, Ray Mantilla led his own group, Space Station, in the 1980s (recording as a leader for Inner City and Red) and has headed the Jazz Tribe since the mid-'90s.

8 *Hands of Fire / Jan. 9, 1984 / Red 123174*
9 *Synergy / Feb. 1986 / Red 123198*
7 *The Next Step / Feb. 2, 1999 / Red 123285*

Ray Mantilla's Space Station (consisting of the leader's percussion, Dick Oatts on saxophones and flute, the talented pianist Eddie Martinez, bassist Peter Barshay, Steve Berrios on drums and percussion, and drummer Joe Chambers doubling on vibes) debuted with 1984's *Hands of Fire*. The opening, "Ode to Vivian," starts out nearly free-form before settling into a Latin groove. Other pieces include numbers in which Chambers' vibes give the group a sound similar to Cal Tjader's, concise percussion displays, and some Latin-flavored bop. *Synergy* has Space Station (which by then was a quintet with Guillermo Edgehill on bass and Steve Berrios as the only drummer) joined on three of the seven selections by the fiery tenor of Steve Grossman (who blends quite well with Oatts) and on "Paisaje" by the haunting voice of Vivien Ara Martinez. Two standards ("Star Eyes" and

Thelonious Monk's "Eronel") are performed along with group originals (mostly by Mantilla and Eddie Martinez), and the music is consistently rewarding. This creative Afro-Cuban Jazz date is highly recommended.

Mantilla's Jazz Tribe is featured on *The Next Step*. This particular unit (a sextet with altoist Bobby Watson, trumpeter Jack Walrath, pianist Ronnie Mathews, bassist Curtis Lundy, and drummer Victor Lewis) is less Afro-Cuban oriented than Space Station, but Mantilla's percussion (which is well featured on a couple of the selections) infuses the largely straightahead music (all originals other than "Good Bait") with some Latin rhythms. A swinging set, with Watson in particular sounding in strong form.

LPs to Search For:

Ray Mantilla's debut as a leader, *Mantilla* (Inner City 1052), is a long out-of-print rarity that features him heading a quintet that also includes flutist Jeremy Steig, guitarist Carl Ratzer, bassist Eddie Gomez, and drummer Joe Chambers; Chambers and Ratzer wrote the five originals for this fine 1978 set.

SABU MARTINEZ

b. July 14, 1930, New York, NY, d. Jan. 13, 1979, Sweden

One of the more valuable conga and bongo players of the Cubop movement of the 1950s, Sabu Martinez appeared on many important record and club dates during that era. Sabu first played professionally in public in 1941, when he was just 11. In 1948 he was the late Chano Pozo's replacement with Dizzy Gillespie's orchestra, following it up by performing with Benny Goodman's Bebop Orchestra of 1949 (when BG was often playing Chico O'Farrill arrangements). During the next 15 years Sabu worked with Charlie Parker, Duke Ellington, Count Basie, trombonist J.J. Johnson (with whom he recorded *The Eminent J.J. Johnson*

Vol. 2), pianist Horace Silver (including a record in 1952), Thelonious Monk, Charles Mingus, Mary Lou Williams, Lionel Hampton, Noro Morales, Marcelino Guerra, Esy Morales, the Lecuona Cuban Boys, Miguelito Valdés, Xavier Cugat, Tito Rodriguez, and the Joe Loco Trio, as well as with Tony Bennett, Sammy Davis Jr., and Harry Belafonte. Sabu first recorded with Art Blakey in 1953 and was part of his special *Orgy in Rhythm* and *Holiday for Skins* projects of 1957-58.

Sabu put together his own quintet in 1957, the year that he led his first recording, a fascinating set for Blue Note called *Palo Congo*. He also led an album apiece for Vik (1957), Alegre (1960), Metronome (1968), and Graamfonverket (1973). The last two sets were recorded after Sabu Martinez in 1967 moved permanently to Sweden, where he recorded with the Francy Boland-Kenny Clarke big band and led a group called Burnt Sugar, staying active into the mid-1970s.

8 *Palo Congo / Apr. 28, 1957 / Blue Note 22665*

Most of the musicians on Sabu Martinez's debut as a leader (and his most widely available release) are either percussionists (Sabu, Caesar Travieso, Quique Travieso, and Ray Romero) and/or singers (Sabu, Caesar Travieso, Willie Capo, and Sarah Baro), so there is a lot of percussion and chanting/singing. Also heard from are Arsenio Rodriguez (on conga, vocals, and most importantly the tres) and bassist Evaristo Baro. Six of the eight songs are Martinez originals, although the most memorable cut is the opening, "El Cumbanchero," which has a memorable melody and a Sabu vocal that in tone sounds oddly like Cab Calloway in spots. Intriguing African-oriented music that grows in interest with each listen.

TONY MARTINEZ

b. Camaguey, Cuba

A talented altoist, tenor saxophonist, flutist, and pianist, Tony Martinez is one of the best reed players to emigrate from Cuba since Paquito D'Rivera. Martinez grew up in rural Cuba, beginning classical lessons at the age of nine, playing saxophone and piano in addition to studying voice. After receiving a teacher's diploma in 1987, he taught music and directed traditional Cuban dance and music ensembles for a few years. In 1990 he moved to Havana in order to study more modern styles. After working with the jazz-oriented group Mezcia and touring Europe three times, he settled in Switzerland in 1993. Tony Martinez, who has kept busy both as a sideman and as a bandleader, has thus far led two superior CDs and seems poised for greatness.

9 *La Habana Vive / 1998 / Blue Jackel 5026*
9 *Maferefun / 1999 / Blue Jackel 5033*

Tony Martinez, whose tone on the alto is sometimes a little reminiscent of Richie Cole's (with touches of David Sanborn) while his tenor looks more towards Michael Brecker, is a brilliant (if relatively little known) improviser whose solos fall between advanced hard bop and Afro-Cuban. For *La Habana Vive,* he wrote all nine pieces, including tributes to both Emiliano Salvador and John Coltrane ("Coltrane My Giant," which is a Latinized "Giant Steps"). The nucleus of Martinez's "Cuban Latin Jazz" is a septet with both Julio Padron and Mathieu Michel on trumpets. There are several guests on this CD (including five vocalists, who are mostly in the background, and several percussionists), most prominent of which is Gonzalo Rubalcaba, whom Martinez regards as a major inspiration. The leader's piano feature on "Tony's Cha Cha Chá" is just one of many highlights to this exciting CD.

Maferefun is at least on the same level. Martinez's band (called Cuban Power by this time) includes the remarkable Gonzalo Rubalcaba as a member, although it is a measure of Martinez's con-

fidence and talent that he plays piano himself (and quite effectively) on two of the eight numbers. Other soloists include trumpeter Padron (who is in top form), Leandro Saint-Hill on soprano (for "Latin Funk"), guitarist Dany Martinez, and the exciting percussion section. There are additional tributes to Salvador and Coltrane plus songs honoring Paquito D'Rivera (the overheated "Tumbao Pa' Mi Timbal") and Chucho Valdés. Tony Martinez is never afraid to let his sidemen take the spotlight, although his soloing ends up stealing the show anyway. The music on both of his CDs is of consistently high quality, quite danceable, and consistently exciting.

BOBBY MATOS
b. New York, NY

A top-notch timbale player who also plays congas and other percussion instruments, Bobby Matos grew up in Harlem. Since moving to the Los Angeles area in the late 1970s, he has been an important fixture in local clubs. Matos has recorded as a leader for Night Life and Cubop, leading his Afro-Cuban Jazz Ensemble and keeping the legacy of Mario Bauzá, Dizzy Gillespie, and Machito very much alive. Bobby Matos has also recorded with vibraphonist Bobby Hutcherson (1975) and Pucho & His Latin Soul Brothers (1999).

8 *Collage—Afro Cuban Jazz / 1993 / Night Life 3011*

Although the vibes of Darrell Harris and (in one case) Angel Pagan are only a small part of the music, the playing of Bobby Matos' Heritage Ensemble on this rewarding CD is often very much in the style of Cal Tjader. Many musicians make appearances on the ten numbers, including flutists Art Webb and Danilo Lozano and several rhythm sections, but there are no real slow moments. Both Bobby Matos and Darrell Harris take some vocals (including on a Latinized version of the Pharoah Sanders/Leon

Thomas song "The Creator Has a Master Plan"); however, the emphasis is mostly on melodic instrumentals and infectious (if often laid-back) Afro-Cuban rhythms. Bobby Matos should record as a leader much more often.

REBECA MAULEÓN

b. San Francisco, CA

An important force in the Afro-Cuban scene of the San Francisco Bay Area, Rebeca Mauleón is a talented pianist in addition to being an enthusiastic and knowledgeable percussionist, author, lecturer, and clinician. As a teenager in the late 1970s, she debuted with Charanga René del Mar. She worked for eight years as a flamenco dancer and was the cofounder and musical director of Orquesta Batachanga (1980-85); the band recorded for Sugarloaf and Earthbeat. Mauleón has worked with Pete Escovedo, Tito Puente (with whom she recorded several albums), Cachao, Santana, Ray Obiedo, and Joe Henderson. She studied dance, percussion, and piano in Cuba starting in 1990. Since the mid-1990s, Rebeca Mauleón has frequently worked with John Santos' Machete Ensemble.

8 *Round Trip / 1998 / Bembe 2023*

It is obvious that the musicians were having fun on Rebeca Mauleón's debut recording as a leader; just listen to how they rip into "Gitana," one of the leader's eight originals on the project (originally released by her Rumbeca Music label). There is impressive variety to be heard, including the R&B tune "I'll Take You There," Thelonious Monk's "'Round Midnight," introspective ballads, and heated jams. Mauleón's playing is impressive throughout without being dominant, the ensembles are clean and spirited, and the pianist is assisted by some strong soloing from trombonist Jeff Cressman and flutist John Calloway. Mauleón's love, respect, knowledge , and joy towards this music are obvious.

AL McKIBBON

b. Jan. 1, 1919, Chicago, IL

Long considered a reliable sidemen in both bebop and Afro-Cuban Jazz settings, Al McKibbon finally had his first opportunity to lead his own record date when he was 80! McKibbon studied bass and piano at Cass Tech High School in Detroit and began playing locally in the late 1930s. After moving to New York, he gained important experience playing with Lucky Millinder's Big Band (1943), altoist Tab Smith (1944-45), drummer J.C. Heard, and tenor great Coleman Hawkins (1946-47). McKibbon became part of jazz history when he replaced Ray Brown in Dizzy Gillespie's orchestra in 1947, just in time to record "Manteca" next to Chano Pozo, remaining with Dizzy until the big band broke up late in 1949. He recorded with Miles Davis' Birth of the Cool Nonet, and worked with Count Basie (1950), Thelonious Monk, pianist Earl Hines, and altoist Johnny Hodges; he also recorded with pianist-composer Herbie Nichols (1955) and at the 1957 Newport Jazz Festival with Coleman Hawkins and Roy Eldridge.

While a longtime member of the George Shearing Quintet (1951-58), McKibbon became particularly adept at Latin rhythms and helped get Cal Tjader (who was with Shearing during 1953-54) initially interested in Afro-Cuban music. After leaving Shearing, McKibbon was a member of one of Tjader's strongest bands during 1958-59. The bassist spent the 1960s mostly on the West Coast, freelancing and working in the studios. He toured with the Giants of Jazz (a group also including Dizzy Gillespie, altoist Sonny Stitt, trombonist Kai Winding, Thelonious Monk, and drummer Art Blakey) during 1971-72, recording with Monk during the pianist-composer's last trio sessions.

McKibbon, who through the years has appeared at countless recording sessions (including with Mongo Santamaria, altoists Cannonball Adderley, Sonny Criss and Benny Carter, singers

Lorez Alexandria, Ruth Brown, Billy Eckstine, Billie Holiday, Anita O'Day, and Sarah Vaughan, drummer Kenny Clarke, trumpeter Buck Clayton, pianists Pete Johnson, Phineas Newborn Jr., and Teddy Wilson, and the Jazz Crusaders), has remained active on the West Coast up to the present time in both Afro-Cuban and straightahead jazz settings.

9 *Tumbao Para Los Congueros di Mi Vida /*
1999 / Blue Lady/Chartmaker 1080

Al McKibbon took this very rare opportunity to lead his own record date and came out with a near-classic. Sticking to Afro-Cuban Jazz (which he helped pioneer), McKibbon is heard in a sextet with Charles Owens (who is mostly on flute), saxophonist Justo Almario, pianist Phil Wright, and two percussionists from Poncho Sanchez's band (Papo Rodriquez and Ramon Banda on congas and timbales). Other than McKibbon's title cut (which in English means "Tumbao for the Drummers of My Life"), the set is comprised of famous standards, including such highlights as Thelonious Monk's "Off Minor," "Tin Tin Deo," "Cubano Chant," and "Seven Steps to Heaven." Owens and Almario blend quite well, and there are some blazing ensembles along with more relaxed moments. A very enjoyable effort.

NORO MORALES
b. Jan. 4, 1911, Puerto de Tierra, Puerto Rico,
d. Jan. 14, 1964, San Juan, Puerto Rico
Leader of one of the most popular Afro-Cuban orchestras of the 1940s (competing for a time with Machito), Noro Morales was an influential force during his prime. The son of a violinist, Morales began playing piano at an early age. In 1924 he moved with his family (which included nine children) to Caracas, Venezuela, where his father was

hired as musical director for the Official Court Orchestra. A few months later, when the older Morales suddenly died, Noro (who was just 13) became his replacement. In 1930 his family decided to return to Puerto Rico, where for the next five years Morales worked as a freelance pianist, including with Rafael Sanchez y Su Sinfonica, the Midnight Serenaders, Carmelo Diaz, and Rafael Munoz. In 1935 he moved to New York, playing with the Alberto Socarrás Orchestra, Augusto Coen, Leo Marini, and Johnny Rodriguez (Tito's brother), making his first recordings with the last in January 1936.

In May 1938 he helped form the Morales Brothers Orchestra, which included his siblings, Humberto and Esy, on drums and flute, respectively. However, within three months the band was renamed the Nino Morales Orchestra. A five-year residency at El Morocco established the ensemble as one of New York's top Latin groups, as did their 1942 hit recording of "Serenata Ritmica" which became their theme song. The orchestra recorded regularly through the years for Columbia, Decca, Seeco, Majestic, MGM, RCA, and Tico, appeared in several movie shorts (including *The Gay Ranchero, Ella,* and *Mexican Jumping Bean*), and its sidemen included Machito (who sang with Morales in 1939), Tito Puente, and Tito Rodriguez (1945). Morales (who wrote most of his band's arrangements and composed "Oye Negra") had other hits in "Tea for Two" and "Bim Bam Bum." In the late 1940s he led a piano-and-percussion quintet in addition to the big band. But as the 1950s progressed and the mambo craze catapulted other Latin bands into fame, Nino Morales faded into obscurity. A greatly overweight diabetic who was rumored to have drunk a bottle of rum a day, Nino Morales in 1960 moved back to Puerto Rico, where he was active (while maintaining a low profile) until his death in 1964 at age 53 from diabetes.

BENY MORÉ

*b. Aug. 24, 1919, Santa Isabel de las Lajas,
Cuba, d. Feb. 19, 1963, Havana, Cuba*

One of the most popular Cuban singers of the 1950s, Beny Moré was especially powerful on slow boleros. He grew up in poverty and learned to play guitar as a child, singing to his own accompaniment. Moré left school when he was 12 to work in sugarcane fields. His singing developed over time (he was completely self-taught), and in 1935 he organized his first band. He sang on a part-time basis for the next five years, struggling a bit. But after he moved to Havana in 1940, Moré was a full-time singer, working with Lazaro Cordero's Sexteto Figaro, Septeto Cauto, and Miguel Matamoros. In 1945 Moré moved with Matamoros' band to Mexico, where he stayed for the next six years and made a strong reputation. Moré recorded with Arturo Nunez (having his first big hit, "Mucho Corazon"), Mariano Merceron (1948), Rafael de Paz (scoring with "Yiri Yiri Bon"), and Chucho Rodriguez. He became quite well known during his period with Pérez Prado (1948-51), and while in Mexico he appeared in several films.

By 1951, when he returned to Cuba, Moré was on the brink of being a national celebrity, and his fame grew during the decade. He worked with the Bebo Valdés Orchestra for a time, formed his own popular orchestra (Banda Gigante) in 1953, and for a time hosted a television series. Nicknamed "El Barbaro del Ritmo" ("The Barbarian of Rhythm"), Moré (who often danced while he sang) was a powerful and exciting singer, with a wide range whose upper-register shouting almost recalled Cab Calloway in spots, but without any "Hi-De-Ho's!" His lack of formal musical training did not seem to matter, and he developed into a talented composer.

One of the few major Cuban performers who chose to stay in Cuba after the Castro revolution, Benny Moré often drank too much, and it eventually caught up to him. After his death from cirrhosis of the liver at age 44, his funeral attracted 100,000 fans.

8 *The Voice and Work of Benny Moré / Milan 35777*

7 *Benny Moré / Javelin 1004*

These two CDs contain music recorded mostly in the 1950s, although the recording dates (and even the personnel) are, inexcusably, not included. While the Javelin disc has a dozen selections, including several in which Moré is joined by a group of singers, the Milan CD (which consists of 19 numbers) is more definitive. Moré is heard on several memorable ballads on the latter set, cooks on the hotter pieces, and is quite passionate throughout, showing why he was considered one of the finest Cuban singers of the '50s. The big band acts as a perfect foil behind him, playing heated riffs and clearly inspiring him. Highlights include "Perdi La Fe," "Mi Amor Fugaz," and "Todo Lo Perdi," with Benny Moré in consistently expressive form throughout.

NETTAI TROPICAL JAZZ BAND

Afro-Cuban Jazz has been popular in Japan since the 1950s, when the Tokyo Cuban Boys were active. Percussionist Carlos Kanno led the Orquesta de la Luz in the 1990s. A few months after leaving the group in December 1994, he formed the Nettai Tropical Jazz Band, an 18-piece Afro-Cuban Jazz big band that has since recorded several albums that have been made available domestically on the RMM label. Listening to the music, listeners would never guess that the musicians were not born in Cuba!

5 *Nettai Tropical Jazz Big Band / Mar. 18-19, 1998 / RMM 84037*

7 *My Favorite / Apr. 4-5, 1999 / RMM 84086*

On *Nettai Tropical Jazz Big Band*, their self-titled RMM release (which was actually their second recording), Nettai comes across as a high-quality stage band, one unusual only in that it includes four percussionists. The musicianship is quite high, but the arrangements sometimes seem a touch corny. The tunes are originals, other than Lalo Schifrin's "Mission Impossible," "Caravan," and "Flamingo," but nothing all that memorable occurs. *My Favorite* is a big improvement, for the arrangements are hipper and the material is fresher. The standards this time include "I Can't Stop Loving You," the Pérez Prado hit "Cherry Pink and Apple Blossom White," "My Favorite Things," and one of the most bizarre versions of "Sing, Sing, Sing" ever recorded. None of the soloists (who are all at least decent) stand out, but the often-jubilant ensembles make *My Favorite* worth picking up.

ARTURO O'FARRILL

b. June 22, 1960, Mexico City, Mexico
Arturo O'Farrill's first solo release (*Blood Lines*) shows that he can have a significant career in Afro-Cuban Jazz separate from his famous father, Chico O'Farrill. Unlike the older O'Farrill, who has been primarily an arranger and composer, Arturo O'Farrill is a strong soloist rather than a writer. He was classically trained as a pianist and grew up in New York City, where he played locally as a teenager and attended the High School of Music and Art, the Manhattan School of Music, and the Brooklyn Conservatory of Music. Although O'Farrill always played jazz, he was one of the founders of a rap group that in 1981 had a release that was number one in England (*Shoot the Pump*).

But more important in the long run was his stint with Carla Bley's big band (1979-83). In the 1980s, O'Farrill freelanced and performed with such notables as Wynton Marsalis, Dizzy Gillespie, Steve Turre, and Jerry González's Fort Apache Band. In 1987 he became Harry Belafonte's musical director, and in 1995 he joined his father, becoming the pianist and musical director for the Chico O'Farrill Afro-Cuban Jazz Big Band. In 1999, at age 39, Arturo O'Farrill finally had a chance to come into his own as he led his first solo recordings.

8 *Blood Lines / Jan. 1999-Feb. 1999 / Milestone 9294*
7 *A Night In Tunisia / Nov. 4, 1999 / 32 Jazz 32202*

Arturo O'Farrill's debut as a leader (*Blood Lines*) puts the emphasis on his fluent and creative piano playing. The music is often not overtly Latin, although Afro-Cuban rhythms are usually felt at least below the surface. The music alternates between straightahead trio numbers and Latin romps, with the pianist joined by drummer Horacio "El Negro" Hernández and either George Mraz or Andy González on bass. Three songs also have Jerry González on conga, two others add trombonist Papo Vazquez, while "Darn That Dream" is taken as an unaccompanied piano solo. Whether cooking on John Coltrane's "Moment's Notice," reviving "Siboney," or performing "Arturo's Closet" (the only song on the date that he wrote, in conjunction with Vazquez), Arturo O'Farrill proves to be an impressive player.

A Night In Tunisia is a mostly straightahead set. Teamed up with bassist George Mraz and drummer Steve Berrios, O'Farrill shows how strong a bop player he is on such numbers as "A Night In Tunisia," "Wave," "On Green Dolphin Street," and "I'll Remember April." Although the liner note writer states that the music succeeds in "proving O'Farrill the equal of almost any of the more widely known Latin jazz keyboard stars," that is an obvious overstatement and there is actually not much Afro-Cuban Jazz on this date. However, the music does not need to be overpraised since it is excellent.

CHICO O'FARRILL

b. Oct. 28, 1921, Havana, Cuba
One of the most important arrangers and com-

posers of Cubop, Chico O'Farrill was a pioneer of the idiom in the late 1940s and is still a significant contributor a half-century later. Born Arturo O'Farrill, he attended a military academy in Georgia during 1936-40. It was during this period that O'Farrill both discovered jazz and began playing the trumpet. After graduating in 1940, he returned to Cuba, where he studied composition, played with René Touzet and Armando Romeu, and led his own band. In 1946 O'Farrill gave up the trumpet altogether to concentrate on arranging, and during 1947-48 he co-led, wrote, and arranged for the Isidro Pérez Orchestra.

In 1948 O'Farrill moved to New York City, where he started off ghost writing some charts for Gil Fuller. He soon met clarinetist Stan Hasselgard, who recommended O'Farrill to Benny Goodman, (at the time the clarinetist was organizing his short-lived bebop orchestra). Goodman, giving O'Farrill his lifelong nickname of Chico, recorded his "Undercurrent Blues," and other bandleaders were soon using O'Farrill's talents, including Stan Kenton ("Cuban Episode"), Dizzy Gillespie, Miguelito Valdés, and Machito (the highly acclaimed "Afro-Cuban Jazz Suite," which featured Charlie Parker, tenor saxophonist Flip Phillips, and drummer Buddy Rich). During 1951-54, O'Farrill made six fiery ten-inch albums of Latin big band jazz for Norman Granz's Clef and Norgran labels, all of which have been reissued on an essential Verve two-CD set, *Cuban Blues*. O'Farrill, who led his own orchestra for a few years and appeared often at Birdland, topped off this fertile period by writing the four-part "Manteca Suite" for Dizzy Gillespie (who recorded it in 1954).

After spending part of 1955-57 back in Cuba, O'Farrill moved to Mexico City, where he worked for eight years in the studios and on television; his son, Arturo O'Farrill Jr., was born during this time. Returning to New York in 1965, O'Farrill worked as arranger and music director for the television

series *Festival of the Lively Arts*. During the next 30 years he freelanced, writing arrangements for many bands, including Count Basie, Buddy DeFranco's Glenn Miller Orchestra, Cal Tjader, Clark Terry, Tito Puente, Candido, Willie Bobo, Stan Kenton, Machito, Dizzy Gillespie, Gato Barbieri (*Chapter Three: Viva Emiliano Zapata*), Paquito D'Rivera, the Mingus Big Band, and Mario Bauzá's orchestra (1989-92). Strangely enough he did not lead any sessions of his own during 1967-94; however, 1995's *Pure Emotion* CD found his writing talents in peak form. Chico O'Farrill has since led a big band (with his son as the pianist and musical director) on a part-time basis.

10 *Cuban Blues / Dec. 21, 1950-Apr. 16, 1954 / Verve 314 533 256*

All six of Chico O'Farrill's early Norgran and Clef dates as a leader are on this unbeatable two-CD set plus a set led by Machito featuring O'Farrill's arrangements. Both of his Afro-Cuban Jazz Suites are here, including the one featuring Charlie Parker, Flip Phillips, and Buddy Rich. Also included in the personnel along the way are such notables as trumpeters Mario Bauzá, Doug Mettome, Roy Eldridge, and Harry "Sweets" Edison, trombonists Eddie Bert and Bill Harris, altoist Herb Geller, pianist René Hernández, bassist Ray Brown, drummers Don Lamond and Jo Jones, and percussionists Candido, José Mangual, Luis Marinda, Carlos Vidal, Chino Pozo, and Machito. Whether it be the suites or the classic miniatures (which include "JATP Mambo," "Cuban Blues," "Flamingo," "The Peanut Vendor," "Malagueña," "Havana Special," and "Siboney"), the music stays consistently at the classic level due to the colorful O'Farrill arrangements.

9 *Pure Emotion / Feb. 1995 / Milestone 9239*
9 *Heart of a Legend / Dec. 1998-July 1999 / Milestone 9299*

The highly influential arranger Chico O'Farrill is one of the unsung heroes of Afro-Cuban Jazz.

After far too long between recordings as a leader, Chico O'Farrill launched his Afro-Cuban Jazz Big Band with the 1995 recording *Pure Emotion.* The very well-respected veteran arranger has his orchestra (which includes such major players as saxophonist Mario Rivera, trombonists Papo Vásquez and Robin Eubanks, trumpeters Victor Paz and Michael Mossman, Andy González, Jerry González, Steve Berrios, and his son, Arturo O'Farrill) interpreting "Perdido," "Get Me to the Church on Time," an obscurity, six originals, plus his witty "Variations on a Well-Known Theme" ("La Cucaracha"). This is a swinging and joyous set. *Heart of a Legend,* comprised of 14 O'Farrill originals, finds his big band (which had experienced a lot of turnover but still included Vásquez, both of the González brothers, and Arturo) joined on various selections by a variety of guests, including Gato

Barbieri, Cachao, Chocolate Armenteros, Freddy Cole (who vocalizes on "Sing Your Blues Away"), Paquito D'Rivera, Arturo Sandoval, Mario Rivera, Candido, and Patato Valdés. Chico O'Farrill's arrangements give the set (which celebrates his productive life) unity and a purpose, resulting in highly enjoyable and memorable music.

LPs to Search For:

Nine Flags (Impulse 9135), from 1966, is a lesser-known release and a bit of an oddity in Chico O'Farrill's career. For this tribute to Nine Flags perfumes, O'Farrill wrote originals inspired, a selection apiece, by the music of Brazil, England, France, Germany, Hong Kong, Ireland, Italy, Spain, and Sweden (but not Cuba) plus "The Lady from Nine Flags." The originals are performed by three different groups, ranging from seven to 15 pieces, with short solos from trombonist J.J. Johnson, Art Farmer and Clark Terry on flügelhorns, and guitarist Larry Coryell, a rare venture for Chico O'Farrill outside of the world of Afro-Cuban music.

MANNY OQUENDO

b. Jan. 1, 1931, New York, NY

Manny Oquendo is best known as a veteran percussionist who has led Libre since the mid-1970s. Born José Manuel Oquendo, at one point the youth lived upstairs from a record store where he was exposed to Cuban music and jazz. He began studying percussion when he was 14, in 1945, and the following year became a professional drummer, working with the Sexteto Sanabria, the Carlos Medina Orchestra, Charlie Valero, singer Luis del Campo, the Marcelino Guerra Orchestra, José Curbelo, and Pupi Campo. Oquendo played bongos with Tito Puente during 1950-54, had short stints with Tito Rodriguez and Vicentico Valdés, and then became a very busy freelance percussionist. In 1962 he started a longtime association with Eddie Palmieri.

In 1974, when Oquendo and Andy González broke away from Palmieri, they started Libre, a band soon led solely by the percussionist. *Libre* means "free" in Spanish, symbolizing that Oquendo and González wanted to play with a rhythm section that was more flexible than Palmieri's had become. In the years since, Libre's alumni have included Steve Turre, Dave Valentin, Néstor Torres, Jerry González, and Papo Vásquez although the group's music is often closer to Salsa than to Afro-Cuban Jazz. Manny Oquendo (who also recorded with Machito, Noro Morales, Billy Taylor, Charlie Palmieri, Mongo Santamaria, the Salsoul Orchestra, Cachao, Chico O'Farrill, and Steve Turre, among others) has led Libre on four albums for Salsoul, two for Montuno, and two thus far for Milestone.

5 *Ritmo, Sonido y Estilo / 1991 / Montuno 522*
6 *Mejor Que Nunca / June 1994-July 1994 / Milestone 9226*
6 *On the Move / May 24, 1996 / Milestone 9263*

Although it has always included some top Afro-Cuban Jazz players, Manny Oquendo's Libre tends to emphasize the Salsa (Spanish-language singing) side of its music, which can be a bit disappointing to those listeners who want to hear the individual musicians stretch out. On the somewhat obscure *Ritmo, Sonido y Estilo,* Libre performs mostly vocal-oriented music (although Freddie Hubbard's "Little Sunflower" is taken as an instrumental), with Tony Torres and Herman Olivera as lead vocalists. The 14-piece group is potentially quite strong from the jazz standpoint, with the musicians including leader Oquendo on timbales and bongo, Andy González, Jerry González on conga and trumpet, Dave Valentin, and four trombonists: Steve Turre, Jimmy Bosch, Dan Reagan, and Reynaldo Jorge. But the band has relatively little to do.

On *Mejor Que Nunca* ("Better Than Ever") the group is also mostly subservient to the vocalists on the majority of the selections. The "Libre Trombone Choir" (Papo Vásquez, Jimmy Bosch, Leonard Pollara, Dan Reagan, William Cepeda, Orlando Pena, Reynaldo Jorge, and José Vidal) get in a few good licks (most notably during "Speak Low") that uplift the music and give this set a stronger jazz content than the Montuno release. *On the Move* sometimes sounds as if it is being played by three groups at once: the rhythm section (pianist Willie Rodriguez, Andy González, Roberto Carrero on congas, and Oquendo), two dominating vocalists (Herman Olivera and Frankie Vazquez), and four trombonists (Dan Regan, Papo Vazquez, Leonard Pollara, and Wayne Wallace). Although there are instrumental stretches and the group's spirit is often quite infectious, one wishes that there was more of a balance between the three parts!

Manny Oquendo's Libre, a Latin music fixture since 1974

JOHNNY PACHECO

b. Mar. 25, 1935, Santiago de los Caballeros, Dominican Republic

Johnny Pacheco's main importance to Latin music has been in two areas: as flutist with Charlie Palmieri's Orchestra and his own early '60s group, and as a founder of the influential Fania label. Pacheco's father was the prominent Dominican Republic clarinetist Rafael Azarias Pacheco who directed Orquesta Santa Cecilia. The family moved to New York City when Johnny was 11, and he quickly became involved in the local music scene, taking saxophone and clarinet lessons in school and playing percussion in groups on weekends. At Bronx Vocational High School, Pacheco learned flute (his most significant instrument in later years)

and organized the Chuchulecos Boys, a mambo band that included trombonist Barry Rogers and pianist Eddie Palmieri. Although he was trained as an engineer, Pacheco soon found out that he could make much more money as a musician. He worked as a percussionist with the Paul Whiteman Orchestra and freelanced, including with Tito Puente, Pérez Prado, and Xavier Cugat (with whom he played flute and sang), and led a quintet with Eddie Palmieri.

Pacheco played conga and bongo with the Charlie Palmieri Quartet in the late '50s. However, he made much more of an impact on flute when Palmieri formed his Charanga Duboney, an influential group consisting of two flutes, two violins, piano, bass, timbales, guiro, and conga that helped lead to the comeback of the charanga (flute-and-strings orchestras). In September 1959, Pacheco went out on his own. His first recording, *Pacheco y su Charanga Vol. 1* (Alegre), sold over 100,000 copies and included a hit in "El Guiro De Macorina." The style of music that he featured was soon nicknamed *pachanga* (a variation of the charanga). The flutist recorded for the Alegre label (including with the Alegre All-Stars) for a few years, switching to a Conjunto band in 1963 that included vocals, trumpets, and a rhythm section.

In 1964 he cofounded the Fania label with attorney Gerald Masucci, and this would be his musical home for the next couple of decades. Recording often for the label, producing dates by other musicians, and forming the Fania All-Stars in 1968 (a full-time band under his leadership during 1971-88), Pacheco was a major force in the rise of Salsa during the 1970s. He also made guest appearances in jazz settings as a percussionist, including with the Erroll Garner Trio, Les McCann, Herbie Mann, McCoy Tyner, and Tito Puente and on Verve dates led by George Benson and Kenny Burrell. Since the late 1980s, Johnny Pacheco has worked for labels other than Fania and become semiretired, having made his impact on Latin music.

CHARLIE PALMIERI

b. Nov. 21, 1927, New York, NY, d. Sept. 12, 1988, New York, NY

Now overshadowed by his brother Eddie Palmieri (who was nine years younger) and in danger of being forgotten, Charlie Palmieri was a top Afro-Cuban Jazz pianist for 40 years.

He began classical piano studies when he was seven, and attended the Juilliard School of Music. As a teenager, Charlie and his brother (who sang) often entered and won amateur contests. Palmieri began playing dances with professional orchestras when he was 14, in 1948 he formed El Conjunto

Pin Pin, and he worked as a sideman with quite a few top bands, including those of Machito, Tito Puente, Tito Rodriguez, Pupi Campo, Vicentico Valdés, Pete Terrace, Rafael Munoz, Xavier Cugat, and Johnny Segui, in addition to recording with Herbie Mann in the late '50s. In 1958 he had a Conjunto band, with trumpets in the lead and Johnny Pacheco on percussion. But later in the year, with Pacheco switching to flute, Palmieri was leading Charanga Duboney, an influential group that helped lead to the comeback (if temporary) of charanga flute and violin bands. That group (which included four violins) recorded *Let's Dance the Charanga* for United Artists. Pacheco left the band after a year, but Palmieri's ensemble continued to grow in popularity for a period. He switched to the Alegre label and became the musical director for the Alegre All-Stars, a jam session band that later inspired similar groups put together by the Tico and Fania labels. An underrated arranger, Palmieri's main influence was considered Noro Morales, although he said that he was also inspired by Art Tatum, Glenn Miller's orchestra, and traditional folkloric music.

By the mid-1960s, Palmieri's charanga had passed its peak in popularity, and he changed his group to the Duboney Orchestra, featuring three trumpets and two trombones. Palmieri recorded a few dates in the boogaloo style (including *Latin Bugalú* for Atlantic in 1968), began a second career in 1969 as a historian and teacher of Latin music history, and started doubling on organ, including playing on some of his brother's records in the early '70s. He also worked as musical director for Tito Puente on his *El Mambo de Tito Puente* television program. Palmieri lived in Puerto Rico for three years (1980-83) but suffered a heart attack shortly after returning to New York. After he recovered, he led various groups, played with Joe Cuba, Ralph Marin, and Joe Quijano, and co-led Combo Gigante with Jimmy Sebater. In 1987 Palmieri recorded with Mongo Santamaria, and the following year he visited England for the first time. But soon after arriving back in New York, Charlie Palmieri died from a second heart attack, at the age of 60.

EDDIE PALMIERI

b. Dec. 15, 1936, East Harlem, NY

A major pianist and bandleader since the early 1960s, Eddie Palmieri has long brought the sound and style of modern jazz pianists (particularly McCoy Tyner and to a lesser extent Bill Evans and Herbie Hancock) into the world of Afro-Cuban Jazz through his playing. His experimenting with instrumentation (starting in the '60s) helped make Cuban bands (such as charangas and conjuntos) more flexible than they had been previously. He started on piano when he was eight and often sang to his older brother Charlie's piano accompaniment at amateur contests. He was also interested in percussion (idolizing Tito Puente) and played timbales with his uncle's orchestra, Chino y Sus Almas Tropicales, during 1949-51; however, Palmieri eventually switched back permanently to piano. Early in his career, Eddie (who became a professional pianist when he was 17) was often recommended for jobs by Charlie when the older Palmieri could not make it, resulting in stints with trumpeter Robertito Santiago, Raul Almo, Bobby Santiago, Eddie Forestier, the Johnny Segui Orchestra, Vicentico Valdés (1956-58), and Tito Rodriguez (1958-61).

In 1961 Palmieri formed an octet called Conjunto la Perfecta that featured an unusual flute-and-two-trombone frontline that brother Charlie dubbed a "trombanga." The popular band (which recorded for Alegre and Tico) played each Sunday at New York's Palladium and lasted until 1968. Palmieri made two notable albums with Cal Tjader during 1966-67: *El Sonido Nuevo* (Verve) and *Bamboleate* (Tico). After La Perfecta broke up in 1968, Palmieri played experimental Salsa that utilized adventurous (sometimes nearly free-form) solos and a wide variety of instrumentation. His 1970s music often mixed Salsa with R&B, rock, pop, Spanish vocals, and jazz solos as he constantly sought to stretch himself. Palmieri, who recorded with both the Tico and Fania All-Stars, Chocolate Armenteros, Cachao, the Tropijazz All-Stars, Dave Samuels, and Conrad Herwig, cut sets as a leader for a variety of labels, including Mango, Coco, Epic, Fania, Elektra, and, more recently, Tropijazz and RMM. He featured Salsa singer India in his group of the early 1990s.

Since then Eddie Palmieri has led a series of impressive Afro-Cuban Jazz groups that at various times have also included David Sanchez, Charlie Sepúlveda, baritonist Ronnie Cuber, trumpeter Brian Lynch, Conrad Herwig, and altoist Donald Harrison.

9 *Arete / 1995 / RMM 81657*
8 *Live! / Oct. 17, 1996 / RMM 82252*

Eddie Palmieri had one of his strongest jazz-oriented groups in 1995, an octet/nonet that included Brian Lynch, Conrad Herwig, Donald Harrison, bassist John Benitez, three percussionists, his piano, and occasionally drummer Adam Cruz. Performing eight of his originals on *Arete,* Palmieri handles lyrical ballads and heated Afro-Cuban romps with equal ease, pushing both himself and his talented sidemen throughout his eight originals and keeping the results from ever getting too predictable while remaining rhythmically accessible. This CD gives listeners an excellent example of Palmieri's talents.

Live! features Palmieri on four of his more extensive works (three of which are over ten minutes) and one other piece, heading a top-notch medium-size group that includes singer Herman Oliveros on two cuts. Among the key soloists are trumpeter Juancito Torres Velez, trombonist J.P.

Torres, Hector Veneros on reeds, and a powerful percussion section. The pianist, who introduces most of the pieces with an out-of-tempo section, uses a lot of variety in his episodic arrangements, and the results are consistently intriguing, unpredictable, and exciting, extending but not breaking the boundaries of Afro-Cuban Jazz.

BOBBY PAUNETTO
b. June 22, 1944, New York, NY

A potentially significant vibraphonist and composer, Bobby Paunetto has had his career mostly stopped by a serious illness. Although he enjoyed music from an early age, Paunetto did not start playing vibes until 1961, when he was already 17. After he befriended Cal Tjader that year, he loved his music so much that he threw himself into the vibes, practicing seven hours a day. Tjader was so impressed that he wrote and recorded "Paunetto's Point" in tribute to his friend in 1962. By then Paunetto was a strong-enough player to form a quintet, and he played regularly in New York, recording for Seeco. After serving in the Army (1965-67), he recorded *The Modern Sound of Bobby Paunetto* for Roulette. He studied at Berklee (1969-73), including with Gary Burton and Dave Samuels, and during the next few years had the opportunity to sit in with Tjader, Clare Fischer, Tito Puente, Buddy Rich, Mongo Santamaria, Armando Peraza, Charlie Palmieri, Eddie Palmieri, and others. He founded the Pathfinder Recording Company and recorded *Paunetto's Point* in 1974 and *Commit to Memory* in 1976, both advanced Afro-Cuban sessions.

But in August 1979 Paunetto was diagnosed as being in the early stages of multiple sclerosis. Other than a brief comeback in 1981, he was forced to give up vibes and a promising career. However, he has continued to compose up to the present time, writing over 200 songs. In 1997 Bobby Paunetto recorded a set of his compositions with his Commit to Memory group (resulting in *Composer in Private*), managing to play vibes and synthesizers on some tracks.

9 *Commit to Memory/Paunetto's Point / Oct. 28, 1974-Aug. 27, 1976 / Tonga 8305*
7 *Composer in Public / 1997 / RSVP 1777*

The history of Latin music might have been a bit different had Bobby Paunetto not been stricken with multiple sclerosis. The music on the two-CD set *Commit to Memory/Paunetto's Point* (which completely reissues all of the performances of his two most significant albums) is both adventurous and grounded in tradition, looking forward without completely discarding the foundation of Cubop. Most of the selections are originals either by Paunetto or members of this group (other than Keith Jarrett's "Coral") and there are many strong soloists, including Paunetto on vibes, trumpeter Tom Harrell, trombonist Ed Byrne, tenor saxophonist Todd Anderson, baritonist Ronnie Cuber, guitarist John Scofield, and pianist Armen Donelian; Andy and Jerry González are also heard from. This music rewards repeated listening.

Twenty-three years later, Bobby Paunetto had not lost either his enthusiasm (despite his illness) or his adventurous spirit. For *Composer in Public,* Bobby Vince Paunetto's writing is just as full of chance taking as his earlier work. The main changes are that the Latin element has been greatly de-emphasized, and the music is a lot more cinematic, showing the influence of Hollywood composers in spots. The 13 originals are complex and tricky but ultimately rewarding (although two vocal pieces are a bit of an acquired taste), with key solos taken by trumpeter Glenn Drewes, Billy Drewes on soprano, tenor and flute, Todd Anderson on tenor and flute, baritonist Gary Smulyan, and either Bill O'Connell or Armen Donelian on keyboards. Paunetto's writing makes the eight- to nine-piece band (which is sometimes joined by a few strings) sound much larger than it actually is.

ARMANDO PERAZA

b. May 30, 1924, Havana, Cuba

Armando Peraza has had a long and productive career. He was self-taught on bongos and congas, working with a variety of bands in Cuba during 1943-49, including with Chano Pozo. Peraza moved to New York in 1949 and within two days was recording with Machito's band on one of his dates with Charlie Parker; he has not been idle since! Peraza toured and recorded with guitarist-singer-comedian Slim Gaillard (1950-51) and then spent a few years (1951-53) living in Tijuana, where he was a baseball and boxing instructor. After he returned to the United States, Peraza moved to San Francisco, recording with Cal Tjader and working with Pérez Prado and Dave Brubeck. He was regularly with George Shearing during 1954-64, often appearing during the second half of the pianist's shows as a "surprise guest"; some of the dates were recorded. Peraza also worked with Stan Kenton, Wes Montgomery, and Mongo Santamaria and was a regular member of Cal Tjader's band during 1966-72. He played with the Latin rock group Azteca in San Francisco and then became a longtime fixture with Carlos Santana's band, appearing on 20 albums with the popular rock guitarist. Armando Peraza has remained quite active up to the present time, and, in addition to the other artists mentioned, he has recorded with Gato Barbieri, Eric Clapton, Herbie Hancock, John Lee Hooker, Peggy Lee, guitarist John McLaughlin, and pianist Randy Weston, among others. His lone album as a leader was made for Skye in 1968.

DANILO PEREZ

b. Dec. 29, 1966, Monte Oscuro, Panama

One of the finest jazz pianists of the past decade, Danilo Perez is a virtuoso who combines the bebop tradition with his Panamanian heritage and a mastery of polyrhythms. He began playing piano when he was eight and studied at the National Conservatory in Panama (1978-82) and Berklee (1985-87). Perez played with Edgardo Quintero's group in Panama (1978-82) and, after moving to the United States, he was featured with Victor Mendoza (1985-86) and Jon Hendricks (1987-88).

The pianist gained initial fame for his work with Paquito D'Rivera (starting in 1988) and with Dizzy Gillespie's United Nation Orchestra (1989-91) and small group. He has since recorded with trumpeters Terence Blanchard, Tom Harrell, Claudio Roditi, Arturo Sandoval, and Charlie Sepúlveda, trombonists Steve Turre, Slide Hampton, and Conrad Herwig, saxophonists David Sanchez, Ricky Ford, Dave Liebman, and Bobby Watson, singer Jeannie Bryson, bassists Ray Drummond, John Patitucci, and Avashi Cohen, vibraphonist Dave Samuels, and drummer T.S. Monk, among others, but has worked primarily with his own trios and quartets.

Danilo Perez, who teaches at the New England Conservatory, has recorded as a leader for Novus, Impulse, and Verve. He grows in power, creativity, and daring each year.

7   *Danilo Perez / Sept. 1992 / Novus 63148*
10   *The Journey / Dec. 19-20, 1993 / Novus 63166*
8   *Panamonk / Jan. 3-4, 1996 / Impulse 190*
7   *Central Avenue / Apr. 7-8, 1998 / Impulse 279*
8   *Motherland / 1999-2000 / Verve 314 543 540*

Danilo Perez's debut as a leader, *Danilo Perez*, finds him in an intriguing quintet with bassist Santi Debriano, drummer Jack DeJohnette, and both Joe Lovano and David Sanchez on tenors and sopranos. The pianist plays three of his originals (including "Panama Libre") and seven obscurities and standards (highlighted by an unaccompanied "Serenata," "Body and Soul," and "Skylark"). Rubén Blades has guest vocals on two selections. But as strong as his sidemen are, Perez is far from overshadowed and shows throughout this early effort that he has limitless potential.

The Journey is a real gem. Divided into "Time Past" and "Time Present," Perez performs music utilizing Afro-Cuban rhythms, complex time signatures, original themes, the influence of bop, and his own very strong technique. The personnel and instrumentation change from song to song, ranging from a septet with both George Garzone and David Sanchez on saxophones (along with two percussionists playing a wide variety of exotic instruments) to a conventional trio, a duet with drummer Ignacio Berroa, and a pair of solo piano pieces. Bassist Larry Grenadier plays very well, always sounding confident during the very tricky music, while Perez displays a highly original yet logical style. Highly recommended.

Panamonk is one of the more interesting Thelonious Monk tribute albums, for Perez does not sound much like Monk (except in a few spots, on purpose), but he plays what he learned from Monk's music, especially in his use of space and quirky dissonances. Performing in a trio with bassist Avashi Cohen and either Terri Lyne Carrington or Jeff Watts on drums, Perez interprets ballads respectfully, Latinizes a few Thelonious Monk tunes (including "Bright Mississippi," "Think of One," and "'Round Midnight"), and contributes some compatible originals. Olga Roman takes a haunting wordless vocal on "September in Rio." Also well worth exploring is *Central Avenue,* which comprises "Lush Life," "Impressions," and five Perez originals, including the three-part "Rhythm in Blue Suite." All but three songs feature Perez in a trio with John Patitucci or John Benitez on bass, and Jeff Ballard or Jeff "Tain"

Watts on drums. "Panama Blues," "Impressions," and "Impromptu" add Latin percussion and vocalists, but, as is often the case, Perez explores the music not only of Cuba, the Dominican Republic, and the United States but also of other lands, including (on one song with a tabla) the Middle East.

Motherland is a very different Danilo Perez recording. The pianist plays brilliantly as usual, but the program (all but one of the 13 pieces are his originals) is less about his improvisations and more about the various folkloric traditions of Central America and Africa. Claudio Acuna and/or Luciana Sauza have vocals (sometimes with chanting and occasionally wordless) on eight of the selections, and a few percussionists (including the versatile Lusito Qintero) are well featured. Perez, who plays electric piano on five numbers, is generous in allocating solo space with violinist Regina Carter and Chris Potter (on alto and soprano) being typically impressive, and bassist John Patitucci and drummer Brian Blade helping out in the supporting cast. If one comes to this set (which includes such titles as the two-part "Suite for the Americas," "Pan Africa," "Rio To Panama" and "Panama 2000") with few preconceptions, the episodic but consistent music will be particularly rewarding.

DAVE PIKE

b. May 23, 1938, Detroit, MI

An exciting vibraphonist, Dave Pike is able to play both hard bop and Afro-Cuban Jazz with equal skill. He started out on drums before becoming self-taught on vibes. After moving with his family to Los Angeles in 1954, Pike worked with many of the top local players including bassist Curtis Counce, tenors Harold Land and Dexter Gordon, and pianists Elmo Hope, Carl Perkins, and Paul Bley. In 1960 he moved to New York and gained his biggest visibility during his period with Herbie Mann's Afro-Cuban band (1961-64).

Pike lived and played in Germany during 1968-73 (where he recorded with the Kenny Clarke-Francy Boland big band) and then later in the 1970s resettled in Los Angeles where he has continued playing locally. As a leader, Dave Pike recorded for Riverside, Epic, New Jazz, and Moodsville during 1961-62, Decca (his 1964 Afro-Cuban Jazz album *Manhattan Latin*), Atlantic (1965), Vortex, Relax, Saba, MPS, Muse, Criss Cross (1986), Timeless (1988), and most recently Cubop (2000), his first Afro-Cuban Jazz project in years.

8 *Peligroso / Feb. 21-22, 2000 / Cubop*

This fine session is dedicated to Cal Tjader and Milt Jackson. The influence of Tjader in particular is felt throughout the catchy boppish tunes, eight of which were written by Pike. With assistance from the excellent trumpeter Carl Saunders, trombonist Rich Pulin, Michael Turre on flute and baritone, and a rhythm section that includes Bobby Matos on timbales and Robertito Melendez on congas, the music is infectious, joyful, and swinging. Cal Tjader would have enjoyed this set. It is long overdue for Dave Pike to be rediscovered!

CHANO POZO

b. Jan. 7, 1915, Havana, Cuba, d. Dec. 2, 1948, New York, NY

Considered one of the founding fathers of Afro-Cuban Jazz and best known for his period as a conga player with Dizzy Gillespie's bebop orchestra, Chano Pozo (born Luciano Pozo y Gonzales) actually had a much more extensive career than is discussed in jazz history books.

A wild child and a street fighter who spent time in reform school in his native Cuba, Pozo worked in street dance groups in his early days and became a skilled choreographer for hotel revues. He belonged to a Nigerian religious cult (the Abakwa), and his drumming and singing were rooted in the Cuban Lucumi faith, which derived from West African rituals. Although he did not know how to write music formally, he was talented at composing songs, singing out melodies for a copyist to transcribe. In the late '30s Pozo wrote several prize-winning carnival tunes, in the 1940s his "Paraparampampin" was in the repertoire of several New York Cuban bands, and his theme, "Nague," became a big hit for Machito. Pozo's songs (which also included "Los Dandies" and "Arinara") were recorded by Orquesta Casino de la Playa, Machito, Xavier Cugat, Miguelito Valdés, and others in New York while he was still in Cuba. During 1940-43, when he co-led El Conjunto Azul with his brother, trumpeter Felix Chappottin, Pozo became quite well known locally for his flashy clothes, songwriting ability, dancing, and hot temper.

In December 1945 Pozo met Mario Bauzá when Machito's orchestra was visiting Cuba; the trumpeter encouraged him to come to New York. Pozo, taking his advice, arrived in New York in May 1946, but at first there was very little work to be found as a dancer or as a conga player and a period of struggle followed. During February-March 1947, Chano Pozo led three little-known record dates for the Coda label that have recently been partly reissued on an Arsenio Rodriguez IMC CD (which is reviewed under Rodriguez's name) and Pozo's *Legendary Sessions*. Miguelito Valdés was successful in convincing Rodriguez (playing tres), members of the Machito Orchestra, and singer Tito Rodriguez to accept two bottles of whiskey as payment for their work on Pozo's sessions! Also participating on some of the selections were Valdés and Marcelino Guerra's band.

The money from those dates did not go very far, so Valdés called Mario Bauzá and asked for help for his friend. Bauzá recalled that Dizzy Gillespie had been showing a strong interest in Latin music, and he introduced Gillespie to Pozo. As it turned out, Dizzy wanted to feature a conga drummer with his band at an upcoming Carnegie Hall concert, and he and Pozo hit it off even though Chano did not speak English. Gillespie would later say that Pozo could play in one rhythm, sing in another, and dance in a third. The Carnegie Hall concert of September 29, 1947, served as the perfect introduction for Dizzy's new Afro-Cuban sound. Ella Fitzgerald, who was on the bill, remarked that a new sound of jazz was born that evening, and it was the first instance of a conga player becoming a regular member of an American jazz big band. On December 22 Pozo recorded four titles with Gillespie: "Algo Bueno," "Cool Breeze," and his two conga and chanting features (composed by George Russell), "Cubana Be" and "Cubana Bop." He topped off the year on December 30 by cutting four more tunes, including "Good Bait" and a number that he cowrote with Gillespie, "Manteca." The eight songs that he performed on these two sessions would be Pozo's only studio recordings with Dizzy's band, although their impact would be enormous.

Pozo toured Europe with Dizzy Gillespie's orchestra in January 1948 and played all over the United States with Gillespie throughout the year; fortunately, several concert appearances were recorded and have since been released. Despite a recording strike, Pozo also appeared on records in 1948, with vibraphonist Milt Jackson, pianist-arranger Tadd Dameron, and tenor saxophonist James Moody. He also co-composed (with Gillespie) "Tin Tin Deo" and "Guachi Guaro."

But it all came to an end suddenly on December 2, 1948. A few hours after he beat up a Cuban who had sold him weak marijuana and had refused to give him his money back, Pozo was fatally shot in a Harlem bar, the Rio Café. The murderer served five years in prison and later on told Machito that he had to kill Pozo because he could not live with the humiliation of having had people see him get hit in the face. Chano Pozo was a month short of his 34th birthday.

8 *Legendary Sessions / Feb. 7, 1947-1953 / Tumbao 017*

Although Chano Pozo is listed first on this CD, he is actually only on the first six selections, which comprise two of the three dates that the conguero led in February 1947; these same selections are also on an Arsenio Rodriguez CD. Pozo is one of the singers (along with Tito Rodriguez and Marcelino Guerra), but Rodriguez's tres playing largely steals the show, including on a number called "Rumba en Swing." Also included are six selections from Rodriguez's band in 1948 (recorded in Cuba) and four tunes from Rodriguez's 1953 group (after he had settled in New York). Although dominated by group singing, Rodriguez's tres has its spots and makes it clear that he is one of the most underrated of all guitarists.

CHINO POZO
b. Oct. 4, 1915, Havana, Cuba, d. Apr. 28, 1980, New York, NY

Although not on the same level as his cousin Chano Pozo, Chino Pozo was able to keep busy in the jazz world as a percussionist after Chano's death. He originally taught himself piano and bass. After switching to percussion, Pozo moved to the United States in 1937 (eight years before Chano) and worked with Machito's early orchestra during 1941-43. He spent the 1943-49 period in a fairly anonymous role accompanying a dance troupe (the Jack Cole Dancers), although he was utilized on a 1948 bop date led by trumpeter Fats Navarro. After Chano's death, Chino found himself in demand in the jazz world throughout the 1950s, and among his many recordings were dates with Dizzy Gillespie, Charlie Parker (his sessions in 1950 with Machito), Louis Jordan, Peggy Lee (with whom he toured during 1954-55), Illinois Jacquet, Stan Kenton (1955), Herbie Mann (1956), the Jazz Modes, Phineas Newborn, Billy Taylor (1959), José Curbelo, Noro Morales, Tito Puente, Tito

Rodriguez, and Pérez Prado. Chano Pozo left jazz in the mid-1960s to work for singer Paul Anka. He was obscure at the time of his death at age 64 and never led his own record date.

PÉREZ PRADO

b. Dec. 11, 1916, Matanzas, Cuba, d. Sept. 14, 1989, Mexico City

Damaso Pérez-Prado was one of the most famous of all the Latin bandleaders in the 1950s and was billed as the "King of Mambo." Although he was not the first to play the mambo rhythm (which was heard as early as 1937 performed by Arcaño's orchestra), he popularized it and led a spirited big band that had several major pop hits. Prado studied classical piano at Principal School of Matanzas and started his career playing locally. He moved to Havana in the late 1930s, made his recording debut in 1940 with Orquesta Casino de la Playa, and also worked with Orquesta Cubaney, Paulina Alvarez, and the CMQ radio band. Prado formed his own band in 1946 and began writing and arranging mambos that he added to his orchestra's repertoire. He moved to Mexico in 1948, teaming up with Beny Moré for tours. Prado's 1949 recording "Mambo No. 5" became a major hit (as did "Que Rico el Mambo," which sold over 4 million copies, and "Mambo Jambo"), and he was already quite well known when he made his United States debut in May 1951.

Prado's Cuban dance band was influenced by swing-oriented jazz and his love for Stan Kenton's music; he even used Kenton's former lead trumpeter Maynard Ferguson on some of his sessions. By 1954, when the mambo craze was at its height, Pérez Prado was a household name. He had two #1 pop hits during 1955-56 in "Cherry Pink and Apple Blossom White" and "Patricia." Although his commercial successes caused a bit of a backlash in the Cuban community and among some fans of Afro-Cuban Jazz, Prado actually had a very spirited

and distinctive orchestra that straddled the boundaries between several styles of music. He also helped keep the big band sound alive in the 1950s, a decade after the swing era had ended. His popularity faded after 1960, but Pérez Prado, who moved to Mexico in 1970, remained active up until his death in 1989 at the age of 72.

7 *Mambos / 1949-mid-50s / Orfeon 801*

Pérez Prado was to the 1950s mambo what Xavier Cugat was to Latin pop music in the 1930s, the most famous figure in the style and the one on whom the mass media tended to focus. This CD has ten of his mambos from the era (including the famous "Mambo No. 5"), but it is packaged like a budget release, with no dates, personnel listing, or liner notes. Prado's big band sound looks a bit toward swing while utilizing well-placed vocal shouts and some occasional gimmicks. All ten selections are under three minutes, making this a rather brief disc. But it does give a sampling of the catchy if sometimes-lightweight Pérez Prado sound.

PUCHO AND THE LATIN SOUL BROTHERS

b. Nov. 1, 1938, Harlem, NY

In the mid-1960s, Henry "Pucho" Brown and the Latin Soul Brothers were one of the top bands exploring Latin boogaloo (which he has described as a slow cha-cha with a backbeat), mixing Afro-Cuban Jazz with funk, Motown, current pop tunes, soul jazz, and rock. Decades later their music was rediscovered and Pucho was able to make a comeback.

As a youth growing up in Harlem, Brown was exposed to jazz, Latin music, and rhythm and blues. Nicknamed "Pucho" by a friend, he started playing timbales when he was 15. Pucho worked with Los Lobos Diablos and spent several years as a member of Joe Panama's band. When that group broke up in

1959, Pucho took over the nucleus and formed his own ensemble, which was originally known as Pucho and the Cha Cha Boys. His early 1960s group included Steve Berrios, Chick Corea, and saxophonist Bobby Capers. But Mongo Santamaria hired those musicians away, and a 1963 single, "Darin's Mambo," did not go anywhere. Pucho had better luck after he reorganized and renamed his band the Latin Soul Brothers. He signed with Prestige in 1966 and recorded seven albums during the next three years that helped define the Latin boogaloo style. Pucho also guested as a percussionist on records by Gene Ammons, King Curtis, and Roberta Flack, among others. After the Prestige period ended, Pucho recorded two albums for the Right On! label and then slipped into obscurity, playing at resort hotels in the Catskills for the next 19 years.

In 1992 the rise of "acid jazz" led British dance clubs to play and sample the old records by Pucho and the Latin Soul Brothers. Because of the rise in interest, Pucho contacted some of his earlier sidemen (including vibraphonist William Bivens, trumpeter Al Pazant, and saxophonist Ed Pazant) and organized a new version of the band. Pucho has since recorded sets for the Milestone and Cannonball labels and has had an active career that has lasted up to the present time, performing in a style largely unchanged from his glory days.

6 *Tough! / Feb. 15, 1966-Nov. 10, 1966 / Prestige 24138*

8 *The Best of Pucho & His Latin Soul Brothers / Aug. 9, 1967-Jan. 12, 1970 / Prestige 24175*

3 *Cold Shoulders / Dec. 5, 1967-Jan. 12, 1970 / Prestige 24240*

Tough! has all of the music from Pucho's first two Prestige albums: *Tough!* and *Saffron Soul.* Heading a band consisting of trumpeter Vincent McEwan, Claude Bartee and Harold Alexander on tenors

(Alexander doubles on flute), vibraphonist William Bivens, pianist John Spruill, Jon Hart or James Phillips on bass, Richard Landrum on conga, Norberto Apellaniz on bongos, and (on the second date) drummer William Curtis, Pucho covers a lot of pop hits from the time. Although "Cantaloupe Island" is fine, these versions of such tunes as "Walk on By," "And I Love Her," "The Shadow of Your Smile," "Goldfinger," "Yesterday," and "Alfie" do sound somewhat dated today. The originals tend to be on a higher level, although overall the music tends to be purposely lightweight, quite worthy of being played on AM radio of the time.

The Best of Pucho & His Latin Soul Brothers lives up to its name, consisting of 16 of the best selections from Pucho's other five Prestige albums. The results are pretty definitive, for Pucho Brown and his band (which during this era often featured trumpeter Al Pazant, trombonist Barry Rogers, Eddie Pazant on alto, tenor, flute, and particularly baritone, keyboardist Neal Creque, vibraphonist Bivens, and, on the last seven selections, three violins) perform a rather eclectic repertoire. Among the selections are group originals (often by Creque), covers of R&B tunes, "Dearly Beloved," Herbie Hancock's "Maiden Voyage," and "Psychedelic Pucho." In contrast, much of *Cold Shoulders* could be subtitled "The Worst of Pucho!" The problem is that the first nine of the 16 selections are dominated by the raspy singing of Jackie Soul (an acquired taste), and the arrangements for those tunes are overly poppish, quite commercial, and very dated. The final seven instrumentals are better, although still not up to the average level of the music on *The Best* CD. *Cold Shoulders* deserves a cold shoulder!

9 *Rip a Dip / June 1995 / Milestone 9247*

7 *Groovin' High / 1997 / Cannonball 27103*

8 *How'm I Doin'? / Dec. 1999-Jan. 2000 / Cannonball 27108*

Although the basic style had not changed that much, the alumni who were gathered to form the new version of Pucho's Latin Soul Brothers in the 1990s had obviously grown through the years. The Pazant Brothers (with Eddie heard on alto and flute) have many fine spots throughout *Rip a Dip,* vibraphonist Bivens is typically tasteful, and the joyous Pucho has four other percussionists to play off of. His comeback disc for Milestone also has six guests, including Steve Berrios on various percussion, saxophonist Mel Martin, and Melvin Sparks singing along with his guitar (à la George Benson) on one number. Whether it be "Milestones," Jack McDuff's catchy "Hot Barbecue," Marvin Gaye's "Trouble Man," or "Caravan," this is one of the strongest jazz sets of Pucho's career.

Groovin' High has a similar group, and, although the repertoire is not quite as worthy (other than the Dizzy Gillespie title cut), the spirit is definitely still present. A "cha-cha rap" on "I Like It Like That" is a misfire, but overall the set has its strong moments as the Pazant brothers, Bivens, and the heated percussion section (with Steve Berrios on guiro) keep the momentum moving. However, *How'm I Doin'?* generally has better material and a stronger emphasis on the Latin side of the music. Although Bivens is missing, there are a lot of intriguing guests, including Dave Valentin, trombonist Fred Wesley, trumpeter Lew Soloff, bassist Harvie Swartz (who contributed "The Dolphy Mambo"), and violinist Louis Kahn. The funky Latin vamps are full of fire, and Pucho's enthusiasm for his group is well placed.

TITO PUENTE

b. Apr. 20, 1923, New York, NY, d. June 1, 2000, New York, NY

The King of Latin music, Tito Puente ("El Rey") was its most famous performer, leader, and personality for 50 years. As a timbale player, an occasional vibraphonist, bandleader, arranger, and composer,

Puente was always near the top of his field, and he was Afro-Cuban music's unofficial goodwill ambassador for years, performing cheerful music for countless dancing and partying audiences. No matter what musical trend was hot at the moment, Puente managed to survive and often flourish. In fact, he seemed so ageless that his sudden death from heart failure on June 1, 2000, was as surprising as the realization that he was still just 77!

He was born Ernesto Puente Jr. and nicknamed Ernestito due to his short stature; his name was eventually shortened to Tito. His mother encouraged Tito and his sister Anna to become performers. In 1935 they became members of the "Stars of the Future," an organization assembled by the director of a local funeral parlor. Each year the "Stars" had a coronation at a local church in which the most talented children were crowned king or queen for their artistic ability. Puente was named king four times due to his dancing skills. However, when he tore a tendon in his ankle, his fledging dancing career came to an end.

Of Puerto Rican descent and growing up in Spanish Harlem, Puente developed an early love for music. He took piano lessons at the New York School of Music for seven years (he would later attend Juilliard), sang with a youth group, learned to play alto sax, and also began playing drums after hearing Gene Krupa on Benny Goodman's recording of "Sing Sing Sing," a solo he memorized. As a teenager, Puente was the drummer with Ramon Olivero's big band.

In 1939, at the age of 16, Tito Puente dropped out of school to become a full-time musician. Puente freelanced and worked with Johnny Rodriguez's Stork Club Orchestra and Anselmo Sacassa's band. On January 27, 1941, he made his recording debut with Vincent López's Suave Swing Orchestra. He spent much of 1941-42 playing drums with Noro Morales' band, not only recording with Morales but appearing in four film shorts.

In June 1942 Puente joined Machito's orchestra on timbales; he was one of the first timbale players to perform standing up. Puente's musical tastes were influenced by the Machito orchestra's mixture of jazz solos with Latin rhythms, but his stay with Machito was brief, for he was soon drafted into the Navy.

Tito's Navy experience was a productive one, since he had an opportunity to play alto and drums with the ship's swing band and he was taught arranging by several other Navy men, including trumpeter Charlie Spivak. While still in the service, he sent his first arrangement to Machito. Puente, who saw combat duty, was honorably discharged in 1945. During the next two years he worked with the José Curbelo Orchestra and Fernando Alvarez's Brazilian band. In September 1947 he became the drummer and musical director of the Pupi Campo Orchestra. Puente's arrangements (including "How High the Moon") plus those of Joe Loco helped make Pupi Campo's orchestra one of the best Afro-Cuban bands of the time.

Tito Puente led his own group, the Piccadilly Boys (after his original song "Piccadillo"), in 1948 for Sunday matinee dances at the Alma Dance Studios. In March 1949 he broke away from Campo and became a full-time bandleader; he would lead ensembles for the remaining 51 years of his life. Playing timbales and vibes (where Lionel Hampton was his main inspiration), Puente started off with a septet consisting of himself, two trumpets, piano, bass, conga, and Manny Oquendo on bongo plus Angel Rosa on vocals. After much rehearsal, the band debuted on July 4, 1949. A third trumpeter was added a few months later, and by the end of the year it was a 16-piece orchestra with four trumpets, three trombones, and four saxophones! Vicentico Valdés was Puente's vocalist during 1949-53, and "Abaniquito" was Puente's first hit. In 1950 Charlie Palmieri became Tito's pianist, and in 1951 Mongo Santamaria joined on conga.

By then, Puente was leading one of the most popular of all Latin bands, and his group's fame would continue to grow throughout the decade.

Puente flourished during the mambo craze, when he was billed as "King of the Mambo" (or "El Rey"). And during the years when the cha-cha-cha was most popular, he successfully transcribed some original Cuban hits from the violin-and-flute charanga format to the brass and reeds frontline of his big band. With the opening of the Palladium, Puente and his childhood friend and close rival Tito Rodriguez had legendary battles over which of the two Titos would be given top billing when they were booked together. "Vibe Mambo" was a popular recording for Puente in 1951. When Willie Bobo joined Santamaria in his band a few years later, Puente had an unparalleled percussion section (informally known as "Ti-Mon-Bo"). Yet when Santamaria and Bobo departed in 1957, eventually to join Cal Tjader, Puente was able to hold onto his popularity. Among his more notable records of the time were the albums *Puente Goes Jazz* (1956) and *Dance Mania Vol. 1* (1958). Other top percussionists who spent time with his band included Ray Barretto, Johnny Pacheco, Candido, and Patato Valdés. When the Cuban government sponsored a "50 Years of Cuban Music" celebration, Puente was the only non-Cuban who was honored.

In the 1960s, Puente was able to weather the changes in Latin music (which included the rise of the pachanga, boogaloo, and Latin soul) without altering his style very much. He recorded many albums with singers Celia Cruz, La Lupe, Abbe Lane, and Santos Colon, cut everything from pop tunes to songs from Broadway shows, and yet held onto his big band's Afro-Cuban sound. A song that he first recorded in 1962 was adopted by Latin rock guitarist Carlos Santana eight years later and became his best-known original, "Oye Come Va"; Santana also successfully recorded Puente's "Para los Rumberos."

Tito Puente, who deserved to be called the King of Latin Music.

Although not as popular in the 1970s as he had been in the 1950s, Puente kept on working, including touring Japan in 1979 with the LP (Latin Percussion) Jazz Ensemble, a quintet that also included Patato Valdés and bongo player Johnny Rodriguez. In the 1980s Puente signed with the Concord Picante label and went back to recording Afro-Cuban Jazz with his combo while leading a big band on a part-time basis. This series for Concord gave Puente a great deal of exposure in the jazz world, where he had often been overlooked or taken for granted. Very proud of his many recordings, Tito Puente in 1991 celebrated the release of his 100th album, *The Mambo King* (RMM). He had recently appeared in the movie *The Mambo Kings* (in which he had an acting role and for which he was the musical coordinator) and also made appearances in Woody Allen's *Radio Days, Armed and Extremely Dangerous,* and *Zoot Suit.* On August 4, 1990, he received a star on the Hollywood Walk of Fame.

Tito Puente did not slow down at all in the 1990s; in fact he seemed to be accelerating his activities. He alternated between three groups: his Latin Jazz Ensemble (which recorded on Concord), his big band, and his Golden Latin Jazz All-Stars, a combo that featured such players as Paquito D'Rivera, Mongo Santamaria, Dave Valentin, Claudio Roditi (later on, Charlie Sepúlveda), Giovanni Hidalgo, Hilton Ruiz, Ignacio Berroa, and Mario Rivera, among others. Through the years Puente also appeared as a special guest on a variety of albums with jazz and Latin greats, including Woody Herman (1958), Cal Tjader (1973), Ray Barretto (1976), Hilton Ruiz, Poncho Sanchez, tenor saxophonist Benny Golson, and the Tropijazz All-Stars. By 1998 he had recorded at least 116 albums for such labels as Seeco, Tico, Tropical, RCA, Gema, GNP, Alegre, Roulette, Misicor, Decca, Fania, Contique, Concord Picante, and Tropijazz/RMM.

So considering all of this, it is very surprising that Tito Puente was still only 77 when he passed away at the peak of his fame!

7 *50 Years of Swing / 1946-1996 / RMM 82050*

8 *El Timbal / 1949-1951 / Greycliff 900006*

7 *Puente Goes Jazz / May 2, 1956-June 2, 1956 / Bluebird 66148*

8 *Night Beat / Feb., 8, 1957-Apr. 12, 1957 / Koch 7847*

The concept behind the three-CD Tito Puente set *50 Years of Swing* has a great deal of potential, picking high points from El Rey's half-century career. Unfortunately the execution is quite flawed. Rather than release the music in strict chronological order (which would make the most sense considering Puente's various periods and his continual evolution), the programming skips around quite a bit. The exact recording dates are not given (just the year), and, quite inexcusably the full personnel is not listed, just the names of a few (but not all) of the featured soloists. The 50 selections do cover a bit of ground, but listening to this set straight through can be confusing. The first disc concentrates mostly on Salsa vocal performances, starting with a number from José Curbelo's 1946 orchestra with Tito Rodriguez doing the singing (Puente wrote the arrangement), and continuing with features for Vicentico Valdés, Graciela, Abbe Lane, Santos Colon, La Lupe, Miguelito Valdés, and even Machito, reaching up to 1981. The second disc is mostly (but not entirely) instrumentals from 1955-1995, including "Ran Kan Kan," "Mambo Herd, 1959" (with Woody Herman), and various features for Mongo Santamaria, Willie Bobo, Candido, Steve Turre, Hilton Ruiz, and even Lionel Hampton and Cal Tjader; that disc concludes with two previously unreleased numbers from 1977. The final CD (from 1956-94) has both Afro-Cuban

Jazz and some Salsa, somewhat randomly programmed; Celia Cruz, Ray Barretto, James Moody, and India are among those making appearances. Although an intriguing set, *50 Years of Swing* could have been so much better with a little logical planning!

Tito Puente's first orchestra is well featured on *El Timbal,* or at least his singers (mostly Vicentico Valdés and Bobby Escoto) are. The 25 selections overflow with mambo pieces and include the hit "Abaniquito." Unfortunately the horns never have an opportunity to solo, but the danceable rhythms, shouting ensembles, spirited vocals, and catchy melodies certainly will hold listeners' interest on this historic set.

Puente Goes Jazz features Puente (doubling on vibes and timbales) heading a big band comprised mostly of studio musicians plus a Latin rhythm section with Willie Bobo (listed as William Correa) on bongo and Mongo Santamaria (listed as Ramon Santa Maria!) on conga. The music (mostly obscure originals plus three standards) swings. And although none of the players in the 14- to 17-piece orchestra became household names (best known is altoist Dave Schildkraut), the musicianship is excellent. Actually the most notable aspects to this enjoyable if conventional outing are two of the song titles: "Tiny Not Ghengis (Kahn)" and "That's a Puente!" *Night Beat* (an RCA album reissued in 1998 as a Koch CD) could almost be called *Puente Goes Jazz II.* The concept is similar, with Puente heading a big band teamed with his Latin percussionists. Actually, with the exception of two pieces, the music is fairly straightahead, featuring such soloists as trumpeter Doc Severinsen (in top form) and tenor saxophonist Marty Holmes, who often recalls Paul Quinichette. The 11 selections (all originals or obscurities except for two numbers) include an uptempo "Carioca," "Flying Down to Rio," and such similar-looking titles as "Night Hawk," "Night Ritual," "Night Beat," "Malibu

Beat," and "Mambo Beat!" A musically rewarding set that is actually a little more creative than the better-known *Puente Goes Jazz.*

9 *On Broadway / July 1982 / Concord Picante 4207*

9 *El Rey / May 1984 / Concord Picante 4250*

8 *Mambo Diablo / May 1985 / Concord Picante 4283*

8 *Sensacion / Dec. 1985 / Concord Picante 4301*

8 *Un Poco Loco / Jan. 1987 / Concord Picante 4329*

10 *Salsa Meets Jazz / Jan. 1988 / Concord Picante 4354*

On Broadway, Tito Puente's first Concord Picante release, is one of the best of the dozen he would record. At the time in 1982, Puente's group included two trumpets (with Jimmy Frisaura doubling on trombone), guitar, electric bass, Mario Rivera on tenor, soprano, and flute, violinist Alfredo De La Fe, pianist Jorge Dalto, Jerry Gonzales on conga and flügelhorn, Johnny Rodriguez on bongos, and the leader on vibes and timbales. The repertoire includes the always-catchy "On Broadway" and Latinized arrangements of "Sophisticated Lady," "Bluesette," and Freddie Hubbard's "First Light." *El Rey* is on the same level, utilizing a similar nine-piece group (no violin this time and with Francisco Aguabella in Jerry González's place) on such unlikely material as "Giant Steps," John Coltrane's "Equinox," and Eddie Heywood's obscure but worthy "Rainfall." This joyous live set also has remakes of "Oye Come Va" and "Ran Kan Kan," often putting the emphasis on Puente's underrated vibes playing.

Mambo Diablo was recorded when Puente's three-horn octet had José Madera on conga and Sonny Bravo as the new pianist. The repertoire is particularly strong on this CD, including "Take

Five," "Lush Life" (probably in its initial treatment as Afro-Cuban Jazz!), "Pick Yourself Up," and "Lullaby of Birdland"; the last song has its composer, George Shearing, guesting on piano. Puente wrote half of the arrangements and is in typically joyful form on timbales and vibes. The same personnel is heard throughout *Sensacion* except that, instead of Shearing, the guest artist is vibraphonist Terry Gibbs. Gibbs is featured on "Jordu" and has a vibes duet with Puente on a tribute to the recently deceased Cal Tjader, "Guajira for Cal." Other highlights include Puente's "Fiesta à la King," "'Round Midnight," Clare Fischer's "Morning," and Chick Corea's "Spain."

For *Un Poco Loco*, his 97th recording as a leader, Tito Puente augments his octet on a few selections with a full big band. Puente, who solos on timbales, marimba, vibes, and the timbalito, performs a wide-ranging set that includes Bud Powell's "Un Poco Loco" (a natural to be turned into Afro-Cuban Jazz), his own spectacular "Machito Forever," "Killer Joe," and "Swinging Shepherd Blues (Goes Latin)." The classic *Salsa Meets Jazz* lives up to its billing, with two pieces that feature a *coro* while three other numbers (George Shearing's "Consternation," Thelonious Monk's "Pannonica," and Neal Hefti's feature for Charlie Parker, "Repetition") put the spotlight on the great bebop altoist Phil Woods. Such songs as "Corner Pocket," "Carioca," and Dizzy Gillespie's "Con Alma" sound quite at home in this setting, and Puente (well featured on vibes and timbales) brought in two originals and wrote seven of the nine arrangements. A definitive outing for the great El Rey.

8 *Goza Mi Timbal / July 31, 1989-Aug. 1, 1989 / Concord Picante 4399*

9 *Out of This World / Dec. 1990 / Concord Picante 4448*

8 *Mambo of the Times / Dec. 1991 / Concord Picante 4499*

8 *Live at the Village Gate / Apr. 27, 1992 / RMM/Tropijazz 80879*

8 *In Session / 1992 / RMM/Tropijazz 81208*

8 *Royal T / Jan. 18-19, 1993 / Concord Picante 4553*

8 *Master Timbalero / Sept. 20-21, 1993 / Concord Picante 4594*

8 *Jazzin' / 1995 / Tropijazz 82032*

7 *Special Delivery / June 11, 1996-July 13, 1996 / Concord Picante 4732*

7 *Party with Puente / July 1982-Sept. 21, 1993 / Concord Picante 4924*

Tito Puente kept up his winning streak with *Goza Mi Timbal,* his 99th release as a leader. There had been some turnover in his group during the past couple of years, and the lineup now consisted of trumpeters Robbie Kwock and Piro Rodriguez, trombonist Sam Burtis, Mary Fettig and Mitch Frohman on reeds, pianist Bravo, bassist Bobby Rodriguez, José Madera on congas, Johnny Rodriguez on bongos, and the always-spirited leader. Two songs feature group vocals that are reasonably infectious, but it is Puente's treatments of such standards as "Airegin," "Pent-Up House," "All Blues," and "Straight No Chaser" that are most memorable. *Out of This World* has Charlie Sepúlveda in the trumpet section, with Rodriguez, Papo Vazquez on trombone, Mario Rivera and baritonist Michael Turre on reeds, and José Rodriguez added on chekere and bongos; at the time the Puente band had four Rodriguezes! The music is consistently exciting, whether it be Thelonious Monk's "In Walked Bud," a modernized "'S Wonderful," or such Puente tunes as "Descarga," "Amanecer Guajira," and "Latin Percussion Summit." One of Tito's most exciting Concord Picante releases. *Mambo of the Times* uses the same musicians, except that altoist Bobby Porcelli is in Turre's place and Brian Murphy adds his synthesizer to some spots. More important is that the material is particularly strong (including "Things to Come," Fats Waller's "Jitterbug Waltz," Puente's "Mambo King," and "If You Could See Me Now") and that the musicians are in superior form, again.

Tito Puente's Golden Jazz All-Stars, as heard on *Live at the Village Gate,* is an all-star nonet overflowing with talent: Puente, Claudio Roditi, Paquito D'Rivera, Dave Valentin, Hilton Ruiz, Andy González, Ignacio Berroa, Giovanni Hidalgo, and Mongo Santamaria! Other than Puente's "Skin Jam" and Ruiz's "New Arrival," the music is all familiar standards (including "Afro Blue," "Oye Como Va" and a pretty flute feature for Valentin on "I Loves You Porgy"), enthusiastically played, with each of the musicians getting his solo spots. For *In Session,* the band uses similar players, except that Charlie Sepúlveda and Mario Rivera (who has a cameo on soprano on the *Village Gate* set) replace Roditi and D'Rivera. The material is more obscure this time around, with six originals by Ruiz, Puente, Sepúlveda, or Marty Sheller plus "Teach Me Tonight," "Flight to Jordan," and "Obsesion" (a bolero from Valentin's repertoire). The music is very jazz-oriented, and, even though most of these musicians were leaders at the time, there was apparently no problem with egos. As a bonus, tenor saxophonist James Moody drops by to sing (and yodel!) his famous "Moody's Mood for Love."

Royal T has an expanded version of Puente's regular group playing such unlikely material as Charlie Parker's "Donna Lee," Horace Silver's "Tokyo Blues," Charles Mingus' "Moanin'," and "Stompin' at the Savoy." Tony Lujan had replaced Sepúlveda in the band, both trombonist Art Velasco and altoist Bobby Porcelli were added to make six horns, and Rebeca Mauleón helps out on synthesizer. *Master Timbalero* has Puente leading a 13-piece band with seven horns (including Ray Vega, Mario Rivera, and Porcelli) and four percussionists. Several of the songs are quite surprising (the traditional Japanese melody "Sakura Sakura," Charles

Mingus' "Nostalgia in Times Square," Erroll Garner's "Crème de Menthe," and Maurice White's "Sun Goddess"), but virtually everything works and Tito Puente once again shows that he deserves the title "Master."

Jazzin' is an unusual project, for Puente not only heads a 12-piece version of his Latin Jazz Ensemble but welcomes Hilton Ruiz, Dave Valentin, and (on four of the ten selections) the Count Basie Orchestra as "guests." But, in reality, this set is dominated by the Salsa singer India. India interprets the lyrics (mostly standards, including "Fever," "Love for Sale," "Wave," and "What a Difference a Day Makes") in both English and Spanish, she scats well, and, even when she goes over the top, she stays consistently musical. This is an intriguing (and now unique) collaboration. On *Special Delivery,* Puente leads one of his largest groups, a 16-piece band that is augmented by a few special guests. On Dizzy Gillespie's "Bebop" and "On Green Dolphin Street," Puente's band is joined by trumpeters Maynard Ferguson and Bobby Shew, trombonist Tom Garling, and tenor saxophonist Don Menza. Ferguson, who is not overly featured despite getting special billing, mostly helps out the ensembles, also popping up on "Flying Home." Hilton Ruiz takes Sonny Bravo's spot on two songs, and the other highlights include "Stablemates," "Misterioso," and Gerry Mulligan's "Venus de Milo."

Finally, the sampler *Party with Puente* has 11 of the hottest and most jazz-oriented selections recorded by Tito Puente during his years on Concord Picante. The packaging is very minimal, for although it tells which CDs the music came from, there is no listing of personnel or recording dates; in fact no liner notes at all. However, the music is quite enjoyable and listeners who do not need to know who the soloists are and just want to be introduced to Puente's music (and desire some hot Latin dance music) will enjoy this CD.

Highlights include "Descarga," "Oye Como Va," "Killer Joe," "Guarjira Soul," "On Broadway," and "Things To Come." Altoist Phil Woods guests on two songs.

QUE CALOR

In 1998 six San Francisco-based jazz musicians with many credits combined their talents to form Que Calor, an Afro-Cuban Jazz sextet. Best known among the players is pianist Mark Levine, who is joined in Que Calor by saxophonist Ron Stallings, trombonist Jeff Cressman, bassist David Belove, drummer Paul Van Wageningen, and percussionist Michael Spiro. Thus far the band has recorded one CD.

5 *Keeper of the Flame / Apr. 1998 / Spirit Nectar 001*

For their debut release, Que Calor performs group originals and Latinized versions of songs by vibraphonist Bobby Hutcherson and pianist Roland Hanna plus four by pianist Mulgrew Miller. Other than "Havana," which is a feature for Ron Stallings' warm voice, the music is essentially post-bop (or advanced hard bop) with Latin rhythms. Trombonist Cressman and pianist Levine are the most distinctive soloists, but the group overall, although quite musical, at this early point in its development did not display its own personality. The music is pleasing but not all that memorable.

JOHNNY RAE

b. Aug. 11, 1934, Saugus, MA, d. Sept. 4, 1993, San Francisco, CA

Johnny Rae was a fine drummer and percussionist who was equally skilled on vibes. Raised in a family of musicians, Rae first played in clubs as a teenager and quit high school at 16 to become a full-time musician. However, he studied piano, timpani, and drums at the New England Conservatory, the Boston Conservatory, and Berklee. As a member of the house band at the Hi Hat Club, he had an opportunity to play with many top jazz musicians, including Charlie Parker. Rae took informal lessons on vibes from Terry Gibbs, gigged in the Boston area with trumpeter Herb Pomeroy and altoist Jay Migliori, and was recommended by pianist John Lewis to George Shearing, who was looking for a successor to Cal Tjader. Rae played vibes next to guitarist Toots Thielemans, Al McKibbon, and Armando Peraza (who taught him timbales) in the very popular George Shearing Quintet during 1955-56.

After leaving Shearing, Rae spent time in the bands of guitarist Johnny Smith, pianist Ralph Sharon, and drummer Cozy Cole. During 1959-61, he was a member of Herbie Mann's influential Afro-Jazz Sextet during a period when Patato Valdés and José Mangual were also in the group. Rae next played drums with Cal Tjader's band for five years, replacing Willie Bobo. He recorded 16 albums with Tjader before he left in 1966 and also played drums with the Gary McFarland Orchestra on Stan Getz's *Big Band Bossa Nova* album. After a period living in Aspen, Colorado, leading his own group and working with guitarist Gabor Szabo (at first on drums before switching to vibes) and Vince Guaraldi, Rae was back with Tjader during 1968-70. In the 1970s he played drums with the team of Herb Ellis and Joe Pass, guitarist Charlie Byrd (1973-75), and the Great Guitars. From the late '70s on he freelanced in the San Francisco area (mostly on drums), working in show bands and with Afro-Cuban Jazz groups. After Cal Tjader's death, Rae put together a memorial band of mostly alumni called Radcliffe (Tjader's middle name), in which he played vibes, a group that lasted until his own death in 1993 at age 61. Johnny Rae led only two albums in his career, both of which featured him on vibes: the straight-ahead *Opus de Jazz* (Savoy) and *African Suite* (United Artists), which found him fronting Herbie

Mann's group (since the flutist was signed to a different label at the time).

HUMBERTO RAMIREZ

b. 1963, San Juan, Puerto Rico

Humberto Ramirez is a talented Latin trumpeter who, although versatile as a producer and arranger, has stuck to recording easy-listening jazz as a leader. His father Humberto Ramirez Sr. was the director of the San Juan Orchestra. At 14 (just two years after he started playing trumpet), the younger Ramirez became a member of his father's band. He also began writing arrangements during that early period. After graduating from the Berklee College of Music in 1984, Ramirez moved to Los Angeles, where he helped form Tolu with Alex Acuña and Justo Almario. After a short time, he returned to Puerto Rico to play with the Salsa orchestra of Willie Rosario (1985-89), for whom he also contributed arrangements. Since then he has produced and arranged for some of the major names in Latin dance music, including Tony Vega, Johnny Rivera, Brenda K. Starr, Cheo Feliciano, Ray Sepúlveda, Willie Colón, and Ismael Miranda. During the past decade Humberto Ramirez (who has a warm tone on trumpet) has led his own group in Puerto Rico (the Jazz Project), recording for the Tropijazz label.

5 *Jazzproject / 1992 / Sony/Tropijazz 80774*
5 *Canciones de Amor / June 3-6, 1996 / Tropijazz 82045*

Considering Humberto Ramirez's obvious talents, these two releases are somewhat frustrating. *Jazzproject* jumps all over the place, from easy-listening ballads, poppish pieces, and music obviously designed for potential airplay to two Afro-Cuban Jazz gems ("Pacifico" and "Cohesion") that contrast with the rest of the CD. Considering that the last two pieces include such players as Justo Almario, David Sanchez, pianists Edsel Gomez and Papo Lucca, Alex Acuña, and Giovanni Hidalgo, it is rather unfortunate that the remainder of the disc is mostly pretty lightweight. *Canciones de Amor* is much more consistent if not much more satisfying. Ramirez plays a set of ballads backed by a large string section and a four-piece rhythm section (with Luis Marin on keyboards). The tempos are all quite slow, nothing unexpected occurs, and Ramirez often sounds like Herb Alpert or Chuck Mangione on a very lazy day. He is certainly capable of much more than this pleasant background music!

LOUIS RAMIREZ

b. Feb. 24, 1938, New York, NY, d. June 7, 1993, Jamaica, NY

Louis Ramirez spent periods of his life as a percussionist (particularly timbales), pianist, vibraphonist, and, most important, arranger and composer. He was so productive at one point that he was called "El Genio de la Salsa" ("The Genius of Salsa"). Ramirez studied classical music as a young child, until 1945 when, after hearing records by Carmen Cavallero and Noro Morales, he decided that he wanted to play Latin music instead. Ramirez was inspired to start playing marimba and vibes in the early 1950s after seeing a Lionel Hampton concert. In 1953, when he was just 15, he was already playing with pianist Gil Suarez and Johnny Pacheco. Ramirez's first important job was as the vibraphonist with the Joe Loco Quintet (1956-59), making his recording debut with Loco in 1957. Ramirez learned to play timbales by taking lessons from Willie Bobo, and in 1959 he organized an Afro-Cuban Jazz octet, leading his first album (*Jazz Espagnole* for the Alegre label) the following year. Ramirez played drums for Charlie Palmieri (1965-66), was in the Joe Cuba Septet during 1967-68, and led his own groups. Along the way he also played with Vicentico Valdés, Sabu Martinez, and the Latin Jazz Quintet, recording with Tito Rodriguez in the early 1970s. However, it was as an inventive arranger that Ramirez primarily worked in the 1970s and '80s, becoming a staff producer with the Fania label in 1975. Ramirez, who considered Tito Puente to be an influence on his writing, produced, arranged, and occasionally played on countless albums, including dates led by Puente, Larry Harlow, Willie Colón, the Fania All-Stars, Willie Rosario, Ismael Miranda, Ray Barretto, Celia Cruz, Rubén Blades, Johnny Pacheco, and many others, recording *A Tribute to Cal Tjader* in 1987 with a group that included Paquito D'Rivera and Mario Rivera. Louis Ramirez was quite active up until his death from a heart attack in 1993 when he was 55.

EMIL RICHARDS

b. Sept. 2, 1932, Hartford, CT

A very valuable studio musician who mastered not only vibes, xylophone, and the standard percussion instruments but such exotic devices as the crotales, the cuica, wind chimes, and the waterphone (!), Emil Richards can play virtually all genres of music and has often been featured in Afro-Cuban settings. Born Emilio Radocchia, he studied xylophone from the age of six. Richards attended the Hartford School of Music (1949-52) and played percussion in the local symphony orchestra (1950-54). During his military service he played in an army band in Japan (1954-55) and worked with pianist Toshiko Akiyoshi. In 1956 Richards moved to Los Angeles, where he has been a busy studio musician on and off ever since.

Outside of the studio, some of Richards' most important musical associations have been with the George Shearing Quintet (1956-59), flutist-altoist Paul Horn (1959-62), trumpeter Shorty Rogers (1963-65), trumpeter Don Ellis (1964-69), Roger Kellaway's Cello Quartet (1970-74), and Frank Zappa (1975-77). Among the many other artists who Richards has recorded with are drummer Louis Bellson, the popular group Shadowfax, Dizzy Gillespie, Nat King Cole, Ella Fitzgerald,

Peggy Lee, Henry Mancini, Mongo Santamaria, baritonist Gerry Mulligan, bassist Charles Mingus, singer Jimmy Witherspoon, tenor saxophonist John Klemmer, and Stan Kenton's Neophonic Orchestra, not to mention Elvis Presley, Frank Sinatra, and even The Monkees! Emil Richards, who recorded as a leader for Del Fi, Impulse (1965-66), and Interworld (1994-95), owns over 350 percussion instruments.

7 *Yazz per Favore / 1961 / Del Fi 71216*
8 *Luntana / Jan. 1996 / Interworld 923*

Emil Richards' "Yazz Band" is heard performing Afro-Cuban Jazz in the early '60s on *Yazz per Favore*. The group, comprising Richards, pianist Paul Moer, Al McKibbon, and three percussionists, interprets three originals, a trio of jazz standards, and a couple of Thelonious Monk tunes; highlights include "Friday the 13th," "Little Niles," and "Half and Half." Unfortunately the original liner notes are duplicated in microscopic fashion on this CD reissue (good luck reading them!), and the recording date is not given, an inexcusably lazy way to reissue enjoyable music.

Luntana, despite being 35 years later, is in a similar style. The highly appealing album has Richards (mostly on marimba and vibes) generally in the lead of the ensembles. The hornless date also includes Michael Lang or Dave Mackay on piano, Al McKibbon or Chuck Domanico on bass, drummer Joe Porcaro, and Luis Conte, Francisco Aguabella, and Efrain Toro on percussion. Highlights include "Well I Didn't" (based on Thelonious Monk's "Well You Needn't"), "Butter Jig Waltz" (which has Richards on the "rattle mallets"), "Little Sunflower," and "A Night in Tunisia."

HÉCTOR RIVERA

b. Jan. 26, 1933, New York, NY

One of the leaders of the "Latin soul," or boogaloo,

movement of the mid- to late 1960s, Héctor Rivera was important as a pianist, bandleader, and arranger. In 1943, after hearing a Machito record, he was motivated to start studying music, inspired particularly by the piano playing of Noro Morales. Rivera attended New York's Lecompte Academy of Music and played early on with José Rodriguez, Eddie Forestier, and Elmo Garcia's band (1951-52) before serving in the military during 1953-55. After his discharge, he studied arranging and composing with Gil Fuller (one of Dizzy Gillespie's top writers in the 1940s) and contributed arrangements for Orlando Marin. Rivera played with Alfredito Levy, Moncho Lena, and singer Mon Rivera.

In 1957 he recorded his debut as a leader, *Let's Cha Cha Chá,* using his own arrangements and many musicians drawn from Machito's orchestra. Despite its success, Rivera continued working as a sideman, with Arsenio Rodriguez, Joe Cuba, Vicentico Valdés' orchestra (1958-64), and Johnny Pacheco (1964-66), arranging for Ray Barretto's *Pachanga with Barretto* record (1961). Rivera's own Epic albums, *Tumba Que Tumba, Viva Rivera, Charanga and Pachanga,* and *Viva Rivera!,* earned him much recognition. He gained his greatest fame with 1966's *At the Party*; the title cut made the R&B top 30. Héctor Rivera also recorded for United Artists and Tico and continued arranging for many of the top Afro-Cuban Jazz performers (including Machito and Tito Puente) but was largely retired by the end of the 1970s.

MARIO RIVERA

b. July 22, 1939, Santo Domingo, Dominican Republic

A valuable saxophonist who has appeared on countless sessions in both Afro-Cuban Jazz and bebop settings, Mario Rivera is a skilled soloist on tenor, alto, baritone, soprano, and flute. Rivera started out playing rock in his native Santa Domingo. After he arrived in New York in 1961, he worked with Puerto Rican singer Joe Valle. His most significant musical associations through the years include Tito Rodriguez (1963-65), Machito, Sonny Stitt, Charlie Palmieri, Eddie Palmieri, Tipica '73, the George Coleman Octet, Dizzy Gillespie's United Nation Orchestra, Slide Hampton's Jazz Masters, the Afro Blue Band, Giovanni Hidalgo, Chico O'Farrill's Orchestra, and especially Tito Puente (with whom he worked on and off for decades). In addition, Mario Rivera occasionally leads the Salsa Refugees, a band whose goal is to mix Dominican Republic folk music with jazz.

CLAUDIO RODITI

b. May 28, 1946, Rio de Janeiro, Brazil

One of the finest trumpeters to emerge from Brazil, Claudio Roditi is equally at home playing bebop-oriented jazz, Brazilian music, or Afro-Cuban. His father played guitar and violin, and Roditi started out on piano and bongos when he was six, switching to trumpet four years later. He worked as a studio musician in Brazil, eventually coming to the United States to study at Berklee (1970-71). Roditi was based in the Boston area for several years (including working with drummer Alan Dawson) before moving to New York City in 1976. He has since played with the who's who of jazz, including tenor saxophonist Charlie Rouse, Herbie Mann, altoist Bob Mover, Dizzy Gillespie's United Nation Orchestra (1988-92), and Slide Hampton's Jazz Masters (starting in 1993), in addition to teaming up often with Paquito D'Rivera. Claudio Roditi, who has led and recorded with his own groups frequently through the years (for the Greene Street, Milestone, Uptown, Candid, Mons, RTE, and Reservoir labels), has also recorded as a sideman with Dave Valentin, harmonica player Hendrik Meurkens, tenors Jimmy Heath and Ricky Ford, altoists Greg Abate and Gary Bartz, baritonist Nick Brignola, singers Mark Murphy and Jeannie

Bryson, guitarist Jim Hall, pianists Horace Silver, Manfredo Fest and McCoy Tyner, the Arkadia Jazz All-Stars, and others.

4 *Gemini Man / Mar. 7-22, 1988 / Milestone 9158*

6 *Slow Fire / Apr. 17-18, 1989 / Milestone 9175*

A good case can be put up that Claudio Roditi's recordings, which are generally either Brazilian-oriented or strictly straightahead hard bop, do not belong in a book on Afro-Cuban music. However, because of his longtime association with Paquito D'Rivera and his ability to sound quite creative in a variety of contexts (including as a sideman in Afro-Cuban groups), it was decided to include Roditi's dates as a leader. Roditi's *Gemini Man* is a mostly easy-listening Brazilian jazz set in which he takes passable but not particularly memorable vocals on several of the eight selections. Roditi is joined by pianist Roger Kellaway, Daniel Freiberg on synthesizers, bassist Nilson Matta, either Ignacio Berroa or Akira Tana on drums, and percussionist Rafael Cruz. A pleasant outing mostly featuring Roditi's originals but largely forgettable overall. *Slow Fire,* which also has three Roditi vocals (on two of those songs he does not even play trumpet), is generally on a higher level, helped by the inclusion of Danilo Perez on piano. Most of the songs are again by Roditi, but this time the music mixes Brazilian rhythms with touches of Afro-Cuban Jazz, and both trombonist Jay Ashby and tenor saxophonist Ralph Moore have their spots. A surprise is Roditi's effective piano playing on "Lullaby for Kristen."

7 *Two of Swords / Sept. 24-25, 1990 / Candid 79504*

8 *Milestones / Nov. 13-14, 1990 / Candid 79515*

7 *Metropole Orchestra / 1994-1995 / Mons 874-767*

9 *Free Wheelin': The Music of Lee Morgan / July 29, 1994 / Reservoir 136*

7 *Samba—Manhattan Style / May 12-13, 1995 / Reservoir 139*

8 *Double Standards / Sept. 30, 1996-Oct. 1, 1996 / Reservoir 148*

On *Two of Swords,* the trumpeter is heard with what is called his "Brazilian Quintet" (Jay Ashby, pianist Edward Simon, bassist Nislon Matta, and drummer Duduka Da Fonseca) and his "Jazz Quartet" (Danilo Perez, bassist David Finck, and drummer Akira Tana). In reality, both groups are similar in style, with hints of Brazilian and Cuban music but mostly playing advanced hard bop. Eight of the 11 concise selections (all but "Airegin," "Secret Love," and Dizzy Gillespie's "Con Alma") are Roditi's, and he plays quite well, melodic yet often burning, equally inspired by both rhythm sections.

Milestones teams Roditi with his occasional employer Paquito D'Rivera in a quintet also including pianist Kenny Barron, bassist Ray Drummond, and drummer Ben Riley. Although Roditi usually plays Afro-Cuban Jazz in D'Rivera's group, this outing (recorded live at Birdland in 1990) is strictly hard bop, with lengthy renditions of five jazz standards (including "I'll Remember April," "But Not for Me," and "Mr. P.C.") plus Roditi's "Brussels in the Rain." Roditi and D'Rivera are both in fine form, uplifting the tunes with their spirit and constant creativity.

On the Mons release, the trumpeter (doubling on flügelhorn) is in the spotlight throughout his meeting with Rob Pronk's Metropole Orchestra, a huge ensemble from the Netherlands. The repertoire balances ballads with medium-tempo pieces, and Roditi (who contributes a few brief, wordless vocals) rises to the occasion, playing quite well on such numbers as "Softly As in a Morning Sunrise," "Airegin," "Speak Low," and "The Night Has a Thousand Eyes."

One of the finest of all Claudio Roditi albums is

Free Wheelin', a tribute to Lee Morgan, his main influence. Roditi, who is joined by baritonist Nick Brignola, Andres Boiarsky on tenor, pianist Mark Soskin, bassist Buster Williams, and drummer Chip White, performs nine of Morgan's compositions plus "A Night in Tunisia." Each of the musicians sounds inspired, with the highlights including "The Sidewinder," "Ceora," and "Speedball." *Samba—Manhattan Style* alternates tunes by Roditi and altoist Gary Abate with obscurities; the only standards on this non Afro-Cuban set are "Footprints," Jobim's "Triste" (which has the trumpeter's lone vocal of the set), and Duke Ellington's "In a Sentimental Mood". Roditi is in typically fine form in a quintet with pianist Helio Alves, bassist John Lee, drummer Duduka Da Fonseca, and either Abate, the tenor or soprano of Andres Boiarsky, or trombonist Jay Ashby. *Double Standards* features the two sides of Claudio Roditi. His renditions of Brazilian tunes (such as "A Felicidade," "Desafinado," which he sings, and "Conceicao") use Boiarsky on tenor, guitarist Marty Ashby, and a Brazilian rhythm section. The straightahead songs (including "Bye Bye Blackbird," "Are You Real," "Bird Like," and "So What") match Roditi with 21-year-old tenor Jimmy Greene, pianist Gil Goldstein, bassist David Finck, and drummer Chip White. Although it is a pity that no Afro-Cuban tunes were also included, the enjoyable set of music is full of spirit and well worth exploring.

LPs to Search For:
Claudio Roditi's debut as a leader is the obscure *Red on Red* (Greene Street 2001), from 1984, which features the trumpeter on some of his originals plus songs by fellow Brazilians (including Ivan Lins, Milton Nascimento, and Edu Lobo); his sidemen include Paquito D'Rivera and Jorge Dalto (on synthesizers). *Claudio* (Uptown 27.27), from the following year, is a straightahead session with Slide Hampton, Howard Kimbo on tenor, pianist

Mulgrew Miller, bassist Rufus Reid, and drummer Akira Tana. Don Sickler's arrangements and the strong playing from the musicians produce swinging versions of "The Eternal Triangle," "My Romance," and Kenny Dorham's "Karioka."

ALFREDO RODRIGUEZ
b. 1936, Havana, Cuba

A pianist, percussionist, singer, and bandleader, Alfredo Rodriguez has perhaps made his strongest contribution in Europe, where he has been based since 1983. He began singing at five and started classical piano lessons at seven. Trained as a concert pianist, he moved to New York in 1960 and soon rediscovered his Cuban roots, switching to Latin music from classical. Rodriguez played with many groups during the next 20 years, including the Vicentico Valdés Orchestra, La Sonora Matancera, Belisario López, Rey Roig's Conjunto Sensacion (with whom he made his recording debut on the Tropical label's *Swing '65*), Willie Rosario, the Joe Cuba Sextet, Justo Betancourt, José Fajardo (1974-76), Patato Valdés, and Tito Puente (1981). Rodriguez, who also recorded with Dizzy Gillespie, has been a major part of the European continent's Latin jazz scene ever since he moved overseas, often leading his own groups.

8 *Cuba Linda / May 1996 / Hannibal / Rykodisc 1399*

Pianist Alfredo Rodriguez returned to Cuba to record this continually colorful set. Jesus Alemany's exciting trumpet sparks "Tumbao a Peruchin," there is some spirited singing on "Cuba Linda" by Gregorio Hernández and a coro, Rodriguez interacts with two violins and flutist Eduard Rubio on a beautiful version of "Vuelvo a Tu Lado" (better-known as "What a Difference a Day Makes"), and "Canto de Palo" has one of Rodriguez's most adventurous and finest piano solos. The second half of the program is not at quite the same height of inspiration, but each selection has its moments. Throughout, Rodriguez shows that he is a superior improviser.

ARSENIO RODRIGUEZ

b. Aug. 30, 1911, Guira de Macurije,
Matanzas, Cuba, d. Dec. 30, 1970,
Los Angeles, CA

Arsenio Rodriguez, a prolific composer who wrote nearly 200 songs, including several standards, was also a master of the tres, a percussionist, and a bandleader who made many contributions to Latin music. The descendent of Congolese slaves, Rodriguez was permanently blinded at the age of three when he was kicked in the face by a horse. He would later be called "El Ciego Maravilloso" ("The Marvelous Blind One"). Despite his handicap, he played a variety of instruments as a child, particularly percussion instruments and the tres. Rodriguez started composing as a teenager and in the early 1930s put together El Sexteto Boston, which lasted until 1937. That year he joined trumpeter José Interain's Septeto Bellamar, and a few of his compositions were recorded by Miguelito Valdés with Orquesta Casino de la Playa.

In 1940 Rodriguez took the standard septeto format (trumpet, guitar, tres, bass, bongos, maracas, and clavés) and added conga, piano, and a second (and later third) trumpet to the ensemble, largely inventing the conjunto, which immediately became popular. Up until then the conga was rarely used in Cuban music because of its African origin and was played mostly in street carnivals. Rodriguez was also among the first in Cuban music to feature improvised vocals by the lead singer over a repeated chorus or vamp (a device also used to back trumpet, tres, and piano solos), and he was one of the first to utilize mambo rhythms.

In the 1940s Rodriguez wrote quite a few Cuban standards, including "A Belen le Toca Ahora," "La Yuca de Catalina," "Juventud

Amaliana," and the bolero "La Vida Es un Sueño" ("Life Is but a Dream"). The last was composed after he came to New York in late 1946 in hopes of having his sight restored only to find out that his case was hopeless. Before returning to Cuba, Rodriguez made several recordings, including with Chano Pozo. In 1952, Rodriguez moved permanently to the United States, living for years in New York. He continued writing popular numbers (including "La Gente del Bronx" and "Como se Goza en el Barrio"), and, although he never caught on in New York at the level he had in Cuba, Rodriguez worked steadily. He recorded as a leader fairly frequently during the 1950s and '60s, was a key sideman on Sabu Martinez's *Palo Congo* recording in 1957, and experimented with the instrumentation of his band, sometimes adding saxophones. His last recording was in 1968, two years before his death from pneumonia at the age of 59. Arsenio Rodriguez, who recorded for RCA from the mid-1940s through 1951, made a series of records in the United States for SMC, Epic, Tico, Bang, and Ansonia.

7 *Con Su Conjunto y Chano Pozo, Machito &*
Orchestra / Feb. 7, 1947-1949 / Musica
Latina 55019

This CD has historic music featuring Arsenio Rodriguez with three different groups. Two of the sessions (six songs) were actually from two of the three dates led by Chano Pozo in early 1947, and these titles feature Rodriguez's tres pretty prominently; other participants include singers Marcelino Guerra and Tito Rodriguez plus many of the key players of Machito's orchestra. The other dozen selections are by Rodriguez's conjunto from 1949, a ten-piece group with three trumpets (including Chocolate Armenteros), pianist Lili Martinez, and vocals by Carlos Ramirez and René Scull. Strangely enough, Rodriguez's tres is much more minor on these numbers, and he composed only two of the

12 tunes. The generally interesting historic music is not as jazz-oriented as would be expected. The Pozo titles are also available on a CD (reviewed under the conguero's name), which actually includes some better titles by Rodriguez's band (from 1948 and 1953).

BOBBY RODRIGUEZ

b. East Los Angeles, CA

An inspiring jazz educator and an exciting conductor, Bobby Rodriguez is a superior trumpeter, influenced by Lee Morgan and Freddie Hubbard. When he was nine, he saw Harry James play on television and immediately knew what he wanted to do with his life. Rodriguez began on the trumpet the following year, and at 14 he was already playing professionally. He was in his high school concert jazz band in the 1960s and was set to sign a contract with Pacific Jazz but was drafted into the Army. After his discharge, Rodriguez studied at Rio Hondo College and Cal State University, Long Beach, spending time working as a disc jockey at Los Angeles' jazz station, KBCA (1969). He toured with the R&B group the Brothers Johnson and has since worked with many top jazz and Afro-Cuban performers in the Los Angeles area, including Lalo Schifrin, Ray Charles, Herbie Hancock, Gerald Wilson's big band, trumpeter Don Ellis, Louie Bellson, Willie Bobo, Poncho Sanchez, and the Clayton-Hamilton Jazz Orchestra.

Rodriguez, who occasionally leads a big band formerly headed by the late trumpeter Bobby Bryant, has recorded as a leader for Sea Breeze, JVC, and his own Latin Jazz Productions label, in addition to appearing regularly with a combo. He has also produced two recordings by the HMA Salsa/Jazz Orchestra. As the enthusiastic director of jazz studies at the Los Angeles County High School of the Arts, Bobby Rodriguez continually introduces younger people to the Afro-Cuban Jazz music that he loves.

8 *Plays Duke Ellington / Apr. 21, 1995-Aug. 15, 1995 / Latin Jazz Productions 123*

9 *A Latin Jazz Christmas / June 9-10, 1997 / JVC 7504*

7 *Latin Jazz Explosion / 1999 / Latin Jazz Productions 124*

The always-enthusiastic Bobby Rodriguez is well featured on each of these releases, playing trumpet in a hard bop style that is also inspired by the Afro-Cuban Jazz pioneers. In 1994 he was invited to play a set for the Los Angeles chapter of the Duke Ellington Society, and he discovered that, by making just a few adjustments, Duke's music sounds quite natural being interpreted as Afro-Cuban Jazz. For the resulting album, *Plays Duke Ellington*, Rodriguez is joined by pianist Serge Kasimoff, bassist Jonathan Pintoff, drummer Russ Henry, and three percussionists. Their versions of such songs as "It Don't Mean a Thing," "Don't Get Around Much Anymore," and "Caravan" sound fresh and lively; Rodriguez contributed one original, "El Duke."

Bobby Rodriguez noticed in the mid-1990s that there did not seem to be any Latin Jazz Christmas albums, so he rectified the situation with his own delightful effort, *A Latin Jazz Christmas*. Joined by the same rhythm section that was on his *Duke Ellington* set plus a trio of percussionists, Rodriguez tackles a variety of Yuletide favorites, often jamming over a vamp or altered chords after stating the melody. In addition, he contributes "Es la Navidad," which he performs (and sings) in both an English version (as "It's Time for Christmas") and a Spanish version. Rodriguez's transformations of such songs as "Have Yourself a Merry Little Christmas," "Jingle Bells," and "Silver Bells" are quite fun, making this a highly recommended disc.

Latin Jazz Explosion has some particularly strong playing by Rodriguez on "Birdland" and "I Remember Clifford" and fine backup work from local musicians. However, the trumpeter's three vocals, which do their best to be inspirational to kids (particularly "East L.A. Blues" and "East L.A. Rasta"), are a bit tiring to hear a second or third time and weigh the set down a little. Next time, someone should record Bobby Rodriguez with his big band!

LPs to Search For:
Bobby Rodriguez's debut as a leader, *Tell an Amigo* (Sea Breeze 2030), from 1986, finds him utilizing different instrumentation on each of the seven songs, three of which are his originals. Rodriguez, who also performs Lee Morgan's "The Double-Up," a Latinized Brahms lullaby, "I Had the Craziest Dream," and a mariachi theme, is assisted by several horn players (including Justo Almario on tenor and flute, and trombonist Art Velasco) and shows that he already had a mature and enthusiastic sound at this early stage of his career.

TITO RODRIGUEZ

b. Jan. 4, 1923, San Juan, Puerto Rico, d. Feb. 28, 1973, New York, NY

In the 1950s the "big three" of Afro-Cuban Jazz and mambos were Machito, Tito Puente, and Tito Rodriguez. So competitive were "the two Titos" that they often had serious fights over their billing at New York's Palladium. Although Rodriguez generally lost, he is still considered one of the most significant (if often overlooked) bandleaders of the era.

Like Machito, Tito Rodriguez was a singer who also played maracas on his band's instrumentals. After working locally in Puerto Rico, in 1939 (when he was 16) Rodriguez moved to live with his brother (singer Johnny Rodriguez) in New York City. He performed with his sibling's band, Conjunto Siboney, and made his recording debut in February 1940. Rodriguez picked up important experience singing with Cuarteto Caney (1940), Enric Madriguera (1941), and Xavier Cugat (1942),

where he replaced Miguelito Valdés. After serving in the U.S. Army (1943-44), he performed with Noro Morales (1945), Eddie LaBarron and José Curbelo (1946-47). Rodriguez also recorded with Chano Pozo, Arsenio Rodriguez, and Machito.

After leaving Curbelo, Rodriguez began his bandleading career. He headed a quintet called the Mambo Devils during 1947-48 and soon expanded his group to an octet. After signing with Tico, he had a hit recording with "La Renta," and his group grew into a big band. Rodriguez would lead his orchestra until 1965, recording not only for Tico but for RCA (1953-56) and United Artists (1960-62). His bigger hits included "Vuela la Paloma," "Cuando, Cuando," "Cara de Payaso," "Mama Guela," and "Inolvidable" (which sold over a million copies), and he was a major attraction for 15 years. As with Tito Puente, Rodriguez's music spanned from what would later be called Salsa and Latin dance music to boppish jazz. Victor Paz was his lead trumpeter for a time, Eddie Palmieri was his pianist, Mario Rivera had a stint on tenor, and his *Live at Birdland '63* LP featured tenors Zoot Sims and Al Cohn, valve trombonist Bob Brookmeyer, and flügelhornist Clark Terry. Rodriguez even learned to play vibes during his Palladium era so as to keep up with Puente.

After breaking up his band in 1965, Rodriguez returned to Puerto Rico in 1966, formed an octet, and starred on a television series. He moved to Miami in the late '60s and founded TR Records in 1971. Stricken with leukemia, Tito Rodriguez performed his last concert at Madison Square Garden in New York with Machito, just 26 days before his death in 1973 at the age of 50.

9 *Tito Tito Tito / 1964 / Palladium 139*
8 *Big Band Latino / 1968 / Palladium 117*
7 *In Puerto Azul, Venezuela / Palladium 148*

Although this trio of CDs does not bother listing

the dates or the personnel and the liner notes (such as they are) are microscopic, they are worthy re-issues of LPs probably from the 1960s. *Tito Tito Tito,* which was originally released by United Artists, has Rodriguez leading a scaled-down group consisting of his very impressive trumpet section (Paz, Tony Cofresi, David González, and Emilion Reales), a percussion-heavy rhythm section, and vocalists. Hernández and Cachao are again prominent, with the bassist saluted on "Descarga Cachao." Tito's singing is superior throughout the set, particularly on the slower material, most notably "Ya Lo Puedes Decir." *Big Band Latino* starts out with "Esta Es Mi Orquesta," a Spanish equivalent of Stan Kenton's "This Is an Orchestra," in which Tito Rodriguez (in Spanish) talks about his music and introduces the members of his band as each plays short spots on a basic theme. It does give brief glimpses of the impressive sidemen in the orchestra (which include pianist René Hernández and Cachao). The other six selections are concise but purposeful, have some group vocals but no solos from Rodriguez, and are most notable for a very impressive trumpet section that is led and inspired by Victor Paz.

For *In Puerto Azul, Venezuela* the balance is upset a bit, with the full emphasis being on Rodriguez's singing and the orchestra almost entirely relegated to an accompanying role. Still, the music is colorful and spirited, with Tito heard in prime form. But a complete reissue of Tito Rodriguez's most significant recordings of the 1950s and '60s is long overdue.

MICHELE ROSEWOMAN

b. Mar. 19, 1953, Oakland, CA

Best known for her adventurous piano playing on dates that range from post-bop to free funk (M-Base), Michele Rosewoman is included in this book because she has led the 12-piece Latin-oriented

New Yor-Uba big band since the mid-1980s, an ensemble that amazingly has yet to make a recording.

Rosewoman came from a musical family in which her parents ran a small record store. She started playing piano when she was six, and as a teenager she studied with pianist Ed Kelly. In addition, she studied congas. After working locally, Rosewoman moved in 1977 to New York, where at first she was a piano tuner and a music teacher for the New York City Parks Department. But soon she was playing music regularly with both avant-garde players (including violinist Billy Bang, altoists Oliver Lake, Greg Osby, Steve Coleman, Julius Hemphill, and Carlos Ward, bassist Reggie Workman, and drummer Ralph Peterson) and Latin bands (Los Kimy, Daniel Ponce, Celia Cruz, Paquito D'Rivera, and Chocolate Armenteros). In addition to heading New Yor-Uba, Michelle Rosewoman has led her quintet Quintessence and recorded stimulating sessions for Soul Note, Enja, Evidence, and Blue Note. But when will New Yor-Uba finally appear on records?

8 *Quintessence / Jan. 27-28, 1987 / Enja 5039*

7 *Contrast High / July 1988 / Enja 79607*

8 *Occasion to Rise / Sept. 13-15, 1990 / Evidence 22042*

9 *Spirit / July 9, 1994 / Blue Note 36777*

Michelle Rosewoman's debut as a leader was 1984's *The Source* for Soul Note. Although she has recorded several impressive discs since, she has not yet been given an opportunity to really display her interests in Cuban rhythms. *Quintessence* teams her with two of the top leaders in the M-Base movement (altoist Steve Coleman and Greg Osby on alto and soprano) along with bassist Anthony Cox and drummer Terri Lyne Carrington. Although the improvising is quite advanced, there is none of the usual free funk rhythms associated with the M-Base players. The solos and ensembles are outstanding and quite original, having a logic of their own far beyond bebop. *Contrast High,* which has Osby, tenor saxophonist Gary Thomas, bassist Lonnie Plaxico, drummer Cecil Brooks III, and Eddie Bobe on bongos, is funkier in spots and denser rhythmically as the group interprets nine of Rosewoman's complex originals.

Occasion to Rise is a mostly straightahead outing for the pianist, in a trio setting with bassist Rufus Reid and drummer Ralph Peterson. The music is never overly safe, because Rosewoman is well acquainted with the innovations of the avant-garde, and her interest in African and Cuban music can be felt here and there; Reid in particular also stretches himself. The pianist sings on "We Are" (one of her five originals) and comes up with fresh statements on John Coltrane's "Lazy Bird," Charles Mingus' "Weird Nightmare," and Lee Morgan's catchy "Nite Flite." *Spirit* is Michele Rosewoman's best all-round outing as a pianist. Playing in a trio with bassist Kenny Davis and drummer Gene Jackson, she sings one number ("For Agayu") that is normally performed by New Yor-Uba and also vocalizes on a gospel ballad "Spirit." Otherwise the emphasis is on her piano playing, where she shows off the influences of Herbie Hancock (particularly on his "Dolphin Dance"), McCoy Tyner, and Cecil Taylor while sounding quite original overall. In addition to her five diverse songs, of particular interest is Rosewoman's colorful transformation of "When Sunny Gets Blue."

GONZALO RUBALCABA

b. May 27, 1963, Havana, Cuba

Gonzalo Rubalcaba is one of the current giants of Afro-Cuban Jazz, a brilliant pianist whose mastery of polyrhythms and dense chord voicings (along with a lyrical side) make him quite notable.

Rubalcaba's grandfather founded a music school that was quite significant in the 1930s; his father, who played violin, saxophones, and especially piano, led the Charanga Tipica Nacional de Conciertos. Rubalcaba studied classical piano extensively from 1971-83 (including at the Havana Conservatory). He worked with Orquesta Cubana de Musica Moderna during 1982-84, toured France and Africa with the Orquesta Aragon in 1983, and also played piano with Los Van Van (1984-87). Rubalcaba formed the Grupo Projecto in 1985 (although it had existed informally as early as 1978) and visited Europe often, even if it would be quite a few years before he was able to play in the United States. In 1986 Rubalcaba met bassist Charlie Haden, who sang his praises and helped arrange his appearances at the Montreal and Montreux festivals, recording *Discovery* (1990) and *The Blessing* (1991) with him. By 1990 the pianist (who had clearly learned from the playing of Herbie Hancock and Chick Corea but always sounded quite original) had been discovered by the jazz world, and his records began to be released on Blue Note. Finally, during 1993-94 he became free to appear in the United States, touring with his quartet Cuarteto Cubano. Since that time, Gonzalo Rubalcaba has had a higher profile in the States, recorded frequently (including with Memo Acevedo, Bob Belden, Jane Bunnett's Spirits of Havana, bassist Ron Carter, Charlie Haden, Joe Lovano, and Tony Martinez plus as a leader for Messidor and Blue Note) and gained recognition as one of jazz's finest pianists.

7 *Live in Havana / Feb. 1986 / Messidor 15830*

8 *Mi Gran Pasion / July 1987 / Messidor 15999*

9 *Discovery / July 15, 1990 / Blue Note 95478*

10 *The Blessing / May 12-15, 1991 / Blue Note 97197*

©Susan Rosmarin

Michele Rosewoman, an inventive pianist who deserves to have her New Yor-Uba big band recorded.

9 *Images / Aug. 24-25, 1991 / Blue Note 99492*

Prior to his being discovered by American jazz fans and having his recordings put out by Blue Note, Gonzalo Rubalcaba recorded three sets (including the electric-oriented *Giraldilla*) that have since been made available by the German Messidor company. *Live in Havana* features the 1986 version of Rubalcaba's Grupo Projecto, a septet with trumpeter Lazaro Cruz, both Manuel Varela and Rafael Carrasco on reeds, Felipe Cabrera playing the unusual double of electric bass and bassoon, drummer Horacio "El Negro" Hernández, and percussionist Roberto Vizcaino. Rubalcaba (who also plays electric piano for this project) and his musicians stretch out on five of his originals plus "On Green Dolphin Street" (which is listed as "Green Dolphin in the Street"). Although the pianist does not show as much restraint as he would by the late 1990s (his playing is frequently overpowering), his solos were already quite miraculous and distinctive at this early point.

Mi Gran Pasion features Rubalcaba's Grupo Projecto a year later, when trumpeter Reinaldo Meliana took the place of saxophonist Manuel Varela. For this set, Rubalcaba pays tribute to the music of his father's era and the style that was popular in Cuba in the 1950s. Five of the six selections are by the pianist, but he often quotes extensively from the music of the time period plus, on "Recordando a Tschaikowsky," classical themes. The colorful arrangements, the three skillful horns (who blend together quite well), and Rubalcaba's creative playing make this a highly recommended and delightful release.

The first Gonzalo Rubalcaba recording to be widely available in the United States was *Discovery*, a trio outing with bassist Charlie Haden and drummer Paul Motian recorded live at the 1990 Montreux Jazz Festival. Rubalcaba tears into "Well You Needn't" and "All the Things You Are," intro-

duces three of his better originals, and is quite sensitive on Haden's "First Song," never letting his impressive virtuosity overshadow his creative ideas. Rubalcaba teams up with Charlie Haden again and drummer Jack DeJohnette for *The Blessing*, a particularly exciting and well-conceived program. Highlights include "Besame Mucho," John Coltrane's "Giant Steps," Ornette Coleman's "The Blessing," and an unusual transformation of Bill Evans' "Blue in Green." Three months later, Rubalcaba collaborated with DeJohnette and John Patitucci (on acoustic bass) for *Images*. This superior live set from the 1991 Mt. Fuji Jazz Festival also has a wide-ranging repertoire, with originals from each of the musicians, John Lennon's "Imagine," a remake of "Giant Steps," and an explosive version of "Autumn Leaves."

7 *Suite 4 Y 20 / May 7-12, 1992 / Blue Note 80054*

7 *Rapsodia / Nov. 15-21, 1992 / Blue Note 28264*

8 *Imagine / May 14, 1993-June 24, 1994 / Blue Note 30491*

8 *Diz / Dec. 14-15, 1993 / Blue Note 30490*

6 *Antiguo / June 1995-July 1996 / Blue Note 37717*

7 *Inner Voyage / Nov. 23-25, 1998 / Blue Note 99241*

Having recorded his last three albums with American all-stars, Rubalcaba had a chance on *Suite 4 Y 20* to document his regular quartet of the period (trumpeter Reynaldo Melian, electric bassist Felipe Cabrera, and drummer Julio Barreto), with Charlie Haden guesting on four of the 13 selections. The pianist performs some superior tunes from other Cuban composers, five of his own originals, "Perfidia," "Love Letters," the Beatles' "Here, There and Everywhere," and Haden's "Our

The Wayne Knight Collection/Photo: Shigero Uchiyama

Gonzalo Rubalcaba, a true piano virtuoso.

Spanish Love Song." The renditions are strong, although Melian does not show much warmth in his tone. The same personnel (without Haden) is heard on *Rapsodia,* which was recorded in Japan. Rubalcaba, who makes some rare appearances on this CD doubling on electric piano, contributed all seven selections (including "Tributo," which was written in honor of the late Dizzy Gillespie) except the bebop standard "Moose the Mooche."

The music on *Imagine* is taken from three sep-arate occasions. The haunting "First Song" is all that was released from a trio concert with its com-poser, Charlie Haden, and Jack DeJohnette (although the rather odd liner notes make it seem as if the entire set is from this New York performance), there are three unaccompanied piano solos (includ-ing an introspective exploration of John Lennon's "Imagine") and also three quartet pieces (with Melian, Cabrera, and Barreto at a Los Angeles con-cert) from Rubalcaba's 1994 tour of the United

States. If there are any doubts that Gonzalo Rubalcaba was a giant with limitless potential, this CD can serve as evidence.

Dizzy Gillespie was an early supporter of Rubalcaba, so *Diz* is a tribute by the pianist to the great innovator. Although Rubalcaba (in a trio with bassist Ron Carter and drummer Julio Barreto) sticks on *Diz* to bebop standards, only four of the songs (including "Woody 'n You" and "A Night in Tunisia") were actually composed by Gillespie, a few ("Donna Lee," Bud Powell's "Bouncing with Bud," Charles Mingus' "Smooch") were never actually played by Dizzy, and the music has been greatly updated. No matter, the spirit of Gillespie is felt. And rather than merely recreate the past, Rubalcaba takes the opportunity to come up with fresh and creative statements.

Antiguo is a very different type of Rubalcaba record, one in which he emphasizes the use of synthesizers. Sometimes the results are memorable (particularly "Eshun Agwe," which means "Party"), but at other times the results are merely haunting mood music. Rubalcaba and his longtime quartet (Melian, Cabrera, and Barretto) are joined in various spots by the voices of Maridalia Hernández and Lazaro Ros, percussionist Giovanni Hidalgo, and violinist Dagoberto González. The influence of Chick Corea is strong in some of the selections and on Rubalcaba's sounds on synthesizers, but the diverse yet mostly quite intriguing music is much more rhythmically complex. Not essential, but worth a few listens.

Inner Voyage is a bit unusual for Rubalcaba in that most of the music is introspective (if not laid back) ballads, all originals by the pianist other than "Here's That Rainy Day" and "Caravan." On all but one selection, he is heard in a trio with bassist Jeff Chambers and drummer Ignacio Berroa. The emphasis is on Rubalcaba's more thoughtful side, and he leaves more space than he would have earlier in his career. The one exception is the uptempo "Blues Lundvall" (named after record company executive Bruce Lundvall), which has a raging tenor solo by guest Michael Brecker. A tasteful effort from a masterful and still-developing pianist.

HILTON RUIZ
b. May 29, 1952, New York, NY

A brilliant pianist equally skilled in hard bop and Latin settings, Hilton Ruiz has been one of the leading soloists in Afro-Cuban Jazz since the 1970s. Born of Puerto Rican parents, Ruiz was classically trained from a very young age and played at Carnegie Recital Hall when he was just eight. He started out working in Latin bands as a teenager, including spending a year with Ismael Rivera. Since 1970, Ruiz (who took extensive lessons from the great pianist Mary Lou Williams) has gigged and recorded with many of jazz's and Latin music's top greats, including tenor saxophonist Frank Foster (1970), trumpeter Joe Newman, Cal Massey's big band (1971-72), tenors George Coleman, Joe Henderson, Pharoah Sanders, Archie Shepp, and Chico Freeman, trumpeters Freddie Hubbard and Clark Terry, altoists Jackie McLean and Greg Abate, Charles Mingus (1973), the remarkable Rahsaan Roland Kirk (1973-77), singers Betty Carter and Abbey Lincoln (1984-85), drummer Rashied Ali, Jerry González, Paquito D'Rivera, Tito Puente's Golden Latin Jazz All-Stars, the Afro Blue Band, Giovanni Hidalgo, Charlie Sepúlveda, J.P. Torres, the Tropijazz All-Stars, Steve Turre, Chucho Valdés, Dave Valentin, Mongo Santamaria, and the Mingus Big Band.

Hilton Ruiz has thus far led albums of his own for Inner City, Steeplechase, Storyville (starting in 1975), Stash, Novus/RCA, Freelance, Telarc, Candid, and RMM. A very valuable pianist!

8 *Something Grand / Oct. 14-15, 1986 / Novus 3011*

8 *El Camino / Oct. 15, 1987 / Novus 3024*

9 *Strut / Nov. 30, 1988-Dec. 1, 1988 / Novus 353*

Hilton Ruiz began his solo career recording for Inner City, SteepleChase, Storyville and Stash. His debut for Novus, *Something Grand*, finds him leading an all-star Afro-Cuban Jazz octet. With such top players as trumpeter Lew Soloff, Steve Turre, Sam Rivers (on tenor, soprano and flute), electric bassist Russell Blake, Ignacio Berroa, Daniel Ponce on conga, and Charlie Santiago on timbales, it is not surprising that the results are stirring and infectious, stretching the boundaries of Latin music a bit. Ruiz wrote all six tunes, and the music reflects the influence of McCoy Tyner and the pianist's Latin predecessors. *El Camino* uses Rivers and Soloff again, but this time Dick Griffin is in Turre's place, guitarist Rodney Jones and bassist Andy

González are assets, and drummer Steve Berrios is joined by Jerry González, Endel Dweno, and José Alexis Diaz on percussion. Once again Ruiz contributes most of the material (although "Come Dance with Me" is by Griffin), and the advanced post-bop Afro-Cuban Jazz is as stirring as the music on *Something Grand*; the nearly 15-minute "Eastern Vibrations" is actually quite free in spots.

Strut brings back the Soloff-Griffin-Rivers frontline along with Rodney Jones (who often comes close to stealing solo honors from Ruiz), while the rhythm section consists of Ruiz, electric bassist Francisco Centeno, drummer Robby Ameen, Steve Berrios on timbales, and Mongo Santamaria. The material is particularly strong on this set (including a fascinating transformation of Lee Morgan's famous "The Sidewinder"). Many of

©Susan Rosmarin

Pianist, Hilton Ruiz's string of recordings are among the finest Afro-Cuban Jazz sessions of the past 15 years.

the other tunes (originals from a variety of places) are catchy too, and the combination of the many very individual voices with the rhythms makes this set a real gem.

7 *Doin' It Right / Nov. 9-11, 1989 / Novus 3085*

9 *A Moment's Notice/ Feb. 25, 1991-Mar. 12, 1991 / Novus 3123*

8 *Manhattan Mambo / Apr. 28, 1992 / Telarc 83322*

8 *Heroes / Nov. 8-9, 1993 / Telarc 83338*

8 *Hands on Percussion / 1994-1995 / RMM 81483*

Although Daniel Ponce's conga is on some selections and Steve Berrios is on drums, most of the music on *Doin' It Right* is straightahead. Ruiz is also assisted by either Jimmy Rowser or (on the title track) Ruben Rodriguez on electric bass. Ornette Coleman's famous trumpeter Don Cherry is on a couple tracks, but his intonation is subpar, even on Ornette's "The Blessing." Ruiz is the star throughout, paying tribute to Thelonious Monk and Bud Powell, displaying the influence of McCoy Tyner, and shining on such numbers as "Stella by Starlight," "Shades of Thelonious," and "I Didn't Know What Time It Was."

It is back to Afro-Cuban Jazz on *A Moment's Notice.* Ruiz is joined by three powerful horn soloists (George Coleman, altoist Kenny Garrett, and Dave Valentin, whose flute solo on "Cuchi Cuchi" is one of his finest on record) plus the rhythm team of Andy González, Steve Berrios, Daniel Ponce, and Endel Dweno. Particularly fun are Latinized versions of two John Coltrane classics ("Moment's Notice" and "Naima") plus revivals of Mario Bauzá's "Mambo Inn" and Kenny Dorham's "Una Mas." A near-classic.

Although Hilton Ruiz switched labels in 1992, his Telarc dates are similar to his high-quality

efforts for Novus. For *Manhattan Mambo,* he is joined by such flexible players as Charlie Sepúlveda, David Sanchez, Papo Vazquez, Andy González, Ignacio Berroa, Steve Berrios (on timbales), Joe González (bongos), and Giovanni Hidalgo (conga). Other than Pérez Prado's "Mambo #5" and Coltrane's "Impressions," the repertoire consists of Ruiz's originals, including "Sure Thing," "Overtime Mambo," and "Giovanni Speaks." Everyone plays up to par on this enjoyable release. Heroes has the same personnel, except that Steve Turre is on trombone and there are guest appearances by Tito Puente (vibes on two numbers and timbales on a third) and Patato Valdés on congas. The music is often quite bop-oriented, with the highlights including Ruiz's "Sonny's Mood," "Little Suede Shoes," "Maiden Voyage," and "Con Alma"; this last is a duet by Ruiz and Sepúlveda.

For *Hands on Percussion*, his debut on RMM, Ruiz once again employed such top musicians as Sepúlveda, Vásquez, Sanchez (on three numbers), Valentin, González, Berroa, Berrios, and Puente (on three cuts) plus cameos for José D'Leon's tenor and flutist Peter Brainin. Four jazz standards (including such unlikely tunes as "Ornithology" and "Cotton Tail") alternate with five catchy group originals (three by Ruiz) for yet another successful mixture of jazz with Latin rhythms. If there is a certain sameness to these reviews of Hilton Ruiz's work, suffice it to say that every one of these CDs is highly recommended to fans of the idiom!

LPs to Search For:

Pianist Hilton Ruiz's first American date as a leader was *Cross Currents* (Stash 248), a now hard-to-find Latin-flavored release from 1984. He performs eight jazz standards (including "Stolen Moments," Charlie Parker's "Confirmation," and "Take the 'A' Train") with the assistance of bassist Major Holley, drummer Ed Blackwell, and percussionists Ray Barretto and Steve Berrios.

OTMARO RUIZ

b. 1965, Caracas, Venezuela

A powerful pianist who deserves to be much better known, Otmaro Ruiz fared quite well during his stint with Arturo Sandoval's group in the early 1990s (appearing on the recordings *Dreams Come True* and *The Latin Train*). Ruiz began as a classical guitarist when he was eight, switching to piano at 15. He was a musical director on television before moving to the United States. Since settling in the Los Angeles area, he has worked with cornetist Nat Adderley, drummer Billy Higgins, Paquito D'Rivera, Sandoval, Alex Acuña, Justo Almario, and bassist Larry Steen in addition to many local musicians. Surprisingly Otmaro Ruiz has led just one CD thus far, *Distant Friends,* for the Moo label.

RUMBA CLUB

Rumba Club was founded in 1986 by bassist Josh "Bermuda" Schwartzman. Based in Baltimore, Rumba Club performed regularly on the East Coast for nearly a decade before the group first recorded. Andy González discovered the band and has thus far produced their first three Palmetto recordings. The ensemble originally consisted of trumpeter Marc Weigel, altoist Paul Hannah, trombonist Craig Considine, pianist Tim Murphy, bassist Schwartzman, and percussionists Steve Bloom, Jim Hannah, and Willie Vazquez. By 1997 Alex Norris was on trumpet and there were four percussionists: Hannah, Vazquez, Rudy Morales, and Orlando Cotto. The only change in the personnel since then is that Sam "Seguito" Turner is in Vazquez's place. Rumba Club plays an infectious variety of Afro-Cuban Jazz with occasional Salsa singing.

8 *Desde la Capital / 1995 / Palmetto 2013*
8 *Mamacita / Jan. 6-7, 1997 / Palmetto 2027*
9 *Espiritista / Apr. 15-18, 1999 / Palmetto 2047*

Rumba Club's recording debut, *Desde la Capital* (which may be from as early as 1993), has two features for a coro but otherwise is full of high-quality hard bop-oriented solos over stirring rhythms. "It's You or No One," Herbie Hancock's "Maiden Voyage," "Moose the Mooche," and "Soul Eyes" are among the songs interpreted. The octet is augmented by several guests, including Andy González (who appears a little bit on each of the three releases) and two future band members: Rudy Morales and Alex Norris. *Mamacita* is the equal of Rumba Club's debut, consisting of obscurities plus rhythmic renditions of John Coltrane's "Countdown," "The Meaning of the Blues," Joe Henderson's title cut, "You Don't Know What Love Is," and Bobby Hutcherson's "Highway One." Of the three Rumba Club releases, *Espiritista* gets a slight edge, only because the group seems a little tighter and there is more of a balance between originals and standards (split almost evenly). In reality, if someone likes one of the Rumba Club CDs, they will like all three! Highlights of *Espiritista* include Wayne Shorter's "Children of the Night," Cedar Walton's "Mosaic," and the closing song, "Things Ain't What They Used to Be," although there is not a slow moment to be heard.

ANSELMO SACASAS

b. Nov. 23, 1912, Manzanillo, Cuba

One of Latin music's most popular pianists of the pre-Cubop era, Anselmo Sacasas was considered an important influence on Noro Morales. At the age of 16 Sacasas graduated from Manzanillo's National Music Conservatory and soon moved to Havana, where in 1929 he worked in the pit orchestra of the Gloria Theatre. In 1932 flutist Luis Carrillo taught Sacasas how to orchestrate music. After freelancing locally during 1933-36 (including with flutist Tata Pereira), Sacasas played with Los Hermanos Castro's band, contributing swinging arrangements. During the 1937-40 period he was with

Casino de la Playa, making eight recordings every two weeks, appearing regularly on the radio and at dance halls, and becoming famous in Cuba. Sacasas emerged as one of the first pianists to solo regularly with a Cuban band, because, before his rise, Cuban bands tended to emphasize guitars, vocals, percussion, and occasional flutes. "Babalu" was a hit recording for the band in 1939, and singer Miguelito Valdés was the Casino de la Playa's other main star. In April 1940, Sacasas and Valdés left Cuba for New York. While Valdés joined Xavier Cugat, Sacasas formed a group that at first played at Chicago's Colony Club, featuring the 17-year-old Tito Puente. In 1941 Sacasas' orchestra became the house band at La Conga Club in Manhattan, and the following year he switched to the La Martinique Club. His recording of "Koki Koka" in 1944 was quite popular.

During the height of his fame, Sacasas spent the 1947-50 period splitting his time between Miami and New York City. In 1950 he moved to Miami, where he became the musical director of the Hotel Fountainbleu and assumed a lower profile. Anselmo Sacasas spent 1963-76 in Puerto Rico as the artistic director of the Hotel San Juan and after retiring moved permanently to Miami.

BOBBY SANABRIA

b. June 2, 1957, Bronx, NY

A versatile conga player also skilled on drums, vibes, and other percussion instruments, Bobby Sanabria has been in strong demand ever since the early 1980s. He grew up in the South Bronx and studied at Berklee (1975-79), forming his own band (Ascension) in 1980; it still exists two decades later. As a sideman, among his many musical associations have been Marco Rizo (1980), Tito Puente (off and on during 1981-99), Mongo Santamaria (1982-84), Perico Ortiz (1986-87), Mario Bauzá (1987-93), Paquito D'Rivera, altoist Henry Threadgill (1988-89), Dizzy Gillespie, tenor saxo-

phonist Chico Freeman, Daniel Ponce, Ray Barretto, William Cepeda, altoist Charles McPherson, Michael Mossman, and even Xavier Cugat (1989-91). He has also worked actively in the studios and is on the soundtrack of *The Mambo Kings*.

Bobby Sanabria has taught drums and percussion at Mannes College of Music since 1990 and has thus far led recordings for Flying Fish and Arabesque. No matter what the situation, his playing adds fire, spirit, and enthusiasm to the proceedings.

9 *New York City Ache / 1993 / Flying Fish 70630*

8 *Afro-Cuban Dream . . . Live & in Clavé!!! / May 20, 1999 / Arabesque 149*

Bobby Sanabria conceived the wide-ranging *New York City Ache* as a tribute to his musical ancestors. Included are homages to the son, the rumba, storytelling, Thelonious Monk ("Blue Monk"), the Palladium, the mambo, the bolero, modern jazz (Joe Henderson's "Caribbean Fire Dance"), and the recently deceased Mario Bauzá ("Adios, Mario"). Intimate vocals alternate with strong Afro-Cuban Jazz performances, and the personnel (which varies from track to track) includes pianist Oscar Hernández, Lewis Kahn on violin and trombone, Tito Puente (who shares the stage with Sanabria on "Two Generations," a pair of duets for drums and timbales), altoist Gene Jefferson, pianist John di Martino, and Paquito D'Rivera, who plays clarinet on "Adios, Mario." A continually surprising and successful set.

Also a little surprising is the power of Sanabria's Afro-Cuban big band that is featured on the Arabesque disc, *Afro-Cuban Dream . . . Live & in Clavé!!!*. The 13 horns (trumpeter Michael Mossman is the biggest name) and six-piece rhythm section are joined by guest tenor John Stubblefield on three numbers and by Candido on congas during the closing cut, "Manteca." A few traditional chants open the live date, which includes a Jay Collins tenor feature on "Angel Eyes," a remake of Sanabria's "Adios, Mario," heated renditions of "Donna Lee" and "Manteca," and some recent originals. There is a great deal of joy to the performance, and Bobby Sanabria sounds very much in his element.

DAVID SANCHEZ

b. Sept. 3, 1968, Guaynabo, Puerto Rico

A talented soloist on tenor and soprano saxophones, David (pronounced dah-VEED) Sanchez can always be counted on to contribute fiery solos and add a Latin feel to every date. He started on conga when he was eight, switching to tenor at 11. Sanchez played Afro-Cuban music before discovering jazz. He attended the University of Puerto Rico, moved to New York in 1988, and attended Rutgers. Among the important musical associations he has had during the past dozen years have been those with Eddie Palmieri, Hilton Ruiz, Daniel Ponce, Paquito D'Rivera, bassist Larry Ridley (1989-90), Dizzy Gillespie's United Nation Orchestra, Gillespie's last regularly working combo (1991-92), the Philip Morris Superband, Slide Hampton's Jazz Masters, and Danilo Perez. Sanchez has led his own group since 1994 and recorded five discs thus far for Columbia. He has also recorded with many top jazz artists, including Gillespie, Ruiz, Perez, Roy Hargrove, Giovanni Hidalgo, Michael Philip Mossman, Claudio Roditi, Arturo Sandoval, Charlie Sepúlveda, Dave Valentin, Lalo Schifrin, pianists Kenny Drew Jr. and Kenny Barron, trombonist Slide Hampton, trumpeter Ryan Kisor, organist Barbara Dennerlein, drummers Roy Haynes and Leon Parker, the Mingus Big Band, and the Tropijazz All-Stars.

7 *The Departure / Nov. 23, 1993-Dec. 7, 1993 / Columbia 57848*

8 *Sketches of Dreams / Dec. 7-9, 1994 / Columbia 67021*

9 *Street Scenes / Feb. 12, 1996-Mar. 1, 1996 / Columbia 67627*

8 *Obsesion / Dec. 10, 1997-Jan. 9, 1998 / Columbia 69116*

7 *Melaza / Feb. 11-14, 2000 / Columbia 62085*

David Sanchez was 25 when he made his recording debut as a leader with *The Departure*. Joined on most selections by Danilo Perez, either Peter Washington or Andy González on bass, and drummer Leon Parker (with trumpeter Tom Harrell heard on three numbers), Sanchez performs originals written by either himself or Perez plus "Woody 'n You," "I'll Be Around," and Jimmy Heath's "CJ." Everyone plays as well as expected, and there is plenty of fire displayed. *Sketches of Dreams* is somewhat episodic. The first two numbers match Sanchez's tenor with trumpeter Roy Hargrove and percussionists Milton Cardona, Jerry González, and Leon Parker. However, the other selections are without Hargrove and only occasionally with percussion, with three songs played with a standard rhythm section. David Kikoski and Danilo Perez share the piano bench, and both take some fine solos. Sanchez (who switches to soprano on two songs) excels at both the Latin romps and such ballads as "Tu y Mi Cancion" and "It's Easy to Remember," sometimes hinting at Joe Henderson and Stanley Turrentine. *Street Scenes* also finds Sanchez exploring both post-bop music and some Latin-flavored songs. He has no problem with Thelonious Monk's rather difficult "Four in One," trades off with guest alto Kenny Garrett on "The Elements," welcomes singer Cassandra Wilson to one number, and also creates some rather crowded music that is reminiscent of the M-Base free funk idiom. With Danilo Perez costarring, this is Sanchez's strongest all-round effort to date.

On *Obsesion,* Sanchez performs one song from Cuba ("Los Aretes de la Luna"), two from Brazil, four from his native Puerto Rico, and one ("Cuban Fantasy") from the United States. The results, which utilize a medium-size band augmented by woodwinds and a few strings, have heated Cuban rhythms intermingling with Brazilian-type melodies and American jazz solos. Most of the spotlight is on the leader, whose tenor solos here sometimes sound a bit influenced by Dexter Gordon. Several of the melodies are quite catchy, and the rhythms are both exuberant and soothing. Overall, even though the Cuban part of this date is a bit short-changed, this is a well-paced set. David Sanchez's recent sextet is featured on many of the selections of *Melaza*: Sanchez on tenor and soprano, altoist Miguel Zenon, pianist Edsel Gomez, bassist Hans Glawischnig, Antonio Sanchez or Adam Cruz on drums, and percussionist Pernell Satumino. There are also appearances by percussionist Hector "Tito" Matos and one by tenor-saxophonist Branford Marsalis (on "Song of the Sugar Cane Field"). The music is adventurous, mixing together the clavé and the heritage of Latin music with stirring post-bop solos.

PONCHO SANCHEZ

b. Oct. 30, 1951, Laredo, TX

Poncho Sanchez deserves the title of "the hardest-working man in Afro-Cuban Jazz." He and his very popular three-horn, three-percussion octet work constantly in every possible venue, from prestigious concert halls and stadiums to free concerts for the poor. Sanchez's men clearly love to play, and their enthusiasm and talent always show.

Poncho Sanchez, the youngest of 11 children, moved with his family to Norwalk, California (where he still lives today), at the age of four. Although Mexican-American, he was very familiar with Cuban music as a child, since his brothers and sisters listened and danced to Latin music. Sanchez bought a guitar for fifty cents in hopes of playing with a band that rehearsed across the street called the Chevelles, but it turned out that his singing was much stronger than his guitar playing and he became the band's vocalist instead for five years. He also played flute a little. But when he had the opportunity to sit behind a set of conga drums while in high school, it felt so natural that he began intensively studying and mastering that instrument. Sanchez played locally in various dance bands (often with his future sidemen bassist Tony Banda and Ramon Banda on timbales) but also had strenuous day jobs, including working in an aluminum foundry.

Sanchez's big break came in 1975, when he was recommended to Cal Tjader, sat in with the vibraphonist, and immediately impressed him. Two weeks later he was hired, and he would be with the busy group until Tjader's death in 1982. In 1980 Sanchez formed his own band, which worked part-time between Tjader's tours, recording two albums for Discovery. Shortly before his death, Tjader convinced Concord's Carl Jefferson to sign Sanchez to his Concord Picante label; 18 CDs have come out thus far. After Tjader's passing, Poncho Sanchez resisted the temptation to form a similar band with vibes and instead put together a unit capable of playing soulful bebop, Salsa, and Afro-Cuban Jazz with equal ability.

Although Sanchez has said that it took a few years for his group to develop its own sound, the Poncho Sanchez band was quite popular from the start, and it has continued working steadily ever since. The Banda brothers are still with the group, as is longtime trumpeter Sal Cracchio, and, other than trombonist Francisco Torres (who joined in 1998), the remaining members of the ensemble have been with the popular conguero for at least 11 years, performing high-quality Afro-Cuban Jazz on an almost-nightly basis for devoted audiences.

The very popular Poncho Sanchez is the hardest-working performer in Afro-Cuban Jazz.

7 *Sonando / Aug. 1982 / Concord Picante 4201*

6 *Bien Sabroso! / Nov. 1983 / Concord Picante 4239*

8 *El Conguero / May 1985 / Concord Picante 4286*

9 *Papa Gato / Oct. 1986 / Concord Picante 4310*

8 *Fuerte / Nov. 1987 / Concord Picante 4340*

7 *La Familia / Nov. 1988 / Concord Picante 4369*

8 *Chile con Soul / Nov. 1989 / Concord Picante 4406*

7 *Cambios / Oct. 15-17, 1990 / Concord Picante 4439*

Listening to *Sonando,* Poncho Sanchez's real debut as a leader (his two earlier Discovery sets were recorded with Clare Fischer), it is striking how similar the music is to what Sanchez would be playing 18 years later. Cut three months after Cal Tjader's death, Sanchez leads a seven-piece group consisting of trumpeter Steve Huffsteter, saxophonist Dick Mitchell, pianist Charlie Otwell, bassist Tony Banda, Ramon Banda on timbales, and Luis Conte on bongos that is augmented by the inclusion of altoist Gary Foster, valve trombonist Mark Levine, and singer José Perico Hernández. Since Sanchez is a superior Salsa singer himself, it would not be deemed necessary in the future (except on special occasions) to use another vocalist. Highlights of this fine date include "A Night in Tunisia," Foster's feature on "The Summer Knows," "Cal's Pals," and "Peruchin." The same musicians (with David Romero for Conte and once again using Levine as a guest) are featured on *Bien Sabroso!,* a decent effort but one in which the horns do not get enough solo space. The percussion section is well featured and the tunes (mostly obscurities and originals other than Kenny Dorham's "Una Mas") are fine, but overall this is a lesser effort for Sanchez.

In 1985 the personnel really solidified as Sal Cracchiolo and Art Velasco joined on trumpet and trombone. Poncho Sanchez considers *El Conguero* to be his first strong CD, and the results do bare him out. Group originals are joined by Latinized versions of "Shiny Stockings" and "Tin Tin Deo," with the Sanchez group sound being very much in place. On *Papa Gato,* Sanchez has the same musicians, except Justo Almario (on alto, tenor, and flute) takes over for Dick Mitchell. One of the strongest of the many Sanchez releases, this set has five excellent originals by the leader and Otwell plus David Torres' "Pan Dulce," "Jumpin' with Symphony Sid," "Manteca," and Horace Silver's "Señor Blues." *Fuerte* (with Kenny Goldberg on tenor and flute taking over for Almario) consists of six group originals, the traditional "Co Co My My," a Latinized "It Could Happen to You," and Clifford Brown's "Daahoud." As usual the music includes some group vocals, excellent jazz horn solos, and infectious rhythms for a typically strong effort.

By the time *La Familia* was recorded, the Poncho Sanchez band was very much like a family and as tight as any working group around. The octet, with guest altoist Gary Foster on two songs, performs originals, some R&B, Eddie Palmieri's "Cuidate Compai," "Mambo Inn," "A Time for Love," and "Well You Needn't" with their usual infectious spirit. *Chile con Soul* has the band (which now had Gene Burkert on alto, tenor, and flute and José "Papo" Rodriguez succeeding David Romero) welcoming one of Poncho's heroes, Tito Puente, to two songs ("Ti-Pon-Pa" and "Lover Come Back to Me") on timbales. This time around Otwell contributed five originals, and the band also performs Cal Tjader's "Soul Burst," "Will You Still Be Mine," and a heated medley of "Cold Sweat" and "Funky Broadway." Trumpeter Freddie Hubbard is the guest artist on *Cambios,* but his three appearances ("Yesterdays," "Sky Dive," and "My Foolish Heart") are average at best, with plenty of cracked notes; he was losing his chops at the time. More important is the change in the piano-musical director chair as David Torres took over for Charlie Otwell (who still contributed a few arrangements to the project). Trombonist Velasco (featured on "In a Sentimental Mood" and particularly strong on "Pique") is the solo star of this CD.

8 *A Night at Kimball's East / Dec. 8, 1990 / Concord Picante 4472*

7 *Bailar / Dec. 8, 1990 / Concord Picante 4558*

7 *El Mejor / Aug. 18-19, 1992 / Concord Picante 4519*

10 *Para Todos / Oct. 25-26, 1993 / Concord Picante 4600*

8 *Soul Sauce / Mar. 7-8, 1995 / Concord Picante 4662*

8 *Conga Blue / Nov. 13-14, 1995 / Concord Picante 4726*

7 *Freedom Sound / Mar. 3-5, 1997 / Concord Picante 4778*

9 *Afro-Cuban Fantasy / June 2, 1998-July 1, 1998 / Concord Picante 4847*

8 *Latin Soul / Apr. 1, 1999 + July 1, 1999 / Concord Picante 4863*

8 *Soul of the Conga / 2000 / Concord Picante*

The music on *A Night at Kimball's East* (which serves as a strong summation of Poncho Sanchez's first eight years as a bandleader) is mostly also available as a video. The band clearly enjoys itself (as does the audience) on such remakes as "Jumpin' with Symphony Sid," "A Night in Tunisia," and a medley of "Cold Sweat," "Funky Broadway," and "Half and Half." *Bailar,* which was released in 1993, is also taken from the same night with a Tito Puente medley (that includes "Oye Como Va"), "Manteca" and "Bien Sabroso" being among the more memorable selections. *El Mejor,* which has the returning Justo Almario and Tom Casey split-ting the saxophone duties, is typical of a Sanchez live date (even though it was recorded in the studios) since it is made up of group originals (including four songs by Torres), a few older tunes, and two standards, although this time around both are obscure: Wes Montgomery's "Angel" and Shorty Rogers' "Just a Few."

Para Todos has the Poncho Sanchez band (with Bruce Paulson taking over on trombone and Scott Martin on tenor and alto) being joined by the great tenor saxophonist Eddie Harris during four songs. Harris is so strong on his "Cold Duck Time," Art Farmer's "Happy Blues," "Rapture," and "Afro Blue" that it is regretful that he is not on the other seven selections (which include Cedar Walton's "Ugetsu" and Gerry Mulligan's "Five Brothers") as well. From start to finish, the band sounds consistently inspired on this particularly fun effort, a CD so strong that everyone should own a copy! On *Soul Sauce* (with Alex Henderson on trombone), the sound of the Sanchez band is purposely altered. The tribute to Cal Tjader logically has Ruben Estrada of the Estrada Brothers (who sounds remarkably close to Tjader) on vibes as Sanchez pays homage to his mentor on such numbers as "Soul Sauce," "Morning," "Poinciana Cha Cha," and three lesser-known Tjader tunes. *Conga Blue* allowed Sanchez to record with another one of his idols, Mongo Santamaria, who plays congas on five of the ten selections, including "Besame Mama" and "Watermelon Man." The horn section is a bit different than usual, since trombonist Alex Henderson and saxophonist Scott Martin are joined by trumpeter Stan Martin (temporarily filling in for Sal Cracchiolo), but the spirit of the infectious group is as high as ever. *Freedom Sound* has Sanchez welcoming the frontline of the Jazz Crusaders (trombonist Wayne Henderson and tenor saxophonist Wilton Felder) to four songs apiece (three together), but it is a pity that the duo is not on more selections. Their renditions of

"Freedom Sound," "MJ's Funk," and "Scratch" work quite well. Otherwise the date alternates as usual between Salsa vocals, Afro-Cuban Jazz, and some fairly straightahead selections.

The 1998 version of Poncho Sanchez's group (with Francisco Torres as its new trombonist) welcomes singer Dianne Reeves to three numbers ("Morning," "Darn That Dream," and "I Remember Spring") on *Afro-Cuban Fantasy*. Reeves' singing is typically excellent, while the band sounds even more infectious than usual on such tunes as "Ritmo Remo," "Subway Harry," "Close Your Eyes," and Torres' title cut. The year 1999's *Latin Soul* (which has baritonist Mike Whitman expanding the group on two cuts) is a typically enthusiastic set that includes "Watermelon Man," "El Conguero," and a medley of "Listen Here" and "Cold Duck Time" among the highlights. Sanchez's singing is warm, his band's ensembles are enthusiastic, and there are plenty of colorful and meaningful solos from his sidemen.

Soul of the Conga, Sanchez's 20th release as a leader (18th for Concord Picante), coincidentally also celebrates his 20th anniversary as a bandleader. Organist Joey DeFrancesco works with the band surprisingly well on seven of the 14 selections, tenor saxophonist Scott Martin is in strong form throughout, the great trumpeter Terence Blanchard is featured on "Stella by Starlight," and four selections match Sanchez with the chanqui sound of the five Ortiz Brothers (featuring tres and group vocals). Afro-Cuban Jazz fans can never own too many Poncho Sanchez records!

ARTURO SANDOVAL

b. Nov. 6, 1949, Artemisa, Cuba

A brilliant trumpeter with a huge range, a fat sound in all of his registers, and the ability to play very fast, and yet also a sensitive interpreter of ballads, Arturo Sandoval has limitless potential. He gives the impression that he can play anything, not just bebop-oriented trumpet but also piano (on which he is a surprisingly capable soloist) and timbales (which he enthusiastically pounds on stage), in addition to being a rapid scat singer worthy of his idol, Dizzy Gillespie.

The son of an auto mechanic, Sandoval began playing classical trumpet at age 12, and he was enrolled in the Cuban National School of the Arts three years later, graduating in 1967. Sandoval became one of the founders of the Orquesta Cubana de Musica Moderna. In 1974 the nucleus of that group (which included Sandoval, Chucho Valdés, and Paquito D'Rivera) became Irakere, Cuba's top band.

Sandoval met Dizzy Gillespie on May 17, 1977, when Dizzy was part of a group of top American musicians (including Stan Getz, pianist Earl Hines, Ry Cooder, and Daniel Amram) who were visiting Cuba. Sandoval, who spoke only Spanish at the time, volunteered to drive Gillespie and Ray Mantilla around Havana. The next day Dizzy was amazed to hear his "chauffeur" playing blazing solos with Irakere!

After appearing on a few of Irakere's albums for Columbia and recording *Havana/New York* with Amram, Sandoval left Irakere in 1981 to tour with his own band. Occasionally the Castro government would allow Sandoval to appear at international jazz festivals or with the BBC Orchestra and Leningrad Philharmonic. In 1982 he recorded *At a Finland Station with Dizzy Gillespie,* which made American audiences aware of the Cuban trumpeter. But Sandoval felt very restrained by the Castro regime, and his touring became more limited as the 1980s progressed. He bided his time until he could get his wife and son out of Cuba. The opportunity arose in July 1990 during a tour with Dizzy Gillespie's United Nation Orchestra. Sandoval and his family defected at the American Embassy in Rome, settling in Florida.

Sandoval's first American concert took place at

On the trumpet, Arturo Sandoval makes the impossible look effortless.

the Village Gate on August 20, 1990, with the orchestras of Tito Puente and Mario Bauzá. Soon he had signed with the GRP label, where his initial album was appropriately titled *Flight to Freedom*. In general his GRP releases are quite rewarding and sometimes stunning. Sandoval, who played again with the United Nation Orchestra during Gillespie's final year, has made other special guest appearances, including with the GRP All-Star Big Band, James Moody, and drummer T.S. Monk, plus being featured on soundtracks with Dave Grusin.

Because he had been registered as a member of the Communist Party in Cuba (specifically because, ironically, it made it easier for him to tour and defect), Sandoval was initially denied U.S. citizenship, even though he played regularly at benefits for the Democratic Party and spoke out constantly against Castro! After a bit of a battle and public outcry, he finally became an American citizen in 1999. Arturo Sandoval, who usually leads his own high-energy Afro-Cuban combo, also occasionally performed with his Cuban big band, Hot House, during 1998-99. In 2000 the trumpeter was the subject of an HBO movie, *The Arturo Sandoval Story*.

7 *Tumbaito / 1986 / Messidor 15974*

7 *No Problem / Aug. 7-8, 1986 / Jazz House 014*

8 *Straight Ahead / Aug. 1988 / Jazz House 008*

6 *Just Music / Aug. 15-16, 1988 / Jazz House 018*

Arturo Sandoval's Cuban recordings, later released by the Messidor and Jazz House labels, are fascinating in their own way, giving listeners an opportunity to hear the talented trumpeter play with few restraints. *Tumbaito* was recorded in Spain, and Sandoval really cuts loose on the six numbers: five originals plus "A Night in Tunisia." The music is high powered and often ferocious, with Sandoval at the head of a sextet also including the great pianist Hilario Duran and guitarist Jorge Chicoy. *No Problem* has the same personnel later in the same tour, with three of its seven songs being repeats from *Tumbaito.* However, these versions, recorded at Ronnie Scott's Club in London, are obviously different. The music is equally as exciting as on the Messidor release, with Sandoval ripping through such tunes as "Night in Tunisia," "Donna Lee," and his own "Nuestro Blues."

Moving ahead two years, *Straight Ahead* is particularly rewarding, because it finds Sandoval in a quartet co-led by Chucho Valdés; this recording was made live in England with bassist Ron Matthewson and drummer Martin Drew. Sandoval is really heated on "Blue Monk" (tearing through the lower register like Al Hirt before jumping into the stratosphere like Maynard Ferguson). Sandoval and Valdés (who is also in fine form) contributed two originals apiece, with the trumpeter sounding quite tender in spots during "My Funny Valentine." In contrast, although *Just Music* has its interesting moments, this outing (using the same group as on his 1986 tour) has weaker material, an emphasis on electronics (with Duran often heard on synthesizer and more solo space than previously for Chicoy's rockish guitar), and less taste than the three other early Sandoval releases. It is sometimes intriguing

to hear, but in general *Just Music* is far from essential.

8 *Flight to Freedom / 1991 / GRP 9634*
10 *I Remember Clifford / 1992 / GRP 9668*
7 *Dreams Come True / 1993 / GRP 9701*
9 *Danzon / Oct. 10, 1993-Nov. 24, 1993 / GRP 9761*
10 *The Latin Train / Jan. 6-11, 1995 / GRP 9818*
10 *Swingin' / Jan. 6-9, 1996 / GRP 9846*
6 *Hot House / 1998 / N2K-10023*
2 *Americana / 1999 / N Coded Music 4205*

Free at last, Arturo Sandoval recorded in 1991 the first of his six GRP CDs. *Flight to Freedom* is primarily boppish jazz with a little bit of rock and Latin percussion. Fiery romps alternate with tasteful renditions of ballads (including "Body and Soul"), with only the closing number, "Marianela," being a bit dull. Sandoval is teamed with the passionate tenor of Ed Calle, the versatile guitarist René Toledo, uniformly strong players, a string section on two pieces, and guest pianist Chick Corea on three others. *I Remember Clifford,* a tribute to trumpeter Clifford Brown, has no Latin rhythms on it at all but is a bebop classic. Sandoval is often wondrous on nine songs associated with Brownie plus Benny Golson's "I Remember Clifford" and his own tender "I Left this Space for You." Sandoval is joined by Ernie Watts, David Sanchez, or Ed Calle on tenor, pianist Kenny Kirkland, bassist Charnett Moffett, and drummer Kenny Washington for such songs as "Daahoud," "Joy Spring," "Cherokee," "The Blues Walk," and "Jordu."

Dreams Come True is one of Sandoval's more restrained sets, although he does get to cut loose on a few numbers. Most of the selections feature his warm tone accompanied by one of two orchestras arranged and conducted by Michel Legrand, including "Little Sunflower," "Once upon a

Summertime," and "To Diz with Love." A duet with pianist Legrand on Dizzy Gillespie's "Con Alma" is touching. In contrast, a 10½-minute version of "Dahomey Dance" (with trombonist Bill Watrous and tenor saxophonist Ernie Watts) and a rapid "Giant Steps" are overflowing with fire, uplifting the otherwise laid-back set.

Danzon returned Sandoval to Afro-Cuban Jazz. Despite some unnecessary guests (including one vocal apiece by Gloria Estefan and Vikki Carr and two cameos by Bill Cosby), the music puts the focus mostly on Sandoval. Heard playing trumpet, flügelhorn, timbales, and on a wee bit of piano, and scatting away on "Groovin' High," Sandoval performs music similar to what he was playing with his working group of the time, even if these particular ensembles are often quite a bit larger, with extra horns and percussion. Danilo Perez, Giovanni Hidalgo, and Dave Valentin are among the more significant guests.

The Latin Train is the one Arturo Sandoval CD that has to be in any serious Afro-Cuban Jazz library, though listeners should not stop with just one! Leading a group that includes Kenny Anderson or Ed Calle on saxophones, Otmaro Ruiz, bassist David Enos, drummer Aaron Serfaty, percussionist Manuel "Egui" Castrillo, and occasional guests (usually background vocalists and percussionists), Sandoval shows throughout why he is one of the greats. "The Latin Train" is a Latinized romp through the supposedly difficult "Giant Steps" chord changes, singers Celia Cruz and Oscar DeLeon share an emotional "La Guarapachanga," Joe Williams drops by to sing "I Can't Get Started," Gillespie's "Be-Bop" is swung hard, and other pieces pay tribute to the Cubop style of the 1950s. *Swingin'* has Sandoval returning to bebop and post-bop playing and is most highly recommended to straightahead jazz listeners who wonder what the fuss is all about. The trumpeter

teams up very successfully with clarinetist Eddie Daniels on two songs, the great tenor Michael Brecker on three (including John Coltrane's "Moment's Notice"), and flügelhornist Clark Terry for a jubilant "Mack the Knife." Sandoval also pays tribute to Woody Shaw, John Coltrane, and Dizzy Gillespie, playing piano on "Street of Dreams," wa-waa-ing with a plunger mute on the humorous "It Never Gets Old," and whipping through "Real McBop."

With the collapse of GRP, Sandoval switched to the N2K label. But thus far there have not been any gems recorded. *Hot House* features Sandoval's spirited big band (or a reasonable approximation, since five of the horns overdubbed additional parts!), but there are a few too many guest soloists (even if Michael Brecker, Tito Puente, and guitarist René Toledo were certainly welcome) and too little heard from Sandoval's sidemen other than in ensembles. "Funky Cha-Cha," "Tito," and of course "Hot House" are highlights, although a "Cuban American Medley" is confusing and a bit frivolous. The full orchestra deserves to be recorded again, preferably live.

Americana is a complete dud. Sandoval had just become an American citizen, so apparently the plot was to pay tribute to recent American songwriters (although it was probably recorded in hopes of getting maximum radio airplay). The problem is that the material is quite weak (including "Just the Way You Are," Janet Jackson's "Come Back to Me," "She's Out of My Life," and "We've Only Just Begun"), the arrangements by Richard Eddy Martinez, Doug Bickel, Ed Calle, and Charles McNeill are as unimaginative and schlocky as the songs, and Arturo Sandoval comes across as a studio musician just going through the motions. This is a pure waste of talent in a commercial project with dubious motives. But there are plenty of other Sandoval CDs that are recommended instead.

MONGO SANTAMARIA

b. Apr. 7, 1922, Havana, Cuba

One of the top conga players of all time, Mongo Santamaria has had a lengthy and productive career, being involved along the way in several different Latin musical styles.

Ramon "Mongo" Santamaria came from a very poor family in Cuba. He started on the violin but switched to drums before dropping out of school in the 7th grade to work as a mechanic. Inspired by Chano Pozo, the teenager was self-taught on conga, bongos, and timbales. Santamaria (who early on was nicknamed "Mongo," which in Senegalese means "chief of the tribe") became a mailman in 1940 but also played music at night, including at the Tropicana Club in Havana. In 1948 he gained a three-month leave of absence from the post office so he could go to Mexico City and accompany a dance troupe called Pablito and Lilon (also known as the Black Cuban Diamonds). That particular job fell through, but it was soon replaced with an opportunity to appear in New York with the dancers. Santamaria played with Miguelito Valdés' orchestra for a week and worked with Johnny Segui's Los Dandies, where he met and befriended Willie Bobo, giving percussion lessons to his new friend. After a period back in Mexico City and Havana (where he arranged to obtain a visa), in 1950 Santamaria moved to New York.

The young conguero made his American debut with Pérez Prado and then spent the 1951-57 period with Tito Puente's orchestra. He cut the notable *Puente in Percussion* in 1955 with Puente and Bobo and recorded with George Shearing in 1953. In 1957, when Santamaria and Bobo made the *Latin Concert* record with Cal Tjader, Puente's jealous anger led both percussionists to depart. Tjader quickly hired them, and they co-led their own group for a short time (El Conjunto Manhattan) while waiting for Tjader to organize his new band. Santamaria and Bobo helped the vibraphonist to have one of his strongest groups, during 1958-61. Santamaria began a series of important recordings for Fantasy in 1958; his second Fantasy album (1959's *Mongo*) featured the debut of his most famous composition, "Afro Blue" (which John Coltrane would soon help make quite famous).

In 1961 Mongo Santamaria went out on his own, forming a variation of a flute-and-violin charanga that became known as a pachanga. With flutist Rolando Lozano, the cool-toned tenor of José "Chombo" Silva, and violinist Felix "Pupi" Legarreta as his main soloists, along with the vocals of Rudy Calzado, Santamaria had a distinctive Latin dance band that was both traditional and distinctive. In 1962 a substitute pianist named Herbie Hancock played his recent song "Watermelon Man" for Santamaria, and soon the conga player had adopted the song as his own; his 1963 recording of "Watermelon Man" for the Battle label was a major hit, reaching #10 on the pop charts. Santamaria shifted the direction of his band (which for a time featured Chick Corea on piano and flutist Hubert Laws) toward a soulful and funky variation of Afro-Cuban Jazz, with increasing commercial success. After recording several albums for the Battle and Riverside labels, he switched to Columbia, where during 1964-69 he was a major part of the boogaloo movement, performing cover versions of current hits (often featuring Marty Sheller arrangements) and creating very danceable music.

Santamaria has kept quite busy in the decades since, recording for Atlantic, Fania (1973-79), Vaya, Pablo (a 1980 album with Dizzy Gillespie and Toots Thielemans), Roulette, Tropical Buddah, Concord Picante (1987-90), Chesky, Tropijazz (with Tito Puente's Golden Latin Jazz All-Stars), and Milestone, performing primarily Afro-Cuban Jazz since the mid-1980s. And as a guest, Santamaria has also recorded with Hilton Ruiz, pianist Valerie Capers, Poncho Sanchez, Steve

Turre, Michel Camilo, the Fania All-Stars, and many others. Now 78, Mongo Santamaria has been semiretired since the late 1990s.

8 *Skin on Skin / Oct. 1957-June 29, 1995 / Rhino 75689*

9 *Afro Roots / Aug. 12, 1958-Mar. 23, 1959 / Prestige 24018*

6 *Our Man in Havana / 1960 / Fantasy 24729*

7 *Arriba / 1961-Aug. 15, 1961 / Fantasy 24738*

8 *At the Blackhawk / 1961-Dec. 19, 1961 / Fantasy 24734*

9 *Sabroso / 1961-1962 / Original Jazz Classics 281*

10 *Watermelon Man / 1962-Feb. 20, 1963 / Milestone 47075*

9 *Skins / July 9, 1962-1964 / Milestone 47038*

8 *Mongo Introduces La Lupe / Dec. 17, 1962-Jan. 9, 1963 / Milestone 9210*

8 *Mongo at the Village Gate / Sept. 2, 1963 / Original Jazz Classics 490*

The Rhino reissue *Skin on Skin* is a strong sampler of Mongo Santamaria's career, a two-CD set that has 34 tracks from 23 albums on seven labels, including a 1957 feature ("Mongorama") with Cal Tjader. "Afro Blue" and "Watermelon Man" are here of course, but so are many formerly scarce selections, including out-of-print titles from his Atlantic years, even if Santamaria's boogaloo period is largely skipped over and there is nothing from 1973-86. *Afro Roots* is a valuable reissue that brings back in full Santamaria's first two albums as a leader: *Yambu* and *Mongo*. The former has six percussionists (including Willie Bobo, Francisco Aguabella, and Carlos Vidal), two singers, and the bass of Al McKibbon, while the latter also features six percussionists (including Bobo, Aguabella,

Vidal, and Armando Peraza) plus three singers (who also double on percussion), McKibbon, vibraphonist Emil Richards, and flutist Paul Horn. One cut, "Mazacote," adds Cal Tjader, Vince Guaraldi, and José "Chombo" Silva. These were particularly significant albums, being among the first largely all-percussion and chant/vocal Afro-Cuban recordings recorded in the United States.

The two records that make up *Our Man in Havana* (the other date is called *Bembe*) were recorded in 1960 during a visit to Cuba by Santamaria and Willie Bobo. The first set is a real gem, one that has an unusual mixture of instruments for a Cuban band: two trumpets, flute, piano, tres (the very fluent Nino Rivera), bass, timbales, bongos, guiro, conga, and two vocalists, essentially combining a charanga and a conjunto. The playing by local musicians is of high quality, and the ten selections are quite enjoyable. Unfortunately, though, that project is combined with the cuts from *Bembe,* which are in a very different style. For the latter set, the music is all performed by vocalists, with the percussion of Santamaria and Bobo being the only instruments. Consisting of folk melodies and religious songs, with the emphasis totally on the chanting and singing, the music is intriguing from a historic standpoint, but the jazz content is nil on this emotional date; Merceditas Valdés has the vocal on four of the numbers.

Arriba has all of the music from two of Santamaria's first records after leaving Cal Tjader: *Arriba* and *Mas Sabroso*. Featured is Mongo's modern charanga band, with appealing flute from Rolando Lozano, occasional tenor solos from José Silva, spots for pianist Joao Donato and violinist Pupi Legaretta, and a bit too much space for singer Rudy Calzado. *At the Blackhawk* has the music from the LP *Viva Mongo* (a somewhat traditional date) and the more jazz-oriented LP *Mighty Mango*. The former session has Santamaria's group with Lozano, Donato, and Legaretta, featuring José Silva on violin, while *Mighty Mango* is generally hotter, with Silva switching to tenor.

Sabroso finds Santamaria's group in transition, a charanga band with two trumpets added. Actually this combination works quite well, for the band features superior playing by José "Chombo" Silva on both violin and tenor (he helps "Para Ti" to be a classic), two little-known but talented trumpeters (Louis Valizan and Marcus Cabuto), the great flutist Lozano, pianist René Hernández, bassist Victor Venegas, and Willie Bobo. Pete Escovedo is one of the background singers as Rudi Calzado takes the lead on a few numbers but does not dominate. There are many fine individual moments on this joyous and infectious set, one of the better Santamaria reissues.

After the surprise of "Watermelon Man," Santamaria's band (with arranger-trumpeter Marty Sheller, two reeds, piano, bass, drums, and three other percussionists) followed it up with a series of singles to consolidate Mongo's success. The CD *Watermelon Man* contains a dozen concise pieces from 1963 (including "Funny Money," "The Boogie Cha-Cha Blues," "Yeh-Yeh," and "The Peanut Vendor") plus six previously unissued selections (including "Afro Blue" and "I'll Remember April") from a live appearance at San Francisco's Blackhawk club in 1962 that had already yielded a full set of material. Featured on the latter is Silva on tenor, Lozano, Legaretta, and singer Rudy Calzado; highly recommended. *Skins,* which reissues in full *Go, Mongo* and *Mongo Explodes,* showcases a couple of Santamaria's strongest groups. *Go, Mongo,* from 1962, has the percussionist heading a nonet with Pat Patrick and Al Abreu on reeds and pianist Chick Corea, while *Mongo Explodes* puts the spotlight on a ten-piece group with trumpeter Sheller, flutist Hubert Laws, Bobby Capers on alto and baritone, and (on three songs) guest cornetist Nat Adderley. The music falls between Afro-Cuban Jazz and the upcoming boogaloo R&B grooves.

La Lupe became a popular singer in New York's Latin music scene of the 1960s. She is heard on five of the nine selections included on *Mongo Introduces La Lupe,* showing lots of spirit along with an appealing voice. However, there are also four strong instrumentals on the date (including the lengthy "Quiet Stroll"), and even the vocal pieces have spots for the instrumentalists. Particularly interesting is hearing the difference between the two trumpet players (Marty Sheller and veteran Chocolate Armenteros) and the fine reed solos from Pat Patrick (Sun Ra's baritonist, who was "on vacation" from the Arkestra at the time) and Bobby Capers; they alternate between various saxophones and flutes. A fine set.

Mongo at the Village Gate finds Santamaria entering the boogaloo era with a variety of funky pieces that show the influence of R&B and soul jazz without losing his roots in Cuban music. This infectious live set teams the conguero with Sheller, Patrick, Capers, pianist Rodgers Grant, bassist Venegas, drummer Frank Hernández, and the percussion of Chihuahua Martinez and Julian Cabrera. Such tunes as "Fatback," "Mongo's Groove," and "Creole," with their happy but soulful and simple melodies, could only have come from this era. Marty Sheller (who would become much better known as an arranger) has rarely sounded better on trumpet, and Santamaria (who takes "My Sound" as an unaccompanied solo) is very well recorded throughout. A remake of "Para Ti" is a welcome bonus track on this enjoyable CD.

8 *Greatest Hits / Mar. 25, 1965-July 29, 1969 / Columbia/Legacy 63920*

9 *Afro American Latin / Oct. 25, 1968-Mar. 5, 1969 / Columbia/Legacy 62220*

Greatest Hits features some of the highpoints from Mongo Santamaria's period on Columbia when he was involved with the boogaloo movement. The first 11 selections are studio selections that sold well at the time, including a remake of "Watermelon

Man," "Fat Back," "Cold Sweat," "Green Onions," and "La Bamba." This 2000 CD also has five numbers that were not on the original sampler LP, including "Mongo's Boogaloo" and a live version of "Afro Blue." Flutist Hubert Laws (also on tenor), trumpeter Marty Sheller, altoist Bobby Capers, altoist Sonny Fortune, and trumpeter Luis Gasca are among the key sidemen on the very accessible, danceable, and fun release.

Afro American Latin was Mongo Santamaria's final full-length album for Columbia, but because several of the selections were not catchy boogaloos (including the spiritual "Obatala"), the music was not released until 2000 and Santamaria soon switched labels. The nine selections that were supposed to be released have Santamaria at the head of a 12-piece band that includes Sonny Fortune, Hubert Laws, trumpeter Lew Soloff, Mark Levine, and Steve Berrios, among others. Ironically, half of the numbers are obvious boogaloos (including "Boogaloo Wow"), the program is one of Santamaria's strongest for Columbia, and the music is sometimes rockish in a Santana vein although Carlos Santana had yet to make an impact. The disc also contains five numbers from a live set (mostly earlier versions of the studio numbers) which was thought of as a type of rehearsal for the ill-fated album. Wonderful music that might have made an impact if Columbia's timid executives had let it be released at the time.

5 *Summertime / July 19, 1980 / Original Jazz Classics 626*

7 *Soy Yo / Apr. 1987 / Concord Picante 327*

7 *Soca Me Nice / May 1988 / Concord Picante 4362*

6 *Ole Ola / May 1989 / Concord Picante 4387*

8 *Live at Jazz Alley / Mar. 1990 / Concord Picante 4427*

7 *Mambo Mongo / Mar. 30-31, 1992 / Chesky 100*

7 *Brazilian Sunset / Oct. 9-10, 1992 / Candid 79703*

8 *Mongo Returns / June 28-29, 1995 / Milestone 9245*

Mongo Santamaria's 1970s recordings for Atlantic and Fania remain quite scarce. *Summertime,* which matches Santamaria with Dizzy Gillespie and the harmonica of Toots Thielemans (plus six other fine players, including Steve Berrios on drums and timbales), does not live up to its potential. The four lengthy jams (which include a 14½-minute "Afro Blue" and a version of "Summertime" that is over 11½ minutes) are too long, Dizzy's trumpet playing was clearly past its prime, and the chemistry that might be expected from the matchup of these three giants does not really occur.

Santamaria recorded four sets for the Concord Picante label during 1987-90. Most of the selections on *Soy Yo* find Mongo heading a tentet with trumpeter E.J. Allen, the saxes of Sam Furnace and Tony Hinson, and four percussionists (counting the leader), conducted and arranged by Marty Sheller. The music ranges from Afro-Cuban to Brazilian, with two songs actually being from the current top-40 charts. A special piece is "Mayeya," which has guest pianist Charlie Palmieri in one of his last recordings. *Soca Me Nice* has a different group (an octet with trumpeter Ray Vega and the reeds of Bobby Porcelli and Mitch Frohman), a couple of tunes with West Indian roots, and a stronger dose of Afro-Cuban music, all originals except for the Beatles' "Day Tripper." The key players return on *Ole Ola,* a surprisingly easy-listening set that emphasizes ballads. Vega and Porcelli have their spots, but none of the overly concise selections exceeds six minutes, and the results are mostly uneventful. *Live at Jazz Alley* is the most exciting of the Concord quartet, featuring Santamaria's band (particularly Vega, Porcelli, and Frohman) stretching out on "Manteca," a few Marty Sheller tunes, and "Afro Blue." Nearly 68 at the time, the conga player sounds quite ageless on this generally high-powered set.

Mongo Santamaria used a very different group for his lone Chesky release, *Mambo Mongo*. Flutist Hubert Laws and Dave Valentin are featured on two songs apiece (it is a pity that they never share the stage), the nine-piece group has trumpeter Eddie Allen, altoist Jimmy Cozier, and Craig Rivers on tenor and soprano, and there are a lot of percussion features, most notably the closing 9½-minute "La Mogolla." A well-played if not quite classic outing. Santamaria leads a similar octet on *Brazilian Sunset*. Eddie Allen (the musical director) is again one of the key soloists, and both Cozier and Rivers are back, although there are no guest soloists this time. Most of the selections are group originals (Santamaria contributed seven of the dozen songs himself), other than catchy reworkings of "Summertime" and "Watermelon Man." The band plays with spirit, and the music is primarily Afro-Cuban Jazz, with a few boogaloo-flavored tunes included.

Mongo Returns has Santamaria at the head of a 12-piece group that includes Allen, three other reed players (including Mel Martin on flutes), either Oscar Hernández or Hilton Ruiz on piano, and up to five percussionists. "Bahia" (with Allen's wa-wa trumpet) is a highlight, Mongo turns a couple of pop tunes (one apiece from Stevie Wonder and Marvin Gaye) into boogaloo jazz, and the originals (which include Hilton Ruiz's "Free World Mambo") are infectious and of high quality. Another winner from the great Mongo Santamaria.

LPs to Search For:

Mongo Santamaria's seven Columbia albums of 1964-68 remain out of print and are long overdue to be reissued in full on CD. Particularly rewarding is 1964's *La Bamba* (Columbia 9175), which features Santamaria's septet when it included Hubert Laws, Marty Sheller, and Bobby Capers. Highlights

include one of the best-known versions of "Watermelon Man," "Fatback," and a surprisingly effective version of "La Bamba"; fortunately those three selections have been reissued as part of Santamaria's *Greatest Hits* CD. Overall, this is a classic boogaloo set filled with infectious and danceable jazz-oriented instrumental performances.

CARLOS SANTANA

b. July 20, 1947, Autlan de Novarra, Mexico

Although he has spent much of his career as a Latin rock (rather than a Latin jazz) guitarist, Carlos Santana has played jazz on an occasional basis (he always considered Miles Davis and John Coltrane to be important influences), and he was responsible for making Tito Puente's "Oye Como Va" a major hit and an Afro-Cuban Jazz standard.

The son of a mariachi violinist, Santana played violin briefly before switching to guitar when he was eight, moving with his family to San Francisco in 1962. He emerged in 1969 with the self-titled *Santana* album, mixing Afro-Cuban rhythms and a blues influence with passionate rock guitar solos. Armando Peraza would become a long-time sideman, and Pete Escovedo also worked regularly with the guitarist. Santana became famous quickly and appeared at Woodstock. Among his more popular songs of the era were "Soul Sacrifice," "Samba Pa Ti," "Black Magic Woman," "Evil Ways," and Puente's "Oye Como Va" (which was included on Santana's second album, *Abraxas*). Santana recorded the spiritual album *Love Devotion and Surrender* with fellow guitarist John McLaughlin in 1973, returned to rock, and was a steady-selling artist throughout the 1970s and '80s. His jazz collaborators included pianist Alice Coltrane, Herbie Hancock, and Wayne Shorter.

Santana recorded a long string of albums for Columbia, switching to Polydor in 1991. His 1999 Arista release, *Supernatural,* was such a big hit that some in the press talked of a "comeback," but in reality Carlos Santana had never lost either his passionate style or his fame as a Latin rock legend. Someone should team him with a group of Afro-Cuban Jazz all-stars sometime and see what sparks fly!

9 *Santana / 1969 / Sony 65489*
7 *Abraxas / 1970 / Sony 65490*
8 *Lotus / July 3-4, 1973 / Columbia 46764*

Carlos Santana's self-titled first release (when his band was known simply as Santana) is still one of his best. Over a rhythm section that is as much soul jazz as rock (organist Gregg Rolie, bassist Dave Brown, drummer Mike Shrieve, Mike Carrabello on conga, and José Chepito Areas on timbales), Santana contributes blazing rockish guitar solos. The vocals (by Santana and Rolie) are not the greatest but are effective on a remake of the Willie Bobo-associated "Evil Ways." Also quite memorable is the organ groove of "Waiting" and the passionate playing on "Soul Sacrifice." The CD reissue adds three selections from Santana's Woodstock appearance to the original program. Is this Afro-Cuban Jazz? Probably not, but it played a part in the continuing evolution of Latin music.

Most of Santana's second album, *Abraxas,* features psychedelic rock with prominent keyboard playing by Gregg Rolie, which sounds close to an organ. However this album will always be best known for its rather out-of-place hit version of Tito Puente's "Oye Come Va" that made the eight-year-old song into an Afro-Cuban Jazz standard. Otherwise, the music is reasonably unpredictable, hinting at jazz on "Incident at Neshabur" but mostly staying in the genre of rock. The timbales of José Areas and the conga playing of Mike Carabello are well buried as part of the group's sound. The CD reissue adds three live selections to the original program. *Lotus,* a double-CD, was recorded live in Japan in 1973 and perfectly sums up the first peri-

od of Santana's career. Most of the music is jazz-influenced psychedelic rock that often crosses over into fusion; Santana was certainly familiar with what Miles Davis was up to at the time. From the Afro-Cuban Jazz standpoint, a remake of "Oye Come Va" is the obvious highpoint. Armando Peraza and Areas add their percussion to the highly electronic ensembles; Santana's fiery guitar stars throughout this strong effort. Santana's later recordings, even the star-filled *Supernatural* from 1999, offer very little Afro-Cuban Jazz.

JOHN SANTOS

b. Nov. 1, 1955, San Francisco, CA

A fine percussionist, John Santos is a significant educator and propagandist for Afro-Cuban music who is based in the San Francisco Bay Area. His step-grandfather had a dance band that performed Puerto Rican and Cuban music. Santos played conga with that ensemble as a teenager during 1968-69. In 1974 he joined Ritmo 74 and the following year was part of La Banda. A major student of African and Cuban music, Santos worked with Tipica Cienfuegos (1977-80), a variety of local groups, Batachanga (1982-85) (with whom he recorded), Pete Escovedo's orchestra, and Tito Puente. Santos first formed the Machete Ensemble in 1986 (Steve Turre and Armando Peraza were early members), and he had his own label, Machete. A serious car accident in 1990 knocked him out of action temporarily and slowed him down for a couple years. Since then, John Santos has recorded with Dizzy Gillespie & Bebop and Beyond, violinist Stephane Grappelli, Bobby Matos, singer Joyce Cooling, guitarist Bruce Forman, singer Mark Murphy, and Omar Sosa, worked with guitarist Charlie Hunter, Bobby Hutcherson, Lalo Schifrin, Santana, Cal Tjader, and Danilo Perez, and led his colorful Machete Ensemble, which has recorded for Xenophile, Bembe, and Cubop.

8   *Africa, Volume 1 / 1986-1987 / Earthbeat 42511*

8   *Machetazo! / 1991-1997 / Bembe 2018*

9   *Tribute to the Masters / 1989-1999 / Cubop 025*

Africa, Volume 1, the debut recording by John Santos' Machete Ensemble, displays the leader's wide taste in Cuban and African music. Among the highlights are "Un Viajea a Oriente" (Afro-Cuban Jazz with prominent roles for violinist Anthony Blea and trombonist Steve Turre), "Oba Lube" (featuring some fine playing by Turre), and the atmospheric blues "Medicine Man" (which has Rebeca Mauleón on the thumb piano and Turre on conch shells). "Africa" puts the spotlight on the vocalizing and chanting of Armando Peraza, while "Asesu" is a four-part suite full of joyous themes featuring the tenor of Melecio Magdaluyo, three trombones, and a large chorus. Stimulating and continually intriguing music played with plenty of enthusiasm.

Machetazo! has 11 performances by several versions of the Machete Ensemble, recorded during 1991-94 and 1996-97. There are a few chanting/vocal pieces, but the emphasis is on Santos' strong soloists, including Melecio Magdaluyo (on soprano, tenor, and alto), trombonists Wayne Wallace and Jeff Cressman, Ron Stallings (on soprano and flute), and Santos' wide array of percussion. The repertoire includes originals by Santos, traditional pieces, Arsenio Rodriguez's "Chango Pachanga," "Footprints," and "Caravan."

Of the three CDs by the Machete Ensemble, *Tribute to the Masters* gets a slight edge, due to the consistently strong material. Most of the selections are from 1998-99, but there are also four cuts from 1989-90, so the personnel varies quite a bit. Ranging from Latin bop (including "Tin Tin Deo," "Moose the Mooche," and "Salt Peanuts") and folkloric chant pieces to Latinized versions of Miles Davis' "So What" and John Coltrane's "Syeeda's Song Flute," the music is continually intriguing.

Among the key soloists are trombonists Wallace and Cressman, Magdaluyo on his reeds, Rebeca Mauleón, and quite a few percussionists, led by the increasingly significant John Santos.

LALO SCHIFRIN

b. June 21, 1932, Buenos Aires, Argentina
Lalo Schifrin has spent much of his professional career writing scores for films and television. But early on and in more recent times, Schifrin has also been involved in Afro-Cuban Jazz. He was born Boris Schifrin (he legally adopted his nickname of Lalo when he became a U.S. citizen in 1968), and his first piano lessons were given him by his father, Luis Schifrin, the concertmaster of the Philharmonic Orchestra of Buenos Aires. Although he won a scholarship to the Paris Conservatory in France, by then the young pianist had discovered jazz. While overseas he often played in clubs at night after studying by day, and in 1955 he represented Argentina at the Third International Jazz Festival. After returning to Argentina, Schifrin became an important studio musician and film writer, in addition to leading a big band that featured his native country's best jazz musicians, including the young Gato Barbieri. When he met Dizzy Gillespie (who was on a South American tour) in 1956, Schifrin was told that if he came to the United States, he would eventually be in Gillespie's band.

In 1958 Schifrin finally moved to the United States, but he had to wait for a period because Junior Mance was the pianist in Dizzy's quintet. Schifrin arranged for Xavier Cugat and led his own trio until he was able to join Gillespie in 1960. During his two years with the trumpeter, Schifrin was constantly encouraged to write new music. His first work for Dizzy was his best: the five-part "Gillespiana," which in its premiere augmented the quintet with 13 brass instruments. While with Gillespie, Schifrin toured the world. And he appeared on quite a few albums with the trumpeter, including one in which his complex six-part work "The New Continent" was recorded.

After leaving Dizzy, Schifrin became a top studio writer and contributed to albums by Cal Tjader, altoist Paul Horn, tenor saxophonist Stan Getz, organist Jimmy Smith (*The Cat*), and altoist Cannonball Adderley. In 1967 he composed the famous theme for the TV series *Mission Impossible* (a Latin melody in 5/4 time). He has since written over 125 film scores and has excelled at a wide variety of commercial assignments, including arranging popular music for the Three Tenors of opera to perform. Occasionally he had a reunion with Gillespie or recorded a jazz album, but it was not until the mid-1990s that Schifrin began to appear more regularly in jazz settings. Since then he has recorded several sets (for Atlantic, Four Winds, and his own label, Aleph) in his "Jazz Meets the Symphony" settings, usually medleys of songs dedicated to different jazz greats. In addition, Lalo Schifrin rerecorded "Gillespiana" (with Jon Faddis in Gillespie's place, Paquito D'Rivera, and the WDR Big Band), performing the work at the 1997 Monterey and Playboy jazz festivals.

9 *Gillespiana / Nov. 30, 1996 / Aleph 002*
7 *Jazz Meets the Symphony / Nov. 1992 / Atlantic 82506*
6 *More Jazz Meets the Symphony / Dec. 1993 / Atlantic 82653*
6 *Firebird / 1996 / Four Winds 2004*
7 *Metamorphosis / May 1998 / Aleph 004*
9 *Latin Jazz Suite / June 18-19, 1999 / Aleph 013*

The new recording of *Gillespiana* that Lalo Schifrin made in 1996 (36 years after the piece's debut) is a real gem. Jon Faddis logically plays in Dizzy's spot, Paquito D'Rivera fills in for the late Leo Wright, Alex Acuña and Marcio Doctor contribute some Latin percussion, and the WDR Big Band swings well. This is a work that grows in interest with each listen; Faddis is quite brilliant throughout. The CD is rounded out by the intriguing but unrelated "Bachianas Brasileiras No. 5" (a Brazilian piece by Hector Villalobos and arranged by Schifrin) featuring Markus Stockhausen's trumpet.

The *Jazz Meets the Symphony* series (which utilizes the London Philharmonic) actually has very little of interest to Afro-Cuban fans. The original *Jazz Meets the Symphony* CD includes such pieces as "Bach to the Blues," "I Can't Get Started," "Brazilian Impressions," "Echoes of Duke Ellington," and "Dizzy Gillespie Fireworks"; the latter two are medleys, and Schifrin is the main soloist. *More Jazz Meets the Symphony* benefits from guest spots by Faddis, D'Rivera (on clarinet and alto), and Ray Brown but has virtually no Latin music. Even Schifrin's original "Chano" is essentially straightahead. There are also tributes to Miles Davis and Louis Armstrong (the latter is a bust, since Schifrin has no real feel for trad jazz) and some shorter pieces. *Firebird* has a medley of "Mission Impossible" and "Take Five," one of "An American in Paris" and "Parisian Thoroughfare," a Fats Waller medley, and a mixture of Charlie Parker tunes with Stravinsky's *Firebird Suite*. *Metamorphosis* is more of the same, including a tribute to Thelonious Monk ("Miraculous Monk"), although the 23½-minute "Rhapsody for Bix (Beiderbecke)" works surprisingly well. But overall the series leaves one unsatisfied as interesting themes are quickly discarded in favor of more routine ones.

The most rewarding of Lalo Schifrin's more recent recordings, *Latin Jazz Suite* is also his most Afro-Cuban-oriented set. Schifrin and his notable guests (Jon Faddis, David Sanchez on tenor and soprano, drummer Ignacio Berroa, and percussionists Alex Acuña, Alphonso Garrido, and Marcio Doctor) join the WDR Big Band of Germany to perform six of his recent originals. The music pays tribute to Cuba, the Caribbean Islands, Argentina, Spanish gypsies, Africa, and Brazil, utilizing rhythms and melodies that are reminiscent of each of these geographical area's musical heritage. Schifrin, Faddis, and Sanchez get in their spots, the ensembles are clean and swinging, and the percussionists uplift the music. Recommended.

SEIS DEL SOLAR

Rubén Blades' principal backup group during the 1980s, Seis Del Solar recorded their first solo album independent of the singer/activist in 1992, and the result was a surprisingly jazz-oriented program, with the music still open to fusion and rock influences. The band in 1992 consisted of pianist Oscar Hernández, bassist Mike Vinus, Ralph Irizarry on timbales, drummer Robbie Ameen, Sammy Figueroa on conga, and Arturo Ortiz on synthesizers, although by the time of its second set three years later, tenor saxophonist Bobby Franceschini was an important new voice, John Benitez was on electric bass, Ortiz was gone, and Paoli Mejias was on congas.

8 *Decision / 1992 / Messidor 15821*
9 *Alternate Roots / 1995 / Messidor 15831*

Decision, the debut recording by Seis Del Solar (which is endorsed by Rubén Blades in his opening liner notes), consists of modern Afro-Cuban Jazz and is often quite stirring. Arturo Ortiz's synthesizers give the band a very contemporary feel, the rhythm section is tight and explosive, the grooves are often funky, and the occasional group vocals add to the music's spirit, even if a rap by Figueroa on "Entregate" is annoying. There are spots where the music (ten group originals, mostly by Ortiz and/or Oscar Hernández) is reminiscent of Chick Corea, and overall this was a very impressive debut. *Alternate Roots* is even better, due to the superior tenor playing of Bobby Franceschini and the con-

sistently strong material; Michael Mossman makes a guest appearance on flügelhorn. Occasional group vocals uplift the music, the rhythm section generally burns, and the band sounds quite tight, holding on to its Afro-Cuban Jazz roots while looking ahead.

CHARLIE SEPÚLVEDA

b. July 15, 1962, Bronx, NY

A fine trumpeter who adds fiery hard bop solos to Afro-Cuban Jazz settings, Charlie Sepúlveda has kept quite busy during the past 15 years. In 1970, when he was eight, his family moved to Puerto Rico, where he studied music extensively. Sepúlveda gained early experience playing with Willie Rosario, Ralphy Levit (1978), Julio Castro (1978-79), Bobby Valentin (1980-83), El Cano Estramera (1983-84), Eddie Palmieri (on and off starting in 1984), Ray Barretto (1985-86), Hector La Voe (1985-87), Tito Puente, Celia Cruz, Johnny Pacheco, Dr. John, and the Fania All-Stars (1990-91). Sepúlveda, who worked with Dizzy Gillespie's United Nation Orchestra in 1991, has headed his own groups since 1989. He has led CDs for Antilles and Tropijazz and recorded as a sideman with Palmieri, Puente, Gillespie, Hilton Ruiz, Dave Valentin, the Tropijazz All-Stars, Manny Oquendo's Libre, and Steve Turre, among others.

8 *The New Arrival / 1991 / Antilles 314 510 056*
9 *Algo Nuestro / Mar. 11, 1992-May 14, 1992 / Antilles 314 512 768*

Throughout *The New Arrival,* Charlie Sepúlveda often sounds a bit like Freddie Hubbard in his prime. A Latin flavor is felt on most of the high-powered cuts (with drummer Adam Cruz, Richie Flores on conga, and sometimes percussionist José Claussel), but in general the music is modern post-bop. David Sanchez has plenty of fiery tenor solos,

Arturo Ortiz is a major asset on piano, and, on "Tid Bits," guest pianist Danilo Perez trades off with Ortiz's electric piano. Completing the group on some of the nine originals are tenorman Ralph Moore plus Ruben Rodriguez or Peter Washington on bass. Even with the impressive supporting cast, the underrated but powerful Sepúlveda is never overshadowed, and his solos are consistently memorable.

Algo Nuestro is even a little stronger, because David Sanchez had grown in power and passion during the past year. For this project, Sepúlveda leads a sextet that includes Sanchez, pianist Edward Simon, Andy González, Adam Cruz on drums, and Richie Flores on congas and bongos, with a few guest percussionists and bassists; Steve Turre sits in on Eddie Palmieri's "Puerto Rico." Once again the music is post-bop jazz with a strong dose of Latin and Puerto Rican rhythms. The solos of Sepúlveda and Sanchez are consistently passionate, while pianist Simon shows a great deal of potential during his spots.

GEORGE SHEARING

b. Aug. 13, 1919, London, England
A famous name in jazz since the late 1940s and the leader of a very popular piano-vibes-guitar-bass-drums quintet for 30 years, George Shearing is still quite active as of this writing. Credited with making bebop more accessible to the general public through his music (which was sometimes quite easy listening, although he was always a virtuoso pianist), Shearing also helped introduce Afro-Cuban Jazz to a wider audience beyond the worlds of jazz and Cuban music.

Born blind, Shearing started playing piano when he was three. Although he took music at the Linden Lodge School for the Blind, he learned as much by studying records, being influenced early on by Teddy Wilson and Fats Waller. Shearing made his first recordings in 1937, was quite active

in his native England, and was a member of violinist Stephane Grappelli's group during much of the World War II years. Shearing first visited the United States in 1947 and was immediately intrigued by bebop, modernizing his style while still remaining a strong two-handed pianist. He worked briefly in the Oscar Pettiford Trio (where he replaced Erroll Garner) and with clarinetist Buddy DeFranco. At critic Leonard Feather's suggestion, in 1949 Shearing led a quintet at a recording session with vibes and guitar (often emphasizing the "locked hands" chordal style that he had learned from pianist Milt Buckner's recordings with Lionel Hampton), and the result was a distinctive group sound that caught on, featuring unisons by the three lead voices. Vibraphonist Marjorie Hyams, guitarist Chuck Wayne, bassist John Levy, and drummer Denzil Best were in the original lineup, recording for Discovery before Shearing settled in at MGM (1950-55) and Capitol (1955-69).

Although the quintet's initial recording date included one number called "Sorry Wrong Rhumba," it was not until Al McKibbon became the group's bassist in late 1951 that Shearing started exploring Latin rhythms, tentatively at first. The pianist had been very impressed by Machito when he first heard him in 1948, and in later years he credited McKibbon, Armando Peraza, and Willie Bobo for having taught him the music.

In 1953 Cal Tjader became Shearing's vibraphonist and Toots Thielemans was on guitar (and occasional harmonica), with McKibbon and drummer Bill Clark completing the group. On the recording session of April 15, Armando Peraza's conga was heard for the first time with the quintet. Peraza would be Shearing's regular "guest" on conga and bongos for the next decade, often appearing during the second half of concerts. The September 2, 1953, recording date also had Candido on bongo (in place of Peraza) and Catalino Rolon on shaker for four pieces; the music, along with a few other selections (usually including Peraza), was released as an MGM ten-inch LP called *Satin Latin.* Although Tjader departed by early 1954, his experience with Shearing was valuable and helped fuel his lifelong interest in Latin music. Other Latin-oriented Shearing albums of the era include 1956's *Latin Escapade* (which sold over 80,000 albums), *Latin Lace* (1957), *Latin Affair* (1959), *Mood Latino* (1961), and *Latin Rendezvous* (1963), the last two including Roland Lozano on flute.

George Shearing would record other projects throughout his career, including bebop standards, mood records (in which his quintet was augmented by brass, strings, and/or voices), dates with singers Dakota Staton, Nancy Wilson, Peggy Lee, and Nat King Cole, and many duet and trio albums, particularly after his quintet was de-emphasized (starting in 1969) and eventually disbanded. His later collaborations with Mel Torme for Concord are often classic. But, although he has not played Latin rhythms all that much since the early 1960s, every once in a while George Shearing will break into a mambo to remind listeners of the legacy that he created in the 1950s.

10 *The Complete Capitol Live Recordings of George Shearing / Mar. 8, 1958-July 6, 1963 / Mosaic 5-157*

Unfortunately, George Shearing's Latin projects have not yet been made available on CD by Capitol. This limited-edition five-CD set put out by Mosaic has all of the Shearing Quintet's live recordings for Capitol. *Shearing on Stage* (1958), *On the Sunny Side of the Strip* (1958), and *San Francisco Scene* (1960) are heard in their original form, while *Jazz Concert* and *Rare Form*, both from 1963, are now double in length. Shearing's sidemen are vibraphonists Emil Richards, Warren Chiasson, and Gary Burton, guitarists Toots Thielemans (who switches to harmonica on "Caravan"), Dick Garcia,

John Gray, and Ron Anthony, bassists Al McKibbon, Wyatt Ruther, Bill Yancey, and Gene Cherico, and drummers Percy Brice, Lawrence Marable, and Vernel Fournier. Shearing sounds in top form throughout, swinging away with his usual charm and showing that he is a strong bop-based improviser. Armando Peraza's congas are added to the quintet on nine selections, but even many of the selections without him have at least a bit of the Latin tinge.

LPs to Search For:
George Shearing's popular series of Latin records add Armando Peraza to Shearing's regular quintet along with other unidentified percussionists. These underrated albums can generally be found in used record stores: *Latin Lace* (Capitol 1082), *Latin Affair* (Capitol 1275), *Latin Escapade* (Capitol 1454), *Mood Latino* (Capitol 1567), and *Latin Rendezvous* (Capitol 2272); this last adds several woodwinds to the instrumentation.

JOSÉ "CHOMBO" SILVA
b. Mar. 27, 1923, Oriente, Cuba, d. July 21, 1995

One of the most respected tenor saxophonists to work regularly with Afro-Cuban bands in the 1950s and '60s, José "Chombo" Silva was called "the Latin Lester Young" by Cal Tjader. Inspired by Jasha Heifitz, Silva originally started on violin, and he would retain the violin as a double on and off throughout his career. In 1938 he began playing tenor and was soon gigging with Peruchin's Trovadores de Tono. At 17 Silva joined the Orquesta Swing Boys and picked up the lifelong nickname of Chombo. After the band broke up in 1942, he became a world traveler, working in Panama (1942-45), Mexico (1945-47), Spain (1948-49), Paris and Germany (1950-54). Returning to Cuba in 1954, Silva gigged with Benny Moré and Armando Romeu's orchestra, appearing on the legendary descarga *Cuban Jam Session, Volume 1* in 1956. He moved to New York in 1957, worked with Machito, and made several notable records with Cal Tjader, including *Mas Ritmo Caliente, A Night at the Blackhawk,* and *Tjader Goes Latin.*

After a period spent freelancing, in 1960 Silva played violin for the first time since 1938, when he joined Johnny Pacheco's popular charanga orchestra. During the 1960s and '70s he worked with Pacheco, Ray Barretto, Mongo Santamaria, Charlie Palmieri (1961-65, including with the Alegre All-Stars), Cachao, Lou Pérez, and other bands on both tenor and violin. Less active by the 1980s when he became semi-retired, Chombo Silva participated on Paquito D'Rivera's *40 Years of Cuban Jam Sessions* recording project in 1993, still displaying his cool tone and inner fire.

MARLON SIMON

A talented percussionist who also plays drums and batá, Marlon Simon is a versatile Afro-Cuban Jazz musician who is also an underrated composer. He came to the United States in 1987, struggled a bit, went to college, and got his first break when Hilton Ruiz hired him. Since that time Simon has worked with Dave Valentin, Chucho Valdés, altoist Bobby Watson, bassist Charles Fambrough (with whom he has recorded), and Jerry González. As a leader, Marlon Simon has thus far recorded for K-Jazz (1998's *Music of Marlon Simon*) and Cubop.

8 *Rumba à la Patato / 1999 / Ubiquity / Cubop 027*

For his second CD as a leader, Marlon Simon (heard on drums, percussion, and batá) utilizes trumpeter Brian Lynch, tenor saxophonist Peter Brainin, Bobby Watson, Luis Perdomo or Edward Simon on piano, John Benitez or Andy González on bass, and Roberto Quintero's congas. His eight originals include tributes to Patato Valdés and Thelonious Monk, while his younger brother,

Michael Simon (who plays trumpet on two songs), contributed one song, "Humble and Innocent." This is an impressive effort overall, with Lynch and Watson fitting in quite well with the Latin grooves.

ALBERTO SOCARRÁS

b. Sept. 18, 1908, Manzanillo, Oriente, Cuba, d. Aug. 26, 1987, New York, NY

Although rarely mentioned in history books, Alberto Socarrás was the first Cuban musician to make a mark in jazz. Wayman Carver often gets the credit for being the first jazz flute soloist. But while Carver played with Chick Webb in the 1930s, Socarrás preceded him by several years. Socarrás was taught the flute by his mother and played in a family band, accompanying silent movies in Cuba. When sound movies were being developed, he quickly realized that he would soon be out of work. Disgusted with the racism against blacks in Cuba and also looking to make a better living, on April 26, 1927, he arrived in New York. He recorded with pianist Clarence Williams on several occasions during 1927-29 (starting with "Bottomland"), including "Have You Ever Felt That Way," which, being from February 5, 1929, may very well be the earliest recorded jazz flute solo. He also can be heard on recordings with singers Lizzie Miles, Eva Taylor, Mary Dixon, and Margaret Webster, Lew Leslie's Blackbirds, the Chicago Serenaders, Carl Webster's Yale Collegians, Bennett's Swamplanders, Russell Wooding's Grand Central Redcaps, and the Lazy Levee Loungers.

Socarrás, who played alto, soprano, and clarinet in addition to flute, worked with trumpeter Vicente Sigler, Nilo Melendez (the composer of "Green Eyes"), and Lew Leslie's Blackbirds (1928-33), touring Europe with the last group in 1929. He was a studio musician for a time and arranged music for quite a few bands, including Vincent López, Cab Calloway, and Tommy Dorsey. In 1934 he formed a rumba band that recorded jazz-flavored Latin music for Brunswick the following year. Socarrás had stints in jazz bands during 1933-37, playing (but not being featured as a soloist) with the orchestras of Benny Carter, Sam Wooding, and Erskine Hawkins. In 1937 Socarrás and his Magic Flute Orchestra had Dizzy Gillespie briefly as a sideman, and his octet played opposite Glenn Miller's at the Glen Island Casino in 1939-40. Socarrás, who earned a degree from the Timothy Musical Conservatory in 1944, recorded *Rumba Classica* for RCA in 1947, was on a jazz date on flute with singer Babs González in 1949, and kept his popular (but rarely documented) Latin band going into the 1950s. In his later years he freelanced as a classical soloist, became a highly respected flute teacher, and recorded with Tito Puente in the 1960s on Tambo (RCA). Throughout his career, Alberto Socarrás generally kept jazz and Latin music separate, and unfortunately he did not record any jazz solos after the mid-1930s, so his valuable contributions to the music have been generally overlooked.

OMAR SOSA

b. 1965, Camaguey, Cuba

A brilliant pianist, Omar Sosa has been making a strong impression in the United States ever since moving to the San Francisco Bay Area in 1995. Originally a percussionist, Sosa was accepted into the National Music School in Havana in 1977. After graduating from that institution and from the Superior Institute of Art in 1984, he worked teaching children. Sosa tried unsuccessfully to master the marimba but had much better luck after switching to piano in the early 1980s. He formed the group Tributo in 1986, toured Africa, and was musical director for singers Vicente Feliu and Xiomara Laugart. A pioneer in utilizing hip hop rhythms in Havana, Sosa has collaborated on an occasional basis with rappers. After leaving Cuba in 1993, he moved to Ecuador, where he led a fusion band, Entrenoz. In 1995 Sosa relocated to San Francisco,

where he played with local Salsa groups and became associated with percussionist John Santos. The two have performed many concerts together during the past few years. Omar Sosa has recorded as a leader for the Price Club and OTA labels.

JUAN TIZOL

b. Jan. 22, 1900, San Juan, Puerto Rico, d. Apr. 23, 1984, Inglewood, CA

The first important valve trombonist in jazz history (although he rarely soloed and never led his own record date), Juan Tizol is significant chiefly as the composer who wrote "Caravan," "Perdido," "Moonlight Fiesta," "Pyramid," and other pieces that usually had a strong Latin feel to them.

The technically skilled trombonist started out working in a municipal concert orchestra in San Juan as a teenager, moving to the United States in 1920. While in the house band at the Howard Theatre in Washington, Tizol first met Duke Ellington. After short stints with Bobby Lee's Cotton Pickers and the White Brothers Band, he became a longtime member of the Duke Ellington Orchestra (1929-44), where his facility often allowed him to fill in for an absent saxophonist without anyone's noticing. Tizol switched to Harry James' big band during 1944-51, and then went back and forth between the two orchestras, playing with Ellington (1951-53), James (1953-60), and finally Ellington for a third time (1960-61). Juan Tizol, who had a hot temper that contrasted with his cool tone and style, spontaneously quit in the middle of Ellington's recording project with Count Basie, permanently retiring to Los Angeles in 1961.

CAL TJADER

b. July 16, 1925, St. Louis, MO, d. May 4, 1982, Manila, Philippines

One of the most popular figures in Afro-Cuban Jazz and a highly influential force as a vibraphonist and as a bandleader, Cal Tjader is still beloved nearly two decades after his death. While it has sometimes been thought (mistakenly of course) that only those with at least some Cuban and Puerto Rican relatives could properly play Afro-Cuban Jazz, how can one explain the success of Tjader, who was of Swedish descent?

Cal Tjader's parents were vaudevillians. His father was a tap dancer and his mother played piano. They happened to be appearing in St. Louis when Cal was born. In 1927 the Tjader family settled in San Mateo, California, where they opened a dance school. Cal began dancing professionally when he was three, he appeared with Bill "Bojangles" Robinson in the film *The White of the Dark Cloud of Joy,* and he was tutored on the piano by his mother. At 14, Tjader discovered jazz and began playing drums. He was in a Dixieland band in high school and made it to the finals of the Gene Krupa drumming contest, losing on December 7, 1941 (!).

After serving in the Navy during 1943-46, Tjader enrolled at San José State College, transferring to San Francisco State College in 1948. At the latter he soon met pianist Dave Brubeck and altoist Paul Desmond, playing and recording with the two future greats in Brubeck's experimental octet. Other than a few tympani lessons, Tjader was self-taught on all of his instruments. He learned bongos literally overnight when he heard that Nick Esposito was looking for a bongo player to make some recordings. After Brubeck's octet (which never worked that much) broke up, Tjader became the drummer with the Dave Brubeck Trio (1949-51), with whom he recorded fairly extensively. During that time he learned vibes, which he soon used as a double.

After a serious swimming accident put Brubeck out of action for a year, Tjader worked with Alvino Rey, gained a teaching degree from college, occasionally led his own group (leading an obscure straightahead trio date for Galaxy during September-November 1951 that found him playing drums and bongos), and was a member of George Shearing's quintet, on vibes and occasional bongos (1953-54). It was during his time with Shearing, working opposite bassist Al McKibbon (who took him to see Machito and Tito Puente), that Tjader began to become quite interested in Afro-Cuban Jazz. While still with Shearing, Tjader recorded an album's worth of material for Savoy (including four songs that had Armando Peraza on conga) and his initial Fantasy set, *Ritmo Caliente,* Tjader's first Afro-Cuban album. A month later he formed his own trio, which soon became a highly influential quintet (composed of his vibes, piano, bass, and two percussionists).

Recording regularly for Fantasy through 1961 and going on tours set up by producer Norman Granz (where his group was billed as "Tjader's Afro-Cuban Jazz" or "Tjader's Modern Mambo Quintet"), the vibraphonist began to build up a loyal audience. Among his sidemen during the 1954-57 period were pianists Manuel Duran and Vince Guaraldi, guitarist Eddie Duran, bassists Carlos Duran and Al McKibbon, Luis Miranda on conga, and tenor saxophonist Brew Moore. In 1958 Willie Bobo and Mongo Santamaria were on Tjader's *Latin Concert* record. Soon they had departed from Tito Puente's band to join Cal and, with José "Chombo" Silva or Paul Horn on reeds, Tjader had one of his strongest bands.

In 1961 Santamaria and Bobo went out on their own and Tjader switched to the Verve label. At first his recordings were in a similar vein as the Fantasy sets, but eventually there were many projects with larger orchestras, some more successful than others. *Several Shades of Jade* sold well but today comes across as dated exotica. However, 1964's *Soul Sauce* not only was very popular (selling over 100,000 copies) but is considered a classic by many, and it helped popularize the word *Salsa.* Also highly rated was Tjader's 1966 collaboration with Eddie Palmieri, *El Sonido Nuevo*. But a trend towards commercialism sank some of Tjader's later recordings from the era, including three rather weak albums for the Skye label during 1968-69.

Tjader returned to Fantasy (a company for whom he recorded a total of over two dozen albums) during 1972-76, and, despite the use of electric keyboards, his music from this era is a large improvement over the Skye dates. After two sets for Galaxy and one for Crystal Clear, in 1979 Cal Tjader entered his final period. He spent his last years happily recording for Concord Picante, a subsidiary of the Concord label that was created by Carl Jefferson specifically to document Tjader's music. His final band was frequently a septet that featured the young Poncho Sanchez on conga along with pianist Mark Levine, flutist Roger Glenn, and sometimes guest altoist Gary Foster.

Cal Tjader, who was born on the road, fittingly died on the road. While on tour in the Philippines he suffered a fatal heart attack at the age of 56.

8 *Los Ritmos Calientes / May 6, 1954-Oct. 11, 1957 / Fantasy 24712*

7 *Tjader Plays Mambo / Sept. 11, 1954-Feb. 21, 1956 / Original Jazz Classics 274*

7 *Mambo with Tjader / Sept. 11, 1954 / Original Jazz Classics 271*

8 *Tjader Plays Tjazz / Dec. 4, 1954 + June 6, 1955 / Original Jazz Classics 988*

8 *Cal Tjader Quartet / May 24, 1956 / Original Jazz Classics 950*

7 *Jazz at the Blackhawk / Jan. 20, 1957 / Original Jazz Classics 436*

Most but not quite all of Cal Tjader's valuable Fantasy recordings have been reissued either as Fantasy CDs or as part of the Original Jazz Classics series. *Los Ritmos Calientes* has all of the music originally on the LPs *Ritmo Caliente* and *Mas Ritmo Caliente*. Included are three sessions from 1954-55 and three from 1957, each one with at least slightly different personnel. Among the key players are flutist Jerome Richardson, Al McKibbon, Armando Peraza, José Silva, Vince Guaraldi, and (on three numbers) Mongo Santamaria and Willie Bobo. Highlights of the enjoyable set include "Cubano Chant," "Mambo Inn," "Bernie's Tune," "Mambo Moderno," "Poinciana Cha Cha," and "Perfidia Cha Cha." On *Tjader Plays Mambo,* the vibraphonist is heard with his regular group of the time, consisting of pianist Manuel Duran, bassist Carlos Duran, Bayardo Velarde on timbales, and Edgard Rosales or Luis Miranda on conga. The music is laid back, sometimes slightly reminiscent of the George Shearing Quintet, and quite pleasing. A quartet of selections add four trumpets (including Al Porcino), which generates a bit of excitement. With the exception of Tjader's "Mambo Macumba," each of the dozen concise performances is a jazz standard, including "Guarachi Guaro," which would be remade eight years later by Tjader as "Soul Sauce." The only minus to the set is the brief playing time: under 34 minutes. *Mambo with Tjader* is taken from the same sessions (but without the trumpets) and consists of two Tjader tunes ("Mamblues" and "Lucero") plus ten more standards (including "Bye Bye Blues," "Chloe," "Tenderly," and "I'll Remember April"), all well played.

Throughout his career, Cal Tjader played straightahead jazz as a change of pace (including a highly rated album with Stan Getz in 1958 that was issued under the tenor's name). *Tjader Plays Tjazz* has two sessions, including a rare occasion on which Tjader plays drums (in a quartet with trombonist Bob Collins, guitarist Eddie Duran, and Al McKibbon). The other tunes feature Tjader on vibes interacting with tenor saxophonist Brew Moore, pianist Sonny Clark, bassist Eugene Wright, and drummer Bobby White. Tjader sounds quite enthusiastic swinging away on such tunes as

The late Cal Tjader was always one of the most famous and beloved figures in Afro-Cuban Jazz.

"There Will Never Be Another You," "Jeepers Creepers," and "Brew's Blues." *Cal Tjader Quartet* is also a strictly straightahead affair as Tjader is well showcased in a group with pianist Gerald Wiggins, Eugene Wright, and drummer Bill Douglass. Despite the identical instrumentation, this group avoids sounding like the Modern Jazz Quartet; Tjader and Wig work together quite well. *Jazz at the Blackhawk* is another cool bop quartet outing without any real Latin rhythms. This fine outing teams Tjader with Vince Guaraldi, Eugene Wright, and drummer Al Torres, jamming such songs as

"I'll Remember April," "Lover Come Back to Me," "Blues in the Night," and Guaraldi's "Thinking of You, MJQ."

- **8** *Latin Kick / Nov. 1956 / Original Jazz Classics 642*
- **9** *Black Orchid / 1956-1959 / Fantasy 24730*
- **9** *Cal Tjader's Latin Concert / Sept. 1958 / Original Jazz Classics 643*
- **8** *Black Hawk Nights / Dec. 1958-1959 / Original Jazz Classics 24755*
- **10** *Monterey Concerts / Apr. 20, 1959 / Prestige 24026*
- **8** *Latino! / 1960 / Fantasy 24732*

Brew Moore returns for *Latin Kick,* showing that he can play Afro-Cuban Jazz too. Tjader's regular quintet of the period (with Manuel Duran, Carlos Duran, Luis Miranda on conga, and Bayardo Velarde on timbales) Latinizes such tunes as "Invitation," "Lover Come Back to Me," "I Love Paris," and "Bye Bye Blues." *Black Orchid* combines the 1956 album *Cal Tjader Quintet* (which again has the Duran brothers, Miranda, and Velarde) with the three sessions that made up *Cal Tjader Goes Latin* (with flutist Paul Horn or tenorman José "Chombo" Silva, Lonnie Hewitt or Vince Guaraldi on piano, and usually Al McKibbon, Mongo Santamaria, and Willie Bobo). The 21 selections (standards and originals) are played with joyful spirit and heated rhythms. The musicians sound even more inspired than usual.

It would be difficult to improve upon the personnel featured on *Cal Tjader's Latin Concert*: Tjader, Guaraldi, McKibbon, Santamaria, and Bobo! They perform four Tjader songs (including "Viva Cepeda"), two by Santamaria, "Cubano Chant," and "The Continental." Cubop as played by some of the very best. *Black Hawk Nights* starts off with the six selections that originally made up *A Night at the Black Hawk,* a superior sextet outing

with Guaraldi, McKibbon, Santamaria, Bobo, and José "Chombo" Silva. Silva, who comes across as a mixture of Stan Getz and Paul Quinichette, has rarely been featured as favorably, digging into such songs as "I Hadn't Anyone Till You" and "A Night in Tunisia." Why was he not given any opportunities to lead his own record date? Also on this CD are six of the seven selections originally on *Live and Direct,* with Tjader on the first five tunes playing conventionally in a quartet with pianist Lonnie Hewitt, bassist Victor Venegas, and Willie Bobo (on drums). The closing number, "Mambo Terrifico," is more exciting, since it adds flutist Rolando Lozano and Mongo Santamaria.

One of the definite high points of the Fantasy years for Cal Tjader was his recorded appearance at a "preview" concert for the 1959 Monterey Jazz Festival. Tjader and his sextet (with Paul Horn, Lonnie Hewitt, Al McKibbon, Willie Bobo, and Mongo Santamaria) are at the peak of their powers throughout *Monterey Concerts,* a single CD that reissues all of the music from the former two-LP set. Whether it be boppish standards (such as "Doxy" and "Love Me or Leave Me") or Latin romps on "Afro Blue" and "A Night in Tunisia," everything works on this exciting live set. *Latino!* features Tjader with five different groups from 1960, all including the soon-to-be-departing team of Santamaria and Bobo. The music, formerly on the albums *Demasiado Caliente* and *Latino!,* has appearances by flutists José Lozano and Paul Horn, pianist Eddie Cano, Al McKibbon, and others. Tjader's Fantasy years are wrapped up nicely with such tunes as "Tumbao," "Cal's Pals," "Afro Blue," "Cuban Fantasy," and "A Night in Tunisia."

- **6** *Talkin' Verve—Roots of Acid Jazz / Aug. 28, 1961-Sept. 19, 1967 / Verve 314 531 562*
- **3** *Several Shades of Jade/Breeze from the East / Apr. 23, 1963-Nov. 26, 1963 / Verve 314 537 083*

9 *Soul Sauce / Nov. 19-20, 1964 / Verve 314 521 668*

8 *Soul Burst / Feb. 9-11, 1966 / Verve 314 557 446*

8 *El Sonido Nuevo / May 24-26, 1966 / Verve 314 519 812*

6 *Compact Jazz / Jan. 28, 1963-Jan. 1967 / Verve 841 131*

Cal Tjader's Verve years (1961-67) found the vibraphonist often interacting with larger orchestras. The sampler *Talkin' Verve* has 16 selections drawn from nine of his Verve albums, with the highlights including "Manteca" (with Oliver Nelson's orchestra), "Mambo in Miami," the famous "Soul Sauce," "Afro Blue," "Picadillo," and "Tokyo Blues" (with a big band arranged by Lalo Schifrin).

Although Tjader's producer during his Verve years (Creed Taylor) deserves credit for taking chances, there were some flops along the way. *Several Shades of Jade* is an ok collaboration with Lalo Schifrin in which they explore nine themes that have something to do with Asian sounds (including four Schifrin compositions). However, much of this music sounds like it was left over from a soundtrack. As for *Breeze from the East,* it is at best corny and at worse nearly unlistenable. Stan Applebaum's arrangements for a string orchestra, even on the better songs ("Black Orchid," "Star Dust," "Poinciana," and "East of the Sun"), are closer to Les Baxter's exotic mood music dates than to the music that Tjader plays best.

Soul Sauce, one of Cal Tjader's most popular recordings, is more like it. The title cut (a remake of the Dizzy Gillespie-Chano Pozo tune "Guachi Guaro") is considered a classic and helped the word *Salsa* come to be used to describe Latin dance music. The sidemen include Lonnie Hewitt, drummer Johnny Rae, Armanda Perazo, and guest Willie Bobo (who adds a great deal to the date's spirit)

plus such unexpected jazz voices as trumpeter Donald Byrd, tenor saxophonist Jimmy Heath, and guitarist Kenny Burrell. "Afro Blue" is given fresh treatment, as is "Tanya" and "Spring Is Here." *Soul Burst* features Tjader playing a few current Latin numbers (including Clare Fischer's famous "Morning"). He revives "Manteca" and also performs a pair of Kurt Weill standards ("My Ship" and "The Bilbao Song"). With Jerome Richardson, Seldon Powell, and/or Jerry Dodgion prominent on flutes, such sidemen as the young pianist Chick Corea, guitarist Attila Zoller, bassist Richard Davis, drummer Grady Tate, and some fine charts written by Oliver Nelson, the music is quite catchy and accessible, commercial but still creative within the genre.

El Sonido Nuevo, a meeting between Tjader and Eddie Palmieri, has been called an all-time classic (the liners of the reissue call this "a landmark in the history of Latin jazz"), but the music is not quite on that level. It is interesting hearing Tjader interacting with Palmieri's "trombanga" band, which has four trombones and one flute in the frontline, and there are some strong selections (including Tito Puente's "Picadillo"). But some of the music is a bit too repetitive, there is a throwaway version of "On a Clear Day," and this CD has been augmented by six additional selections actually recorded for the *Breeze from the East* and *Along Comes Cal* albums. There are some heated and memorable moments along the way, but *El Sonido Nuevo* (which has a lot of fadeouts) does not quite reach greatness.

Compact Jazz has five songs apiece from Cal Tjader's Verve albums *Sona Libre* and *Soul Burst* plus three from *Along Comes Cal.* The music (which features such sidemen as pianists Chick Corea and Clare Fischer, flutist Jerome Richardson, Armando Peraza, and Patato Valdés) is excellent, with the highlights including "Los Bandidos," "Samba do Sueño," "Descarga Cubana," "Soul

Burst," and "Manteca." However, the original albums (only *Soul Burst* is currently in print) are naturally preferred.

3 *Sounds Out Burt Bacharach / Aug. 6-19, 1968 / DCC Jazz 633*

5 *Plugs In / Feb. 20-21, 1969 / DCC Jazz 622*

7 *Descarga / 1971-1972 / Fantasy 24737*

8 *Primo / Feb. 8-9, 1973 / Original Jazz Classics 762*

5 *Tambu / Sept. 18-20, 1973 / Original Jazz Classics 891*

6 *Amazonas / June 1975 / Original Jazz Classics 840*

7 *The Grace Cathedral Concert / May 22, 1976 / Fantasy 9677*

6 *Here and There / Sept. 1976-June 18, 1977 / Fantasy 24743*

Two of Cal Tjader's three Skye albums have been reissued by the audiophile DCC Jazz label, a definite mistake! Tjader's *Sounds Out Burt Bacharach,* finds the vibist joined by up to ten horns, a few strings, and an electric rhythm section. The results are overly commercial and pretty abysmal; with few exceptions, these are not even the better Bacharach songs! *Plugs In,* recorded live at the Lighthouse, is the best of Tjader's Skye sets, with mostly obscure material being interpreted by the vibraphonist with a rhythm section that includes the electric piano of Al Zulaica and electric bassist Jim McCabe. Tjader plays reasonably well, even if the electronics now sound dated, but the brief playing time and even briefer moments of excitement make this a rather forgettable effort.

Tjader's second period with Fantasy was much more rewarding than the Skye ventures. *Descarga* brings back the music originally released as *Agua Dulce* and *Live at the Funky Quarters.* The former is an intriguing outing with a 14-piece big band of West Coast (mostly San Francisco) players, includ-

ing trumpeter Luis Gasca, saxophonist Bill Perkins, and both Pete and Coke Escovedo. While that date features mostly obscurities (other than "Morning" and "Invitation"), the second half of the CD, a quintet outing with keyboardist Zulaica, has some old favorites (including "Cubano Chant," a remake of "Soul Sauce," and "Manteca") and is a happily spontaneous outing, though it is a pity that Zulaica was not persuaded to play acoustic piano. *Primo* finds Tjader joined by four horns, the keyboards of Charlie Palmieri, electric bassist Bobby Rodriguez, and six percussionists. Tito Puente makes an appearance on "Tanga" and, along with Palmieri, contributed all the arrangements. The music is definitely jumping, quite rhythmic, and fun. The songs include "Vibe Mambo," "El Watusi," and two versions of "Bang Bang."

Tambu, a rare meeting between Tjader and Brazilian jazz guitarist Charlie Byrd, is an interesting clash between two styles. Actually Tjader mostly meets Byrd in the guitarist's home field, adding his vibes to Brazilian-flavored tunes. Mike Wolff on electric piano sounds a bit dated, and there are times when the vibraphonist also seems a little ill at ease. A historical curiosity. *Amazonas,* which continues the "experiment" by teaming Tjader with such modern Brazilian players as pianist Egberto Gismonti, flutist Hermeto Pascoal, guitarist David Amaro, and keyboardist Dawilli Gonga, is better if still not essential. George Duke's arrangements are modern and funky, Tjader doubles on marimba, and the results are interesting if not completely successful.

Much more comfortable is *The Grace Cathedral Concert,* which, despite its setting, is not a religious concert. Cal Tjader (doubling on timbales) leads his regular mid-'70s quintet, which consists of Lonnie Hewitt (unfortunately on electric piano), bassist Rob Fister, drummer Pete Riso, and the young conga player Poncho Sanchez. Together they perform a basic original, "Bluesology," "Body and

Soul," and a medley from *Black Orpheus* that ironically works better than anything on the two previous Brazilian albums. *Here and There* has Tjader's final Fantasy album (*Guarabe*) and one of his two Galaxy dates (five of the six tracks from *Here*). The most unusual aspect to this otherwise conventional set is that Clare Fischer (usually more associated with Brazilian jazz) is on keyboards. Otherwise Tjader leads a no-name sextet/septet, with Poncho Sanchez often taking the most exciting spots.

6 *La Onda Va Bien / July 1979 / Concord Picante 4113*

7 *Gozame! Pero Ya… / June 1980 / Concord Picante 4133*

7 *The Shining Sea / Mar. 1981 / Concord Jazz 4159*

8 *A Fuego Vivo / Aug. 1981 / Concord Picante 4176*

6 *Heat Wave / Jan. 1982 / Concord Jazz 4189*

9 *Good Vibes / Sept. 1981 / Concord Picante 4247*

Cal Tjader's final period resulted in six albums as a leader, two for the Concord label and four for its Concord Picante subsidiary. The Concord Picante subsidiary began with *La Onda Va Bien,* an ok but not too essential sextet outing. Actually Tjader and flutist Roger Glenn fail to generate any real excitement, so drummer Vince Lateano and Sanchez easily take honors. *Gozame! Pero Ya* has the same musicians on a more inspired outing, with three ballads finding the group joined by the lyrical guitarist Mundell Lowe (including "This Is Always"). Other highlights include "Bye Bye Blues" and "Will You Still Be Mine." *The Shining Sea* is notable for teaming Tjader with the warm swing tenor of Scott Hamilton in a straightahead quintet with pianist Hank Jones, bassist Dean Reilly, and drummer Lateano. All eight songs were composed by Johnny Mandel, so the emphasis is on ballads, including

"Quietly There," "Emily," and "A Time for Love." *A Fuego Vivo* is a live set featuring Tjader's working band of 1981 (a quintet with keyboardist Mark Levine, bassist Rob Fisher, Lateano, Sanchez, and guest Gary Foster on flute, soprano, and alto, plus Ramon Banda on timbales). These versions of "The Continental" and "Serenata" are quite joyful, and this set gives one a good idea what it was like to see Tjader live during his final period. Tjader's last recording, *Heat Wave,* was cut just four months before his death. It is an ok collaboration with singer Carmen McRae, although Tjader's band (which bears a strong similarity to the nucleus of Poncho Sanchez's upcoming group) has relatively little to do. McRae sounds cheerful but not particularly inspired on such tunes as "Besame Mucho," "Evil Ways," a couple of Stevie Wonder songs, and "Heat Wave."

But to end this section on a higher note, Tjader's next-to-last recording, *Good Vibes,* is a must. His band of the early 1980s (Levine, Fisher, Lateano, Sanchez, and both flutist Roger Glenn and Gary Foster on reeds) rarely sounded better, and the vibraphonist is quite inspired. The well-rounded outing (which includes "Soul Sauce," "Doxy," "Speak Low," "Broadway," and "Cuban Fantasy") is a highly recommended gem that wraps up Cal Tjader's important career with one last burst of glory.

LPs to Search For:

A few of Cal Tjader's Fantasy records were reissued on LP in the Original Jazz Classics series but are not yet on CD, including 1960's *Concert on the Campus* (OJC 279), which gives listeners additional titles from the Tjader-Hewitt-Bobo-Santamaria quintet (with Eddie Coleman on bass). *West Side Story* (Fantasy 8054) is a real obscurity (also from 1960). Tjader plays songs from the famous musical with his quintet plus a large string orchestra arranged by Clare Fischer; interesting even if nothing all that unusual occurs. *Breathe Easy* (Galaxy 5107), from 1977, is a decent boppish non-Latin quintet outing with pianist Hank Jones, bassist Monty Budwig, drummer Shelly Manne, and the obscure trumpeter Allen Smith.

J.P. TORRES
b. Puerto Padre, Cuba

One of the top Cuban trombonists, Juan Pablo Torres has appeared on over 25 CDs as a valuable sideman. He was a member of the Orquesta Cubana de Musica Moderna (which later became Irakere) in the 1970s. Torres formed Algo Nuevo in 1976 and later became the musical director of Estrellas de Arieto. After defecting from Cuba, Torres was greatly in demand for recording dates in the 1990s, including appearing on important albums by Paquito D'Rivera, Chico O'Farrill, Eddie Palmieri, Tito Puente, the Tropijazz All-Stars, and Bebo Valdés. J.P. Torres has also recorded as a leader for Tropijazz and RMM.

9 *Trombone Man / Mar. 22, 1995-Apr. 11, 1995 / Tropijazz 81601*

One of the few major trombonists to emerge from Cuba, J.P. Torres is heard in superb form throughout this boppish set. The music is primarily straightahead despite the utilization of two percussionists (Gabriel Machado and Pernell Saturnino) on many of the selections. The repertoire consists of compositions by Torres, Paquito D'Rivera (who plays alto on two tracks and clarinet on three others), Hilton Ruiz (heard on piano on three numbers) plus Miles Davis' "Four," which is performed simultaneously with Ernesto Duarte's "Como Fue." Torres scats masterfully on the latter selection and also sings on his own "Banana Split." Other key soloists include pianist Ed Simon, trumpeter Diego Urcola, and altoist Manuel Valera; these last two deserve to be much better known. Andy González and Oscar Stagnaro alternate on bass. But even with

a partly all-star cast, J.P. Torres emerges as the star, contributing many extroverted and passionate solos, showing that he is a master of bebop while remaining tied to the Cuban music tradition.

NÉSTOR TORRES
b. Apr. 25, 1954, Puerto Rico

Although his roots are in Afro-Cuban Jazz and salsa, Néstor Torres has made his fame as a pop/jazz crossover flutist who nevertheless remains a strong player. He was originally inspired by Cal Tjader, Dave Brubeck, and Tito Puente. Torres started playing drums at five, switching to flute at 12. After high school, he moved at first to New York and then studied at Berklee and the New England Conservatory of Music. In 1977 he returned to New York, working with a variety of lesser-known Cuban groups in addition to sitting in with Tito Puente and Eddie Palmieri and gigging with Manny Oquendo's Libre. He recorded three little-known Afro-Cuban Jazz albums during 1980-81 that did not sell much (*Colombia En Charanga, Orchestra Afro-Charanga*, and *No Me Provoques*).

In 1981, Torres started working with a Latin act (Hansel and Raul) in Miami, where he still lives. He became popular at first on the local scene and then in 1989 signed with Verve/Forecast. His debut for the label, the crossover *Morning Ride*, was a big seller. A serious accident in a celebrity boat race knocked him out of action in 1990, but after a year he returned with *Dance of the Phoenix* and has since made a full comeback. His other recordings as a leader are 1994's *Burning Whispers* (Sony Latin Jazz), 1996's *Talk to Me*, and 1999's *Treasures of the Heart* (the last two for Shanachie). Néstor Torres has also appeared on recordings by Cachao, Gloria Estefan, Larry Harlow, and saxophonist Billy Ross.

7 *Morning Ride / 1989 / Verve Forecast 839 387*

7 *Burning Whispers / 1994 / Sony Discos 469698*

4 *Treasures of the Heart / 1999 / Shanachie 5055*

Morning Ride, which helped make Néstor Torres a strong name in the jazz crossover field, has aged fairly well. Torres' mastery of the flute uplifts even his weaker originals, the rhythm section (which includes either Satoshi Takeishi or Juan Vicente Zambrano on keyboards) is a bit faceless but displays spirit, and the closing acoustic rendition of "Seven Steps to Heaven" shows how strong a player Torres can be. *Burning Whispers*, recorded after Néstor Torres had recovered from his accident, finds the flutist playing quite well. Some of the music is poppish or a bit slick and the Afro-Cuban elements are watered down, but no one can deny that Torres is a masterful flutist, often building a great deal out of practically nothing. Keyboardist Zambrano and guitarist Manny López are the key players in the backup group, which includes an oversized rhythm section, occasional horns, and background vocalists. Torres performs eight group originals plus a lyrical version of "Over the Rainbow." Pleasing as the music is, it is still a pity that the arrangements are not more creative or the material quite a bit stronger.

Treasures of the Heart is actually much more commercial, with plenty of electronic rhythms, poppish melodies, and only slight hints here and there of how good a player Torres can be. "Luna Latina," "Ain't No Sunshine," and "Casey's Garden" are not bad, but most of this CD is quite forgettable, music recorded specifically in hopes of getting radio airplay. At this time, Néstor Torres' most exciting playing seems reserved for his guest appearances on other artists' sessions.

BEBO VALDÉS

b. Oct. 9, 1918, Quivican, Havana

Bebo Valdés (the father of Chucho Valdés) was a major pianist, composer, and arranger in Cuba before the Castro revolution. He first started studying piano in 1931, moved with his family to Havana in 1936, and two years later made his professional debut with Happy D'Ulsasia. Valdés played piano with Wilfredo Garcia-Curbelo's orchestra (1943-45) and Julio Cuevas (1945-47), appearing on records with the latter. During 1948-57 Valdés worked as the arranger for singer Rita Montaner and was the musical director for the nightclub shows at the famous Tropicana in Havana, leading his own orchestra and recording quite regularly. His October 1952 recording for producer Norman Granz with a sextet has been cited as possibly the first Cuban jazz jam session (*descarga*) on record.

In 1960 Valdés defected from Cuba and relocated to Mexico, where he played and wrote for television. A couple of years later he played for two weeks in Los Angeles with Miguelito Valdés (no relation), moved to Spain, accompanied singer Lucho Gatica for nine months, and then toured Europe. In 1963 he met his future wife in Sweden and settled permanently in Stockholm. Maintaining a low profile for decades, Bebo Valdés played an eclectic variety of music until he was rediscovered in 1994. After 34 years off of records, he cut the very successful *Bebo Rides Again* for the Messidor label.

10 *Bebop Rides Again / Nov. 1994 / Messidor 15834*

Although musically active since settling in Stockholm in 1963, Bebo Valdés went completely unrecorded until this project, which was organized by Paquito D'Rivera. Valdés certainly rose to the occasion, because not only is he heard playing piano very well, but he composed eight numbers and arranged ten of the eleven songs in the 36 hours before the first session; he was 76 at the time! This recording is particularly significant for it was one of the first times that Cuban exiles were allowed to record with Cuban musicians still living under Castro's rule (guitarist Carlos Emilio Morales and percussionist Amadito Valdés). The fresh new music is full of strong melodies, stirring rhythms, exciting ensembles, and lots of variety. The instrumentation differs on each track, with plenty of solo space for D'Rivera (on both alto and clarinet), trombonist J.P. Torres (who takes "Veinte Años" as a duet with Valdés), trumpeter Diego Urcola, and the apparently ageless pianist. The percussionists (which include Patato Valdés, also of no relation!) work together quite well behind the lead voices, and every selection is well worth hearing. This is simply one of the finest Afro-Cuban Jazz recordings of recent times.

CHUCHO VALDÉS

b. Oct. 9, 1941, Quivican, Havana, Cuba

One of Cuba's great pianists and long an important bandleader, Chucho Valdés has in recent years also been an important goodwill ambassador for his native country, not through his words but through his consistently exciting music and professionalism. The son of Bebo Valdés and a mother who was a singer and pianist, Chucho was taking piano lessons by the time he was four. He grew up listening to both Cuban music and jazz and was already directing bands as a teenager. He worked very early on with Ernesto Lecuona and Beny Moré and led a trio when he was 16. In 1957 (the year that Chucho made his recording debut), Bebo Valdés organized a group (La Orquesta Sabor de Cuba) for his son to play in. However, after Bebo's defection in 1960, it would be decades before Chucho saw him again.

The younger Valdés had a quartet, was the pianist for El Teatro Musical in 1963, and during 1965-67 worked with the Elio Reve Orchestra. In 1967 Cuba's best musicians were selected to form La Orquesta Cubana de Musica Moderna. Although it was originally directed by Armando Romeu, the main stars were soon Valdés, Arturo Sandoval, and Paquito D'Rivera. In 1973 Valdés, Sandoval, and D'Rivera, along with the nucleus of the orchestra, broke away to form the smaller and more adventurous Irakere. Although started as a co-op, within a year the pianist was Irakere's leader.

Valdés ran, arranged, and played piano for Irakere for the next 25 years. Thought of by some as the McCoy Tyner of Cuba, Valdés has a modern style that displays his wide knowledge of other jazz pianists plus his grounding in Cuban folk music. In addition to his work with Irakere (which included many tours of Europe and finally, by the mid-1990s, the United States), Valdés founded the Havana International Jazz Festival in 1980, led a combo, and occasionally performed solo. He also recorded and toured with Roy Hargrove's Cristol in 1996. In 1998, Valdés left Irakere (although he occasionally makes guest appearances) so as to pursue his own solo projects. In addition to his recordings with Irakere and Sandoval (for Jazz House), Chucho Valdés has led sessions for Messidor, Blue Note, and various Cuban and European companies.

8 *Lucumi / Nov. 15, 1986 / Messidor 15976*
10 *Solo Piano / Sept. 1991 / Blue Note 80597*
9 *Pianissimo / 1994 / Musique 3006 040*
8 *Bele Bele en la Habana / Jan. 12-13, 1998 / Blue Note 23082*
9 *Briyumba Palo Congo / Nov. 23-25, 1998 / Blue Note 98917*
8 *Live at the Village Vanguard / Apr. 9-10, 1999 / Blue Note 20730*

The first three Chucho Valdés CDs reviewed here are all unaccompanied solo sets. *Lucumi* is an often-thoughtful recital by Valdés. Part of the time he sounds a bit like a Latin Ray Bryant, displaying his two-handed style and a slight tie to the swing tradition in a relaxed fashion. Valdés' nine originals are full of rich melodies, are often wistful, and are explored with taste and subtle creativity. Listen to how he builds up his solo on "Mambo Influenciado," showing in spots that he is quite aware of McCoy Tyner.

The Wayne Knight Collection/Photo: Juliana Thomas

Chucho Valdés, the Art Tatum of Cuba.

Solo Piano, from five years later, finds Valdés playing adventurous and unpredictable solos on eight pieces [seven originals, including "Bill (Evans)" plus the lone standard "My Foolish Heart"]. He shows off the influences of Tyner, Lennie Tristano, and Cecil Taylor in spots while still sounding quite original. Valdés' improvisations are frequently dazzling (check out "Blue Yes," which is based on Charlie Parker's "Confirmation"), sometimes quite free, and never dull. The final two pieces ("When I Fall in Love" and "Blues Untitled") get away from the solo format as Valdés interacts closely with bassist Dave Green, drummer Enrique Pla, and percussionist Miguel Diaz.

The obscure but rewarding *Pianissimo* is a bit unusual for Chucho Valdés in that he performs exclusively older material (most songs dating from the 1950s or before) and the performances are quite concise, with only two of the dozen pieces exceeding five minutes; four are under three minutes in length. There are many beautiful melodies on this set, including "Linda Cubana, "Guantanamera,"

"Son de la Loma," and Ernesto Lecuona's "La Comparsa." Valdés' loving variations uplift the music.

Bele Bele en la Habana is highlighted by Valdés' interpretations of "Tres Lindas Cubanas," "La Sitiera," "But Not for Me," and his own "Lorraine." The pianist is heard in top form, stretching out on a set of mostly little-known material (including "Con Poco Poco," by his father, Bebo Valdés) in a quartet with bassist Alain Rodriguez, drummer Raul Roque, and percussionist Roberto Guillot

Briyumba Palo Congo, which is mostly a quartet date with bassist Francisco Pampin, drummer Roque, and Guillot on conga and batá drums, certainly has its memorable moments. Valdés' "El Rumbon (The Party)" lives up to its name, his rendition of "Caravan" is dense and explosive, "Embraceable You" is, in contrast, quite relaxed and melodic, and "Rhapsody in Blue" is completely transformed into a 1920s/'30s-style Cuban dance number. The last song has Joaquin Gavilan guesting on flute while a chorus chants and sings a little bit on one segment of the title cut. A typically impressive effort.

Live at the Village Vanguard finds Valdés, at age 57, still in peak form. Matched with the same quartet that is featured on *Briyumba Palo Congo*, Valdés performs a set of colorful originals (including "To Bud Powell") along with "My Funny Valentine." His sister, Mayra Valdés, sings "Drume Negrita," a very emotional lullaby that is a bit of an acquired taste. However, Chucho Valdés' mastery of polyrhythms is always quite remarkable. His playing is very difficult not to appreciate and enjoy throughout this spirited program and all of the other sets reviewed in this section.

MIGUELITO VALDÉS

b. Sept. 6, 1910, Havana, Cuba, d. Nov. 8, 1978, Bogota, Columbia

Known as "Mr. Babalu," Miguelito Valdés was one of Cuba's most famous singers for decades. Born Eugenio Zacrias Miguel Valdés, he worked as an automobile mechanic at the age of 11 and as a teenager was a prize fighter, eventually becoming Cuba's amateur welterweight champion. When Valdés was being interviewed on the radio after his 23rd win in the ring, he asked if he could sing a song for the audience; a new career was born! In 1927, he became a professional singer, working with El Sexteto Habanero Juvenil and taking guitar lessons. He was part of Maria Teresa Vera's chorus in 1929 and freelanced. Valdés spent 1933-36 in Panama, at first singing with a Cuban band at a carnival and working as a singing waiter before landing a job with Lucho Azcarraga's band (1934-36). He became quite popular in Panama. When he returned to Cuba in 1936, he was considered a star.

Valdés sang with Los Hermanos Castro for a year and then helped organize Orquesta Casino de la Playa. The band caught on and signed with RCA; Valdés recorded around 200 titles during 1937-40. In 1939 his recording of Margarita Lecuona's "Babalu" became a big hit; Desi Arnaz in New York would turn it into a sensation. In May 1940, Valdés moved to the United States, where he was a major attraction as the main singer with Xavier Cugat's orchestra, having hits with a remake of "Babalu," "Negra Leona," "Bambarito," "Yo Ta Namora," and "Anna Boroco Tinde." After singing "Bim Bam Bum" in the background of a scene in the Fred Astaire film *You Were Never Lovelier* in 1942, he left Cugat due to a dispute over money. Right before the Musicians Union recording strike of 1942, Valdés recorded 24 songs while accompanied by Machito's orchestra. He spent most of the next two years in Mexico, where he appeared in a dozen motion pictures (mostly cameo roles). Valdés moved to Los Angeles in September 1944 and is featured singing "Babalu" in the so-so 1945 film *Pan Americana*. He also appeared with Machito in *Night in the Tropics* (1946).

After years as a single, he formed an orchestra in 1948 that lasted for six years and employed Stan Getz on tenor for a few months in 1949. Valdés broke up his band and retired in 1955 (when he was just 45). In 1963 Valdés was lured back to music to record the album *Reunion* with Machito. The success of that recording revived his career, and he worked on a part-time basis from then on, including having his own television show in Mexico during 1966-76. On November 8, 1978, 68-year-old Miguelito Valdés died of a heart attack in the middle of a performance onstage in Columbia.

PATATO VALDÉS

b. Nov. 4, 1926, Havana, Cuba

A very busy conguero since his arrival in the United States, Carlo "Patato" Valdés (not "Potato," as is sometimes listed) has been an asset to hundreds if not thousands of sessions through the years. His father played the tres guitar in Cuba with Los Apaches. Patato began playing the tres and also learned thumb piano and washtub bass before switching to conga. He worked in Cuba with La Sonora Mantancera (starting in 1944), Conjunto Kubavana, Conjunto Azul, and Chano Pozo. In 1947 Valdés was supposed to go to New York with Miguelito Valdés (no relation) but, when his father would not let him travel (he was not quite 21), Chano Pozo took the job in his place. In 1950 Patato discovered a way of tuning his congas by turning a key to tighten a metal ring, essentially inventing the tuned conga drum and making the instrument much more melodic than it had been previously. Valdés played with Conjunto Casino starting in 1949 and finally visited New York in 1952 when Conjunto Casino had an American engagement. In 1954 Valdés, who had in the meantime also played with Pérez Prado and Beny Moré, moved to the United States permanently and immediately got busy.

Valdés' first American record date was trum-peter Kenny Dorham's *Afro-Cuban*. During the next decade he also recorded with Dizzy Gillespie, Art Blakey (*Orgy in Rhythm*), Willie Bobo, Charlie Palmieri, Max Roach, Cal Tjader, Billy Taylor, Grant Green, altoist Sonny Stitt, trombonist J.J. Johnson, and Quincy Jones, among others. He joined Tito Puente's band in 1955 and recorded *Cuban Carnaval* (RCA) and *Puente in Percussion* (Tico). Valdés spent three years (1956-59) working with Machito (recording *Kenya*) and then gained a lot of recognition during his long period with Herbie Mann's Afro-Cuban band (1959-68). Mann wrote "Patato" and "Cuban Patato Chips" to feature Valdés. In 1967 the conguero co-led an album for Verve with vocalist Totico (a childhood friend), *Patato y Totico*, which included Arsenio Rodriguez on tres and Cachao.

Freelancing after leaving Mann, Valdés played with the Latin Percussion Jazz Ensemble in the 1970s, was featured with Cachao on *Cachao y Su Descarga '77* (Salsoul), and during 1978-80 lived in Paris, where he played with Alfredo Rodriguez's band. He worked with Jorge Dalto during the first half of the 1980s (recording with Dalto for Concord Picante) and in the late '80s was featured with Machito's orchestra (when it was led by Machito's son, Mario Grillo). Valdés toured Europe with Mario Bauzá's Big Band in 1991 and during the past decade has recorded with Bauzá, Bebo Valdés, Roy Hargrove, tenor saxophonist Benny Golson, and Hilton Ruiz, among others. Patato Valdés has led relatively few record dates through the years, but in recent times he recorded as a leader for Messidor and Six Degrees. He can also be seen giving Bridget Bardot a mambo lesson in the film *And God Created Woman*!

7 *Masterpiece / 1984-1985 / Messidor 15827*
8 *The Legend of Cuban Percussion / 1995-1996 / Six Degrees 657036 1027*

Masterpiece is a mixed bag in terms of style. Several

of the numbers are dominated by group singing/chanting, and both Vicentico Valdés ("Reflexionando") and Patato Valdés himself ("A Los Pianistas") have individual features. In contrast, "Cute" and "Comelon" are straightahead showcases for Ronnie Cuber (on soprano and baritone) and Michel Camilo, while flutist Artie Webb is heard in top form on "Adios Pampa Mia" and a cooking version of Horace Silver's "Nica's Dream." Other participants include pianist Jorge Dalto (on his next-to-last recording), Nicky Marrero on timbales, drummer Steve Berrios, Andy González, and Jerry González on trumpet. Everything is done well, but the music reaches surprisingly far beyond Afro-Cuban Jazz.

The Legend of Cuban Percussion draws its dozen selections from a pair of albums called *Ritmo y Candela* and *Ritmo y Candela II*. A more jazz-oriented disc (with fewer vocals) than *Masterpiece*, this set has plenty of features for Valdés, pianist Rebeca Mauleón, and Enrique Fernandez on flute, alto, baritone, and tenor. Fernandez sometimes overdubbed his horns to achieve what was called a "wall of wind." Among the highlights are Mauleón's "Descarga en Faux," "Yo Tengo Ritmo" ("I Got Rhythm"), "Son de Patato," and "Señor Blues." Patato Valdés at 70 shows that he had lost nothing and was still capable of playing exciting music.

DAVE VALENTIN

b. Apr. 29, 1952, Bronx, NY

Flutist Dave Valentin is best known for his extensive series of recordings for the GRP label, music that was slickly produced and had a commercial bent to it (adding elements of pop, R&B, and Brazilian music) although also including plenty of moments of stirring Afro-Cuban Jazz. Valentin started on congas and bongos at the age of 7, playing with a local group on timbales when he was 13. However, when he attended the High School of Music and Art, Valentin switched permanently to flute, and he

took lessons from Hubert Laws. He made his first recordings with Ricardo Marrero and violinist Noel Pointer in 1977. Producers Dave Grusin and Larry Rosen were impressed, and, when they started the GRP label, Valentin was the first artist they signed. Valentin recorded 16 albums for the label and became quite popular. In addition, he had opportunities to record with many other artists, including Steve Turre, the GRP All-Star Big Band, Memo Acevedo, Justo Almario, Conrad Herwig, Giovanni Hidalgo, Ralph Irizarry, Humberto Ramirez, Hilton Ruiz, Arturo Sandoval, Mongo Santamaria, Charlie Sepúlveda, vibraphonist Jay Hoggard, bassist Charles Fambrough, singers Adela Dalto, Chris Connor, and Nnenna Freelon, keyboardist Don Grolnick, Dave Grusin, and the Tropijazz All-Stars.

Valentin played with McCoy Tyner's Afro-Cuban All-Stars in the mid-1990s and, after the collapse of the GRP label, switched to the Concord Vista label. During the second half of the 1990s the flutist also worked as the musical director of Tito Puente's Golden Latin Jazz All-Stars. Recently Dave Valentin became a member of the Caribbean Jazz Project, taking over Paquito D'Rivera's spot.

7 *Kalahari / 1984 / GRP 9508*
7 *Jungle Garden / 1985 / GRP 9523*
7 *Light Strike / 1986 / GRP 9537*
8 *Mind Time / 1987 / GRP 9554*

Kalahari, Dave Valentin's 7th of 16 recordings for the GRP label, is typical of his output for the company. The music is expertly played, melodic, lightly funky, has subtle Latin rhythms, and is quite musical, if mostly absent of surprises. Valentin's long-time group of the period consisted of Bill O'Connell on keyboards, electric bassist Lincoln Goines, and drummer Robert Ameen, with occasional percussion by Roger Squitero. Keyboardist Dave Grusin and guitarist Kevin Eubanks make a guest appearance on "September Nights." *Jungle Gardens* has the same personnel except with Frank

The colorful Dave Valentin has always been a crowd-pleaser.

Malabe in Squitero's place. Tania Maria sings on her "Very Nice Indeed," and the group's originals are joined by a Stevie Wonder tune, Ron Carter's "81," and "I Loves You Porgy."

It can be said without exaggeration that listeners who like one Valentin record will like them all! *Light Strike* has the Valentin-O'Connell-Goines-Ameen quartet assisted by percussionist Rafael de Jesus, a few substitutes in the rhythm section, and Angela Bofill, who sings Ivan Lins' "Can't Change My Heart." Nothing surprising occurs outside of the inclusion of a mellow version of Duke Ellington's "Prelude to a Kiss." *Mind Time* has different personnel on each of the selections and more variety than usual. Earl Klugh adds his acoustic guitar to "Feel Like Jazz" (unfortunately his only appearance on the disc). Valentin takes two duets (one on pan pipes) with the synthesizers of Richard Martinez, has "Passion Flower" as his overdubbed solo feature, duets with the acoustic piano of Bill O'Connell on "It Might As Well Be Spring," and jams with three very different quartet/quintets. A strong release overall.

9 *Live at the Blue Note / May 31, 1988-June 1, 1988 / GRP 9568*

4 *Two Amigos / 1990 / GRP 9606*

6 *Musical Portraits / July 10, 1990-1991 / GRP 9664*

7 *Red Sun / 1992-1993 / GRP 9699*

9 *Tropic Heat / 1994 / GRP 9769*

7 *Sunshower / June 6-9, 1999 / Concord Vista 4872*

Live at the Blue Note was Valentin's first in-concert recording, and he puts on a colorful show, playing not only the usual group originals but Wayne Shorter's "Footprints," the Beatles' "Blackbird," and "Afro Blue." The Valentin-O'Connell-Goines-Ameen quartet is assisted by Giovanni Hidalgo on congas, and the result is one of their strongest jazz-oriented sets.

In contrast, *Two Amigos* is a disappointment. Valentin meets up with fellow flutist Herbie Mann on five selections, but the material is forgettable (the first number starts out being dominated by electronic percussion), the flutists recorded their parts on a different day than the rhythm section (which sounds a bit obvious), and the expected sparks are missing. Instead of being a historic flute summit, the weak arrangements sink the effort. Valentin is actually heard at his best on the four songs that he recorded without Mann (particularly "First Date" and "Obsession")! *Musical Portraits* is a little stronger but not particularly memorable. Valentin's brand of Latin-tinged funky jazz was often quite predictable by this time. The best cut on *Musical Portraits* is "Firecracker," which allows the flutist to stretch a bit. By the time that *Red Sun* was recorded, the drum slot in Valentin's band was being shared by Robby Ameen and Richie Morales, while Sammy Figueroa was usually on percussion. Steve Turre sits in on "Little Sunflower," and Arturo Sandoval takes a tasteful flügelhorn solo on "We'll Be Together Again," a tribute to the recently deceased Dizzy Gillespie. Those two selections uplift the otherwise fairly conventional set.

Tropic Heat, Dave Valentin's 16th and final GRP recording as a leader, is different from the previous 15 in that this date is mostly straightforward Afro-Cuban Jazz, without the funk or pop rhythms. Two percussionists and seven horns (saxophonists Dick Oatts, Mario Rivera, and David Sanchez, trumpeters Piro Rodriguez, Ray Vega, and Charlie Sepúlveda, and trombonist Papo Vásquez) are added to the quartet, and each of the horn players gets at least one solo! Although most of the tunes (other than "My Favorite Things") are originals, the music is very much in the Afro-Cuban tradition.

In 1999 Valentin debuted for a new label (Concord Vista), but his sound and style were virtually unchanged from his GRP days. *Sunshower* is mostly pretty safe (particularly the first few selections), with the music being lightly funky and all of the musicians playing well without taking any real chances. Valentin, O'Connell, and Ameen are joined in their quintet by electric bassist Ruben Rodriguez and percussionist Milton Cardona.

Guest spots are taken by Ed Calle (on his R&Bish alto and tenor), percussionist Rafael de Jesus and two of Valentin's fellow members of the Caribbean Jazz Project: vibraphonist Dave Samuels (a strong asset) and guitarist Steve Khan. "I Got It Bad" and "Subway Six" are highlights, as is the closing number, "Space Cadet," which shows how adventurous a soloist Dave Valentin can be when inspired.

ORLANDO "MARACA" VALLE
b. Sept. 1966, Havana, Cuba

A superb flutist best known thus far for his period with Irakere, Orlando Valle came from a musical family. At ten Valle began studying flute at the Manuel Saumell Conservatory. In 1987 he worked with the Bobby Carcasses Orchestra in Panama and with pianist Emiliano Salvador. While with Irakere (1988-94), Valle played flute and occasional keyboards. Valle began his solo career in 1994, producing CDs by his brother, singer Moises "Yumuri" Valle, and Tata Guines. The flutist led his own album, *Formula Uno*, wrote several songs for the 1996 album *Cubanismo*, and recorded with Roy Hargrove (*Cristo*), Jane Bunnett, and Steve Coleman. Also in 1996, Maraca Valle recorded *Havana Calling* with his group, Otra Vision. He has great potential and deserves to be much better known.

9 *Havana Calling / 1996 / Qbadisc 9023*

Orlando "Maraca" Valle may not be a household name in jazz circles yet, but he ought to be. His flute playing throughout this CD is on the level of a Hubert Laws (making fast, complex passages sound effortless), and he is a particularly strong improviser. With his wife, Celine Valle, on second flute, guest altoist Lenny Pickett, such soloists as Irving Acao (alto and tenor), German Velazco (soprano and tenor), and trumpeters Luis Valle and Alexander Brown plus a fine rhythm section that includes up to four percussionists, this is a rewarding effort. In addition to Valle's originals, his band (Otra Vision) also performs a heated version of Cedar Walton's "Bolivia," and his brother, Moises Valle, is featured on "La Vela." Orlando Valle is a name to look for in the future.

PAPO VAZQUEZ

b. Feb. 24, 1958, Philadelphia, PA

One of the best trombonists active today in Afro-Cuban Jazz, Papo Vazquez began playing trombone in local dance bands when he was 13. A few of his early role models were trombonists José Rodriguez and Barry Rogers (both of whom were featured with Eddie Palmieri) and Willie Colón. After Vazquez discovered jazz, J.J. Johnson became an important influence. In the early 1970s, he moved to New York, where he worked with Chocolate Armenteros. Vazquez made his recording debut with Manny Oquendo's Conjunto Libre in 1974, at age 16, and has continued working with that band up to the present time. He also freelanced, playing with Hilton Ruiz, Jorge Dalto, tenors George Coleman and Pharoah Sanders, Willie Colón, Ray Barretto, and the Fania All-Stars. Vazquez has had important associations with Jerry González's Fort Apache Band and Mario Rivera's Salsa Refugees. Vazquez studied with Slide Hampton in 1979 and became a member of Hampton's The World of Trombones. He spent the 1980-85 period living in Puerto Rico, where he founded, played, and arranged for the Salsa group Batacumbele. Since returning to New York, Papo Vazquez has sought to utilize the rhythms of Puerto Rico (the bomba and plena) in his own jazz group.

8 *Breakout / Feb. 18-19, 1991 / Timeless 311*
9 *At the Point, Vol. Two / Nov. 11-12, 1997 / Cubop 016*

Breakout, Papo Vazquez's debut as a leader, finds him showing off his talents in both straightahead boppish jazz and Cuban music, sometimes combin-ing the two idioms and at other times completely separating them. "Chango y Yemeya" goes back and forth between folkloric singing (by percussion-ist Milton Cardona) and heated jamming over a walking bass. Vazquez shows off his warm trom-bone tone on "I Thought About You" and then sounds like a completely different person singing "Bomba Voulez," with equal success. He is joined by a mostly all-star crew that includes Bill O'Connell or Larry Willis on piano, guitarist Edgardo Miranda, Andy González or Lincoln Goines on bass, drummer Steve Berrios, Cardona, and the excellent tenor saxophonist Mario Rivera. Vazquez ranks with J.P. Torres and Steve Turre as one of the finest trombonists active today in Afro-Cuban Jazz, as he shows on "Girl Talk" and "Fiesta Cika," the latter being one of five originals that he brought to this stimulating set.

Vazquez is also in top form throughout the six selections on *At the Point, Vol. Two*. Tenor saxo-phonist Michael Brecker guests on two songs and Dave Valentin is on one, but Vazquez is not over-shadowed. Assisted by a rhythm section that includes pianist Arturo O'Farrill, percussionist Richie Flores, and sometimes Andy González, Vazquez romps through such songs as "The Reverend," "It's Only a Paper Moon," and the exu-berant "Capullito de Aleli" with spirit and confi-dence. There are no slow moments on this enjoy-able set.

RAY VEGA

b. Apr. 3, 1961, New York, NY

A powerful trumpeter who has never lost sight of his Puerto Rican roots, Ray Vega has played with the who's who of Afro-Cuban Jazz during his career. He originally wanted to play alto in junior high school, but the only instruments he had to choose from were trumpet and trombone, so he chose the former. His early inspiration was Freddie Hubbard. Vega attended The School of Music and

Art; at the Johnny Colon School of Music his trumpet teacher was Jerry González. Vega worked early on with altoists James Spaulding and Wessell Anderson, Louie Ramirez (1985), the Luis "Perico" Ortiz Orchestra, and Hector Lavoe (1987). Since then Vega has been an important part of many bands, including Mongo Santamaria (1987-92), Johnny Pacheco, Eddie Palmieri, Ray Barretto's New World Spirit (1990-94), Pete Rodriguez (1991-92), Mario Bauzá's orchestra, and Tito Puente (1994-99), for whom he played both first trumpet and solos. In addition, Vega has worked with Jimmy Bosch's Masters, the Joe Henderson Big Band, Chico O'Farrill, and the Lincoln Center Jazz Orchestra, also recording with Giovanni Hidalgo, Conrad Herwig, and the Bronx Horns. As a leader, Ray Vega thus far has two CDs out on the Concord Picante label.

8 *Ray Vega / May 21-22, 1996 / Concord Picante 4735*

9 *Boperation / Apr. 13-17, 1999 / Concord Picante 4867*

Best known for his work in Afro-Cuban Jazz settings (including with Mongo Santamaria, Ray Barretto, and Tito Puente), Ray Vega proves to be a superior hard bop trumpeter on his self-titled debut, particularly on such numbers as "Greenhouse" (based on "What Is This Thing Called Love") and a medium-slow "Alone Together." However, his Latin heritage is not neglected, since Wilson "Chembo" Corniel is prominent on conga. And the band (keyboardist John di Martino, electric bassist Jairo Moreno, drummer Vince Cherico, and tenor saxophonist Roger Byam) is quite adept at switching between the two overlapping styles.

Boperation finds Vega paying tribute on a dozen songs to 13 different trumpeters: Freddie Hubbard, Kenny Dorham, Fats Navarro, Howard McGhee, Dizzy Gillespie, Eddie Henderson, Clifford Brown, Miles Davis, Woody Shaw, Chet Baker, Art Farmer, Donald Byrd, and Lee Morgan. Assisted by Byam (on tenor, alto, and soprano), pianist Igor Atalita, bassist Bernie Minoso, drummer Cherico, and percussionist Corniel (with guest spots for guitarist Steve Khan and vibraphonist Joe Locke), Vega does not try to copy his trumpet heroes but instead plays in his own sparkling, Latin-tinged hard bop style. Highlights include a slower-than-usual rendition of "Boperation," "Daahoud," "Tangerine," and "Social Call." A delight from start to finish.

PAMELA WISE

Pamela Wise, a talented composer and pianist, has been associated with Detroit-area clarinetist Wendell Harrison since 1979. Harrison has recorded several of her compositions, some of which trumpeter Freddie Hubbard also performed. Wise made her debut as a leader for Harrison's Wenha label in 1994 with *Songo Festividad* and also has appeared on a couple of his CDs (on piano, keyboards, and vibes).

7 *Songo Festividad / Mar. 7, 1994 / Wenha 210*

Pamela Wise's first recording project as a leader features six of her compositions, one Wendell Harrison piece ("Pamela's Holiday"), an obscurity, and "I Didn't Know What Time It Was" (a vocal feature for Valencia Edner). Each selection has one or two Latin percussionists, including, quite often, Jerry González on congas or timbales; he also plays flügelhorn on "Hasta Mañana." Also quite prominent in the supporting cast is Harrison on tenor and clarinet (stretching himself on the latter, if sometimes sounding a bit out of place in this Afro-Cuban date) and Brad Felt on baritone horn (not baritone sax) and tuba. Although none of the songs are destined to become standards, they are enjoyable enough, with Pamela Wise's piano solos and accompaniment fitting the music well.

CONVERSATIONS WITH
FOUR AFRO-CUBAN JAZZ GREATS

Each of the four musicians—whom I had discussions with—have made strong contributions to Afro-Cuban Jazz. Jane Bunnett has used many talented (if otherwise rarely heard) Cuban musicians in her band, Danilo Perez is the cultural ambassador to Panama (a unique and prestigious position for a jazz musician), Susie Hansen has been a fixture on the Los Angeles music scene for quite a few years, and to many people Paquito D'Rivera absolutely symbolizes Afro-Cuban Jazz. Each had rather interesting stories to tell.

PAQUITO D'RIVERA

A very distinctive alto-saxophonist and clarinetist, Paquito D'Rivera is also a fine improviser on soprano and tenor. Born in Cuba where his father was a highly respected classical saxophonist, D'Rivera performed as a child on soprano and clarinet with orchestras. He became a professional when he was 14, recorded with Chucho Valdés while a teenager, and served in the Cuban Army. He was a member of the Orquesta Cubana de Musica Moderna and its successor Irakere, where during 1973-80 he was one of the star soloists. Since moving to the United States in 1980, D'Rivera has been one of jazz's top altoists and clarinetists, not only playing bebop and Afro-Cuban Jazz but also exploring music from other Latin and South American countries.

I know you've been traveling a lot lately.
PAQUITO: Ahh, yes, for the last 20 years! That's the story of my life, but it's fun.

What is the earliest music that you remember hearing?
PAQUITO: My father was a classical saxophone player who also loved jazz music. So I grew up listening to many types of music, from Mozart to Pérez Prado. One of the most influential records for me

was the one that Benny Goodman did at Carnegie Hall in 1938, which today is one of my favorite records. My father was also the representative for the Selmer company in Havana and used to import musical instruments and accessories. Some of his friends and clients were people like Cachao, Chico O'Farrill, Chocolate, and Mario Bauzá. I grew up listening to what they had to say. So music was my background; I had no choice!

Did you start on the clarinet and the alto?
PAQUITO: No, I actually started on the curved soprano. I still have that instrument. I began on the soprano when I was five and started on clarinet when I was 12.

Did you originally plan to become a classical player?
PAQUITO: Yes, at first. Actually until I was 11 or 12, I didn't know the difference between Mozart and the Machito Orchestra or Cab Calloway. It was all just music to me. I still look at it that way.

I know that you served in the Cuban Army and played in an Army band. What kind of music did you play there?
PAQUITO: That was against my will; I didn't want to be in the Army. There was a point where the Army band was really good and they recruited some excellent young players. We mostly played classical

transcriptions adapted for a stage band, music by Mozart, Wagner, Rossini, Puccini, and other classical composers.

Tell me a little bit about the Orquesta Cubana de Musica Moderna.

PAQUITO: That was a big band that the government put together in order to erase a little bit of the bad image that Castro had created around the world with his repression of jazz music.

Did the Orquesta Cuban de Musica Moderna have opportunities to record?

PAQUITO: Yes. We started out with a live recording, but then after that the recordings were very commercial. Still, there were always elements of jazz music to be heard.

Were those your first records?

Paquito: No, my first recording as a professional musician was with Chucho Valdés and his combo in 1963 or '64. It still sounds good to me.

How did Irakere's music differ from the Orquesta Cuban de Musica Moderna?

PAQUITO: Irakere was a lot more creative. Irakere was a combination of our jazz roots with the Cuban tradition, along with some classical influences. Irakere was a unique group of musicians, a very creative unit that kept on adding more and more elements from different styles of music. Jazz for a long time in Cuba under Castro was considered a four-letter word. So Chucho avoided the word jazz with Irakere even when we played it.

Tell me about how you first met Dizzy Gillespie in 1977.

PAQUITO: There was a cruise boat that stopped by Havana with a bunch of jazz musicians including Dizzy, Stan Getz, David Amram, and Earl "Fatha" Hines. We had a jam session in a theatre, a closed session just for people that the government selected. Dizzy Gillespie was a very important figure in our life. When he went back to the United States, he

and Stan Getz contacted Bruce Lundvall to let him know what they had seen in Havana.

After moving to the United States, did it take you long to get established?

PAQUITO: No. My mother had lived here since 1968 so I had some family. I had the help of Dizzy Gillespie and I also had the intention to make it; I wanted to make it very bad. I was so happy to be playing jazz in the land of jazz.

What are some of the things that you learned from Dizzy Gillespie?

PAQUITO: His concept of a real jazz player is one who not only shines by himself but wants others to shine around him with their own light. He was very generous. Other bandleaders should learn that from him and convince themselves that they have nothing to lose by helping others.

How would you say your playing has evolved since coming to the United States?

PAQUITO: I've learned a lot in the United States because here you have the opportunity to meet people from other nationalities and I use that as a contribution to my own playing. The whole idea is to have a recognizable style. I base my style partly on the classical French school of the saxophone, which is a very interesting way to play, and of course my Cuban and jazz roots. It is a combination of all that.

I saw you a couple times in recent years with the United Nation Orchestra. Is that orchestra working very much these days?

PAQUITO: It just got to the point where I did not have enough time to pay attention to the orchestra and write for it. I decided to quit finally. Every time I want to have some fun and lose some money, I put together a big band!

Do you think it is getting easier for Cuban musicians to play in other countries and get to return home now than it was when you left?

PAQUITO: In some ways, that is a very good way to

Whether on alto or clarinet, Paquito D'Rivera is a modern master with a sound of his own.

support the regime. The musicians go out and then bring back money to the government. They are feeding dollars to the dictatorship. Of course it is very hard to tell a person what is the right thing to do. As long as they don't talk against the government, they are allowed to go. They can talk about the schools and the free hospitals but not about the government. It is a very hard situation. It is about time to end all that.

What have been some of your favorite personal recordings of your own playing?
PAQUITO: I like *Tico! Tico!* and *Portraits of Cuba.*

Of the Latin and South American countries, Cuba and Brazil get the most publicity in music, but you are also involved in exploring music from other countries.
PAQUITO: The music of Cuba and Brazil is so strong that it has overwhelmed the other countries, but each of the countries has had interesting elements to their music, too, particularly Venezuela, Mexico, and especially Argentina. It is like the same tree but with different branches; some branches are bigger and stronger than the others, but all of the branches are worth exploring. That is what I really call Latin Jazz, when one mixes all of the elements of the different countries together. Many people are starting to finally open their eyes to the music of Latin America. There is an awful lot happening south of the border.

JANE BUNNETT

Although she had originally hoped to become a concert classical pianist, Jane Bunnett's career took some unexpected turns after she developed tendonitis. During a vacation in San Francisco, she saw the Charles Mingus band at the legendary Keystone Korner and was amazed by the power, passion, and spontaneity of the music. Having been forced to give up playing piano, she took up the soprano sax and doubled on flute (which she had played earlier), burying herself in jazz. Bunnett quickly developed into an adventurous improviser, who was able to hold her own with pianist Don Pullen and tenor-saxophonist Dewey Redman on her debut recording. A 1982 vacation to Cuba with her husband trumpeter Larry Cramer was a major turning point in her life. Bunnett discovered Cuban music and, although she still performs in other types of jazz settings, she became determined to both master her adopted music and make the world aware of the tremendous amount of talent hidden in Castro's Cuba. Through her group Spirits of Havana (an ensemble filled with fellow Canadians and Cubans, which constantly tours) and her recordings, Jane Bunnett has found her own unique niche in the music world.

What is the earliest music that you remember hearing?

JANE: My next-door neighbor was a concert pianist so I heard her practice. There was a rock band that lived around the corner from my house that kind of mesmerized me. On the way home from school at lunchtime, I'd hear them rehearsing. As a kid I loved the records of shows that my parents had including *South Pacific, The Wizard of Oz,* and *My Fair Lady.*

Even though you had planned to become a classical pianist, do you think you would have gravitated to jazz eventually anyway?

JANE: I think I probably would have. I don't think I could have really expressed myself fully in classical music. I alternated between music and art for a time, and in art I really liked being able to create something out of nothing, from scratch. I think to an extent that is what jazz is about too, the spontaneity of improvisation.

How long did you play piano?

JANE: I started when I was small, in public school, eight or nine, but I wasn't very successful because it was a half-hour lesson at lunchtime with ten of us having to share one piano. In grade six I started on clarinet, which I played for a couple years. I gave up on the piano around that time, played it briefly when I was 13 or 14, quit again, and then when I was 16, I went to a teacher who was very strict. There was a lot of friction between us partly because I was lazy. I quit after about a year, but then two years later I went back to him when I realized that he was good for me. I worked really hard for three years, devoting myself to the piano and playing eight hours a day. Even during that period, I gravitated towards the Latin American composers. Eventually all of that playing did my hand in, because I was playing too hard, probably sitting too low at the piano, resulting in tendonitis.

Tell me about going to San Francisco and seeing Charles Mingus.

JANE: When I first heard Mingus, I thought that he and his musicians were simply classical musicians playing a different style. I thought that if they could do it, I could do it. In other words, I didn't have a clue! Their music was so powerful and there was such interaction between the players and such excitement. It was like nothing I had ever heard before.

What made you decide to start playing soprano and flute?

JANE: The first flute record I heard was the Herbie Mann/Bill Evans record *Nirvana,* and that made

Jane Bunnett's Spirits of Havana have exposed countless North Americans to top Cuban Musicians.

me want to play flute during my last year of high school. With the soprano, it was really hearing Steve Lacy's early record *Evidence.* I loved Lacy's sound. I started on soprano in 1978, during my first and only year at York University. It only took me about two years before I was playing in public. I lived in Toronto in the Greek section where there are a lot of Greek coffeehouses. Even though I was learning standards and playing at jam sessions,

some guy heard me and I was hired for three nights a week (from midnight until five in the morning) playing Greek music, none of which was written down. From that, I began playing duo gigs with pianist Marilyn Lerner at restaurants and coffeehouses.

You had a pretty strong career going with several records out before you became involved in Cuban music. How did you originally get interested in Afro-

Cuban Jazz and what is it about the music that makes you want to play it?

JANE: It was really going to Cuba that made me want to play it. I had played a little bit in Salsa bands early on. Although the rhythm sections would be from Cuba, Peru, Ecuador, and other Latin countries, the horn sections were filled usually with gringos in those days, because they could improvise and play jazz, so I got occasional calls to fill out horn sections. In 1982 Larry and I took our first trip to Santiago, Cuba, and that was what really opened me up. The moment we landed in Cuba we saw music everywhere; it was overwhelming: all kinds of groups from jazz and Salsa to the Afro-Cuban folkloric bands. When we came back from that trip, which was for a week, we immediately tried to figure out how to get back to Cuba to learn more. Three weeks later we returned, staying for two weeks and seeing Havana.

This time we had some phone numbers and met Merceditas Valdés and Guillermo Barreto, who were both very important to us. Guillermo was a huge jazz fan and had played drums with Nat King Cole and Sarah Vaughan when they visited Cuba. He knew every Dizzy Gillespie solo note-for-note, and he loved to sing them. When Dizzy Gillespie visited Cuba in 1977, Guillermo was in tears meeting Dizzy, he was so touched. He amazed Dizzy by singing his solos to him. Merceditas had been a popular singer, even appearing with a Cuban all-star group at the Apollo in the 1940s. But she was also a very important interpreter of the Afro-Cuban folkloric music and was regarded very highly in the religious community, singing religious material over the radio, which was controversial at first. We learned a great deal from Merceditas and Guillermo. It was within a year of meeting them that we began planning on doing a project with them, which ended up being *Spirits of Havana*.

It took us about three years to pull that off. We were really up against a lot with a great deal of red tape on both Canada and Cuba's side. For example, we used Grupo Yoruba Andabo, a group of singers and percussionists. At the time they were dock workers and were not considered musicians. They were not even allowed to go into the recording studios because they were not registered with the state as professional musicians so that was a struggle.

Since then, how many times have you been to Cuba?

JANE: Over 40 times so far. We just finished a documentary filmed by the National Film Board of Canada that is a kind of a road trip of our collaborations with a lot of different Cuban musicians, with interviews about the music and its history.

How has the music scene changed in Cuba since you first started going there?

JANE: The roof has just blown off. There are many more musicians now than there were awhile ago, and such an abundance of music and styles. Cuba has 25 conservatories so there is an incredible outpouring of musicians, and that is not even counting the folkloric and rural musicians.

It seems that, up until at least the mid-1990s, Cuban musicians had to defect in order to move and play freely in other countries, but now that is changing a little, particularly with Chucho Valdés and Gonzalo Rubalcaba who seem to be free to move around. Is it getting better?

JANE: Before, everyone was in the same boat; nobody was really going anywhere! But now there are a lot of gray areas today, as opposed to everything being black and white. The political nature of things has changed a little bit since Arturo Sandoval defected, and now for some there are alternatives. If you can hook into somebody who is able to help you (an agent or a record label), it is much easier. With Larry and I, there are only so many musicians who we can put in our group, so we can only help a few. Chucho Valdés and Gonzalo Rubalcaba have paid their dues, both having had difficult times in the past. Things have loosened up now for them, their reputations are big, and they have lawyers and record companies behind them. So for some musicians, it is possible to live in the country and maintain their Cuban citizenship but be fairly free to travel. A lot has to do with building up a reputation outside of the country.

But for the average musician, it must be difficult to leave the country to travel. You deal with that all of the time.

JANE: It is really difficult. Unless there is a lifeline for a musician outside of Cuba, they can't get out. For myself, if I want to go play at a club in France, I can go. But for Cubans, they cannot leave the island without permission from the government. In the case of the musicians I work with, I've been doing it for a long time, but I still have to go through all of these formalities to get musicians out so they can tour in my band, and I have to pay a lot of money.

Tell me a bit about your efforts to raise money to buy musical instruments for Cuban players.

JANE: We've been doing that for five years now. A while ago we went to a school in Cuba to hear the kids play, and they were really disciplined and wonderful players. But their instruments were a mess and, when I tried a couple kids' flutes after the recital, I couldn't get any notes on them; they were atrocious. We felt a bit sad, knowing how important the music is to those kids. So after returning to Canada, we did a fundraiser and raised around $7,000. With that money we were able to invite two technicians from Toronto to come down and repair instruments. We also brought along some donated instruments and parts that are in short supply in Cuba. We have continued to do this year after year. With some schools having 14 kids using one flute, this is really necessary. It is really worth it because there is so much musical talent in that country.

DANILO PEREZ

The last decade has been a musical golden age with many brilliant Afro-Cuban pianists (ranging from Chucho Valdés and Gonzalo Rubalcaba to Hilario Duran and Hilton Ruiz) playing at the peak of their powers. Danilo Perez belongs in that elite group, although he is actually from Panama rather than Cuba or Puerto Rico. The son of a singer, Perez heard Latin music from an early age, moved to Boston in 1985 to study at Berklee College of Music, and has since had important associations with singer Jon Hendricks (1987), trumpeters Terence Blanchard and Claudio Roditi, and altoist Paquito D'Rivera, in addition to being Dizzy Gillespie's last pianist (1989-92). Since leaving Gillespie, Perez has primarily led his own groups, although he also makes many sideman appearances on records. His mastery of polyrhythms and ability to infuse advanced bebop with his Panamanian heritage gives him a distinctive style. Recently Danilo Perez was officially named the cultural ambassador of Panama.

I know that your earliest instrument was the bongos. How young were you when you started playing piano?

DANILO: My father bought me some mini-bongos when I was three years old. He sang with a great Afro-Cuban-influenced orchestra in Panama and I used to perform with him. I played bongos until I was seven and also played a little bit of guitar. When I was seven, my uncle gave me a little keyboard and that is when I switched to piano.

What were some of the most important musical lessons that you learned from your father?

DANILO: The most important thing he told me was that if I didn't learn the clavé, I wouldn't have any swing. I learned a lot of Latin American standards from him.

How did you happen to discover jazz?

DANILO: We just had one jazz record in the house, Louis Armstrong's *Hello Dolly*. But a neighbor of mine blasted out jazz records all the time when I was around ten, so I couldn't miss it! I heard a pianist from Puerto Rico, Papo Lucca, who mixed in Cuban music with Bud Powell and Oscar Peterson. He did not play the typical Latin piano style and his approach appealed to me. That eased me into jazz.

Did you work much in Panama before you moved to the U.S.?
DANILO: Yes. I worked with my father early on and played percussion with his orchestra when I was 11 or 12. But by then, I was concentrating more on piano. I did a lot of work for commercial television, made many records in Panama, was part of the commercial pop scene, and led a band that played all kinds of music.

What made you decide to go to Berklee?
DANILO: I went to Indiana University in Pennsylvania first, but a friend talked me into applying for a scholarship at Berklee and I was accepted.

When you moved to New York, did it take you long to get established?
DANILO: I first came to New York on the recommendation of pianist Donald Brown to audition for Jon Hendricks. So when I moved to New York, I had a gig. After a year, I moved back to Boston for a little while longer.

What were some of the things that you learned from playing with Jon Hendricks?
DANILO: Singers have a different perspective about the music than players. He taught me a lot about jazz's history, about Art Tatum, Thelonious Monk, and Duke Ellington. We had a huge repertory. I remember us doing the Nat King Cole songbook and having to learn 50–60 songs. It was like a speeded-up seminar for me. He threw an awful lot of information at me. I learned from him how to accompany singers, and the function of the piano in that setting.

How did you join Paquito D'Rivera's band?
DANILO: It was through Claudio Roditi. I had

worked with Claudio and he has been very influential in my career. He was working with Paquito and called me one day, inviting me to the Blue Note where they were playing so Paquito could hear me. I was afraid but Claudio got me to sit in and Paquito soon said, "OK, now I have my piano player!"

That must have been an important experience for you, traveling and playing with major musicians.
DANILO: That period of life from 1986 until the time that I played with Dizzy, I was involved in so many projects with major jazz musicians. After Jon Hendricks, I was with the Terence Blanchard Quintet and then Paquito's band. I also started working with Tom Harrell. Learning from those masters meant so much.

You and Paquito share some important musical interests in pursuing not just the music of Panama and Cuba but that of many Latin and South American countries. Are there some countries where the music has been a bit overlooked, since Brazil and Cuba tend to get the most publicity?

DANILO: Yes. Both Paquito and I have made the commitment to bring a much stronger awareness to Latin American music. Each country has a beauty to it. Every country in Latin and South America has its own flavor. I think it is time for people to open up a little more and find out that Venezuela, Argentina, Uruguay, Bolivia, Columbia, and Panama also have strong contributions to make to music. Cuba and Brazil have opened the door for this discovery to take place.

What would you say have been some of the most important contributors of Panama to music?
DANILO: Luis Russell, a Panamanian pianist-arranger, was the musical director for Louis Armstrong in the 1930s and later in his career gave drummer Roy Haynes his first break. Other top Panamanian players include Billy Cobham, Santi Debriano, Alex and Russell Blake, Carlos Ward, Carlos Garnett, and flutist Mauricio Smith.

Danilo Perez, the cultural ambassador of Panama.

Since your period with Dizzy Gillespie, you've been on many recordings, as a leader and sideman. What do you think are the ones that best show off your playing?

DANILO: I think some of my best playing has not been recorded! It is difficult going to a studio, feeling that one has to come up with musical magic on that particular day. My recordings are totally honest. I don't overdub or "fix" solos later on. I think one of my most important recordings was *The Journey* as far as being ambitious. For my piano

playing, I would go with *Panamonk*. There are different things on different records. I enjoy being part of a group and teaming different players together rather than just focusing on my piano playing. I like my recordings with Tom Harrell and Paquito and a recent one with John Patitucci and Roy Haynes. My newest record *Motherland* has some free playing but also relates to music from other countries and from Panama. It is always a dream of mine to play something in which it is difficult to know whether it was written-out or not.

At the New England Conservatory of Music where you are a professor, what are the general lessons that you try to get across to students who want to play jazz and Latin music?

DANILO: First of all you have to love what you do. That makes everything you do have a conviction to it and a joy. If you don't love the music, there's no point to it. A lot of people go to school sometime and don't even know if they love what they are trying for or not. Everything else is clearer. I try to have musicians add more of a dance experience to their playing, returning to the swing period when people danced to the music. In general I try to inspire my students so they can inspire me; I teach them so I can learn from them.

Tell us about being appointed Cultural Ambassador of Panama.

DANILO: Wow, that is an incredible honor. Basically what I'm doing is to try to bring the awareness of my country to the world. Hopefully people tomorrow will have more knowledge about our little country Panama; little in geography but giant in emotions and heart. Panama is full of a lot of dimensions with musicians, classical composers, baseball players, singers, boxers, and actors. We have a complex history and hopefully I can help promote the culture. At the same time, I want to take the music out of our culture and display it to the world. I'm so thankful to be around in this era because there are going to be all kinds of new mixtures in the near future between the music of South and Latin America and jazz, all kinds of new discoveries.

SUSIE HANSEN

Although the violin is a key part of charanga bands, very few violinists today lead Afro-Cuban Jazz groups. Susie Hansen, a white female who has no direct link to the Latin world except for her love and dedication to the music, breaks the rules on several levels. The Susie Hansen Latin

Band plays between 175-200 gigs a year, mostly in the Los Angeles area.

What originally attracted you to the violin and how did you happen to begin playing it?

SUSIE: My father was a violinist with the Chicago Symphony and he put one in my hand when I was five. Although I played a little bit of mandolin and guitar while growing up, the violin was always my main instrument.

When did you know that you were going to try to be a professional musician?

SUSIE: I didn't know until I was out of graduate school, where I had earned a masters degree in computer science and electrical engineering. I had played violin on and off through the years. I put it aside several times, but it wouldn't stay silent; it is part of my being. I studied primarily with my father, later on at the New England Conservatory, and with Max Hobath from the Boston Symphony Orchestra.

How did you originally get interested in jazz?

SUSIE: When I came back to music when I was 21, after not playing for seven years, I played some folk music and classical. A friend of mine invited me to play with his rock band. I didn't have any idea what to do since there was no music. They just pointed to me when it was time to play, and told me when to stop. I discovered that I had a natural instinct for it, that I could play by ear, and that I loved to improvise. It took me about a year to get bored with rock and roll, but in the meantime I'd been exposed to Miles Davis, Chick Corea, Jean-Luc Ponty, John McLaughlin, and many others. I never really looked back and stayed with jazz after that. I played jazz gigs in Boston and I was in an acoustic quartet called Strings Attached that mostly played original string band music. After moving back to Chicago, I played in various jazz bands before I started leading one of my own.

The Wayne Knight Collection/Photo: Joe La Russo

Violinist Susie Hansen's band is a popular attraction in the Los Angeles area.

How did you discover Afro-Cuban Jazz and what is it about this music that made you want to play it?

SUSIE: I was playing with my own jazz band in Chicago, a six-piece group, at a big festival at Grant Park. The group before us was a mambo band and they stayed to hear my band. The leader, Victor Parra, told me that he liked my playing and wanted me to play with his group, since he had just fired his violin player. Although I told him that I didn't know anything about mambos, he told me not to worry, that I'd get it. I found that I just loved it. I loved the rhythms and found them so much more irresistible and compelling than the swing rhythms I had been playing with. Although it took me around two years from that point before I was playing Latin jazz full-time, I knew that I'd found my home.

Were there any violinists in Latin jazz who inspired you?

SUSIE: Alfredo De La Fey from Columbia, the best-known violinist in charanga and Salsa music. Also the violin players from Los Van Van and the ones in Orquesta Aragon.

Why did you move to Los Angeles in 1988?

SUSIE: The bulk of the work that I had in Chicago that paid well was society dinner dances and jobs like that. I didn't really want to be a society band-leader. Since I had a sister out in Los Angeles and I loved the city and the weather, I decided to move and play the music that interested me. I worked with Bobby Matos, Long John Oliva, and other Afro-Cuban bands while I was out here, before forming my own band in September 1989.

Is it difficult being a female instrumentalist and playing Latin music without being Latin yourself?

SUSIE: There are some problems inherent in all this. Some men find it difficult to take orders from a woman, and I do know how I want to run my band. Also, if you're not Latino, there are certain gigs that won't come your way. Because I don't speak good Spanish, there are certain promoters who I have trouble communicating with. But that being said, the fact that I'm white and blond and play violin in Latin music brings me a lot of attention. People don't forget me! It's more of a benefit than a detriment. People often disregard me before they hear me play, but afterwards I'm totally accepted. I've gotten many compliments from Cubans telling me that they recognize that I really love their music, that I can play their music, and that I'm respectful of their tradition.

How would you describe the music of your band?

SUSIE: It's Latin jazz and Salsa. We accommodate the kind of event that we are playing. If we are performing at a dance, we focus more on Salsa and vocal music. But there is not a song that we play that does not have at least one jazz solo in it.

What have been some of the highpoints of your group's existence so far?

SUSIE: We have appeared at most of the jazz festivals in town, and we love playing every Friday night before 300-400 people at the Whittier Hilton Hotel. We also enjoy performing at Mr. E's, Pete Escovedo's club in San Francisco.

Tell me about your trip to Cuba.

SUSIE: I was there for two weeks in 1997 and had a chance to play with Los Van Van three times. Cuba is a very interesting place; it is like walking into the 1950s. It doesn't have a lot of modern buildings and certainly does not have very many modern cars. The place is kind of falling apart. I was just in Havana and the whole city is in need of a serious facelift; [it is] crumbling away. But on the other hand, the people are really healthy. They walk all over because they have no choice, and they don't eat junk food because it is not available, so they are all thin; you don't see anyone fat. Everyone seems to be in robust good health. I loved the fact that it seems like everyone is acquainted with the clavé, the basic rhythm of the music. It is wonderful to walk down the street past outdoor stalls where paintings or artifacts are being sold, and next to that will be a stall selling percussion instruments with the owner sitting there playing the clavés. There are many little ensembles playing for their own fun on street corners. Musicians are held in high esteem, people are very well educated in Cuba, and they have an excellent medical system. However, it is a country of great contradictions. The Cubans are not allowed in hotel rooms; they are repressed and not free. People are not that forthcoming about their lives, particularly if you don't speak the language. They do not have much money and that is a tough fate. But I loved visiting Cuba and it is impossible for me to resist their music.

THEY ALSO RECORDED AFRO-CUBAN JAZZ

What do Louis Armstrong, Count Basie, Art Tatum, Miles Davis, John Coltrane, and Cecil Taylor have in common? They never recorded an Afro-Cuban Jazz album! However, in addition to the major contributors who have entries in the main part of this book, there were other great jazz musicians who recorded in Afro-Cuban Jazz settings on rare occasions. This is not too surprising considering that the style has become such a significant part of the jazz scene. Some value judgment was necessary to decide what to include; Randy Weston's African-oriented dates and Miles Davis' *Sketches of Spain* fell just outside the boundary lines of this study, although it is possible to argue for both.

This book would certainly not be complete without mentioning the "part-time" Afro-Cuban Jazz musicians (and their important recordings), who are discussed in this section.

GENE AMMONS

> b. Apr. 14, 1925, Chicago, IL, d. Aug. 6, 1974, Chicago, IL

- **10** *The Happy Blues / Apr. 25, 1956 / Original Jazz Classics 013*
- **7** *Blue Gene / May 3, 1958 / Original Jazz Classics 192*
- **9** *Boss Tenor / June 16, 1960 / Original Jazz Classics 297*
- **8** *The Gene Ammons Story: Organ Combos / June 17, 1960-Nov. 28, 1961 / Nov. 28, 1961 / Prestige 7238*
- **7** *Jug / Jan. 27, 1961 / Original Jazz Classics 701*
- **6** *Late Hour Special / June 13, 1961-Apr. 13, 1962 / Original Jazz Classics 942*
- **8** *Up Tight! / Oct. 17-18, 1961 / Prestige 24140*

A tenor saxophonist with a huge tone who could play bebop with the best of them, Gene "Jug" Ammons was also very influential in R&B and symbolized soul. He was a major figure in jazz from the time he emerged with Billy Eckstine's orchestra in 1944 (trading off with Dexter Gordon on "Blowin' the Blues Away") until his death in 1974, taking time off for a long prison sentence (due to drug abuse) that stole 1963-68.

Ammons never really played Afro-Cuban Jazz, but he was one of the first straightahead jazz combo leaders to use congo players fairly often. He utilized congo players on seven of his recordings during the 1956-61 period; Ray Barretto is on six albums, while Candido makes his presence felt on *The Happy Blues* . Fortunately all have been reissued on CD. In each case, the conguero (whether Barretto or Candido) gives a Latin flavor to the music without getting in the way of the swinging rhythm section; Jug just liked the sound of a conga!

Ammons led a series of high-quality studio jam sessions for Prestige during 1956-58. *The Happy Blues* was the first and best, with the title cut in particular having memorable solos and subtle but exciting riffing by the ensemble. In addition to the leader, the group includes trumpeter Art Farmer, altoist Jackie McLean, pianist Duke Jordan, bassist

Addison Farmer, drummer Art Taylor, and Candido for four lengthy selections. The final one of the jam sessions, *Blue Gene,* was Ammons' first recording with Ray Barretto. The material (three blues plus pianist Mal Waldron's ballad "Hip Tip") is just ok but the solos are worthwhile; the all-star group consists of Ammons, Waldron, Barretto, trumpeter Idrees Sulieman, baritonist Pepper Adams, bassist Doug Watkins, and drummer Art Taylor.

Ray Barretto helps add to the rhythm section's fire on five other Gene Ammons dates. *Boss Tenor* is one of the tenor's stronger efforts from the period, a quintet outing that also includes pianist Tommy Flanagan, Watkins, and Taylor. Most notable are Ammons' popular version of the ballad "Canadian Sunset" and a swinging "Hittin' the Jug." The *Organ Combos* CD, which has over 77 minutes of music, includes all of the performances from the album *Twistin' the Jug* (a solid sextet outing with organist Jack McDuff, trumpeter Joe Newman, bassist Wendell Marshall, and drummer Walter Perkins along with Barretto). In addition there are six numbers from another, unrelated session (originally out as *Angel Eyes*) without Barretto; Frank Wess (on tenor and flute), organist Johnny Hammond Smith, and Art Taylor are in that band. Ammons shows that he has no difficulty sounding quite creative and comfortable playing standards, blues, or ballads. *Jug* is uneventful but worthwhile, a typical date, with Ammons showcased on six standards and two originals, assisted by Richard Wyands or Sleepy Anderson on piano, Doug Watkins, drummer J.C. Heard, and Barretto. Late Hour Special is a bit run-of-the-mill. Ammons is featured on three numbers with the Patti Bown Trio (Barretto is not on that date) and for four songs as part of a ten-piece group arranged by Oliver Nelson and including Barretto. Clark Terry has a fine flügelhorn solo on "Things Ain't What They Used to Be," but the brief playing time (35 minutes) keeps this CD from getting a higher rating. Ammons' last meeting on records with Barretto resulted in two albums of material (the LPs *Up Tight!* and *Boss Soul*), made during a two-day period; they are reissued as the single CD *Up Tight!.* Ammons and Barretto are joined by Walter Bishop Jr. or Patti Bown on piano, Art Davis or George Duvivier on bass, and Art Taylor for 14 selections, including "The Breeze and I," "I'm Afraid the Masquerade Is Over," "Jug's Blue Blues," "Lester Leaps In," and "Don't Go to Strangers."

Although they are not landmarks in Afro-Cuban Jazz, these recordings helped jazz listeners become accustomed to the sound of the conga.

DAVID AMRAM
b. Nov. 17, 1930, Philadelphia, PA
9 *Havana/New York / May 18, 1977-June 1977 / Flying Fish 057*

A busy traveler, both geographically and musically, David Amram has always believed in breaking down walls and boundaries between jazz and classical music, and between American music and folk music from other countries. A French horn player who has also been heard on piano, recorder, Spanish guitar, penny whistles and percussion, Amram is a skilled arranger and composer too.

In 1977 Amram was on the cruise ship Daphne that visited Cuba with Dizzy Gillespie, Ray Mantilla, Stan Getz, and Earl Hines. Unlike the others, Amram actually recorded in Cuba, to memorialize the trip, and the result was *Havana/New York.* "En Memoria de Chano Pozo" features Amram (on guitar, piano, flute, penny whistles, French horn, percussion, and xylophone!) heading an octet that includes Arturo Sandoval (20 at the time), Paquito D'Rivera, bassist John Ore, drummer Billy Hart, and three percussionists, including Mantilla. The historic (and exciting) performance is joined by two selections recorded a month later in New York by

Amram in a group with trumpeter Thad Jones, baritonist Pepper Adams, tenor saxophonist Billy Mitchell, and a Latin rhythm section with Candido and Mantilla, plus a short number from the streets of New York in which Amram sits in with a Cuban group. A special set.

LPs to Search For:
Latin-Jazz Celebration (Elektra/Musician 60195), from 1982, is well worth a search, for Amram (on nearly all of his instruments) heads a 14-piece orchestra that includes such notables as D'Rivera, tenor saxophonist David "Fathead" Newman, baritonist Pepper Adams, and six percussionists, including Machito, Machito Jr., Candido, and Steve Berrios. The music consists of seven Amram compositions (including a remake of "En Memoria de Chano Pozo") plus "Take the 'A' Train."

ART BLAKEY

b. Oct. 11, 1919, Pittsburgh, PA, d. Oct. 16, 1990, New York; NY

7 *Orgy in Rhythm Vols. One & Two / Mar. 7, 1957 / Blue Note 56586*

8 *The African Beat / Jan. 24, 1962 / Blue Note 22666*

One of the most explosive of all bop-era drummers, Art Blakey became famous for leading the Jazz Messengers (a virtual school for up-and-coming hard bop musicians) during 1955-90. Blakey, who first gained recognition for his playing with Billy Eckstine's bebop orchestra during 1944-47, spent some time in Africa in the late '40s soaking up the native rhythms. He never forgot this period, and on a few special occasions through the years, he was involved in percussion-oriented projects.

The first hint of Blakey's interest in this part of his heritage took place on November 23, 1953, when, after recording the unaccompanied drum

solo "Nothing but Soul," he played a duet ("Message from Kenya") with Sabu Martinez (on conga, bongo, and vocal). There would be four full-length percussion projects, two of which have been reissued on CD thus far. The intriguing single-CD *Orgy in Rhythm* has all of the music from two former LPs. The results are quite spontaneous, since Blakey and Sabu Martinez quickly explained the eight pieces to the musicians before everything was played just once. The music (which includes three vocals/chants by Sabu and one by Blakey) is often explosive and always stimulating. The band consists of Blakey and Art Taylor on drums, Jo Jones and Specs Wright doubling on drums and tympani, Sabu on bongo and timbales, the conga playing of Patato Valdés and José Valiente, Ubaldo Nieto on timbales, Evilio Quintero on cencerro, maracas and tree log, plus Herbie Mann (mostly on African wood flutes), pianist Ray Bryant, and bassist Wendell Marshall. The music is more African- than Cuban-oriented but often crosses the boundary and is quite rewarding on its own level.

The African Beat, from five years later, is similar in intent but a little more successful. This time around the percussionists are from both the United States and Africa, and the two melody instrumentalists (Yusef Lateef on oboe, flute, tenor, cow horn, and thumb piano, and bassist Ahmed Abdul-Malik) were very familiar with African and Eastern music. Blakey (who in addition to drums plays tympani, gong, and telegraph drum) is joined by Solomon G. Ilori (on vocal and talking drum), Chief Bey on conga, Montego Joe and Garvin Masseaux on various percussion, James Ola and Folami on congas, Robert Crowder on batá drum and conga, and trombonist Curtis Fuller, who sticks on this date exclusively to tympani. In addition to Ilori's occasional vocals/chants and some colorful solos by Lateef, there are many outbursts by the large percussion section that are consistently exciting.

LPs to Search For:

Drum Suite (1002), which was recorded a few weeks before *Orgy in Rhythm*, has "the Art Blakey Percussion Ensemble" performing three numbers (including Ray Bryant's "Cubano Chant" and Oscar Pettiford's "Oscalypso") that flow together quite well. Pianist Bryant and bassist Pettiford are joined by Blakey and Jo Jones on drums, Specs Wright on tympani, Candido's conga, and Sabu's bongos. The second half of this album is more conventional: three straightahead numbers by the 1956 edition of Blakey's Jazz Messengers (with trumpeter Bill Hardman, altoist Jackie McLean, pianist Sam Dockery, and bassist Spanky DeBrest). *Holiday for Skins* (Blue Note 4004 and 4005) is particularly scarce these days, a 1958 set in which trumpeter Donald Byrd, pianist Bryant, and bassist Wendell Marshall play mostly minor roles behind the drums of Blakey, Art Taylor, and Philly Joe Jones and the percussion of Sabu, Ray Barretto, Chonguito Vincente, Victor Gonzales, Andy Dellannoy, Julio Martinez, and Fred Pagani. Pretty wild stuff!

DAVE BRUBECK

b. Dec. 6, 1920, Concord, CA

9 *24 Classic Original Recordings / Sept. 1949-Nov. 1950 / Fantasy 24726*

7 *Bravo! Brubeck! / May 12-14, 1967 / Columbia / Legacy 65723*

It seems odd, considering all of his work through the years with polyrhythms, that pianist Dave Brubeck has never recorded an out-and-out Afro-Cuban Jazz record. Famous for leading the Dave Brubeck Quartet (particularly the 1952-67 version with altoist Paul Desmond and later units with either clarinetist Bill Smith or altoist Bobby Militello), Brubeck has been a highly original pianist throughout his long and productive career.

Brubeck first recorded with his adventurous octet, a unit that during 1946-49 sought to combine aspects of classical music (plus polytonality and polyrhythms) in a swinging jazz context. Cal Tjader was the group's drummer, making his recording debut. During 1949-51, Brubeck led a trio consisting of Tjader and bassist Ron Crotty. They recorded 24 concise selections for Fantasy, all of which are reissued on the single CD, *24 Classic Original Recordings.* Tjader mostly plays drums, but he is also heard a bit on vibes (which he was just learning) and bongos. Most of the music (all of it standards) is straightahead, other than a few moments where Tjader plays one of his then-secondary instruments.

The closest that Brubeck came to Afro-Cuban Jazz was on *Bravo! Brubeck!,* which was performed live in Mexico. Brubeck's longtime quartet (with altoist Paul Desmond, bassist Eugene Wright, and drummer Joe Morello) is joined by acoustic guitarist Benjamin "Chamin" Correa, and Salvador "Rabito" Agueros on bongos and conga for a set of melodic tunes that are mostly associated with Mexico or Central America. Brubeck, who contributed "Nostalgia de Mexico," plays such traditional melodies as "Cielito Lindo," "La Paloma Azul," "Besame Mucho," "Perfidia" (which is given a light Latin rhythm), "Frenesi," and "Estrellita"; Desmond's playing is typically beautiful. But it is a pity that Brubeck has never collaborated with a Cuban band.

CAB CALLOWAY

b. Dec. 25, 1907, Rochester, NY, d. Nov. 18, 1994, Hockessin, DE

10 *1930-1931 / July 24, 1930-June 17, 1931 / Classics 516*

7 *1938-1939 / Mar. 23, 1938-Feb. 20, 1939 / Classics 576*

9 *1939-1940 / Mar. 28, 1939-Mar. 8, 1940 / Classics 595*

8 *1940 / Mar. 8, 1940-Aug. 28, 1940 / Classics 614*

7 *1940-1941 / Aug. 28, 1940-July 24, 1941 / Classics 629*

7 *1941-1942 / July 24, 1941-July 27, 1942 / Classics 682*

One of the great personalities of the 1930s and '40s and an underrated jazz singer who was highly influential (including on Latin performers), Cab Calloway led a major big band during 1930-47. Fortunately, all of the recordings from his prime years are available on a dozen Classics CDs that are covered in full in the book *Swing*.

Through the years, Calloway performed an occasional number that showed off pop music's current interest in the rumba, the conga, and Latin rhythms in general. "Doin' the Rhumba" (reissued on *1930-1931*), from March 3, 1931 (the same session that resulted in the original "Minnie the Moocher"), has Calloway's band hinting slightly at "The Peanut Vendor," even if their swing rhythms have little to do with the rumba. On August 30, 1938, Calloway's "The Congo-Conga" (released on *1938-1939*) finds Cab sounding a bit like Desi Arnaz and the band (with Leon Maxey on drums) having a better feel for the basic Latin rhythms. Mario Bauzá joined the band in time for their July 17, 1939, recording session, and Dizzy Gillespie came aboard in August. "Chili Con Conga" (on *1939-1940*) is referred to by Cab as "Cuban jive." He has an extended vocal backed by the rhythm section, which includes Cozy Cole and several band members playing percussion. Although a little silly, the rhythms sound mostly in the genre. Also on this CD is Gillespie's "Pickin' the Cabbage," a mysterious-sounding piece that hints a little at the yet-unwritten "A Night in Tunisia."

"Rhapsody in Rhumba" (on *1940*) from June 27, 1940, is a throwaway that is mostly lightweight swing, but "Yo Eta Cansa," from August 5, 1940, has an eerie Calloway vocal over a repetitious vamp and a Latin-based rhythm. The most exuberant of Cab's "exotic" Latin numbers was "Goin Conga" (included on *1940-1941*), with both the singer and his orchestra really romping on the final of his three "conga" songs. The last of Calloway's "south-of-the-border" numbers, "Conchita (Cares Nothing About Love)," which is included on *1941-1942,* is spirited, if a bit anticlimactic. It is a pity that the classic singer never recorded a full-length set of Cuban songs, for he was flexible enough to have succeeded if he had had the interest.

NAT KING COLE
b. Mar. 17, 1917, Montgomery, AL, d. Feb. 15, 1965, Santa Monica, CA

10 *The Complete Capitol Trio Recordings / Oct. 11, 1942-Mar. 2, 1961 / Mosaic 138*

One of the great swing pianists and leader of the King Cole Trio during 1938-51, Nat King Cole was too talented a ballad vocalist for his talents to be confined to the jazz world forever. His warm voice became so popular after the 1950 hit "Mona Lisa" was released that he spent his last 14 years primarily singing in front of orchestras, playing piano on only an occasional basis.

Cole recorded a few albums in Spanish (which he sang phonetically) and even recorded in Cuba, but those sets (albums that sold quite well in the Spanish speaking world) are primarily pop music. The closest that Cole came to Afro-Cuban Jazz was during 1949-50, when his trio became a quartet (being billed as Nat King Cole and His Trio) with the addition of Jack Costanzo on bongo and conga. On numbers such as "Bop Kick," "Go Bongo," "Rhumba Blues," "Calico Sal," "Ooh Kickeroonie," and especially "Calypso Blues" (a duet between Cole's voice and Costanzo's bongos), the Latin percussion is quite prominent. All of the music was made available as part of the limited-edition and now out-of-print 18-CD *The Complete Capitol Trio Recordings* box, a magnificent package well worth bidding on; most of the numbers have yet to be reissued in a smaller sampler.

CHICK COREA

b. June 12, 1941, Chelsea, MA

9 *My Spanish Heart / Oct. 1976 / Verve 314 543 303*

Latin music has been part of the life of Chick Corea (born Armando Corea) from the near the start. Although his career has found him playing a wide variety of music, including hard bop, post-bop, avant-garde (with his group Circle), fusion (Return to Forever), and straightahead, the pianist/keyboardist often hints at Latin rhythms in his playing. As a sideman in the 1960s Corea spent time playing Afro-Cuban Jazz with Pucho and the Cha Cha Boys, Mongo Santamaria, Willie Bobo, and Herbie Mann.

In 1976, right after the breakup of the most popular version of Return to Forever (the fusion quartet with guitarist Al DiMeola, bassist Stanley Clarke, and drummer Lenny White), Chick Corea recorded a Spanish-oriented double LP (now reissued as the single-CD *My Spanish Heart*) that found him exploring his roots in Latin-style jazz. None of the music is conventional Afro-Cuban Jazz, but it does show the influence that that music has always had on Corea's style. He alternates between acoustic piano and synthesizers (being one of the most distinctive soloists of all on the latter) and uses a variety of different instrumental combinations while mostly being the lead voice. Such notables as Stanley Clarke, drummer Steve Gadd, and violinist Jean-Luc Ponty (featured on a previously unreleased trio number with Corea and Clarke called "The Clouds") are heard from, along with an occasional string quartet, a four-piece brass section, percussionist Don Alias, and the background voice of Gayle Moran. The three-part "El Bozo" is quite catchy, and the other highlights on this memorable all-original program include "Armando's Rhumba" and "Night Streets."

EDDIE "LOCKJAW" DAVIS

b. Mar. 2, 1922, New York, NY, d. Nov. 3, 1986, Culver City, CA

9 *Afro-Jaws / May 4 + 12, 1961 / Original Jazz Classics 403*

One of the toughest of the tough-toned tenors, Eddie "Lockjaw" Davis never played an unemotional note or phrase. He came up at the tail end of the swing era (playing with Cootie Williams' orchestra during 1942-44), recorded a series of very passionate R&B sessions, and then slightly tempered his sound in the 1950s. He was with Count Basie's orchestra during 1952-53, 1957, and 1964-73, collaborated with organist Shirley Scott during 1955-60, had an exciting two-tenor quintet with the equally competitive Johnny Griffin during 1960-62, and in later years often teamed up with trumpeter Harry "Sweets" Edison.

Although his sound would seem ideal for Afro-Cuban Jazz dates, the only full-fledged effort in Lockjaw's discography resulted in *Afro-Jaws*. Davis is joined by three trumpeters (including Clark Terry, who has a few solos), the rhythm section of his band with Griffin (pianist Lloyd Mayers, bassist Larry Gales, and drummer Ben Riley), Ray Barretto on conga, bongos, and quinto, plus an unfortunately unidentified "Latin percussion section." Gil López provided both the arrangements and four of the seven numbers (including "Gunaco Lament" and "Jazz-a-Samba"); the other selections are "Tin Tin Deo," "Star Eyes," and Davis' "Afro-Jaws." Lockjaw's passionate tenor is inspired by the oversized rhythm section, making this an underrated (if little-known) gem in Afro-Cuban Jazz history.

LOU DONALDSON

b. Nov. 1, 1926, Badin, NC

10 *Blues Walk / July 28, 1958 / Blue Note 46525*

The lively Jack Costanzo made the Nat King Cole Trio into a quartet during 1949-1950.

8 *Gravy Train / Apr. 27, 1961 / Blue Note 53357*

A bop-based alto saxophonist with a soulful sound of his own, Lou Donaldson has straddled the boundaries between several styles throughout his career. In the 1950s he played primarily bebop, in the '60s he was involved in hard bop and soul jazz, his work later in the decade and in the 1970s was more commercial (often being melodic electric funk), but since the 1980s he has returned to the hard bop/soul jazz idiom that best fits his thoughtful and bluesy solos.

During 1958-61, Donaldson frequently used a conga player in his combos. *Blues Walk* is a bebop classic, with Donaldson, pianist Herman Foster, bassist Peck Morrison, drummer Dave Bailey, and Ray Barretto on conga jamming on such numbers as "Move," "The Masquerade Is Over," "Autumn Nocturne," and the title cut. *Gravy Train* uses the same instrumentation (with Foster, bassist Ben Tucker, Bailey, and Alec Dorsey on conga) with "South of the Border," "Avalon," and "Candy" being the high points; two alternate takes were added to this CD reissue. Soon after *Gravy Train* was recorded, Donaldson moved on to soul jazz, adding an organ to his band and dropping the conga spot, but these two CDs are highly recommended.

LPs to Search For:

Midnight Sun (Blue Note 1028), from July 22, 1960, repeats "Candy" and "Avalon" from the *Gravy Train* date, but with the personnel of Donaldson, pianist Horace Parlan, Tucker, drummer Al Harewood, and Ray Barretto. This strong set (originally unreleased until 1980 and long overdue to be reissued on CD) also has such tunes as "The Squirrel" and "Exactly Like You."

KENNY DORHAM
b. Aug. 30, 1924, Fairfield, TX, d. Dec. 5, 1972, New York, NY

9 *Afro-Cuban / Jan. 30, 1955 + Mar. 29, 1955 / Blue Note 46815*

Throughout his career (the prime years of which were 1946-65), Kenny Dorham was one of the finest jazz trumpeters around, making the transition from bebop (he was a member of Charlie Parker's quintet during 1948-49) to hard bop, leading a series of rewarding Blue Note albums, and helping to discover tenor saxophonist Joe Henderson. Dorham did not play Afro-Cuban Jazz very often, but certainly an album with the title *Afro-Cuban* belongs in this book! The first four titles ("Minor's Holiday" is heard in two versions) features Dorham in an octet with trombonist J.J. Johnson, tenor saxophonist Hank Mobley, baritonist Cecil Payne, pianist Horace Silver, bassist Oscar Pettiford, drummer Art Blakey, and Patato Valdés (on his first American recording) on conga. That session (from March 29, 1955) introduced Dorham's "Lotus Flower" and, due to the inclusion of Patato, has a strong Latin flavor. The remainder of the CD (four selections, including a previously unreleased "K.D.'s Cab Ride") is straightahead hard bop, with Valdés and J.J. absent and Percy Heath in place of Pettiford. Excellent music, one of Kenny Dorham's finest sessions of the era.

DUKE ELLINGTON
b. Apr. 29, 1899, Washington D.C., d. May 24, 1974, New York, NY

8 *Afro-Bossa / Nov. 29, 1962-Jan. 5, 1963 / Discovery 71002*

8 *Latin American Suite / Oct. 1968 / Original Jazz Classics 469*

Duke Ellington had an incredible career, one with 50 years of constant creativity, an enormous quantity of accomplishments, and nonstop music. As a bandleader (from 1925 until his death in 1974), pianist (starting in stride, yet always evolving and sounding quite modern), arranger (not so much breaking the rules as working around them!), and composer (writing thousands of pieces, including hundreds that became standards), Ellington was in his own category.

In the 1930s and '40s, valve trombonist Juan Tizol wrote several "exotic" Latin-flavored pieces for Ellington, including "Caravan," "Perdido" (which became a jam session favorite but whose lyrics are worth exploring), "Conga Brava," "Moon Over Cuba," and "Moonlight Fiesta"; Duke himself wrote "The Flaming Sword." In the 1960s, Duke Ellington began occasionally to explore music influenced by sounds he heard while touring in other countries. For *Afro-Bossa,* Duke Ellington and Billy Strayhorn wrote 11 new pieces inspired by their worldwide travels. In addition to the lone standard "Pyramid," the most notable selections are "Purple Gazelle," "Eighth Veil," "Silk Lace," and "Bonga." On some numbers, Strayhorn and trumpeters Cat Anderson, Roy Burrowes, and Cootie Williams play "auxiliary percussion." *Latin American Suite,* from 1968, is a seven-part work. None of the individual pieces caught on, but all are worth hearing. The key soloists include Ellington (who is well showcased throughout the album), tenor saxophonist Paul Gonsalves, trombonist Buster Cooper, and altoist Johnny Hodges.

These two albums are the closest that Duke Ellington came to performing Afro-Cuban Jazz.

JON FADDIS

b. July 24, 1953, Oakland, CA

8 *The Dizzy Gillespie Alumni All-Stars / June 19-20, 1997 / Shanachie 5040*

9 *The Dizzy Gillespie Alumni All-Stars: Dizzy's World / May 12-13, 1999 / Shanachie 5060*

The first trumpeter who could really emulate Dizzy Gillespie closely (after others tried for decades), Jon Faddis is a brilliant technician with a very wide

range (he can pop out high notes effortlessly), the ability to also do close imitations of Roy Eldridge and Louis Armstrong, and a master of bebop who gradually developed his own sound. After his close friend Dizzy Gillespie's death in 1993, Faddis was a natural to fill in for Dizzy on tribute albums and when Lalo Schifrin revived "Gillespiana."

Both of the two Shanachie CDs feature some of Dizzy's alumni on a variety of tunes associated with the great trumpeter. The earlier set has Faddis joined by altoist Antonio Hart or tenor saxophonist Andres Boiarsky, pianist Cyrus Chestnut, bassist John Lee, drummer Ignacio Berroa, Gabriel Machado on congas, and Duduka Da Fonesca on percussion. The music (which includes "Salt Peanuts," "Birk's Works," "Manteca," and "A Night in Tunisia") is mostly straightahead, with a strong Latin tinge on some of the more Afro-Cuban-oriented numbers. *Dizzy's World* is actually a little stronger, due to the more offbeat material and the greater emphasis on music from South America. Faddis, Lee, Berroa, and Da Fonseca are assisted by either tenor saxophonist Don Braden (doubling on soprano) or altoist-flutist James Moody, pianist Mulgrew Miller, guitarist Chuck Loeb, Duke on conga, and (for three numbers) trombonist Slide Hampton. The material includes three of the five movements from Schifrin's *Gillespiana Suite,* "Tin Tin Deo," "Guarachi Guaro," and "Algo Bueno." Faddis plays brilliantly throughout both sets.

CLARE FISCHER

b. Oct. 22, 1928, Durand, MI

6 *Lembrancas / June 1989 / Concord Picante 4404*

Clare Fischer has certainly had an interesting career, as pianist, organist, electric keyboardist, composer, and arranger in straightahead, big band, Brazilian and Afro-Cuban settings. He wrote two standards ("Pensativa" and "Morning") and has long been interested in Latin rhythms and music.

Most of Clare Fischer's music is more Brazilian than Afro-Cuban (other than some of his long out-of-print Discovery LPs), but *Lembrancas* is an exception. Fischer (sticking to synthesizers) performs a pleasing, easy-listening Latin set with Dick Mitchell on reeds, bassist Brent Fischer, drummer Tris Imboden, Luis Conte on timbales, and Michito Sanchez on congas. The music (eight Fischer originals, two obscurities, and "On Green Dolphin Street") is enjoyable but not overly memorable, light rather than fiery, soothing rather than exciting. Worthwhile music but not essential. Clare Fischer's definitive Afro-Cuban recording is hopefully still in the future.

RED GARLAND

> b. May 13, 1923, Dallas, TX, d. Apr. 23, 1984, Dallas, TX

9 *Manteca / Apr. 11, 1958 / Original Jazz Classics 428*

8 *Rediscovered Masters, Vol. 1 / June 27, 1958 / Original Jazz Classics 768*

8 *Rojo / Aug. 22, 1958 / Original Jazz Classics 677*

Pianist Red Garland, whose frequently heavy chord voicings were quite original, is best known for his period with the Miles Davis Quintet and Sextet (1955-58). He led a large number of small group recordings (the majority with a trio) during 1956-62 for the Prestige, Jazzland, and Moodsville labels, most of which have been reissued in the OJC series. He drifted into semiretirement in his native Texas after 1962, other than a brief comeback during 1977-79.

On three recording dates in 1958, Garland's trio was augmented on recordings by Ray Barretto on conga. *Manteca* (which gained a lot of recognition at the time) finds Barretto fitting in quite easily with Garland, bassist Paul Chambers, and drummer Art Taylor, adding a bit of fire without significantly altering the music. "Manteca," "Lady Be Good," and "Exactly Like You" are highlights of that recommended disc. *Rediscovered Masters, Vol. 1,* which went unreleased for decades, uses the same musicians on swinging renditions of "Blues in Mambo," "Estrellita," "East of the Sun," and four other songs. *Rojo* has Garland and Barretto joined by bassist George Joyner and drummer Charlie Persip and includes faster-than-usual versions of the ballads "We Kiss in a Shadow" and "You Better Go Now." Throughout, Ray Barretto presents a strong case for the acceptance of the conga as a jazz instrument.

ERROLL GARNER

> b. June 15, 1921, Pittsburgh, PA, d. Jan. 2, 1977, Los Angeles, CA

9 *Mambo Moves Garner / July 27, 1954 / Mercury 834 909*

8 *That's My Kick & Gemini / Apr. 1966-Dec. 21, 1971 / Telarchive 83332*

One of the all-time great jazz pianists and quite popular throughout his career, Erroll Garner emulated an orchestra, often achieving an echo effect by stating the chords on the beat with his left hand (like a rhythm guitar) while his right played just a tiny bit behind the beat. He did not read music or look much at the keyboard while he was playing, but Garner could spontaneously create a classic performance at any time.

Garner mostly utilized a trio throughout his career when not performing solo concerts. For *Mambo Moves* Garner, he added Candido on conga to his rhythm section (bassist Wyatt Ruther and drummer Eugene Heard) and shows that, had he chosen to pursue it, Garner could have been a masterful Afro-Cuban pianist too. Highlights include "Mambo Garner," "Night and Day," "Cherokee," and "Sweet Sue."

During his later years, Garner occasionally utilized a conga, particularly for recording projects. The 1966 album *That's My Kick* and 1971's *Gemini* have been combined on a single CD. Both have José Mangual on conga (two cuts on the former set substitute Johnny Pacheco instead), although Garner is the main star throughout. He is typically exuberant on such selections as "That's My Kick," "Autumn Leaves," "Blue Moon," "Nervous Waltz" (one of his eight originals that are included), "It Could Happen to You," and "Tea for Two."

TERRY GIBBS

b. Oct. 13, 1924, New York, NY

An exciting bop vibraphonist whose playing is usually quite hyper, Terry Gibbs was a member of the Tommy Dorsey (1946 and 1948), Chubby Jackson (1947-48), Buddy Rich (1948), Woody Herman (the 1948-49 Second Herd), and Benny Goodman (1950-52) orchestras before going out on his own. He led his Dream Band in the late '50s/early '60s, was associated with Steve Allen's *Tonight Show*, has teamed up frequently with clarinetist Buddy DeFranco during the past 20 years, and is still a very colorful and hard-swinging performer.

LPs to Search For:

The Latin Connection (Contemporary 14022), from 1986, finds Gibbs sounding quite at home in a band with altoist Frank Morgan, pianist Sonny Bravo, bassist Bobby Rodriguez, José Madera on congas, Johnny Rodriguez on bongos, and either Orestes Vilato or Tito Puente (who is on three numbers) playing timbales. The music is primarily swing and bop standards (including "Scrapple from the Apple," "Sing Sing Sing," and "Good Bait") and, typical for Gibbs, swings up a storm. It is surprising that this exuberant date has not yet been reissued on CD.

GRANT GREEN

b. June 6, 1931, St. Louis, MO, d. Jan. 31, 1979, New York, NY

10 *The Latin Bit / Apr. 26, 1962 + Sept. 8, 1962 / Blue Note 37645*

Guitarist Grant Green was everywhere in the 1960s, recording hard bop, adventurous jazz, R&B-oriented sessions, a set of spirituals, and plenty of soul jazz. His single-note lines (he rarely ever played chords) were very hornlike and, coupled with an appealing sound, made him one of the more distinctive guitarists of the era.

One style of music that Grant Green did not explore very much was Afro-Cuban Jazz, with the exception of *The Latin Bit*. A real gem, this date teams Green with pianist Johnny Acea, bassist Wendell Marshall, drummer Willie Bobo, Patato Valdés on conga, and Carvin Masseaux on chereke (an African shaker). These renditions of such songs as "Mambo Inn," "Besame Mucho," "Brazil," "My Little Suede Shoes," and particularly "Tico Tico" are quite memorable, with Green "singing" his heart out and creating a classic. For the CD reissue, two slightly later selections by a pianoless quintet with Green, tenor saxophonist Ike Quebec, Marshall, Bobo, and Valdés were added to the program. Get this one!

GRP ALL-STAR BIG BAND

9 *GRP All-Star Big Band / Jan. 12, 1992 / GRP 9672*

8 *Live! / Jan. 31, 1993 / GRP 9740*

6 *All Blues / Jan. 8-9, 1994 / GRP 9800*

With the great commercial success of the GRP label, producers Dave Grusin and Larry Rosen decided to fulfill a longtime dream and form a big band comprising most of their label's stars. Three recordings over a four-year period feature the notable musicians mostly performing jazz standards of the 1950s and '60s. Along with the many crossover and hard bop players, the band often included Arturo Sandoval, Dave Valentin, and guest Chick Corea but only slight touches of Afro-Cuban Jazz.

The debut release, *GRP All-Star Big Band,* is their best. With a saxophone section made up of Eric Marienthal, Nelson Rangell, Bob Mintzer, Ernie Watts, and Tom Scott, trumpeters Sandoval, Randy Brecker, and Sal Marquez, trombonist George Bohanon, bassist John Patitucci, drummer Dave Weckl, Russell Ferrante, Kenny Kirkland, Grusin, and David Benoit sharing the piano bench and guitarist Lee Ritenour, Dave Valentin, vibraphonist Gary Burton, clarinetist Eddie Daniels, and percussionist Alex Acuña as guests, this orchestra is top-heavy with solo talent. The Latin element is pretty light (other than on "Manteca" and Chick Corea's "Spain"), but Sandoval gets in his spots. Other highlights include "Blue Train," "Donna Lee," "The Sidewinder," and "Footprints." Live! has similar personnel and a few repeats ("Manteca" and "Blue Train") but is full of lively solos, including a version of "Cherokee" that has tradeoffs by trumpeters Sandoval, Brecker, Byron Stripling, and Chuck Findley. The audience is rightfully enthusiastic throughout this spirited set.

All Blues unfortunately is a bit of a disappointment. Added to the lineup of all-stars are the tenors of Michael Brecker and Bob Mintzer, Chick Corea, pianist Ramsey Lewis, and even B.B. King (who is featured on "Stormy Monday Blues"). But the material is mostly pretty well worn, and the arrangements offer very few surprises. The novelty of hearing crossover players stretch out on hard bop tunes was wearing off. And why revive such common songs as "All Blues," "Goodbye Pork Pie Hat," and "Stormy Monday Blues" yet again?

VINCE GUARALDI
b. July 17, 1928, San Francisco, CA, d. Feb. 6, 1976, Menlo Park, CA

7 *The Latin Side of Vince Guaraldi / 1964 / Original Jazz Classics 878*

Pianist Vince Guaraldi accomplished a great deal in a relatively brief period of time. He was in Cal Tjader's first band (1950-51), led a fine San Francisco-based trio in the 1950s, was with the Woody Herman Orchestra twice (1956-57 and 1959), was a strong asset while back with Tjader (1957-59), recorded Brazilian music on several occasions, often teamed up with guitarist Bola Sete in 1963, composed the hit "Cast Your Fate to the Wind," and wrote the music for the Charlie Brown animated television series.

Vince Guaraldi was more involved with Brazilian music during his solo career than Afro-Cuban music, but he never lost his love for the latter either. On this 1964 recording, Guaraldi is joined by guitarist Eddie Duran, bassist Fred Marshall, drummer Jerry Granelli, Bill Fitch on congas, Benny Velarde on timbales, and a string quartet arranged by Jack Weeks. The music alternates between bossa novas (such as "Corcovado") and hotter, Cuban-style arrangements (including "Work Song"). Overall this is a relaxing, rhythmic set of melodic music.

SLIDE HAMPTON
b. Apr. 21, 1932, Jeannette, PA

7 *Dedicated to Diz / Feb. 6-7, 1993 / Telarc 83323*

A fluent bop trombonist and a very musical arranger, Slide Hampton gained some recognition for his contributions to Maynard Ferguson's big band during 1957-59. He led impressive octets in the 1960s and spent the 1968-77 period writing and playing music in Europe. Since his return home, he has led The World of Trombones (a 12-piece group with nine trombones!), played with Dizzy Gillespie's United Nation Orchestra, and has participated in many Gillespie tribute projects, often with his Jazz Masters.

The Jazz Masters' *Dedicated to Diz* certainly boasts an impressive lineup of musicians: Hampton, Jon Faddis, Roy Hargrove, Claudio Roditi, Steve Turre, trombonist Douglas Purviance, altoist Antonio Hart, tenors David Sanchez and Jimmy Heath, Danilo Perez, bassist George Mraz, and drummer Lewis Nash. Hampton's arrangements are solid, but somewhat predictable to those quite familiar with Dizzy's music. An 11-minute "Overture" (which starts out with short quotes from other Gillespie-associated songs) becomes a cooking "Blue & Boogie," and, with the exception of "Lover Man," all of the music on this set was composed by Gillespie. "Bebop," "Tour de Force," and "A Night in Tunisia" are the high points. Most of the musicians (particularly Faddis) are well featured, although the project would have benefited from some surprises along the way.

HERBIE HANCOCK

b. Apr. 12, 1940, Chicago, IL

7 *Inventions and Dimensions / Aug. 30, 1963 / Blue Note 84147*

Herbie Hancock's career has been very productive and eclectic, to say the least. Emerging as a Bill Evans-influenced pianist in the early 1960s, Hancock played with the Donald Byrd-Pepper Adams Quintet and scored with a major hit on his first solo record. *Takin' Off* included his composition "Watermelon Man," a tune soon adopted by Mongo Santamaria and considered an Afro-Cuban Jazz standard ever since. Hancock's style became more distinctive and adventurous as the 1960s progressed, and his long period as a member of the Miles Davis Quintet (1964-68) would have made him immortal even if he had not been recording a series of brilliant dates for Blue Note (one of which resulted in "Maiden Voyage") during the same period. Hancock led an adventurous sextet in the early 1970s, switched to funky jazz with the Headhunters during 1973-76, explored both electronic funk and

World music, and since then has gone back and forth between acoustic post-bop jazz and funkier electric sounds.

Inventions and Dimensions is an unusual recording, because most of the five compositions were freely improvised in the studio. The reason it is included here is that Hancock is joined not only by bassist Paul Chambers but by Willie Bobo on drums and Osvaldo "Chichuahua" Martinez on conga and bongos. The improvisations are often quite free, with Bobo and Martinez giving the performances a Latin flavor even though the overall rhythms are not very danceable! An intriguing set that was one of the first times that Latin rhythms were heard in a fairly avant-garde jazz setting.

ROY HARGROVE

b. Oct. 16, 1969, Waco, TX

7 *Habana / Jan. 5-6, 1997 / Verve 314 537 563*

One of the most promising of the "Young Lions" to emerge in the late 1980s, trumpeter Roy Hargrove came up as a hard bop soloist but has kept his mind open to other developments along the way. A bandleader since 1990 (when he was 20), Hargrove mixes passionate straightahead jazz in with showmanship and occasional funk tunes. He has also appeared as a featured sideman now and then, including with Superblue, Sonny Rollins, altoist Jackie McLean, and Jazz Futures.

In 1996 Hargrove became interested in exploring Cuban music. In February he visited Havana for 11 days, playing with local musicians (including sitting in with the band Los Van Van) and learning a great deal about the music's rhythms. Later in the year he formed Cristol (Spanish for "melting pot"), an all-star group that toured the United States (including the Playboy Jazz Festival in Hollywood) during 1997. Their one recording was unfortunately made before the tour. Since the ten-piece group would grow and develop in future months, it is a pity that a later live session was not released instead. This CD is well worth picking up anyway since it features such notables as Hargrove, Chucho Valdés, trombonist Frank Lacy, altoist Gary Bartz, guitarist Russell Malone, David Sanchez on tenor and soprano, and bassist John Benitez along with three drummer/percussionists. The music (by Hargrove, Lacy, Bartz, and Valdés plus a couple of tunes by Kenny Dorham) is excellent and often catchy although not played as comfortably or with as much fire as it would be a few months later. Hopefully a later live recording will come out eventually.

JOE HENDERSON

b. Apr. 24, 1937, Lima, OH

8 *Canyon Lady / Oct. 1973 / Original Jazz Classics 949*

A major tenor saxophonist ever since he was sponsored by trumpeter Kenny Dorham in the early 1960s, Joe Henderson has always had his own inside/outside sound and style, able to play hard bop and in freer settings with equal facility. He recorded a string of impressive albums for Blue Note in the 1960s, had a long association with the Milestone label, was taken for granted for years, was "rediscovered" in an inspired marketing campaign by the Verve label in the 1990s, and finally received the recognition that he deserved. To his credit, whether in obscurity or world-famous, Henderson always played the same way, not straying far from his own singular musical path.

Canyon Lady is an underrated set from 1973, one of Joe Henderson's few albums in an Afro-Cuban Jazz setting. "Tres Palabras" features a large group arranged by trumpeter Luis Gasca, "Las Palmas" teams Gasca with Henderson and a Latin rhythm section, and two other songs have a frontline of Henderson, Gasca, trumpeter Oscar Brashear, trombonist Julian Priester, and sometimes Hadley Caliman on second tenor. The percussion-

ists include Francisco Aguabella, Carmelo Garcia, and Victor Pantoja. Throughout, Henderson plays typically well, stretching himself and riding confidently above the rhythms.

WOODY HERMAN

b. May 16, 1913, Milwaukee, WI, d. Oct. 29, 1987 Los Angeles, CA

7 *Herman's Heat & Puente's Beat / Sept. 1958 / Evidence 2208*

A major big bandleader for 51 years (1936-87), Woody Herman played clarinet, alto, and soprano in addition to singing but was most significant as a constant encourager of young talent. His bands almost always sounded modern, and he loved to play new material by his sidemen. Herman's most popular groups were the First Herd (1944-46) and the Second Herd, or Four Brothers Band (1947-49), orchestras that set the standard for his many swinging bands to come.

Woody Herman's contributions to Afro-Cuban Jazz were not much bigger than that of most other swing-era big-band leaders. His First Herd did record an eccentric rumba named "Bijou" that was a feature for Bill Harris' expressive trombone, and "Sidewalks of Cuba" (a straightahead piece) had one of Sonny Berman's most famous trumpet solos. For a period during January-March 1953, Herman's Third Herd was expanded with the inclusion of Candido and José Mangual on percussion, but that experiment did not last long. In September 1958, Herman recorded his only real Afro-Cuban session, half of an LP for Everest that was reissued by Evidence. Half of the six selections are conventional, featuring Herman's new big band, which was set to soon tour Europe, playing such numbers as "Woodchopper's Ball" and "Lullaby of Rhythm." However, two numbers ("Tito Meets Woody" and "Carioca") have the orchestra augmented by Tito Puente's rhythm section, with Puente on timbales, bassist Robert Rodriguez, Ray

Barretto on conga, and other percussion played by Gilbert López and Raymond Rodriguez. The remaining four songs have a partly all-star studio group, with Herman also assisted by Puente's rhythm section. Those titles are "Latin Flight," "New Cha-Cha," "Mambo Herd," and "Cha-Cha Chick." The results are a little lightweight, with the rhythm section sometimes sounding grafted on, but the "experiment" was largely successful. Pity that it was never repeated again.

CONRAD HERWIG
b. Nov. 1, 1959, Oklahoma

9 *The Latin Side of John Coltrane / Mar. 15-16, 1996 / Astor Place 4003*

A top-notch trombonist who has freelanced in the New York area since the early 1980s, Conrad Herwig has appeared with Joe Henderson, drummer Jack DeJohnette, Paquito D'Rivera, the Toshiko Akiyoshi Orchestra, and many others in the jazz and Latin music world.

Strange as it seems, Herwig's *The Latin Side of John Coltrane* was the first full-length exploration of the great saxophonist's music in a Latin setting. Herwig varies the instrumentation on each selection, features such top players as trumpeter Brian Lynch, Dave Valentin, baritonist Ronnie Cuber, pianists Danilo Perez, Eddie Palmieri, Richie Beirach, and Edward Simon and three percussionists, including Milton Cardona, who opens and closes the program with a brief sung "Blessing." Among the ten Coltrane-associated songs that are explored are "Blue Train," "Naima," "Impressions," "India," and of course "Afro Blue." An inspired idea, expertly executed, highly recommended.

LIGHTHOUSE ALL-STARS
6 *Mexican Passport / July 22, 1952-Oct. 2, 1956 / Contemporary 14077*

During 1949-62, former Stan Kenton bassist Howard Rumsey led the Lighthouse All-Stars, the definitive West Coast "cool jazz" band. Based at the Lighthouse in Hermosa Beach, such major players as trumpeters Shorty Rogers and Conte Candoli, trombonist Frank Rosolino, altoist Bud Shank, tenors Jimmy Giuffre and Bob Cooper, and drummer Shelly Manne were among the many top musicians who spent important periods with the popular band which recorded regularly for the Contemporary label. In the late 1980s the group was reformed for a few years under Shorty Rogers' leadership.

Mexican Passport is a sampler that collects together the Lighthouse All-Stars' occasional Latin recordings. The ten selections (taken from five albums) are a bit limited since there are two versions of "Viva Zapata," three of "Witch Doctor," and several of the other songs are just one-chord vamps. A few different versions of the Lighthouse All-Stars are heard from, including such players as Rogers, Candoli, trumpeter Chet Baker, Rosolino, Cooper, Giuffre, Shank, altoist Herb Geller, drummer Max Roach, and pianists Sonny Clark, Hampton Hawes, and Claude Williamson. In addition, Carlos Vidal on conga and Jack Costanzo on bongos are added to two songs apiece and quite often the horn players bang on percussion instruments when they are not soloing. The music is good humored overall and, although not essential, the results are fun.

JOE LOVANO
b. Dec. 29, 1952, Cleveland, OH

8 *Flying Colors / Jan. 11, 1997 / Blue Note 56092*

Tenor saxophonist Joe Lovano, who began to impress listeners in the 1980s with his solo projects and his work with drummer Paul Motian, bassist Charlie Haden's Liberation Music Orchestra, guitarist John Scofield, and drummer Elvin Jones, was recognized as a giant in the 1990s. He popped up in many settings, and his own recordings were quite rewarding and unpredictable.

Flying Colors is an unusual duo date with the great pianist Gonzalo Rubalcaba. Lovano is heard playing tenor, soprano, alto clarinet, drums, and gongs, sometimes utilizing some overdubbing (particularly for the gongs). Rubalcaba and Lovano had played together previously only during a single week a couple of years earlier at Yoshi's in Oakland and had just one rehearsal before this very spontaneous date. Whether it be a few standards (including "How Deep Is the Ocean," "Hot House," and "I Love Music"), some obscurities (tunes by Ornette Coleman, Paul Motian, and Scott LaFaro), or four of their originals, the music relies heavily on the musicians' ears and their close interplay. There are plenty of sparks along the way with some surprises, making this a continually interesting listen.

SHELLY MANNE

> *b. June 11, 1920, New York, NY, d. Sept. 26, 1984, Los Angeles, CA*

A popular drummer for nearly four decades, Shelly Manne appeared on countless sessions, whether in the studios, with Stan Kenton's orchestra (1946-48 and 1950-52), as a sideman in jazz bands, or as leader of his own West Coast quintet.

LPs to Search For:

In 1952 Manne led his only out-and-out Afro-Cuban Jazz date, although (due to his Contemporary contract) he was listed as "guest star." *Hot Skins* (V.S.O.P. 29) brings back the music recorded for the long-defunct Interlude label, nine selections performed in an octet with guitarist Tony Rizzi, pianist Robert Gil, both Tony Reyes and Julio Ayala on bass, second drummer Frank Guerrero, Mike Pachecho on bongos, and Carlos Vidal on conga. Robert Gil contributed four of the nine songs (including "Rhumba by Candlelight"), the band plays a Xavier Cugat number ("Nightingale"), and the other four tunes are jazz standards, including "Caravan" and "Move." Needless to say, the music is quite rhythmic!

CHARLES MINGUS

> *b. Apr. 22, 1922, Nogales, AZ, d. Jan. 5, 1979, Cuernavaca, Mexico*

10 *New Tijuana Moods / July 18, 1957-Aug. 6, 1957 / RCA 68591*

7 *Cumbia and Jazz Fusion / Mar. 31, 1976-May 1, 1977 / Rhino 71785*

One of jazz's greatest bassists, bandleaders, and innovators, Charles Mingus was highly emotional and unpredictable. He often inspired his sidemen to play above their limitations, but also was the cause of many of them quitting his band! Mingus' music looked both backwards (toward group improvising, stop-time rhythms, the feel of New Orleans jazz, blues, and spirituals) and ahead, to sound explorations and the avant-garde. Mingus' prime period was 1955-65, but he also led impressive bands during 1970-77, before his worsening health forced him to quit.

Twice in Mingus' career he explored music from south of the border. *Tijuana Moods* (renamed *New Tijuana Moods* when it was reissued with alternate takes) features his 1957 band (trumpeter Clarence Shaw, trombonist Jimmy Knepper, altoist Shafi Hadi, pianist Bill Triglia, and drummer Danny Richmond) plus percussionists Frankie Dunlop and Ysabel Morel. With the exception of Knepper and Richmond, all of Mingus' sidemen on this project played way above their heads, and this would be the recording that they would be remembered for. Inspired by a somewhat-riotous trip to Mexico, this date has many intense moments, some fairly free improvisations, and is quite memorable overall, particularly "Ysabel's Table Dance" and "Tijuana Gift Shop." Earlier, a two-LP set reissued the five original selections plus alternates to each of the songs; due to lack of space, the lengthy alternate for "Los Mariachis" has been left out of this single CD, but otherwise the release is quite definitive. An exhilarating set that at times gives the feeling that the musicians were almost on the verge of getting out of control.

Cumbia and Jazz Fusion is from Charles Mingus' final period. He performed the 22-minute "Music for 'Todo Modo'" in 1976 and the 28-minute "Cumbia & Jazz Fusion" in 1977 with larger than usual ensembles. In both cases, the music was written for films, and the results are quite episodic. "Music for 'Todo Modo'" has Mingus leading a tentet that includes his regular musicians (trumpeter Jack Walrath, George Adams on tenor, pianist Danny Mixon, and drummer Danny Richmond) plus five Italian horn players. "Cumbia & Jazz Fusion" (which is more Latin-oriented) also has a tentet (Walrath, trombonist Knepper, Ricky Ford on tenor, pianist Bob Neloms, and Richmond plus four woodwinds) in addition to four conga players, including Candido and Ray Mantilla. The CD reissue is rounded out by a couple of brief and previously unissued piano solos by Mingus of a "Wedding March/Slow Waltz."

MINGUS BIG BAND

9 *Que Viva Mingus / Sept. 8-9, 1997 / Dreyfus 36593*

Formed in 1991, a dozen years after Charles Mingus' death, the Mingus Big Band is the kind of orchestra the bassist should have had during his lifetime but probably could not have held on to due to his temper. Playing weekly at the Time Spot Café in New York, this very impressive ensemble has mastered and developed the many compositions of Mingus, bringing back his spirit and chance-taking legacy.

The Mingus Big Band's fourth release for Dreyfus focuses on Mingus' Latin compositions. They perform four of the five selections from New Tijuana Moods (everything but "Flamingo"). The group revives "Cumbia & Jazz Fusion" (in a version that tops the original) and also performs "Far Wells Mill Valley," the out-of-place "Eat That Chicken," and such obscurities as "Love Chant," "Slippers," and "Moods in Mambo." Among the key soloists are trumpeter Randy Brecker, altoist Chris Potter, Steve Slagle on soprano and alto, tenors John Stubblefield and David Sanchez, baritonist Ronnie Cuber, and pianist Dave Kikoski. Steve Berrios and Milton Cardona help out on percussion during some of the songs. Stirring and exciting music.

JELLY ROLL MORTON

b. Oct. 20, 1890, New Orleans, LA, d. July 10, 1941, Los Angeles, CA

10 *Jelly Roll Morton / June 9, 1923-Feb. 2, 1926 / Milestone 47018*

Jelly Roll Morton stated early on that what he called "The Spanish Tinge" is an essential ingredient to all jazz, separating it from ragtime. A pioneering jazz pianist, composer, arranger, and bandleader, Morton was among the first jazz greats to emerge, recording a series of brilliant piano solos during 1923-24, and leading his Red Hot Peppers on many classic recordings during 1926-30. Unfortunately his tendency to brag and exaggerate his own formidable talents hurt him in the long run, resulting in his being largely friendless when hard times struck in the 1930s, and being underrated by some in jazz history books. But a close listen to his music makes it clear that he was one of the true giants.

"The Spanish Tinge" can be heard on several of Morton's early piano solos, particularly "New Orleans Joys," "Mama Nita" (which he recorded twice), "Jelly Roll Blues," "Tia Juana," and, later on, "Creepy Feeling" and "The Crave." Morton used a habanera or tango rhythm on at least part of each of these solos, a device rarely utilized in jazz that early on. The CD called simply *Jelly Roll Morton* has all 20 of Morton's piano solos from 1923-24 plus a few rather primitive band numbers and two charming duets with cornetist King Oliver. The music is essential for all jazz collections, and it illustrates the early use of Latin rhythms, 20 years before the rise of Cubop.

MICHAEL PHILIP MOSSMAN

b. Oct. 12, 1959, Philadelphia, PA

8 *Springdance / May 9-10, 1994 / Clavés Jazz 50-1094*

8 *Mama Soho / Dec. 3-4, 1995 / TCB 9810*

A top-notch hard bop trumpeter, Michael Mossman has played with Art Blakey's Jazz Messengers (for a month), Machito, baritonist Gerry Mulligan, Out of the Blue, Toshiko Akiyoshi's Jazz Orchestra, Horace Silver, Dizzy Gillespie's United Nation Orchestra, Slide Hampton's Jazz Masters, Michel Camilo, Mario Bauzá, and Eddie Palmieri, among many others. His wide range, attractive sound, and knowledge of several styles are always strong assets.

Springdance features the trumpeter (who also plays some effective trombone) in a sextet with David Sanchez, pianist Kenny Drew Jr., bassist James Genus, drummer Marvin "Smitty" Smith, and percussionist Bobby Sanabria. Other than one piece by Slide Hampton and a medley of Bill Evans' "Peace Piece" and Horace Silver's "Peace," Springdance is made up of Mossman's originals. These include several Latin pieces (most notably "Chachanita" and "Mambo Ala Jo") along with a few numbers very much in the hard bop vein of Art Blakey's Jazz Messengers and Horace Silver. *Mama Soho* utilizes a similar group (with Bob Mintzer on tenor and flute in Sanchez's place and Mark Walker on drums). This time around, all of the nine selections (except "All the Things You Are") were arranged and composed by Mossman, and these include tributes to Michel Camilo ("Ronita's Fantasy"), Clare Fischer ("No Peeking"), and Duke Ellington and Miles Davis ("My Sentiments"). The playing throughout *Mama Soho* is equal to that on *Springdance* and shows the apparent ease that Mossman has in quickly shifting back and forth between straightahead and Afro-Cuban Jazz.

ANITA O'DAY

b. Oct. 18, 1919, Kansas City, MO

One of the top singers to emerge from the swing era, Anita O'Day had hits with Gene Krupa's orchestra (1941-43), spent a year with Stan Kenton's big band, and recorded her finest performances in the 1950s, being one of the few swing singers to sound quite comfortable performing bop. She survived harrowing episodes with drugs in the 1960s to make a full comeback in the '70s, but her voice has gradually faded away since then, although she is still active as of this writing.

LPs to Search For:

In 1962 O'Day teamed up with Cal Tjader's band for *Time for Two* (Verve 8472), a set currently available only on CD as part of the nine-disc *Complete Anita O'Day Verve/Clef Sessions* (Mosaic 9-188). Backed by Tjader (whose vibes add a lot of atmosphere to the music) and his rhythm section (with Johnny Rae on drums and usually Wilfredo Vicenti on conga), O'Day sounds in prime form on a wide-ranging repertoire that includes "Peel Me a Grape," "Spring Will Be a Little Late This Year," "Your Red Wagon," and even a worthwhile rendition of "Mister Sandman."

CHARLIE PARKER

b. Aug. 29, 1920, Kansas City, KS, d. Mar. 12, 1955, New York, NY

10 *South of the Border: The Verve Latin-Jazz Sides / Dec. 20, 1948-Jan. 23, 1952 / Verve 314 527 779*

Jelly Roll Morton was among the first jazz musicians to recognize the potential of Latin rhthyms.

Charlie "Bird" Parker was one of the most important jazz musicians of all time, a masterful improviser whose every phrase was copied and eventually became part of the mainstream of music. The altoist could play perfectly coherent solos at ridiculously fast tempos, he was a master at creating new melodic phrases over chord changes, and yet he was a blues player at heart. Along with Dizzy Gillespie, Bird largely founded bebop. His prime years (1945-54) may not have been long, but this period was full of enough innovations, adventure, drama, and excess to fill in several lifetimes!

Unlike Gillespie, Parker flirted with Afro-Cuban rhythms only on a very occasional basis. He did record with Machito's orchestra on two different occasions in 1948 and 1950 (including Chico O'Farrill's "Afro-Cuban Suite"). For two of his small-group recording sessions of 1951-52, he utilized José Mangual on bongos and Luis Miranda on conga. The latter dates are highlighted by "Tico Tico," "Mama Inez," "Estrellita," and the original version of Bird's "My Little Suede Shoes." All of the master takes from these four sessions are on South of the Border. Due to its historic nature and Parker's always-brilliant playing, this CD is well worth picking up.

BUD POWELL

b. Sept. 27, 1924, New York, NY, d. July 31,
1966, New York, NY

10 *The Amazing Bud Powell, Vol. 1 / Aug. 8,*
1949-May 1, 1951 / Blue Note 81503

Bud Powell changed the way that the piano is
played in jazz. Instead of keeping time while strid-
ing, Powell's left hand stated the chords on an erratic but forceful basis while his right emphasized
speedy single-note lines. Jazz piano was never the
same after the rise of this troubled genius, who
fought mental illness throughout his tragic but often
musically rewarding life.

Bud Powell had no real involvement with Afro-
Cuban Jazz, with the exception of having composed
"Un Poco Loco," a complex and fiery rhythmic
piece. On *The Amazing Bud Powell, Vol. 1,* Powell is
heard on three versions of that original in 1951 in a
trio with bassist Curly Russell and Max Roach.
Also included is a very exciting quintet session from
two years earlier that features trumpeter Fats
Navarro and tenor saxophonist Sonny Rollins playing other Powell compositions, including "Dance of
the Infidels" and "Bouncin' with Bud."

SONNY ROLLINS

b. Sept. 7, 1930, New York, NY

10 *The Complete RCA Victor Recordings / Jan.*
30, 1962-July 9, 1964 / RCA 68675

By the mid-1950s, when he was considered the top
young tenor saxophonist in jazz (prior to the rise of
John Coltrane), Sonny Rollins had the reputation of
always being willing to expand the repertoire of
jazz, whether it meant reviving forgotten show
tunes, playing an obscure Al Jolson-associated
song, or writing some standards of his own. On
June 22, 1956, he recorded the first (and definitive)
version of an old calypso tune that he called "St.
Thomas." Throughout his lengthy career (which
was interrupted by three retirement periods),

Rollins has recorded countless colorful dates, ranging from bebop and ballads to calypso and R&Bish
funk.

Not counting the calypsos, which would be part
of his repertoire for decades, Rollins' only album in
which he explored South American rhythms is
1962's *What's New,* which is currently available
only on CD as part of Rollins' six-disc *The
Complete RCA Victor Recordings* box. Guitarist Jim
Hall, bassist Ben Cranshaw, and drummer Ben
Riley are on most of the selections. Rollins introduced "Don't Stop the Carnival" on this album
(with his group joined by three percussionists and
six background singers), "Jungoso" and
"Bluesongo" are played in a trio with Cranshaw and
Candido (on conga and bongos), and Rollins is also
showcased on "Brown Skin Gal," "The Night Has
a Thousand Eyes," and a lengthy "If Ever I Should
Leave You." The great tenor hints at the avant-
garde in places through his intense tone, even when
he emphasizes the melody. Also on the magnificent
six-CD set is his classic album with Jim Hall called
The Bridge, an eccentric meeting with tenor saxophonist Coleman Hawkins, some music influenced
by Ornette Coleman, and lots of adventurous performances by the unique Sonny Rollins.

DAVE SAMUELS

b. Oct. 9, 1948, Waukegan, IL

6 *Tjader-ized / 1998 / Verve 314 557 086*

Vibraphonist and marimba player Dave Samuels
has gained his greatest fame for his work with Spyro
Gyra (1979 to mid-'90s). Although he played early
on in bop and post-bop settings (including co-leading Double Image with fellow vibist Don
Friedman), most of his own solo recordings have
been a bit commercial, even if he always solos well.
Samuels has in recent times been one of the leaders
of the Caribbean Jazz Project.

In 1998 Dave Samuels recorded a tribute to the

great Cal Tjader, bringing back such songs as "Soul Sauce," "Viva Cepeda," and "Triste." In addition, Samuels performs two Eddie Palmieri compositions (including "Tjader-ized") and co-wrote "Duo Plus Four" with Palmieri. For this well-conceived outing, Samuels is joined by Dave Valentin, David Sanchez, either Palmieri, Michael Wolff, or Alain Mallet on piano, guitarist Steve Khan, John Benitez or Joe Santiago on bass, drummer Horacio "El Negro" Hernández, and several percussionists, including Ray Barretto. The music is pleasing, although not quite as stirring as Cal Tjader's best sets. But this CD might serve as a way for Samuels' fans from Spyro Gyra to make their way toward Tjader and Afro-Cuban Jazz.

BOBBY SHEW

b. Mar. 4, 1941, Albuquerque, NM

8 *Salsa Caliente / May 19-20, 1998 / Mama Foundation 1023*

A versatile trumpeter with impressive technical skills and a creative hard bop style, Bobby Shew is equally skilled playing lead in big bands or being featured as a soloist with combos. During his productive career, Shew has worked in the big bands of Woody Herman, Buddy Rich, Toshiko Akiyoshi, Louie Bellson, and the Frank Capp Juggernaut. In addition, he has worked extensively in the studios and been an important jazz educator even though, ironically, he was largely self-taught!

Although he has had few opportunities to record it through the years, Bobby Shew has always had a strong fondness for Afro-Cuban Jazz. *On Salsa Caliente,* he teams up with quite a few notables from the field: Art Velasco, Justo Almario (on tenor and flute), Mark Levine, bassist Eddie Resto, Papo Rodriguez on bongos, Tiki Pasillas on timbales, and Michito Sanchez on congas along with guest trumpeter Sal Cracchiolo. On such tunes as "Cubano Chant," Cal Tjader's "Paunetto's Point,"

and Harold Ousley's "Elation" (plus several newer songs), Bobby Shew shows that he is an even more versatile trumpeter than expected. The high-quality results are delightful and infectious.

HORACE SILVER

b. Sept. 2, 1928, Norwalk, CT

9 *Six Pieces of Silver / Nov. 10, 1956 + June 15, 1958 / Blue Note 81539*

The definitive funk pianist, Horace Silver has had a very original style since the early to mid-1950s and has also been one of jazz's top songwriters of the past half-century. His piano playing in a hard bop context led the way toward soul jazz, and his best songs (including "Song for My Father," "The Preacher," and "Doodlin'") have long been jazz standards. The original co-leader (with Art Blakey) of the Jazz Messengers in 1955, Silver has led his own bands (usually quintets) since 1956.

Although his funky style has not been featured in an Afro-Cuban Jazz setting, a few of Silver's tunes have been used by Latin bands. *Six Pieces of Silver,* the first classic album by the Horace Silver Quintet (which at the time consisted of trumpeter Donald Byrd, Hank Mobley on tenor, bassist Doug Watkins, and drummer Louis Hayes) is most notable for introducing "Señor Blues." The CD reissue not only has the original recording and the slightly shorter "45 version" but the first rendition with lyrics, a 1958 recording in which Bill Henderson takes the vocal. Also on this enjoyable set are several other Silver tunes (including "Cool Eyes" and "Tippin'") plus the standard "For Heaven's Sake."

HARVIE SWARTZ

b. Dec. 6, 1948, Chelsea, MA

6 *Havana Mañana / Feb. 1999 / Bembe 2024*

A versatile bassist, Harvie Swartz has performed voice-bass duets with Sheila Jordan, played advanced jazz with arranger Gil Evans, altoist Lee Konitz, Double Image, pianist Steve Kuhn, and drummer Paul Motian and led his own bands, including a 1980s group called Urban Earth.

Swartz became quite interested in Latin music a few years ago and has devoted himself to studying and playing the rhythms. His new group, Eye Contact, debuted on *Havana Mañana*. The music will not please Afro-Cuban purists, for Bruce Arnold's guitar is frequently rockish (although he does a remarkable imitation of steel drums on "Cubalypso"), and Gregor Hubener's violin and piano playing (although he is talented) is mostly outside of the genre. However, drummer Ed Uribe and Memo Acevedo (on congas, bongos, and guiro) work together quite well, and Swartz forms a strong rhythm section with them. Trombonist Barry Olsen is a guest on two cuts ("Descarga Y2K" and the last part of the three-movement "Havana Mañana Suite"). The music on this CD sounds like a work-in-progress. Harvie Swartz's future projects in this field, as he continues to become immersed in Afro-Cuban Jazz, should be well worth following.

BILLY TAYLOR
b. July 24, 1921, Greenville, NC
8 *Cross-Section / May 7, 1953-Sept. 30, 1954 / Original Jazz Classics 1730*
7 *The Billy Taylor Trio with Candido / Sept. 7, 1954 / Original Jazz Classics 015*

Dr. Billy Taylor has long been jazz's most articulate spokesperson, whether profiling jazz artists on CBS's *Sunday Morning* television series, speaking on the radio, or as a busy jazz educator. However, his verbal talents should never be allowed to overshadow his consistently swinging and inventive piano playing. Whether playing with swing greats on 52nd Street in 1944, being the house pianist at Birdland in 1951, performing on the Jazzmobile (which he founded) in 1965, leading the orchestra for *The David Frost Show* in 1970, or playing around the world with his trio during the past 50 years, Billy Taylor is one of the finest pianists in jazz.

During 1951-54, Taylor utilized Latin percussion on a few of his recordings. The earliest album (Roost 409) had Frank Conlon on conga and Manny Oquendo joining Taylor's quartet, but this set has been out of print for decades. *Cross-Section* has eight straightahead numbers by Taylor's 1954 trio (with bassist Earl May and drummer Percy Brice). However, there are also four originals ("I Love to Mambo," "Early Morning Mambo," "Mambo Azul," and "Candido") performed by a sextet with May, Charlie Smith on conga, and Machito's rhythm section: José Mangual on bongos, Uba Nieto playing timbales, and Machito himself on maracas. The mambos work well both for close listening and as backgrounds for dancing.

The collaboration with Candido (*The Billy Taylor Trio with Candido*) finds Taylor, May, and Brice teaming up successfully with the percussionist (heard on conga and bongos). Both Taylor and Candido get plenty of solo space on four of the pianist's boppish themes ("Bit of Bedlam" finds Taylor sounding like Bud Powell), "Love for Sale," and "Mambo Inn." This is a happy set, although it is unfortunate that only 32 minutes of music was recorded.

CLARK TERRY
b. Dec. 14, 1920, St. Louis, MO

Flügelhornist Clark Terry has long had the happiest sound in jazz. His very distinctive and joyous tone has been on countless recordings through the years, whether with the orchestras of Count Basie (1948-51) and Duke Ellington (1951-59) or with his many combos. Although he came up in the bebop era and could fit into nearly any modern musical situation, C.T. has an unclassifiable style that falls between

©Susan Rosmarin

Jazz's first virtuoso of the conch shells, Steve Turre is also a brilliant trombonist.

bop and swing. Fifty-three years after he first joined Charlie Barnet's band, Terry still remains greatly in demand for concerts and recordings.

LPs to Search For:
Although his highly expressive tone would seem to be a perfect match for an Afro-Cuban setting (why wasn't he ever recorded with Tito Puente?), Clark Terry has rarely been heard with any Latin musicians. An exception is the out-of-print *Spanish Rice* (Impulse 9127), a 1966 album in which Terry is joined by three other trumpeters, two guitars, bassist George Duvivier, drummer Grady Tate, and four percussionists, including Chino Pozo. Chico O'Farrill provided the arrangements for some new songs and such vintage material as "The Peanut

Vendor," "Mexican Hat Dance" "Say Si Si," and "Tin Tin Deo." Unfortunately only two of the dozen performances exceed three minutes, so these renditions are overly concise. But the music is fun.

STEVE TURRE
b. Sept. 12, 1948, Omaha, NE

7 *Right There / Mar. 30, 1991-Apr. 10, 1991 / Antilles 314 510 040*

7 *Sanctified Shells / Jan. 31, 1992-May 11, 1992 / Antilles 314 514 186*

9 *Rhythm Within / 1995 / Antilles 314 527 159*

10 *Steve Turre / May 7, 1996 + June 20, 1996 / Verve 314 537 133*

9 *In the Spur of the Moment / Aug. 14, 1999-Oct. 8, 1999 / Telarc 83484*

A versatile trombonist, Steve Turre excels at every musical style that interests him. He has sounded quite credible and creative playing with Rahsaan Roland Kirk, Ray Charles, Santana, Art Blakey's Jazz Messengers, McCoy Tyner, tenor saxophonist Dexter Gordon, Poncho Sanchez, Hilton Ruiz, Tito Puente, Dizzy Gillespie's United Nation Orchestra, and Lester Bowie's Brass Fantasy, not to mention his own bands. In addition to his fluent trombone playing, Turre introduced the conch shells to jazz, which he uses both to evoke a mysterious atmosphere and to take solos.

Although many of his sideman appearances have found Turre sounding quite at home in Afro-Cuban Jazz settings, his own albums as a leader have included swing, bebop, and adventurous explorations in addition to Latin music. *Right There* is primarily a straightahead set featuring Turre on trombone and shells in a sextet with violinist John Blake, cellist Akua Dixon Turre, pianist Benny Green (who here often sounds surprisingly close to McCoy Tyner), bassist Buster Williams, and drummer Billy Higgins. Two of the first seven selections have guest spots for Wynton Marsalis, and tenor saxophonist Benny Golson is on one of those cuts. Highlights include "Woody & Bu," Duke Ellington's "Echoes of Harlem," and "Duke's Mountain." From the Latin standpoint, the closing eight-minute "Descarga de Turre" is of greatest interest, since it features the leader in a group with Dave Valentin, pianist Willie Rodriguez, Andy González, George Delgado on conga, Manny Oquendo on timbales, and Herman Olivera on clavé.

Sanctified Shells is recommended primarily to listeners who enjoy Turre's work with shells, because his trombone playing takes a back seat throughout the set. In fact, Turre is often joined by fellow trombonists Robin Eubanks and Reynaldo Jorge on additional shells. The leader wrote or cowrote all ten selections, and these include an ok guest appearance by Dizzy Gillespie on "Toreador" and spots for Charlie Sepúlveda, trombonist Clifton Anderson, and several percussionists.

Rhythm Within is a very strong CD, with each of the nine selections having different personnel and its own purpose. In various spots Turre utilizes a "shell choir," several other trombonists (including Britt Woodman, Frank Lacy, and Robin Eubanks), Jon Faddis, tenor saxophonist Pharoah Sanders, pianist Herbie Hancock, Andy González, and Milton Cardon on conga, among others. Among the more memorable selections of this eclectic but consistent set are "Funky-T," "Twilight Dreams," "Since I Fell for You," "All Blues," "Motuno Caracol," and "African Shuffle."

The CD called *Steve Turre* is even better. It is more successful than it is ambitious, and it is a lot of both! Once again the personnel changes constantly. Cassandra Wilson sings "In a Sentimental Mood" with a group that includes a string quartet, Turre holds his own with the great trombonist J.J. Johnson on "The Emperor" and "Steve's Blues," violinist Regina Carter has a few good solos, Graciela Perez sings the Marty Sheller-arranged "Ayer Lo Vi Llorar," and Mongo Santamaria, Chocolate Armenteros, Manny Oquendo, and Jimmy Bosch drop by for "Mongo 'n McCoy." Other notables who make appearances include trumpeter Randy Brecker, Andy González, Jon Faddis, Milton Cardona, pianist Willie Rodriguez, and vibraphonist Stefon Harris. An exciting set—Turre's classic thus far.

Steve Turre is featured in three very different quartets on *In the Spur of the Moment*. The first four numbers are quite unusual, because Turre's group includes not only bassist Peter Washington and his son, Peter Turre, on drums but Ray Charles in a rare sideman appearance on piano! Charles shows that he is still an excellent jazz pianist on such numbers as "The Way You Look Tonight," "Duke Rays," and his "Ray's Collard Greens." Turre plays a Duke Ellington medley and a couple of modern modal pieces with pianist Stephen Scott, bassist Buster Williams, and drummer Jack DeJohnette. The final three selections are the Afro-Cuban portion of the CD, with Turre assisted by Chucho Valdés (in mostly restrained but creative form), Andy González, and Horacio "El Negro" Hernández on congas, bongos, and timbales; Valdés' beautiful "Claudia" has the group joined by a string quartet, Quartette Indigo. A successful project in all three settings.

McCOY TYNER

b. Dec. 11, 1938, Philadelphia, PA
9 *McCoy Tyner and the Latin All-Stars / July 29-30, 1998 / Telarc 83462*

John Coltrane's pianist in his classic quartet during 1960-65, McCoy Tyner's powerful style (which utilizes very original chord voicings) is still very much intact after 35 years as the leader of his own important bands. Any list of the all-time great jazz pianists has to include Tyner, who is still very much in his musical prime.

McCoy Tyner used Johnny Pacheco and Willie Rodriguez on Latin percussion for four selections in his 1964 Duke Ellington tribute album, and he occasionally utilized a percussionist in his later projects. However, his first real Afro-Cuban Jazz album, *McCoy Tyner and the Latin All-Stars,* was not recorded until he was 59, in 1998. The "All-Stars" in the title is not inaccurate, since Tyner's specially assembled band also includes Claudio Roditi, Steve Turre, Dave Valentin, altoist Gary Bartz, bassist Avery Sharpe, Ignacio Berroa, Giovanni Hidalgo, and Johnny Almendro on timbales. The octet performs three Tyner originals

(including "Festival in Bahia"), one song by Avery Sharpe, "Blue Bossa," "Poinciana," and "Afro Blue" (which Tyner played many times with Coltrane) with infectious joy. Fortunately McCoy Tyner has occasionally toured in a similar format during the past two years when not performing with his regular trio, so hopefully further recordings will come out eventually.

GERALD WILSON

b. Sept. 4, 1918, Shelby, MS
9 *Moment of Truth / Sept. 1962 / Capitol / Pacific Jazz 92928*

A major arranger since the 1940s, Gerald Wilson started out as a trumpeter with Jimmy Lunceford's orchestra (1939-42), settled in Los Angeles, led a bebop big band in the '40s, and played with the orchestras of Count Basie and Dizzy Gillespie (1947-48). After working as a freelance arranger, Wilson in 1961 formed a big band and began recording regularly for Pacific Jazz. After giving up playing trumpet, Wilson has led his orchestra on a part-time basis ever since, and he is today still considered one of the top arrangers in jazz.

Gerald Wilson has always had a love for the music of Mexico, and on several occasions he has recorded both original and traditional themes inspired by Mexico. *Moment of Truth* is most notable for including the earliest version of his best-known original, "Viva Tirado," which the Latin rock group El Chicano would make a hit in 1970. In addition to that catchy number, Wilson contributed all but two of the songs on this big band set, including "Latino" and "Moment of Truth"; this driving arrangement of "Milestones" has remained in Wilson's book up to the present time. The key soloists on the easily recommended set are trumpeter Carmell Jones, tenors Teddy Edwards and Harold Land, guitarist Joe Pass, and pianist Jack Wilson.

LPs to Search For:

The Golden Sword (Discovery 901), from 1966, is Gerald Wilson's tribute to Mexico. Of his six originals that are included, best known is his famous tribute to a bullfighter, "Carlos," which features Jimmy Owens' dramatic trumpet. Also on this date is Ernest Lecuona's "The Breeze and I" and a few traditional songs; the other soloists include trumpeters Conte Candoli and Nat Meeks, Roy Ayers or Victor Feldman on vibes, guitarist Laurindo Almeida, and both Harold Land and Teddy Edwards on tenors.

VARIOUS ARTISTS

8 *Afro Blue Band: Impressions / Sept. 1994-*
   May 1995 / Milestone 9237

The Afro Blue Band, an all-star ensemble, was put together by tenor saxophonist Arthur Barron to play both modern Afro-Cuban Jazz and post-bop. The eight selections on their CD (John Coltrane's "Impressions" and "Lonnie's Lament," "Afro Blue," Horace Silver's "Señor Blues," and four originals by Barron and/or Hilton Ruiz) are often challenging, yet they always swing. Fifteen musicians participated in this project, with no more than eight on a single selection. Among the key soloists are Barron (on tenor and alto), tenor saxophonist Mario Rivera, trumpeter Melton Mustafa, pianists Ruiz and Mark Levine, Papo Vásquez, Jerry González on conga, Mel Martin on various reeds, and the adventurous soprano saxophonist Dave Liebman. Nicole Yarling, who plays violin on "Impressions," also sings on "Lonnie's Lament." The music, which is mostly post-bop, will be of strong interest for fans of Cubop due to its consistently high quality.

7 *Afro-Cubano Chant / Sept. 1995 / Hip Bop*
   8009

This Afro-Cuban-flavored set features a leaderless all-star sextet consisting of Gato Barbieri (who is showcased on around half of the selections), vibraphonist Mike Mainieri, pianist Bob James, Andy González, drummer Lenny White, and percussionist Steve Berrios. "Cubano Chant" and Horace Silver's "Nica's Dream" are performed along with some more recent pieces, with the music sticking mostly to Cubop. Bob James, best known for his commercial crossover recordings, is a bit of a wild-card here but mostly fares pretty well, showing that he is comfortable with Latin rhythms. It is also a pleasure to hear Barbieri in this fairly spontaneous setting.

8 *The Afro-Latin Groove: Sabroso / June 30,*
   1954-June 16, 1972 / Rhino 75209

The excellent Rhino sampler (which has three cuts from the 1950s, 13 from the '60s, and the remaining two from 1972) consists of selections by Willie Bobo ("Fried Neck Bones and Some Home Fries"), Willie Rosario, Tito Rodriguez ("Descarga Cachao"), Joe Cuba, Mongo Santamaria ("Sweet 'Tater Pie"), Cal Tjader with Eddie Palmieri, Ocho, Ray Barretto, Machito ("Relax and Mambo"), Pucho and the Latin Soul Brothers, Cal Tjader, Tito Puente ("Hong Kong Mambo"), Charlie Palmieri, the Har-You Percussion Group, and Kako ("Shingaling, Shingaling"). Most of the selections were quite popular during the era, and the emphasis is on catchy melodies, heated rhythms, and concise performances. A perfect introduction to the more accessible side of Afro-Cuban Jazz.

8 *The Conga Kings / Dec. 6-9, 1999 / Chesky*
   193

This historic set is a summit meeting between congueros Candido, Giovanni Hidalgo, and Patato Valdés. The traditional music (half of which is comprised of rhythmic originals) teams the three conga players (all of whom sing) with Nelson González or John Benthal on tres, flutist Mauricio Smith, bassist Guillermo Edghill, Joe González on bongos, José Francisco Valdés on clavés, and three coro singers. With ten congas in all (four for Patato and three apiece for Candido and Hidalgo), it is fortunate that the co-leaders each have their own sounds. The final piece (a 7½ minute "Conga Kings Grand Finale") is the highlight of this rhythmically exciting set.

6 *Corcovado! / Concord Special Products 5305*
6 *Cubop! / Concord Special Products 5301*
6 *From Samba to Bomba! / Concord Special Products 5303*
6 *A Latin Vibe! / Concord Special Products 5300*
6 *Sabroso! / Concord Special Products 5304*
6 *Soul Sauce! / Concord Special Products 5302*

Celebrating the richness of both the Concord and Concord Picante catalogs, these six sampler CDs were released in 2000 as a new "The Colors of Latin Jazz" series. All of the material is currently available elsewhere in more complete form, but the idea of an introductory series is a good one. Unfortunately, though, both the recording dates and the personnel are not included, which greatly lowers the quality of the packaging. The selections, however, are mostly pretty enjoyable, if somewhat randomly programmed.

Corcovado! concentrates on Brazilian music, with performances from singers Karrin Allyson, Susannah McCorkle, and Tania Maria, Manfredo Fest, Marcos Silva, Charlie Byrd (with Ken Peplowski), Hendrik Meurkens, and Trio Da Paz. *Cubop!* has a selection or two apiece from the who's who of Afro-Cuban Jazz, including Poncho Sanchez, Mongo Santamaria, Tito Puente, Ray Barretto, the Caribbean Jazz Project, Ray Vega, and of course Cal Tjader, for whom the Picante subsidiary was originally formed. *From Samba to Bomba!* has both Cuban and Brazilian-styled performances with appearances from Trio Da Paz (with Claudio Roditi), Puente, Sanchez, Santamaria, Fest, Tjader, Meurkens, Pete Escovedo, Barretto, the

Caribbean Jazz Project, Monty Alexander's Ivory & Steel Band, and Tania Maria. *A Latin Vibe!* focuses on vibraphonists, with examples of the playing of Puente, Meurkens, Tjader, Dave Samuels, Ruben Estrada (with Poncho Sanchez), Joe Locke (with Ray Vega), and Terry Gibbs (with Puente on "Jordu"). *Sabroso* emphasizes the more poppish side of Latin jazz, with moderately commercial performances by Jeff Linsky, Tania Maria, Escovedo, Meurkens, Sanchez, Fest, Santamaria, Marcos Silva, Ed Calle, and Dave Valentin. Finally, *Soul Sauce!* contains funky Afro-Cuban Jazz, with heated selections from Sanchez ("Watermelon Man"), Barretto, Santamaria, Meurkens, Monty Alexander, Puente, Vega, Escovedo, Tania Maria, Ed Calle, and Tjader (playing "Soul Sauce").

Serious Afro-Cuban Jazz collectors will want to go elsewhere, but there are gems scattered throughout these samplers.

6 *The Cuban All-Stars: Pasaporte / 1994 / Enja 9019*

Recorded in Havana, this CD features some of the top musicians playing in Cuba in the mid-1990s, nearly all of whom are unknown outside of the country. Although percussionists Miguel Anga and Tata Guines are listed as co-leaders and they have their spots, the most impressive soloists are flutist Orlando Valle, saxophonist Cesar López, and trumpeter Juan Munguia. Unfortunately the final three selections get bogged down in so-so vocal features (Merceditas Valdés sounds a bit past her prime on "Blem Blem Blem") that are not at the same level as the earlier, blues-based instrumentals. But this CD does have its moments.

8 *Cuban Big Sound: Tumbao Cubano / 1959 / Palladium 160*

A year before Castro's Cuba became locked away from the Western world, an impressive big band full of top local performers recorded the 28 selections on this generous (77½ minute) CD. With arrangements by pianist Pedro "Peruchin" Justiz, Chico O'Farrill, René Hernández, Obdulio Morales, and Severiano Ramos, the music very much fits the time period. There are not too many big names among the personnel (Chocolate Armenteros and Peruchin are the best known) or any lengthy solos, but the musicianship is impressive, the band swings, and the music is both danceable and occasionally exciting. A perfect example of what a high-quality Cuban dance band sounded like in the late 1950s, a largely lost style.

4 Cuban Nights / Jan. 15, 1968-Aug. 9, 1968 / DCC Compact Classics 148

This frivolous audiophile release (which, other than on the back cover, substitutes food-related titles for the original song titles!) draws its music from the short-lived Skye label. There are four cuts from two of guitarist Gabor Szabo's albums, four from Cal Tjader's *Solar Heat* LP, and "Red Onions" from a set led by Armando Peraza; all date from 1968. The Szabo titles, although sounding mysterious and exotic, have little if anything to do with Cuban music; the guitarist is from Hungary! The brief liner notes talk as much about food as about the performances and do not bother mentioning where these selections came from. The music overall is worthwhile. But why reissue it this way?

8 Cuban Revolucion Jazz / 1988-1997 / Milan 35880

This two-CD sampler has such strong performances (17 in all) that it seems a shame not to give it a higher rating. But unfortunately, despite some liner notes, the personnel, along with the recording dates, are mostly not listed. The music was leased from such catalogs as Messidor, Egrem, Ashe, Ayva Musica, Qbadisc, and Milan, so some of the recordings are quite rare, making this twofer well worth

picking up despite the faulty packaging. Most of the selections are originals by the bandleaders (other than "A Night in Tunisia"), and these performances from Irakere, Mario Bauzá, Frank Emilio, Chucho Valdés, Paquito D'Rivera, Arturo Sandoval, Gonzalo Rubalcaba, Orlando "Maraca" Valle, Carto Espacio (a quartet led by pianist Ernan López-Nussa), conguero Ramon Valle, and pianist Emiliano Salvador are uniformly exciting. If the necessary information had been supplied, this twofer would have given listeners a fairly definitive look at the Cuban jazz scene of the past decade.

3 Fania All-Stars: Rhythm Machine / 1977 / Columbia/Legacy 57666

It is ironic that one of the few easily available CDs by the Fania All-Stars is one of their weakest. The problem is that the potentially impressive group (which includes such notables as Johnny Pacheco, pianist Papo Lucca, and Mongo Santamaria, with Rubén Blades taking the vocal on "Juan Pachanga") was produced for this project by Jay Chattaway for Bob James' Tappan Zee label. Lots of New York studio musicians were added, the arrangements (which have little to do with Latin music) are quite commercial, and the results are extremely watered down. Occasionally Santamaria, Pachecho, and the core musicians emerge, but not for long, since making a hit was the main priority. Other than an eccentric version of "The Peanut Vendor," the results are largely a waste.

7 Fiesta Picante / July 1979-May 22, 1996 / Concord Picante 4782

Subtitled *The Latin Jazz Party Collection*, this two-CD set is an excellent "best of" sampler that has 23 selections that have appeared on 19 different Concord Picante releases. The first CD is called "Choice Cha Cha Chá" while the second is "Mostly Mambo." Though the recording dates are not given, the personnel is included along with photos of the original album jackets. Heard from are the bands of Poncho Sanchez, Tito Puente, Mongo Santamaria, Pete Escovedo, Jorge Dalto, Cal Tjader, Ray Barretto, and Ray Vega. Such favorite songs as "Watermelon Man," "Killer Joe," "Soul Sauce," "Oye Como Va," "Things to Come," "Work Song," and "Manteca" are included along with some lesser-known but highly danceable selections. This is fun music, although true collectors will want the 19 CDs instead!

9 Havana Jazz Summit / Apr. 3-5, 1996 / Naxos 86005

Jane Bunnett has done a great deal to publicize and document the important music scene of Cuba. The original idea for this CD was to team her (sticking to flute) with fellow flutist Orlando Valle. However, it was soon decided to add Valle's wife Celine Valle and the veteran Richard Egues (who was well respected in Cuba back in the 1940s) on additional flutes, having the four interact in different combinations. Assisted by Hilario Duran, bassist Oscar Rodriguez, and three percussionists, this set (recorded in Cuba) is quite delightful. The flutists blend quite well, performing melodic group originals with joy and creativity. No one flutist stands above the rest, because the abilities of the players are fairly even and because the performances are complementary rather than competitive. A flute fan's delight, available at a budget price from Naxos.

8 Jammin' in the Bronx / Oct. 19, 1995 / Tropijazz 82044

Recorded at a benefit concert for the Bronx-Lebanon Hospital Center, this CD boasts a rather impressive lineup. The Machito Orchestra (under the direction of Machito's son, Mario Grillo) sounds fine during its three selections, although it is a pity that they were not featured more extensively; Chocolate Armenteros is one of their soloists. Papo Vazquez's octet (with Arturo O'Farrill, tenor saxo-

phonist Peter Brainin, and three percussionists) digs into their three numbers, Dave Valentin takes "Kalahari" as an opportunity to show off his virtuosity on flute, and there are unaccompanied solo features for Giovanni Hidalgo and Patato Valdés. But best are three selections from an "All Star Ensemble" featuring Chucho Valdés (quite passionate on "Neurosis"), who contributed the haunting "Claudia." Worth searching for.

8 Jazz on the Latin Side All-Stars / Jan. 7, 2000 / Cubop 029

One of the finest Afro-Cuban radio shows around is José Rizo's Jazz on the Latin Side, which is broadcast by KLON-FM in Long Beach, California. On January 7, 2000, a special tribute performance took place at B.B. King's in Universal City, featuring many of Los Angeles' top Afro-Cuban performers. What is particularly unusual about this release is that Rizo himself wrote five of the six selections that are performed (all but "Descarga Cachao"). The songs all serve as very viable devices for the strong playing of the all-stars. Among the many soloists heard from during this happy occasion are violinist Susie Hansen (in top form), trombonist Art Velasco, flutist Danilo Loranzo, altoist Robert Incelli, Justo Almario on tenor, trumpeter Ramon Flores (who in a couple of cases almost steals the show), pianist Otmaro Ruiz, drummer Cougar Estrada, Alex Acuña, and Francisco Aguabella on conga. Al McKibbon and Poncho Sanchez are also heard from in supportive roles. Recommended.

8 Latino Blue / Mar. 29, 1955-1968 / Blue Note 21688

Blue Note was never a major Afro-Cuban Jazz label, so the 14 selections on this sampler CD are drawn from the catalogs of Liberty, Roulette, World Pacific, Pacific Jazz, Jubilee, and Roost, with just one number (Kenny Dorham's "Afrodisia") that actually originated at Blue Note. Most of the performances are rather rare (just a few have been reissued on CD thus far), and the quality is consistently high despite the wide variety. Included are performances by Jack Costanzo (the exciting "Latin Fever"), Willie Bobo, Machito, Joe Torres (a fine timbales player), the Jazz Crusaders, vibraphonist Bobby Montez, Candido, organist Charles Kynard with flutist Buddy Collette, Clare Fischer, altoist Sonny Stitt and Art Blakey's Jazz Messengers with Sabu Martinez.

7 *Mambo Mio / Rhino 7456*

Fourteen rather diverse selections are reissued on this interesting sampler CD, although unfortunately the recording data (personnel and dates) is not included. Despite that flaw, general listeners in particular will probably enjoy this wide-ranging program. It starts out with Machito's orchestra performing "Tanga" (Is this the original 1943 version?) and has selections from Desi Arnaz, Pérez Prado ("Cherry Pink and Apple Blossom White"), Nat King Cole (singing "Perfidia" in Spanish), Tito Puente, Machito with Graciela, Beny Moré ("Como Fue"), Mario Bauzá (an exciting rendition of "Azulito"), Dean Martin ("Cha Cha Chá D'Amor"), Xavier Cugat, Celia Cruz ("Guantanamera"), Charlie Palmieri, Johnny Pacheco, and Pérez Prado with Rosemary Clooney ("Adios"). This is a colorful set that really deserved better packaging.

5 *Mamborama—Talkin' Verve / June 30, 1959-Aug. 28, 1968 / Verve 314 557 363*

There are many valuable Afro-Cuban recordings in Verve's vaults, but this CD is a confusing way to acquire some of the performances. Released as part of Verve's absurd "Talkin' Verve" series, nevertheless there are some decent performances included here (mostly from 1966-67) by Chico O'Farrill, Miguelito Valdés (who has three vocals), Wes Montgomery, the team of Patato and Totico, the Francy Boland-Kenny Clarke big band, Lalo Schifrin, Cal Tjader, and Herbie Mann's 1959

band. This CD could serve as an introduction to the genre, except that most of the performances are not all that essential! Common recordings are mixed in with out-of-print items, so this disc will be sure to annoy completists.

9 *The Music of Cuba / 1909-July 26, 1951 / Columbia/Legacy 62234*

This intriguing historical sampler is filled with many very rare performances long gathering dust in Sony's vaults. Programmed in chronological order, the 25 selections trace the early history of Cuban music, only some of which are jazz-oriented. The opening track, an unknown tune performed by Orquesta Tipica in 1909, is particularly exciting. Counting an early example of songs from 1919, there are seven selections from the 1919-31 period by a variety of Cuban bands and the radio star Maria Cervantes. There are two very rare numbers from Alberto Socarrás's 1935 orchestra (he plays flute on "Masabi" and alto on "Pacio Con El Diablo") and performances from Augusto Coen's Golden Casino Orchestra (a pair of swinging tunes from 1936), Johnny Rodriguez, the Lecuona Cuban Boys, Desi Arnaz (two cuts from 1939-40), and some lesser-known bands dating up to 1942. The CD concludes with Conjunto Cubakonga's "Como Ayer" in 1951. Not much jazz overall but this CD allows one to get a strong idea what Cuban music sounded like before the rise of Afro-Cuban Jazz.

7 *Rumbajazz—Tribute to Chombo / 1999 / Sunnyside 1084*

José "Chombo" Silva was supposed to record with Jerry González's Fort Apache band, but a stroke in 1994 ended his career and, a year later, his life. *Rumbajazz* is a tribute to the late tenor saxophonist and violinist, consisting mostly of songs that he had previously recorded (along with a few tributes), including "Perfidia," "Perdido," "Mongorama," and "Guajira at the Blackhawk." Victor Payano and David Sanchez are heard on tenors, Ricardo Davia Canino plays violin on one song, and the other musicians include both Andy and Jerry González along with various percussionists; two pieces have vocals. The final two selections are trios by Jerry González (on cornet), Andy González, and drummer Jimmy Rivera. A heartfelt and mostly lightly swinging set of melodic music.

7 *Tropijazz All-Stars / Apr. 10, 1996 / RMM 82028*

7 *Tropijazz All-Stars, Vol. II. / Apr. 10, 1996 / RMM 82061*

It is not an understatement to say that this concert features an all-star group, for the collective personnel consists of Charlie Sepúlveda, Humberto Ramirez, J.P. Torres, David Sanchez, Dave Valentin, pianists Michel Camilo, Eddie Palmieri, and Hilton Ruiz, bassist John Benitez, drummer Horacio "El Negro" Hernández, and percussionists Tito Puente, Giovanni Hidalgo, Richie Flores, and Johnny Almendro. Both of these CDs follow similar formats. They each start out with a long pronouncement (an overly lengthy introduction of the players on the first set and an endless poem on the second CD) by a rather obnoxious announcer (Felipe Luciano) with a pushy and rather strident delivery. Fortunately there is some excellent music along the way, with virtually every musician being featured somewhere. The first disc has showcases for Camilo ("On Fire"), Torres ("Rumba de Cajon"), an unnecessary singer (Jillian on "Everyday I Have the Blues"), and Tito Puente and the percussionists ("Five Beat Mambo") along with Palmieri's adventurous if wandering 16-minute "Suite 925-2828." *Vol. II* is highlighted by Camilo on "And Sammy Walked In," Valentin and Ruiz during "Oh My Goodness Baby," and Sanchez on a relatively brief "Jumpin' at the Woodside." The grand finale is Palmieri's 29½-minute "Noble Cruise," which is rather episodic and takes some

time to get going, starting out surprisingly free and spacey and not really cooking until 11 minutes into the song. After spirited solos from both trumpeters, Sanchez, Torres, Valentin, Palmieri, and the percussionists, the piece ends quite inconclusively. However, due to the accumulated talent on these two discs, there are enough bright moments to justify their purchase.

7 *United Nations of Messidor / 1983-1994 / Messidor 15840*

This expertly conceived two-CD set not only has 22 selections from the rich Messidor catalog but serves as a fine cross section of today's Latin music scene, with the great majority of the performances falling into Afro-Cuban Jazz. Represented in a song apiece (all previously released) are Charlie Palmieri, Gonzalo Rubalcaba, Irakere, Chucho Valdés, Spanish guitarist Agustin Carbonell, Argentinean charanga player Jaime Torres, Astor Piazzola on bandoneon, and altoist Paulo Moura. In addition there are two songs by Bebo Valdés, Patato Valdés, Giovanni Hidalgo, and Seis Del Solar and three from Mario Bauzá and Paquito D'Rivera. Happily for a sampler such as this, the personnel and recording dates are given. A solid introduction to the music.

7 *Viva Cubop 2—Dance the Afro-Cuban Way / 1999-2000 / Cubop 033*

This sampler CD has a dozen selections taken from 11 of the Cubop label's recent releases. The music is consistently high-powered, infectious, and exciting, and the packaging gives both the personnel and a paragraph or two about each of the performances. Heard from are Jack Costanzo, Dave Pike, London's Grupo X (who are featured on two songs), drummer Marlon Simon, Bobby Matos, Snowboy, percussionist Ray Armando, the Jazz On The Latin Side All-Stars, percussionist Babatunde Lea, Arturo Sandoval, and Afroshock. A strong introduction to the important label.

LPs to Search For:

In May 1979, historic concerts were held at the Karl Marx Theatre in Havana, Cuba. There had been a temporary easing in the tensions between the United States and Cuba, so these events (listed on one album as taking place March 2-4 and on the other as March 3-5) featured both American and Cuban musicians. A pair of two-LP sets, *Havana Jam* (Columbia 36053) and *Havana Jam II* (Columbia 36180), were released during the era with highlights from the concerts. *Havana Jam* has quite a wide variety of performers: Weather Report ("Black Market"), Irakere, Stephen Sills, Cuban folk singer Sara González, the traditional charanga band Orquesta Aragon, a duet by Kris Kristofferson and Rita Coolidge, the Fania All-Stars (with Rubén Blades), the "Trio of Doom" (a jam band consisting of guitarist John McLaughlin, electric bassist Jaco Pastorius, and drummer Tony Williams), and the Cuban Percussion Ensemble, which teams pianist Frank Emilio with 30 conga players. In addition, there are two numbers by the CBS Jazz All-Stars, an ensemble with up to six horns (the tenors of Dexter Gordon, Stan Getz, and Jimmy Heath, altoist Arthur Blythe, trumpeter Woody Shaw, and flutist Hubert Laws), and an oversized rhythm section that includes Willie Bobo. *Havana Jam II* sticks exclusively to jazz with additional selections from Irakere (Arturo Sandoval takes a heated solo on "Mil Ciento de Junedad"), the CBS Jazz All-Stars (Getz and Gordon both have lyrical spots on the ballad "Polka Dots and Moonbeams"), the Trio of Doom, the Cuban Percussion Ensemble, and Weather Report. It is lucky that this music was recorded when it was, for the atmosphere between the two countries would soon go back to being quite frosty.

Although all of the music on the two-LP set *Afro-Cuban Jazz* (Verve 2-2322) has been reissued on CD, this attractive twofer is still worth getting. Included are Machito's two collaborations with Charlie Parker (including Chico O'Farrill's five-part "Afro-Cuban Suite"), a set of music by O'Farrill's 1951 orchestra, and a Dizzy Gillespie-led big band in 1954 performing O'Farrill's four-part "Manteca Suite." Classic music no matter what the format!

RECOMMENDED BOOKS

Normally in each of the style books in this series, I provide a lengthy list of other recommended books that have additional information about the genre. In the case of Afro-Cuban Jazz, it is surprising how little has been written about this idiom, at least in English.

John Storm Roberts has written the only full-length overviews of the Latin music scene that I have been able to locate. *The Latin Tinge* (Oxford University Press, 1979) is an excellent work that goes into great detail about the influence of Latin music on American styles, and it is particularly valuable in discussing the events that occurred during the decades prior to the birth of Afro-Cuban Jazz. The same description and praise applies to Roberts' *Latin Jazz* (Schirmer Books, 1999), which covers a similar subject but takes the story into the 1990s; he has also written a related book, *Black Music of Two Worlds*.

Also worth picking up is Steven Loza's *Tito Puente and the Making of Latin Music* (University of Illinois Press, 1999), a loving but informative book on El Rey that not only covers Puente's life (including interviews with Puente and some of his associates such as Jerry González, Poncho Sanchez, and Hilton Ruiz) but covers other related topics and even has transcriptions of some of his songs.

But going to a local bookstore at this point in time in hopes of finding *The Tito Rodriguez Story*, Ray Barretto's memoirs, or *The Life and Times of Mongo Santamaria* will only result in disappointment!

THE FUTURE OF AFRO-CUBAN JAZZ

Afro-Cuban Jazz and Latin music in general seem to be everywhere these days. No longer thought of as a stepchild or an oddity, Afro-Cuban Jazz is ever so gradually being accepted by the mainstream jazz world. Most modern jazz musicians utilize Latin rhythms now and then, at least as spice in their performances. It is difficult for any contemporary musician to neglect the potential of those Cuban polyrhythms, even when performing music without a percussionist.

The increase in the number of Spanish-speaking people in the United States has had a strong effect on pop, rock, dance music, and other current styles, not just in the use of Spanish vocals but in the rich melodies and rhythms that have been imported. A glance at the pop charts makes it obvious that the growing number of Latin artists (compared to 20 or 30 years ago) has made a major impact.

The death of Tito Puente in recent times made major headlines, for he was the most famous living Afro-Cuban Jazz artist. But unlike many in other idioms who survive to a reasonable age, there is nothing nostalgic or dated about Puente's later recordings. While jazz in general rushed ahead during the 1915-75 period, constantly discarding the old in favor of the new, Afro-Cuban Jazz has developed at a slower pace since it exploded in 1947, and its traditions remain very much a part of even the most modern artists. Veterans who play in the style of the 1940s (think of pianist Ruben González) or the earlier folkloric idiom are recognized as contributing to the modern literature and considered relevant to the music's present and future.

Afro-Cuban Jazz has gradually modernized through the years, having a parallel development to mainstream jazz. Whether it be post-bop saxophone solos that reflect the influence of John Coltrane and beyond, electronic keyboards, funkier rhythms, or a remarkable rise in the technical prowess of the players, Afro-Cuban Jazz has adjusted, held on to its roots in the clavé rhythm, and given listeners the feeling of being part of an extended joyous family.

This book is full of the names of the music's great innovators and practitioners of the 20th century, and so many are currently active. There are also many others, in the early stages of their careers, who will be in similar books in the future. The excitement, danceability, and sheer fun of this dynamic music guarantees that Afro-Cuban Jazz will always be a major part of the American and world music scene.

ABOUT THE AUTHOR

Scott Yanow has been writing about jazz since 1975. Jazz editor of *Record Review* during its entire publishing history (1976-84), he has written for *Downbeat, JazzTimes, Jazz Forum, Jazz News,* and *Strictly Jazz* magazines. Yanow currently is a regular contributor to *Cadence, Jazziz, Coda, L.A. Jazz Scene, Mississippi Rag, Jazz Improv, Jazz Now, Jazz Report,* and *Planet Jazz.* He compiles the jazz listings for the Los Angeles Times, and has written over 200 album liner notes. Editor of the *All Music Guide to Jazz* and author of *Duke Ellington,* Yanow also wrote *Swing* and *Bebop* for the Third Ear—The Essential Listening Companion series.

INDEX

Fresh perspectives, new discoveries, great music.

Third Ear—The Essential Listening Companion is a new series of music guides exploring some of the most compelling genres in popular music. Each guide is written or edited by a leading authority in the field, who provides uncommon insight into the music. These books offer informed histories, anecdotal artist biographies, and incisive reviews and ratings of recordings. In-depth essays explore the roots and branches of the music. Easy to use and fun to browse, *Third Ear* guides are visually inviting as well, with evocative artist photos.

Swing
By Scott Yanow

Swing explores the musical phenomenon that has younger listeners up and dancing, and older ones fondly looking back. From the 1930s' classic sound of Duke Ellington through today's retro-swing movement with Big Bad Voodoo Daddy, this guide covers every era of swing. It profiles over 500 band leaders, players, vocalists, sidemen and composers, and the recordings that make (or don't make) the cut. Plus—it covers swing in the movies, books, hard-to-find recordings, and more.
Softcover, 514 pages, ISBN 0-87930-600-9, $22.95

Bebop
By Scott Yanow

On the heels of swing in 1945, bebop changed everything. This is the insightful guide to the innovators, tunes, and attitudes that evolved jazz from a dance music to an art form. *Bebop* portrays the lives and work of the daring musicians who became virtuosos in their own right: the bebop giants, like Charlie Parker and Dizzy Gillespie; the classic beboppers, like Sarah Vaughan and Dexter Gordon; and such later bebop figures as Oscar Peterson and Sonny Rollins.
Softcover, 391 pages, ISBN 0-87930-608-4, $19.95

Alternative Rock
By Dave Thompson

Alternative Rock looks inside the music that transformed the soundscape of the late '70s, '80s and '90s, and is still evolving today. Detailed essays delve into the meaning of "alternative," exploring topics ranging from primary musical influences to cultural trends, sampling, lo-fi, and more. Featured artists include The Beastie Boys, The Clash, The Cure, Green Day, PJ Harvey, Jane's Addiction, Nirvana, Smashing Pumpkins, The Smiths, Sonic Youth, and hundreds more.
Softcover, 837 pages, ISBN 0-87930-607-6, $27.95

Celtic Music
Edited by Kenny Mathieson

Today's Celtic music hails from its traditional homelands but also embraces new fusions from around the globe. Featuring 100 color photos, this guide captures the flavor of this widely enjoyed music in all its forms—traditional, new Celtic, and Celtic-influenced music. It describes known and lesser-known solo artists, groups, singers and players, ranging from Irish piper Johnny Doran to the Chieftains. Plus—essays explore Celtic's regional variations and unique instrumentation such as harp, pipe, fiddle, and squeezebox.
Softcover, 192 pages, ISBN 0-87930-623-8, March 2001, $19.95

Miller Freeman Books

AVAILABLE AT FINE BOOK AND MUSIC STORES EVERYWHERE. OR CONTACT:

Miller Freeman Books • 6600 Silacci Way • Gilroy, CA 95020 USA •
Phone: Toll free (866) 222-5232 • **Fax:** (408) 848-5784 •
E-mail: backbeat@rushorder.com • **Web:** www.backbeatbooks.com